Social Class in Modern Britain

Social Class in Modern Britain

Gordon Marshall,
David Rose,
Howard Newby
and
Carolyn Vogler

First published in 1988 by Hutchinson Education
Reprinted 1989,1991

Reprinted in 1993
by Routledge
11 New Fetter Lane, London EC4P 4EE

Transferred to Digital Printing 2004

British Library Cataloguing in Publication Data
Social class in Modern Britain.
    1. Great Britain. Social class
    I. Marshall, Gordon
    305.5′0941

ISBN 0–415–09876–9

The Authors

Gordon Marshall is Senior Lecturer in Sociology at the University of Essex. His previous publications include *Presbyteries and Profits* (Oxford University press, 1980) and *In Search of the Spirit of Capitalism* (Hutchinson, 1982).

David Rose is Lecturer in Sociology at the University of Essex and Executive Director of the Committee on Advanced Research at Essex. He is a former Convenor of the ESRC Research Seminar in Social Stratification. He is the editor of *Social Stratification and Economic Change* (Hutchinson, 1988) and co-author of *Property, Paternalism and Power* (Hutchinson, 1978).

Howard Newby is Chairman of the Economic and Social Research Council. He was formerly Professor of Sociology at the University of Essex and Director of the ESRC Data Archive. His previous books include *The Deferential Worker* (Penguin, 1977), *Green and Pleasant Land?* (Hutchinson, 1979), and *Country Life* (Weidenfeld and Nicolson, 1987).

Carolyn Vogler is Senior Research Officer at Nuffield College, Oxford. She was formerly Senior Research Officer for the Economic Stagflation and Social Structure Project at the University of Essex and is the author of *The Nation State* (Gower, 1985).

For John H. Goldthorpe and Erik Olin Wright

Contents

List of tables   viii

Preface   xiii

1   Social class and social inequality   1

2   When is a social class?   13

3   Constructing the Wright classes   31

4   Class formation and social mobility   63

5   The structure of class processes   98

6   The moral order of a capitalist society   143

7   Making and unmaking class consciousness   168

8   Goodbye to social class?   196

9   Class politics   225

10   Conclusion   264

Bibliography   276

Appendix: Technical details of the British survey   288

Coda: Constructing the Goldthorpe classes   305

Index   311

Tables

2.1 Distribution of respondents into the Registrar-General's class categories

2.2 Distribution of respondents into Goldthorpe class categories

2.3 Distribution of respondents into Wright class categories

2.4 Overall logic of Wright's class categories

2.5 Cross-classification of respondents into Registrar-General, Goldthorpe, and Wright class categories

3.1 Distribution of respondents into revised Wright class categories

3.2 Overall logic of Wright's revised class categories

3.3 Wright I (original) by Wright II (revised) classes

3.4 Distribution of Respondents into Wright II (revised) classes according to (1) socio-economic group and (2) American occupational variable

3.5 Wright II (revised) classes by Goldthorpe classes

3.6 Selected characteristics of Wright semi-autonomous employees who are in Goldthorpe service class or working class

3.7 Selected characteristics of Wright capitalist class

4.1 Distribution of cohabiting men and women, where both partners are gainfully employed, by Goldthorpe social class of both partners

4.2 Proportions of cohabiting couples, of which both partners are gainfully employed, by Goldthorpe social class pairings

4.3 Type of employment of wives of men with differing class mobility experience

4.4 Interrelationship between vote and class

4.5 Interrelationship between educational qualifications and class

4.6 Distribution of respondents by Goldthorpe social class and sex

4.7 Class composition by sex and class of chief childhood supporter at same age as respondent – Goldthorpe class categories

4.8 Class distribution of respondents by sex and class of chief childhood supporter at same age as respondent – Goldthorpe class categories

4.9 Market and work situations of women and men in Goldthorpe social classes

4.10 Constraints imposed by domestic responsibilities on men and women in Goldthorpe classes

4.11 Goldthorpe social classes by educational qualifications and sex

4.12 Relative sizes of Goldthorpe classes for men and women

4.13 Distribution of respondents by Wright social class and sex

5.1 Distribution of respondents and of respondents' chief childhood supporters (at same age as respondents) by Goldthorpe class and sex

5.2 Goldthorpe class distribution of Wright proletariat, by sex
5.3 Relative mobility chances in terms of odds ratios, by Goldthorpe class and sex
5.4 Interrelationship between class on entry into employment, class of origin, and sex
5.5 Interrelationship between present class, class on entry into employment, class of origin, and sex
5.6 Class on entry into employment by class of origin and sex (Goldthorpe class categories)
5.7 Present class by class on entry into employment by class of origin and sex (Goldthorpe class categories)
5.8 Relationship between class of origin, class destination, and sex
5.9 Class distribution of respondents by class of chief childhood supporter and age-groups (Goldthorpe class categories)
5.10 Interrelationship between class of origin, class destination, and age-group
5.11 Deskilling (job technique) by Goldthorpe class and sex
5.12 Deskilling (job autonomy) by Goldthorpe class and sex
5.13 Career paths of men and women by Goldthorpe class (collapsed)
5.14 Self-assigned class by Goldthorpe class and sex
5.15 Current trades union membership by Goldthorpe class and sex
5.16 Previous trades union membership (among current non-members) by Goldthorpe class and sex
5.17 Vote by Goldthorpe class and sex
5.18 Class identity by family type of respondent
5.19 Self-assigned class by family type of respondent
5.20 Perceptions of class structure by family type of respondent
5.21 Perceptions of distributional justice by family type of respondent
5.22 Vote by family type of respondent
6.1 Self-assigned class
6.2 Ways in which class processes have changed
6.3 Popular perceptions of social class
6.4 Factors perceived as determining class membership
6.5 Sources of social identity other than class
6.6 Others voting for same political party as respondent and for same reasons
6.7 Sources of work-centred social identities
6.8 Suggested reasons for industrial conflict
6.9 Suggested common interests of those who run industry and those who work for them
6.10 Issues perceived as causing class conflict
6.11 Reasons for trades union membership
6.12 Issues on which unions should concentrate
6.13 Perceptions of other important conficts in Britain today
6.14 Perceptions of distributional justice
6.15 Perceptions of Britain's economic problems

6.16 Proposed solutions to Britain's economic problems
6.17 Responses to cuts in government expenditure
6.18 Reasons for accepting cuts in government expenditure
6.19 Stated reasons as to why it makes no difference which party runs the country
6.20 Membership distribution of those actively involved in political associations
6.21 Reasons for leaving trade union
6.22 Reasons for not joining trade union
7.1 Consistency of attitudes to economic recovery
7.2 General attitude to tax and welfare benefits by willingness to finance increased welfare benefits personally
7.3 General attitude to incomes policies favouring the low paid by willingness to finance income redistribution personally
7.4 Support for tax increases to create jobs by support for wage restraint to create jobs
7.5 Association between normative items
7.6 Association between class items
7.7 Association between fatalism items
7.8 Responses to individual items in the class consciousness scale by Goldthorpe class
7.9 Mean scores on class consciousness index for principal explanatory items
7.10 Attitudes to distributional justice by Goldthorpe class
8.1 Types of distributional struggle
8.2 The meaning of work
8.3 Meaning of job by social class and sex
8.4 Meanings of work by Goldthorpe class and sex
8.5 Respondents' explanations for pecuniary attitude to work by social class
8.6 The meaning of home
8.7 Meaning of home by Goldthorpe class
8.8 Associational activities by Goldthorpe class
8.9 Associational activities by longevity of residence
8.10 Work-based friendships by Goldthorpe class
9.1 Vote by class in Britain, May 1979
9.2 Alford indexes for Britain, 1959–79
9.3 Voting intention by Registrar-General's social class
9.4 Voting intention by state benefits
9.5 Voting intention by housing tenure
9.6 Voting intention by sector of employment
9.7 Voting intention by Goldthorpe social class, and by Wright social classes
9.8 Partisanship by Goldthorpe social class, 1970–84
9.9 Voting intention by Goldthorpe social class by Goldthorpe class of origin

9.10 Salience of class, and political partisanship, by family type of respondent

9.11 Reasons for choice of party by family type of respondent

9.12 Voting intention by Goldthorpe social class by self-assigned class

9.13 Voting intention by self-assigned class by attitudes to class

9.14 Housing tenure by Goldthorpe class

9.15 Production sector by Goldthorpe class

9.16 Voting intention by Goldthorpe social class and housing tenure

9.17 Voting intention by sector of employment by Goldthorpe social class

9.18 Interrelationship of voting intention, class, class of origin, class identification, housing tenure, and state benefit dependency

9.19 Relationship between voting intention, class variables, and sectoral variables

9.20 Attitude to party differences by Goldthorpe social class

9.21 Attitude to party differences by voting intention

9.22 Patterns of vote switching by Goldthorpe social class

9.23 Reasons for choice of party

9.24 Goldthorpe service class voting intention by impact of economic recession

Appendix

A.1 Basic statement of response

A.2 Basic response by standard region

A.3 Socio-economic characteristics of the sample

Coda

C.1 Class distribution by sex and class of chief childhood supporter at same age as respondent – Goldthorpe class categories revised

Preface

This book forms part of an international project researching class structure and class consciousness in a number of countries throughout North America, Europe, and Australasia.[1]* The project was initiated in the United States by Erik Olin Wright and had the minimal aim of replicating questions about work, home, and political life in different national contexts in order to enable strictly comparable analyses to be made of class processes in separate countries. Most participating academics have explored their results using the class schema devised by Wright himself, although some studies, our own included, have incorporated alternative conceptions of class alongside Wright's structural Marxist account. From the outset, therefore, one objective of the British team has been to field common questions about production, ownership, and labour which would form the basis for the comparative element in the different national projects. Some comparative as well as national studies have already been published,[2] although more remain to be done, and we will be reporting on these in future publications in conjunction with our colleagues abroad.

However each project within the international effort has been free to pursue additional goals limited only by the constraints of available research resources. In the British case we found ourselves embarking on a major study of social class at precisely that moment in the national sociology when a consensus seemed to be emerging about the demise of class as an important factor structuring economic, political, and social life in this country. The study of structured social inequality was increasingly dominated by new theses which emphasized the reorganization of capital and labour; different forms of sectionalism among the work-force; privatism of families and individuals; and fatalistic acceptance of social inequality shaped less by class processes than by gender, state dependency, or sectoral production and consumption cleavages. In this context our commitment to class analysis began to look incongruous if not downright obstructive. We therefore set ouselves the further task of investigating these newer arguments by adding to our interview schedule questions about sectionalism, privatism, and fatalism, as far as our budget would allow this. Already in a strong position to evaluate the strengths and weaknesses of class analysis because of our involvment in Erik Wright's enterprise, we then reinforced this by collecting sufficient occupational data to permit a replication of the Oxford Mobility Study of the 1970s, so testing

* Superior figures refer to the Notes and references sections following each chapter.

John H. Goldthorpe's occupational class schema alongside the Marxist categories used by our international collaborators.

These twin objectives required data collection via a complex and lengthy questionnaire and we are much indebted to the staff of Social and Community Planning Research, particularly Patricia Prescott-Clarke and Steve Elder, for invaluable assistance in designing and fielding our national sample survey.[3] The research was supported by the Economic and Social Research Council (Grant HR 8633) who have tolerated with admirable good humour the delays and confusions occasioned by our involvement in a project spanning a dozen or so languages. Along the way we have accumulated numerous debts to colleagues and friends. This is an appropriate place to acknowledge the help given by Gerda Loosemore-Reppen, Andrew Abelson and Neil Price at the Economic and Social Research Council; Mike Kenning, Charles Bowman, Shirley Kettle, Mary Toussaint, Sandy Holder, Paul Smith, Peter Allott, Miles Welsh and Jane Howard, all of the Essex University Computing Service; Phil Fox, Eric Roughley, Bonnie Amim, Jean Shearman, Melvyn Read, David Broughton, David Sanders, Eric Tanenbaum, Andrew Briggs, Jose Abud, Shalini Buell and Wycliffe Chilowa, who assisted in coding and data preparation; Graham Upton and Oriel Sullivan, who helped with the loglinear modelling; Ted Benton, David Lockwood, George Kolankiewicz, Ray Pahl and David Lee, with whom we have enjoyed friendly (if sometimes heated) conversations; John Robertson, Jill Scott, Peter Allington, Nick and Liz Cope, and David Potter, who helped with pre-piloting of the questionnaire.

John Goldthorpe and Erik Wright must be singled out for special thanks. Both have given freely of their time and expertise in a spirit of academic fraternity – despite our often explicit disagreements about the nature of social class and class analysis. We are deeply grateful to them both.

Our research is collaborative in another sense, in that it results from work undertaken jointly by four researchers, each with rather different interests and expertise. To some extent this has been reflected in a division of labour and responsibilities already evident in the previous publications of the group. Rose and Vogler have addressed themselves to arguments about the restructuring of capital and labour, Newby has discussed privatism and fatalism, while Marshall has written about social class and class analysis more generally. However the present text, like all previous publications by the group, is the result of genuinely co-operative efforts. The various drafts have been commented on and modified by all four contributors. In any case we have long since ceased to be able to identify individual authorship of our arguments.

This book was preceded by a number of position papers in which we set out our approach to the theoretical and conceptual issues encompassed by our project[4] This, however, was the rare case of a piece of sociological research which did not confirm all of the researchers' preconceptions. We therefore acknowledge that we have modified some of our early views in the light of our findings; this, after all, is the purpose of empirical research. The arguments in

Chapters 8 and 9 have, in particular, been affected by the necessity to rethink our position. It is also important to emphasize that this volume does not cover all of the themes which we pursued in our study. We have concentrated here on the issue of class but do not wish to imply that this has exhausted the substantive content of the stratification of contemporary British society. Other predominantly non-class issues will be explored in a second volume which will be a companion to this one.

In the light of the discussion of proletarianization in Chapter 5 below it may or may not be worth recording here that the entire manuscript was typed by Gordon Marshall on an Amstrad PCW8256. His secretary, meanwhile, spent considerable amounts of time and money entertaining a long list of interesting visitors to the Sociology Department. If asked about the matter she will say that she doesn't think she has been deskilled. Marshall thinks he can understand why. Thanks anyway to Mary Girling, Linda George, Brenda Corti, Sandra Dyson and Carole Allington, for barring the way to Marshall's door so that he could work without interruptions.

Finally, we should acknowledge that the history of our study is one of three very pleasant years of close co-operation, not only among ourselves, but with all our colleagues in the international study of class structure and class consciousness. We extend our warmest thanks to everyone who has advised and encouraged us along the way.

Gordon Marshall, Wivenhoe
Howard Newby, Great Bentley
David Rose, Colchester
Carolyn Vogler, Oxford

Notes

1 At the time of writing the full list of participating countries is as follows: Australia, Brazil, Canada, Denmark, Finland, France, Great Britain, Greece, Hungary, Israel, Italy, Japan, Netherlands, New Zealand, Norway, Poland, Portugal, Sweden, and West Germany. The various national studies are in different stages of completion. So far the data from some six or so surveys have been fully merged for the purposes of comparative analyses.
2 These include Wright (1982, 1985), Blom (1985), Ahrne and Wright (1983).
3 Technical details of the survey are given in the Appendix.
4 See Rose et al. (1984, 1987), Newby et al. (1985), Marshall et al. (1985, 1987).

Acknowledgements.

Parts of the present volume have appeared in articles in the *British Journal of Sociology* and *Sociology*. We are grateful to the Editors of these journals and to Routledge and Kegan Paul for permission to reprint this material in revised form.

1 Social class and social inequality

To what extent are disparity and discord in British society still shaped by familiar processes of social class? The answer to this question is by no means obvious, for it is now widely argued that fundamental shifts in the structure of social hierarchy have generated new forms of sectionalism that replace earlier solidaristic class struggles. Associated and complementary swings in social values have allegedly intensified individualism and privatism. Structural shifts and changing values are also evident in the decline of class-based politics in the United Kingdom. The concept of class is therefore obsolete. The proletariat and bourgeoisie have had their day.

In Eric Hobsbawm's version of this argument a solidarity of shared life-style and political objectives among the traditional British working class has been undermined since the 1950s by the growth both of public sector employment and multinational corporations. The majority of employees now bargain for wages under conditions other than those of the free market. This, together with the increased but uneven participation of women in paid labour, expansion of nonmanual employment and post-war immigration from the New Commonwealth, has encouraged 'a growing division of workers into sections and groups, each pursuing its own economic interest irrespective of the rest'. Everywhere, according to Hobsbawm, solidaristic forms of political consciousness have given way to 'the values of consumer-society individualism and the search for private and personal satisfactions above all else'.[1]

In similar vein, Steven Lukes has concluded from his review of the social and occupational structures of Britain in the 1980s that

the . . . distinction between manual and non-manual labour is less and less relevant. . . . Labour or work itself, and the sphere of production, seems to be becoming less central to the identity and consciousness of workers, while consumption, especially with respect to housing and transport, has become more central to their basic interests.

Britain is a society divided against itself in new ways: those with a stake in property markets and those without; the self-sufficient on wages versus welfare claimants; the populations of declining regions against those resident in economically buoyant areas; and so on. These changes are reflected in the extent to which the mentality of the market has come to dominate the consciousness of the majority. In Lukes' view,

There appears to have been a reactive growth (encouraged by a combination of recession and inflation) of instrumental, pecuniary, egoistic, in short capitalist values and attitudes, and a disintegration of various moral frameworks within which these had a subordinate place and faced various countervailing forms of commitment, loyalty and discipline – whether based on unionism, locality or class.

Ordinary people are now convinced that there is no alternative to the morality of the acquisitive society; that Britain's seemingly intractable economic problems are quite beyond human control; that social inequalities are therefore unalterable. As a result, they have settled down in a mood of quiet disillusionment to seek their private satisfactions and pursue conflicting sectional demands.[2]

According to Lukes, Hobsbawm, and others, the new sectionalism and self-interest have had important political consequences, evident in particular in the breakdown of class-based politics. This claim is supported by a number of studies which suggest that the electorate is now fragmented along unfamiliar lines. There is some disagreement about whether established patterns of class voting have been undermined specifically by partisan dealignment, the disaggregation of economic interests, cognitive consumer voting, or the development of sectoral production and consumption cleavages, but in every case structural shifts in the ordering of stratification are seen to generate new conceptions of self-interest and intensify the vigour with which these are then pursued.[3]

These general arguments about the demise of social class as a force structuring British society in the 1980s find their logical conclusion in epitaphs both for the proletariat and the concept of class itself. Andre Gorz, for example, has argued that the traditional working classes of western industrial societies are now no more than a privileged minority. True, an aristocracy of tenured workers do still 'identify with their work, define themselves through it and do or hope to realise themselves in their work'. But few today are engaged as autonomous labourers, both in control of production and finding personal fulfilment in it. An increasingly complex division of tasks, necessary automation and standardization of tools, procedures, and knowledge, have relegated the majority of white-collar and blue-collar workers alike to a 'post-industrial proletariat which, with no job security or definite class identity, fills the area of probationary, contracted, casual, temporary and part-time employment'. Work, for this group, is merely 'a blank interval on the margins of life, to be endured to earn a little money'. Members no longer seek liberation within production. Rather, they wish to free themselves from it, to create a private haven at home, in family life or leisure, into which can be poured all aspirations for individual autonomy and personal satisfaction. Class membership, among this atomized mass of consumer-oriented individuals, is lived only as a 'contingent and meaningless fact'. The idea of class consciousness, like that of the proletariat itself, is an illusion long since shattered by changes in science and technology that have destroyed the power of skilled industrial workers. Only the dinosaur of class analysis persists and perpetuates the mythology.[4]

II

The evidence that is normally cited in support of this general interpretation of events is drawn from fields as diverse as those of human geography, social policy, and industrial sociology. However a number of themes can be identified which are common to the several obituaries that have been published for social class and social class analysis. The most important of these in the British context are those of restructuring capital and labour; the growing complexity and consequent opacity of class processes; emergence of instrumental collectivism as the epitome of increasingly sectional distributional struggles; privatization of individuals and families; and fatalistic acceptance of structural inequality allied to an inability to conceive of any alternative. Of course different accounts interrelate these in different ways. Moreover the literature is as voluminous as it is diverse. We should make it clear at the outset, therefore, that our restatement of these themes in the present context necessarily takes the form of an heuristic device rather than a comprehensive review. Nevertheless ours is, we would argue, a fair summary of the principal tenets of the argument against conventional class analysis and it is these that will be investigated more closely in subsequent chapters.

The focal point of discussion is, of course, social class. However, critics of class analysis usually begin from observations about the economy and the impact of economic or technological change on occupational structure. The analyses that sustain the various accounts are diverse and often complex, but commonly emphasize economic recession, deindustrialization, or industrial restructuring. It is not necessary to pursue these in detail here, since most accounts offer variations on the theme that relatively recent and radical changes in market conditions have necessitated a large-scale reorganization of capital and labour, as the former has moved from less to more profitable sectors and technologies. The ownership and control of profits, plant, and investment have therefore taken new (and generally more complex) forms. Labour, too, is constantly reorganized as a result of international and sectoral movements of capital and the adoption of new technologies and forms of work organization. Thus, for example, we have witnessed in recent years a decline in the relative importance of the manufacturing sectors in most advanced western economies. (In the case of Britain this has been particularly marked.) As a result there has been a commensurate growth in public sector and service employment. Industrial manufacture is increasingly carried out in certain so-called developing countries – South Korea, Brazil, or India for example – while western economies form the world's financial and commercial centre. Moreover, these processes are generally seen to have restructured those societies involved in a fundamental rather than temporary fashion, so that the simple reversal of economic recession will not significantly alter the underlying occupational and social trends.[5]

These changes in the national and international direction of investment and division of labour have had three generally recognized consequences from the point of view of class structure. The first concerns the ownership and control of capital, which has become more involved as pension funds, multinational corporations, horizontally and vertically integrated companies and cartels have replaced local family proprietorship as the prevailing form of business organization.[6] Moreover, sectoral shifts in the economy and in the reorganization and restructuring of labour itself have, on balance, created a more diverse and sectorally uneven economic structure, and one in which the differences between workers in different economic sectors are tending to increase.[7] Finally, the shedding of 'surplus' labour during the present recession has reinforced labour market segmentation, in particular the boundary between those in relatively secure occupational or company careers and the unemployed or subemployed.[8]

The decomposition of the relevant changes in occupational structure into distinct 'shift effects' provides an illustration of the processes that are said to have rendered the theoretical frameworks of conventional class analysis inadequate to the study of contemporary social inequalities. 'Industry shift effects' refer to that part of the overall change in the class structure which is due to shifts in the labour force from industrial sectors with one distribution of classes, into sectors with a different distribution of classes. Rapid deindustrialization and the growth of the service sector has brought about such a transformation in Britain during the past two decades. 'Class composition shift effects', on the other hand, stem from the transformation of class relations within industrial sectors and are evident in the alleged proletarianization or deskilling of tasks and workers. Some analysts claim also to have identified 'interaction effects', which are the result of simultaneous shifts in employment across industrial sectors with different class structures, and shifts in the internal class structures of these sectors themselves. The net effect of these several processes is to fragment traditional 'bourgeois' and 'proletarian' groupings and redraw the boundaries of common interest in new ways not specifically reducible to established differences of class. Myriad 'new middle' and 'new working' classes have been created. Their conceptual locations and political proclivities are objects of intense speculation.[9]

This already complex picture is further complicated by the contextual dimensions of gender and geography. Industry and class composition shifts both affect, and are in turn affected by, the sexual composition of the labour force, since the terms under which different categories of labour are available is an important factor influencing investment decisions as well as changes in the labour process; and, conversely, these processes also have effects on the composition of the labour force itself. Industry shift effects, for example, have been associated with a decline in male jobs in the manufacturing sector, and a large increase in less skilled, low paid, and often part-time female jobs in the service sector. Similarly, with regard to changes in the labour process, it has been argued that the deskilling of clerical work in the banking and insurance sectors has been associated with its feminization, so that women are largely restricted to the deskilled tasks, while men continue to be promoted through the internal clerical and administrative labour market.[10]

4

These processes also have a geographical dimension, since industry shift effects in part reflect a trend towards an increasingly international economy, involving direct investment by multinational companies as well as trade and international finance. Since the early 1970s this has been associated with a restructuring of the division of labour on an international level. Multinational companies have been relocating the capital intensive stages of production and research and development to countries with the highest labour productivity and the best markets, while transferring labour intensive stages of production to underdeveloped countries where labour is relatively cheap. This has been linked to the phenomenon of deindustrialization in the advanced countries, although its precise effects are likely to vary according to the extent to which countries are dependent on the international sector, and according to each country's competitive position in the world market. Since Britain is particularly dependent on an advanced multinational sector and also relatively uncompetitive in relation to other states, international restructuring is more likely to result in higher levels of unemployment, especially in the traditional skilled and semi-skilled areas, which is not compensated for by new inward investment or an expanding state sector.[11]

Within Britain this is creating a much more diverse and uneven economic structure in which differences between workers in different economic sectors (and thus also geographical locations) may well be increasing. Workers in the advanced multinational sector, for example, are now dependent on economic enterprises operating in rather different economic circumstances from those in the national and state sectors. Although these various changes are sometimes conceptualized and interrelated in different ways their composite effect is commonly seen to be one of rendering class structures and class processes increasingly opaque.

Class is objectively opaque to the extent that forms of ownership and control are distant, more impersonal, and less concrete. The occupational structure has become progressively more complex as the numbers in traditional proletarian occupations are decreased and those in services increased.[12] This generates both theoretical and subjective opacity. In effect the conventional distinction between manual and nonmanual labour becomes less salient sociologically and socially. Theoretical opacity means simply that the intricacies of modern class arrangements create problems for sociological analysis. This is evident in the plethora of recent attempts by Marxists and sociologists alike to come to terms with the class structures of contemporary societies both conceptually and empirically. These have yielded an *embarras du choix* among occupational classifications and boundary-mapping schemata; a choice, it must be said, in which one can as yet be guided by little beyond personal preference.[13] Similarly, the very complexity of contemporary class structures renders class processes ever more inscrutable to the population at large. This makes it less likely that individuals, especially those who are relatively disprivileged, will perceive a common class cause as informing their interests and action. It can be argued, therefore, that the degree of ambiguity, ambivalence, and contradiction which emerges from the literature on, for

5

example, working-class images of society is not merely the result of cognitive mystification. It reflects many of the objective characteristics of the contemporary class structure.[14]

This raises the issue of the extent to which social class has retained its coherence as a strong source of social identity. By definition sociology is less concerned with who a person thinks he or she is in a highly personal sense (Who am I?) than with who that person identifies with (Who are we?). Such social identities can be thought of as important intervening elements in the sociological equation of social structure, social consciousness, and social action. Social identity intercedes between structure on the one hand and consciousness and action on the other. One such identity is with class. Does this identity extend into any sense of what Mann has called totality, opposition, and alternative?[15] Do people see their interests as being in concert with those of others among their class and, moreover, as antagonistic to the interests of other classes?

The evidence seems to suggest that class identity is still reasonably widespread but, critics have argued, merely formal. Class has become less relevant as a basis of social schism as the economic structure of Britain has become more diverse and uneven, with increasing differences between workers in different economic sectors, labour markets, and geographical locations. These differences are said to be evident in changes in the nature and organization of collective action. Increasingly class conflicts have taken the form of sectional distributional struggles. These are as likely to embrace intra-class conflict as conflict between classes. During the last ten years, for example, centralized industry bargaining between national trades union leaders and nationally organized employers has been almost completely replaced by sectional, decentralized, single-employer bargaining on the basis of the market position of individual companies. This form of bargaining is particularly prevalent in the multinational sector comprising mainly high wage industries which tend to take the lead in pay bargaining. There have also been increasing regional and sub-regional disparities in employment and wages, since multi-employer bargaining tends to be concentrated in the declining regions, whereas company bargaining is more prevalent in the relatively buoyant south-east.[16]

It is further argued that, against this background of increasing heterogeneity and diversity among the work-force, the class structure comes to be perceived by most people as an opaque hierarchy based on distributional competition over income. In the distributional conflicts which characterize the market situation of the working population, the lesson which has been learned from the apparent ubiquity of capitalist social relations is that moral restraints upon acquisitiveness have no part to play, and that one's market situation must be exploited to the full. Under these circumstances particular groups are more likely to look after their own interests than consider their possible common cause with those who happen to share the same class position. Rather than an oppositional political and economic consciousness the working population has developed institutions which reflect its pervasive absorption of capitalist values; of individualism, egoism, and economic calculation. Instrumental collectivism, based on sectional self-interest, has become the order of the day.[17]

Evidence on instrumental collectivism is matched by that on orientations to work. It seems that a lengthy period of inflation and recession during the past twenty years has exacerbated rather than diminished the pecuniary attitude to work which, together with an instrumental orientation to class organizations, was regarded as the hallmark of the 'affluent workers' of the 1960s. Indeed, when it is recalled that the impact of recession has been thrown principally on to the unemployed and unwaged and that many of those continuously in work will have experienced an increase in real living standards, then arguments about affluence and recession in fact converge. For example Brown and his colleagues, in their comparison of studies of work carried out in the period 1963 to 1972 with those undertaken since 1973, found 'no clear evidence that there have been general changes in orientations to paid work'. However their own recent studies in Tyneside provide 'some evidence . . . for orientations to work to become more narrowly preoccupied with pay and security and similar "economistic" reasons . . . [which may] reflect the declining proportion of workers who have a sense of a distinctive "occupational identity"'. In other words industry shift effects are reducing the numbers of workers in traditional proletarian occupations which, in turn, 'could give rise to an increasingly calculative involvement in work and attachment to the employing organisation, and lower levels of satisfaction with work'.[18]

But the predominant mood among British workers, of whatever type, is seen by many to be not only one of instrumentalism, but also of stoicism. Compared with their counterparts in other advanced industrial societies, British workers seem more commonly to be motivated by the achievement of material success, but are also characterized by a very high rate of failure to achieve their (limited) aspirations for autonomy at work. Finding their jobs to be boring, most people do not seek personal fulfilment through paid labour, but elsewhere. Moreover, evidence has been adduced which suggests to many that the element of fatalism which informs resignation to the cash nexus in the workplace, extends also to the economy as a whole. The apparent intractability of Britain's economic problems has led to increasing fatalism about their solution. The economic well-being of the country is seen to be dependent on market forces, or the equally impersonal activities of largely uncontrollable external agencies (the Japanese, the Common Market), so that even the British government is powerless to rearrange matters (if indeed it is inclined to do so). This results not in a politics of protest but of quiet disillusion and cynicism, of which lack of partisanship, indifference to organized party politics, and a marked decline in support for altruistic social policies are the common features. It is not that people are unaware of inequalities. They simply judge them to be unassailable. The economy and, in broad outline, the class structure are, like the weather, beyond human volition.[19]

Increasing sectionalism and perceptions of the public world as being

7

intractable are often related to a further process which some believe has come to characterize social relationships. This is the process of privatization or privatism – the growth of increasingly individualized, home-centred, and family-centred life-styles.

In so far as people have any sense of control over their own destinies this is more likely to be experienced in the private than in the public domain. The private domain may therefore be as crucial for the formation of social identities as the more public milieux of work and community. These social identities will play a crucial mediating role in any analysis of the relationship between social structure and social action. Structural locations create arrays of potential interests, but interests depend upon people's perceptions of their social identity for their realization in action. Class analysts have tended to assume what is undoubtedly often the case: that social identities arise primarily from the sphere of production. However this is not always true, nor does it have uniform consequences. Sectional as well as class identities can arise from particular work experiences but they need not be durable or permanent. They may be acted upon in particular situations, say in the context of an industrial dispute, but may at other times remain latent. At such times non-work areas of life are more likely to be most salient for active social identities. Indeed for some individuals such identities may generally override other potential identities. In this sense, sectionally based social identities may simply be an extension of a more basic social identity which is derived from the private, non-work sphere. Even the various forms of militant collective action may be so many collective means to individual ends; that is, the improvement of the position of separate individuals, rather than of the collectivity or class as a whole.[20]

Increasingly, privatized or individualized life-styles are also a reflection of the increasing diffuseness of the capitalist economic system. This system involves, of course, not just a sphere of production but also spheres of civil society and consumption. Moreover the sphere of civil society has expanded and a consumer society has emerged. Both developments have affected people's experience of the sphere of production. For example, people now spend fewer hours at work, have paid holidays, and benefit from legislation specifically to protect them as workers; in addition the economic returns from work in combination with the social wage guarantee for most people a full sense of participating in society as citizens and consumers. Other changes, such as those associated with the dilation of locality-based status orders, tend to reinforce the trend towards more privatized life-styles and individualized home-centred or family-centred social identities based on them. For many people, therefore, privatized social identities may be more significant in mediating political interests than the public social identities deriving from the sphere of production. Changes in non-work life may be contributing to a decline in the experience of class identity and solidarity outside work and in the community, so that even the effects of recession do not result in the emergence of widespread class struggle or politics, but in further disillusion and fatalism towards class politics and a retreat into the privatized world within home and family.[21]

These changes may also have been reinforced by changes in consumption which have affected social identities and thus conceptions of political interest in a similar manner. Moorhouse has argued, for example, that rising living standards have come to integrate people into the capitalist market economy as individual consumers, thus reducing the coherence of their experience of society as fundamentally class-divided.[22] One particularly important feature of changes in consumption patterns which is commonly seen to be of crucial importance in the formation of social identities is the growth of home-ownership. This is particularly noticeable among the skilled working class. By 1981 more than half of all households headed by skilled manual or junior nonmanual workers owned or were buying their homes, as were more than one third of all semi-skilled households and about one quarter of all unskilled households. The broad effect, according to some observers, has been to produce a new dividing line between home-owners and others which is now affecting voting patterns in particular and social values more generally.[23]

The link between changing patterns of consumption (especially home-ownership) and politics also emerges clearly in a number of recent studies which claim that the electorate is now fragmented by what is referred to, following Dunleavy, as 'sectoral consumption cleavages'. For example, the evidence seems to suggest that private market-based consumption of housing and transport have come to divide the working class, so undermining the strength and extent of its support for the Labour Party's traditional policies of increasing state provision in these spheres. Both party alignment and variation in support for Labour's policy of increasing state spending are affected more by how people consume housing and transport (that is by their consumption location) than they are by their location in the sphere of production. As expected those most dependent on state provision are most supportive of state spending. The Labour Party thus appears to be representing a shrinking minority rather than a clear majority of the working class. Post-war patterns of consumption have thus served to integrate workers into capitalism as individuals, and in a directly economic (rather than simply ideological) way, so providing them with a stake in the system of financial and property markets which in turn undermines their sense of class identity and hence their participation in class politics. This helps explain a reported ambivalence in working-class attitudes both towards the welfare state and towards the traditional policies of the Labour Party.[24]

The most powerful image of modern Britain thus created by contemporary writings on social inequality is one of a society peopled largely by materialistic citizens progressively inclined towards instrumental pursuit of growing expectations for personal satisfaction. In the absence of an agreed morality for rendering distributive issues principled, fatalistic beliefs about the national economy combine with the pursuit of self-interest to generate sectional distributional struggles. These then surface, as opportunities to exploit one's market position happen to present themselves. The material basis of the society is thus reflected in its moral order. Capitalist relations of production and the capitalist market, their logics rooted in the 'natural' self-interest of individual actors, have apparently created a truly selfish society.

<h1 style="text-align:center">III</h1>

These, then, are the propositions that the present study sets out to test against the data generated by our national sample survey. The case against class analysis seems clear. In summary, recent findings seem to suggest that class analysts exaggerate the extent to which the sphere of production generally, and paid labour in particular, now provides individuals with a clear sense of social identity which could form the basis for class action. For many people, work is part of a world which is not regarded as amenable to either personal or collective control, and thus is approached instrumentally and fatalistically. Such empirical data as are available appear to indicate a combination of sectionalism and fatalism in the sphere of production. These may well be causally related; the British economy, indeed distributional order generally, is seen as unalterable precisely because of the high degree of sectionalism and lack of common identity and purpose between different groups of workers in different companies and sectors. Similarly, in the sphere of consumption, post-war changes in patterns of working-class culture and community are apparently tending towards a relative privatism of individual households or families, which is in turn reinforced by patterns of private consumption, particularly in housing. In the spheres both of production and consumption therefore, groups of employees are coming to occupy increasingly diverse social positions (in terms of their potential interests), which traditional class organizations such as the Conservative and Labour Parties or the trades unions can no longer articulate or constitute in terms of class identities. These diverse potential interests have thus come to be mediated through non-class sectional identities (in the sphere of production), and privatized home-centred or family-centred identities (in the sphere of consumption), both of which are associated with increasing fatalism and instrumentalism in relation to the structure of the wider economy and society.

Are these arguments sound and is the critique of class analysis therefore justified? In the following two chapters we take up the preliminary task of identifying social classes. The class theories of Marx and Weber are examined briefly, but greater emphasis is placed on the operational procedures by which modern class analysts allocate individuals to the various social classes. Sociological, Marxist, and official approaches are explored in some detail, as these are represented in the strategies adopted by John Goldthorpe, Erik Wright, and the Registrar-General. Chapters 4 and 5 extend this inquiry by pursuing two of the currently most contentious issues in class analysis; namely, those of identifying the appropriate unit for study, and of determining the significance of putative trends in occupational mobility. These are evident in ongoing debates about 'gender and class' and 'proletarianization'. To anticipate our findings, we shall argue that Britain remains a capitalist *class* society, and that the various attempts to identify 'post-industrial' (and post-capitalist) features in the social developments of recent years are not at all convincing. Neither, on the other hand, are arguments about the proletarianization of the class structure. We shall try to show that the reality is more complex than this.

These chapters offer a modest contribution to class analysis that is set squarely within the established framework of that enterprise. We then extend our investigation to consider the broader issues raised by the literature that challenges that framework itself. Chapters 6 and 7 explore the nature of the moral order in modern Britain. Questions of social identity and social consciousness are to the fore. In this way the arguments about class imagery, sectionalism, fatalism, and pecuniary instrumentalism can be set against our fairly extensive data on social values, beliefs, and attitudes. Of course these chapters are based on cross-sectional rather than longitudinal data so we have included in our study a review of the historical context into which any conclusions about fatalism, privatism, and class action must be set (Chapter 8). In this way we hope to enhance our own arguments as well as suggesting that a certain lack of historical sensitivity may have led critics of class analysis to overstate their case. The parameters of class action, as these can be established using the admittedly limited example of voting behaviour, are then examined in Chapter 9. Are we witnessing the demise of class politics and corresponding ascendancy of sectoral cleavages in structuring party preferences? We think not.

This is an ambitious programme to undertake in one volume and we would be the first to concede that many of the issues here addressed should be pursued in more depth. Additional data and further analysis are warranted throughout. This most common of conclusions to sociological research reflects, in our particular case, the commitment to explore a broad though clearly interrelated set of issues hitherto raised in somewhat discrete literatures. Of necessity, therefore, our research instrument elicits rather less information on occupational trajectories than does the Oxford Mobility Survey, contains far fewer questions on political partisanship than will be found in the British Election Studies, and so forth. However, to the extent that the data lack detail on particulars, they exhibit the alternative virtue of scope. The potential of our study lies in exploring connections between phenomena that are normally considered in isolation. Our achievement in this direction may be modest – but we make no apology for extending the scope of our discussion to embrace so much of worklife, home situation, and political beliefs alike. This is not to suggest that the following chapters exhaust the material collected in our sample survey. They offer, rather, the firm outlines of the picture we would wish to paint of social class in modern Britain. We shall fill in such fine detail as we can in due course.

Notes

1 Hobsbawm (1981).
2 Lukes (1984).
3 For example, structural Marxists (Dunleavy, 1979, 1980a), mainstream sociologists (Saunders, 1978, 1984), and political scientists (Finer, 1980), as well as those interested in social policy (Duke and Edgell, 1984), have all argued the case. In psephological studies the thesis has been embraced by those working within social psychological (Alt, 1979; Crewe *et al.*, 1977; Sarlvik and Crewe, 1983), rational choice (Robertson, 1984), societal psychological (Himmelweit *et al.*, 1984), and radical structural (Dunleavy and Husbands, 1985) perspectives.
4 Gorz (1982). See also Bauman (1982), Offe (1985), and Lipset (1981).
5 A detailed account of these aspects of the debate is available in Rose *et al.* (1984). The papers in Roberts *et al* (1984) and Newby *et al.* (1985) are representative of the relevant literature.
6 Scott (1979, 1982), Ingham (1984).
7 Routh (1980), Fothergill and Gudgin (1982), Thatcher (1979).
8 Sinfield (1981), Kreckel (1980), Blackburn and Mann (1979).
9 On shift effects see Wright and Singelmann (1982), and Lee (1981).
10 Garnsey (1978), Crompton and Jones (1984).
11 Amin (1979), Pratten (1976), Massey (1984).
12 Routh (1980).
13 See, for overviews of the different class schemata, Wright (1980a), Abercrombie and Urry (1983), and Carter (1985).
14 For a review of this literature see Marshall (1983).
15 Mann (1973).
16 Daniel and Millward (1983), Brown (1981).
17 Goldthorpe (1978).
18 Brown *et al.* (1983). See also Sparrow (1983).
19 Alt (1979), Sarlvik and Crewe (1983), Daniel (1975), Purcell (1982), Cashmore (1984).
20 Pahl (1985), Goldthorpe (1979).
21 Gorz (1982).
22 Moorhouse (1983).
23 Westergaard (1984), Dunleavy (1980b).
24 Taylor-Gooby (1982, 1983).

2 When is a social class?

Our first task must be to provide a clear picture of what is to be understood by the term social class. Only then will it be possible to evaluate the significance of class processes, alongside that of alternative mechanisms structuring consensus and conflict, as these have been identified in recent accounts of social inequality in modern Britain. What, then, are social classes?

I

Social class is, of course, one of the fundamental concepts of sociology. Class analysis at present is characterized by a diversity of competing models of class, and over the years has sponsored vociferous debates on the relationship between different conceptualizations of class and other dimensions of power and inequality, such as those of sex, race, and social status. It is but a slight exaggeration to say that there have been almost as many theories of class as there have class analysts observing the phenomenon.

In some texts the various class models are presented as if they are wholly antagonistic and mutually exclusive. If we consider the class theories of Marx and Weber, for example, it has been argued at length that

it is a mistake to try to synthesise the concept of class of these two theorists. In particular the emphasis on distribution and the associated phenomenon of the market in Weberian theory gives only a partial and at times misleading account of the class structure of capitalist industrial societies.[1]

Crompton and Gubbay, on reaching this conclusion, would prefer to 'follow Marx in grounding the class structure in relationships of production'. Another reviewer has judged social class, rather more despairingly, to be an 'essentially contested concept', subject to endless and irresolvable disputes about its meaning and proper use, and therefore wisely to be abandoned altogether.[2]

Elsewhere, however, sociologists have attempted to synthesize the insights of Marx and Weber – an exercise seen by Crompton and Gubbay as 'doomed to failure because of the fundamental differences between the two theorists'. Abercrombie and Urry, for example, find it difficult to determine which among contemporary class analyses are Weberian and which Marxian in provenance. In their view, these labels often 'indicate differences in analytical style or emphasis rather than a conflict of principle', and they conclude therefore that 'a separation of Marxist and Weberian theory is not now theoretically profitable and . . . an adequate theory may well seem eclectic, incorporating and rejecting elements of both approaches'.[3]

Where then does class analysis stand at present? Have we reached an impasse in which the different approaches must exist within closed theoretical universes justifying incompatible and incomparable *modi operandi*? Or is a *rapprochement* of the major traditions possible?

At the level of social theory the issues seem straightforward enough. Clearly, there is an unbridgeable epistemological gap between the Marxian and Weberian frameworks for the study of society generally, since Weber's insistence on the logical and methodological separation of fact and value ultimately cannot be reconciled with Marx's philosophy of praxis.[4] Yet their respective accounts of class mechanisms appear to be not wholly dissimilar. Since subsequent discussion of class matters – at least among European sociologists – has been conducted within the parameters established by these early theorists it is apposite here to consider their accounts in some detail.[5] Erik Wright, after all, derives his class schema straight from the pages of *Capital* while that of John Goldthorpe is explicitly Weberian in conception.

In fact both Marx and Weber focused their discussions of social class on the correlates of industrialization and market capitalism. The former term refers to a threefold process embracing the development of technology (technical division of labour), growth of manufacturing industry (sectoral division of labour), and changes in the organization of production (social division of labour). The three dimensions of the division of labour raise issues primarily of co-ordination and control as these emerge from the differentiation, allocation, and negotiation of roles and tasks. The development of market capitalism, on the other hand, describes the extension of market principles to social life in general and the consequences of this for the distribution of wealth in society. It pertains to issues arising out of the ownership and exchange of private property.

These two processes are in principle distinct and often, in practice, empirically discrete. If capitalism is defined as the private ownership of property and transaction of social relations through the market by way of a cash nexus then Rome during the last two centuries of the Republic and the first two of the Principate was no less capitalist than was England during the sixteenth and seventeenth centuries. Indeed it could be argued that urban markets in the former were subject to fewer external constraints (enforced monopolies, prices, or trading practices) than were those of the English towns and cities. Nevertheless the development of machine technology and growth of large-scale production had reached levels in early-modern England that were unimagined and unimaginable in classical Rome.[6]

Of course it is a commonplace observation that both Marx and Weber wrote extensively about the progressive commercialization of life in general and the social consequences of the development of machine technology in particular. But one often overlooked consequence of this is that each refers their analysis of social class to aspects of both processes. Their discussions of class mechanisms are, in fact, generally held to be quite dissimilar. Above all else, Marx's account of social class relationships is said to differ from that of Weber in that Marxism postulates an explicit theory of the relationship between market capitalism and the division of labour whereas Weberian sociology takes the occupational structure as given, 'as the starting point for the analysis of social stratification, not as a phenomenon requiring explanation in its own right'.[7] But we shall argue that this is, indeed, a misconception. Let us examine each contribution in turn.

For most commentators Marx is the theorist *par excellence* of social class relationships. Almost everything he wrote is directly or indirectly concerned with social class and this renders concise summary of his position understandably difficult.[8] Nevertheless it can reasonably be claimed that his conception of class relationships involves the three dimensions of ownership, production, and struggle.

In Marx's early writings relations of ownership and production are merged into a single dimension of exploitation. Thus, for example, the analysis of alienation that is offered in the *Economic and Philosophical Manuscripts of 1844* describes a proletariat that is simultaneously deprived both of property and of unified (and therefore meaningful) work. The accumulation of capital and division of labour conjointly impoverish the workers, polarize the classes, and destabilize capitalist society by generating a crisis of industrial overproduction. At this stage Marx offers no theory of the relationship between the two processes. He merely asserts that they are empirically inseparable. In *The German Ideology* he returns to this theme, insisting that the social relations which are the fundamental determinants of class structure embrace private property and the division of labour as 'identical expressions'.[9]

However Marx cannot be said to have been consistent about this. Elsewhere in *The German Ideology* he seems to accord priority to the division of labour by deriving from its structure both the general forms of social ownership and the specific distribution of particular goods. Two years later he reverses this relationship, now conceding only that the division of labour can produce diverse occupations within social classes, so bringing members of these classes into conflict (but not *class* conflict) with each other. This is probably the position Marx would have developed in *Capital III*. There too he insists that

the owners merely of labour-power, owners of capital, and landowners whose respective sources of income are wages, profit and ground-rent, in other words, wage-labourers, capitalists and landowners, constitute then three big classes of modern society based upon the capitalist mode of production.

Within these social classes the social division of labour separates labourers, capitalists, and landowners into an 'infinite fragmentation of interest and rank'.[10]

In his later works, therefore, Marx maintained an analytical distinction between ownership (which separates social classes) and the social division of labour (which delineates strata or fragments within classes). Moreover,

15

because his account of the capitalist mode of production rests upon the labour theory of value, he can offer a concise statement of the relationship between the two; the division of labour (in the specific form of machine-based large-scale factory production) is the instrument by which the capitalist class maintains the extraction of surplus value despite the inherent tendency of the rate of profit to fall.[11] In fact the relevant passages in Marx's texts are sufficiently ambiguous to have permitted the development of two such formulations and these are neatly reflected in contemporary literature on the labour process. In Braverman's interpretation of the deskilling and labour displacing features of modern technology, subdivisions of the work process are an attempt to reduce skill levels, so cutting wage costs and protecting 'efficiency' (or in other words maintaining the rate of profit). Others, Stone and Edwards for example, have argued that the introduction of the factory system of manufacture, application of new technologies, subdivision and hierarchical organization of tasks are all attempts to control labour irrespective of the issue of profit. These theories can, of course, be rendered complementary since they differ only in the extent to which there is an explicit reliance on the labour theory of value in reconstructing the motives of capitalists and managers. It can reasonably be argued that the whole point about controlling labour is that this is a prerequisite to extracting a surplus from it.[12]

Finally it must be recognized that Marx envisages class relations existing at a political and ideological level, quite independently of the relationships that inhere in the labour process. This is the Marx of *The Eighteenth Brumaire of Louis Bonaparte* and *The Class Struggles in France, 1848 to 1850*. It is sufficient for our purposes simply to note that the elements of economic, political, and ideological struggle separately and together pervade his account of class relations. Since Marx is irretrievably ambiguous, both about the respective parts played by economics, politics, and ideology in the determination of classes, and about the roles of people, surplus value, and the relations of production generally as the makers and bearers of history, we do not intend to pursue these questions here.[13] The metaphysics of relative autonomy appear simply to have translated the problems of the *an sich/fur sich* transformation into another vocabulary without in any sense resolving them. Likewise the problematic of the subject remains, indeed, problematic. In short, Marx's own writings are sufficiently inconsistent to ensure that the different interpretations of Hirst and Cohen, Althusser and Thompson, are inseparable if adjudication is attempted merely by appeal to original sources.[14]

But what of Weber? His theory of social class is usually contrasted with that of Marx since the two are held to be more or less diametrically opposed. In fact, for Weber as for Marx, social class relationships embrace the same three dimensions of ownership, production, and struggle. This is nowhere more apparent than in Weber's definition of class itself which employs the criteria of private ownership of property, possession of and control over marketable skills, and association of class members in class organizations.[15]

Like Marx, Weber makes a fundamental distinction between propertied and propertyless classes, and allows for a similar differentiation of individuals into social strata within these according to the different types of property, services, and skills that each person possesses or controls. It is at this point, however, that Marx and Weber are commonly judged to have parted company. Central to Weber's conception of class is the market. It is differential life-chances distributed by the capitalist market that distinguish the various social classes. Marx, guided by his interpretation of the labour theory of value, was unhappy with this formulation since, at least as it appears in classical economics, the implication is that the contract between capital and labour is in some sense an exchange of equivalents. But, for Marx, the proposition that the market is the basic driving force in capitalism mistakes the level of appearances for that of reality. Symmetrical exchanges in the market are an illusion behind which surplus value is extracted from labour power in the process of production.[16]

While this commonly held perception of the difference between the two approaches is indeed accurate it also serves, at the same time, to undermine the claim that Weber offers no theory of the division of labour (and hence of the occupational structure). In fact, for Weber, the same mechanism stands behind the social division of labour as generates the distribution of property in the form of capital and land; namely, the capitalist market itself. It is the operation of the capitalist market that determines the sectoral and technical divisions of labour (whether or not new technologies will improve efficiency or profits), and indeed determines the social division of labour itself, since this is nothing more than the bargain struck by employer and employee in the unequal exchange of more or less scarce formal job opportunities against more or less scarce socially agreed skills. As Braverman's critics constantly remind us the social division of labour is negotiated between management and workers. It is 'a continual process of conflict, compromise and even co-operation between capitalists and workers, over the form and content of the components of technical change'.[17] It is structured, in short, by market exchanges of the same order as determine the distribution of property. Labour power, and the different skills embraced by it, are simply forms of property which offer variable life-chances on the market.[18]

If the idea that private property and the division of labour interchangeably structure class relations through the medium of market exchanges seems familiar this is perhaps because we have earlier encountered this same proposition. Karl Marx offered precisely such an interpretation of class processes in the Paris Manuscripts and *The German Ideology*. In other words, as far as the ownership and production dimensions of social class relationships are concerned, the young Marx and the mature Weber are indistinguishable. It is only in Marx's later texts, beginning with the *Grundrisse*, that his treatment of class can be said in any sense to diverge significantly from that of Weber. The principal distinguishing feature would seem to be the theory of surplus value.

Finally, in respect of Weber's treatment, it is worth noting that, like Marx, he perceives class relations as existing at the political and ideological as well as economic levels, and insists that the relationships between these are a matter for empirical investigation in each case. Class position (commonable life-chances) provides no necessary basis for collective action. Whether or not members of a class recognize and act upon class interests as a class 'is linked to general cultural conditions . . . and is especially linked to the transparency of the connections between the causes and the consequences of the class situation'. In fact, since classes tend not to be groups or communities, it is more often the case that the social sources of shared identity and collective action are located in status groups, these being defined in terms of 'a specific, positive or negative, social estimation of *honour*', normally expressed in 'a specific *style of life*'. Weberian classes, like their Marxian counterparts, are autonomous at the political and ideological levels. The classes which emerge in the class struggle, the antagonistic social relations between people, have an indeterminate and empirically variable relationship to the classes that are defined in material life by relationships between people in the market.[19]

It is clear, then, that such differences between Marxian and Weberian theory as are conventionally identified – Weber's emphasis on market processes as compared to that placed on the sphere of production by Marx for example – can be magnified or minimized according to which of the several Marxian and Weberian accounts of class one elects to pursue. At the level of social theory, social classes can be almost all things to all people, most of whom will be able to claim a respectable classical pedigree for their favoured approach. In practice, therefore, the differences between Marxist and Weberian frameworks are more obvious from the details of research procedure than from the axioms of class theory itself. This can be illustrated by examining three discrete approaches to class analysis – those of the Registrar-General, John Goldthorpe, and Erik Wright. These are official, sociological, and Marxist perspectives respectively.

II

The Registrar-General's class schema rests on the assumption that society is a graded hierarchy of occupations ranked according to skill. Occupations are allocated to social classes commensurate with the degree of expertise involved in carrying out their associated tasks and the resulting categories are assumed to be homogeneous in these terms. In fact, the five basic social classes recognized by the Office of Population Censuses and Surveys were, from 1921 to 1971, a classification of occupations according to their reputed 'standing within the community'. In 1980 this was changed so that social class was equated instead with occupational skill. Unfortunately, OPCS have not explained the principles behind this reconceptualization, so it is not clear how the earlier 'lifestyle and prestige' categories relate to the newer 'occupational skill' ones. Since only about 7 per cent of cases are awarded different class codes when the same data are coded according to both procedures and then cross-classified, it seems that in practice, the changes in the mechanism for allocating occupations to classes have achieved little beyond further obfuscation of the already somewhat unclear class categories themselves.[20]

Since occupations are placed in social classes on the basis of judgements made by the Registrar-General's staff, and not in accordance with any coherent body of social theory, the classification has rightly been described as an intuitive or a priori scale.[21] This is not to suggest that it makes no assumptions about the structure of society and the nature of social stratification. In fact the scheme embodies the now obsolete and discredited conceptual model of the nineteenth-century eugenicists; namely, that of society as a hierarchy of inherited natural abilities, these being reflected in the skill level of different occupations. Although the first published application of the class schema in 1911 was, as is commonly known, to the interpretation of infant mortality statistics, the real inspiration for its construction came from the nineteenth-century debate about differential fertility, between hereditarian eugenicists on the one hand and environmentalists on the other. The eugenicists were concerned that interventionist public health measures would lead to the survival of greater numbers of physically and mentally inferior children among the lower orders in society. The long-term implication, they argued, was a deterioration in the average national physique and intellect, as the population came increasingly to be recruited from 'inferior' grades. T. H. C. Stevenson, an environmentalist and advocate of interventionist public health measures, developed the social class schema in order to test and disprove these theories. To do this he had actually to measure fertility in the different occupational groups – and this is why occupation came to be used as the crucial indicator for the measurement and construction of social grades. In fact, those working on the issue of infant mortality had previously established that occupational categories were less useful as a measure of a household's social position than quite different indicators, in particular those of residential overcrowding and numbers of servants retained. Yet Stevenson's refutation of biological theory did not lead to the abandonment of this model of society. On the contrary, eugenicist assumptions about society as a graded hierarchy of inherited natural abilities reflected in the skill level of occupations, remain embedded in the official, and most commonly used, measure of social class in Britain today.[22]

Over the years a number of changes have been implemented both in the method of classifying occupations and in the allocation of particular occupations to social classes. These make time-series comparisons extremely difficult. In 1931, for example, male clerks were demoted from class 2 to class 3; in 1960 airline pilots were promoted from class 3 to class 2; and in 1961 postmen and telephone operators were demoted from class 2 to class 4. However, while individual occupations have been reallocated to different classes, the overall shape of the model has changed very little during the past fifty years. In practice individuals are assigned to social classes by a threefold process. First, they are allocated an occupational group, defined according to 'the kind of work done and the nature of the operation performed'. Each occupational category is then assigned 'as a whole to one or other social class and no account is taken of differences between individuals in the same occupation group e.g. differences of education or level of remuneration'.[23] Finally, however, persons of particular employment status within occupational groups are removed to social classes different to that allocated the occupation as a whole. Most notably, individuals of foreman status whose basic social class is 4 or 5 are reallocated to social class 3, and persons of managerial status are (with certain minor exceptions) placed in social class 2 (see Table 2.1 which shows the composition of our own sample).

Table 2.1 *Distribution of respondents into the Registrar-General's class categories*

Class		N	%
1	Professional, etc., occupations	48	3.7
2	Intermediate occupations	327	24.9
3N	Skilled occupations, nonmanual	294	22.4
3M	Skilled occupations, manual	358	27.2
4	Partly skilled occupations	212	16.1
5	Unskilled occupations	67	5.1
6	Armed forces	9	0.7
		1315	100.0

This strategy has been widely criticized in sociology on both practical and theoretical grounds. The coding of occupational groups and employment statuses produces notoriously unreliable results. The categories themselves are imprecisely formulated, and this in turn leads to considerable coding error, both between different coders using the same data and particular researchers allocating individuals to common categories on the basis of different answers. Quality checks of the 1966 Census, for example, showed that 10.7 per cent of occupations had been coded to the wrong occupational unit group because the categories were unclear, too general, or confused with grade titles. Similarly, by using data from the official records of a 1 per cent sample of the population, Leete and Fox were able to test the reliability of the 1971 Census, comparing the class position of men who registered the birth of a child between census day 1971 and the end of December of that year, with their class position as recorded at the census itself. Only about 81 per cent of the sample were assigned to the same class at both events; at birth registration 10 per cent were placed in a higher social class and 9 per cent in a lower social class than at the census. The proportion in the same social class was over 80 per cent for classes 1, 2, and 3, 70 per cent for class 4, and only 51 per cent for class 5. The authors concluded that, while a small part of the discrepancy would be explained by genuine social mobility, most was the result of inconsistency in occupational descriptions and of coding or punching errors. More recently, the *1981 Census Post-Enumeration Survey* suggested that the gross error in the census occupational and class allocations was about 20 per cent and 13 per cent respectively, though in the latter case discrepancies were due less to differences in coding procedures and rather more to the fact that inadequate information had been provided by respondents to the census itself.[24]

While random punching errors will occur in any mechanical operation it is reasonable to argue that the reliability and coding problems encountered in using the Registrar-General's classification stem largely from the fact that it fails to conform to any consistent theory of social class. It is this which accounts for imprecision both in the categories themselves and in the principles governing the allocation of occupations to classes. In other words the unreliability of the schema is a direct function of its invalidity as a measure of social class. This, of course, was exactly Hindess's argument with regard to the Indian Census in his critique of the use of official statistics in sociology.[25] Not surprisingly, therefore, some sociologists have sought to develop measures of social class that rest on explicit sociological reasoning rather than taxonomic fiat. Most prominent among such schemata are the class categories developed by John Goldthorpe for the Oxford study of social mobility in England and Wales.

Although the construction of Goldthorpe's original sevenfold class schema was informed by the earlier Hope–Goldthorpe scale of the social desirability of jobs,[26] the theoretical justification for the categories themselves derives from a Weberian conception of class, as defined by the market and work situations of particular occupations. The classification attempts

to combine occupational categories whose members would appear . . . to be typically comparable, on the one hand, in terms of their sources and levels of income, their degree of economic security and chances of economic advancement; and, on the other, in their location within systems of authority and control governing the process of production in which they are engaged, and hence their degree of autonomy in performing their work-tasks and roles.[27]

Goldthorpe has now refined this schema by subdividing three of the original classes, and details of the eleven-category version are given in Table 2.2, together with the frequency distribution for our own respondents.

But Goldthorpe has always maintained that an exclusively structural approach to class is inadequate to the explanation of social order and collective action. Specific historical forms of the division of labour do generate a structure of positions – typically those of employer, self-employed worker, domestic labourer, and employee – with the last of these in particular differentiated into a complex hierarchy according to varying conditions of employment. And, of course, certain positions within the structure – manager, supervisor, own account worker – typically accrue similar returns in terms of income, job autonomy, and so forth. However, a satisfactory class analysis must take seriously the issues of process and agency, hence class formation.

For any such structure of positions, the empirical question can then be raised of how far classes have in fact formed within it, in the sense of specific social collectivities; that

Table 2.2 *Distribution of respondents into Goldthorpe class categories*

Class			N	%
Service	I	Higher-grade professionals, administrators, and officials; managers in large establishments; large proprietors.	123	9.4
	II	Lower-grade professionals, administrators, and officials; higher-grade technicians; managers in small business and industrial establishments; supervisors of nonmanual employees.	235	17.9
Intermediate	IIIa	Routine nonmanual employees in administration and commerce	198	15.1
	IIIb	Personal service workers	58	4.4
	IVa	Small proprietors, artisans, etc., with employees	45	3.4
	IVb	Small proprietors, artisans, etc., without employees	59	4.5
	IVc	Farmers and smallholders; self-employed fishermen	11	0.8
	V	Lower-grade technicians, supervisors of manual workers	107	8.1
Working	VI	Skilled manual workers	165	12.5
	VIIa	Semi-skilled and unskilled manual workers (not in agriculture)	307	23.4
	VIIb	Agricultural workers	7	0.5
			1315	100.0

is, collectivities that are identifiable through the degree of continuity with which, in consequence of patterns of class mobility and immobility, their members are associated with particular sets of positions over time; and, in turn, the further issue may be pursued of the degree of distinctiveness of members of identifiable classes in terms of their life-chances, their life-styles and patterns of association, and their socio-political orientations and modes of action.[28]

Class analysis within this perspective therefore calls for explicit consideration of the question of social mobility and its impact on demographic class formation.

This is an elegant argument firmly grounded in the mainstream of sociological theory, combining as it does the twin themes of Weber's influential discussion of class situation, namely those of position in the market and of social closure around 'class situations within which individual and generational mobility is easy and typical'.[29] However, within sociology, both the Weberian tradition of class analysis in general, and Goldthorpe's interpretation of it in particular, have been subject to extensive criticism on the grounds that the conditions of the market-place fragment society into innumerable divisions so that it is hard to see where one class begins and another ends.[30] Most Marxists argue further that, boundary problems aside, this approach to the study of class places too much importance on the distributive system and too little on processes of production – a serious limitation in their view, of course, since Marxian theory suggests that it is relations of production which are the determining element in class structures.[31] But it is not necessary to pursue these issues here, since it is the practice of class analysis that forms the object of our concern, rather than its theoretical rationale. And, although Goldthorpe's schema emerges from a developed theory of class processes, in practice individual respondents are given a Goldthorpe class standing via a procedure analogous to that followed in official circles. First, they are placed in occupational groups according to the content of their jobs, then given an employment status that reflects their social relationships at work (self-employed without employees, manager in large establishment, and so forth). In both cases the categories and definitions used are those adopted by the Registrar-General. The *Classification of Occupations 1980* lists 549 occupational groups, aggregated under 161 key occupational headings, together with nine employment statuses. Finally, a social class position is obtained for each individual by cross-classifying his or her occupation and employment status, each possible legitimate combination having previously been allocated a place within one of the eleven Goldthorpe social class categories.

Not surprisingly, Marxists are critical of any approach, Goldthorpe's own included, that retains occupation as the basis for class analysis. To do so is, in their view, to mistake categories defined by technical relations of production (the prevailing state of technology) for those defined by social relations of production (ownership and non-ownership of productive means).[32] Consider, therefore, by way of comparison, the class schema developed by the American Marxist Erik Wright – here applied in its elaborated form to our sample as shown in Table 2.3.

Wright argues that, in each mode of production, certain basic social classes are defined by being completely polarized within the relevant social relations of production. Under capitalism, for example, the working class is wholly dispossessed of the means of production, must sell its labour power to the bourgeoisie, so is both exploited and dominated by it. However, in the absence of wholesale polarization, contradictory locations within a mode of production also arise. Managers, for example, are simultaneously in two classes. They are workers, since they are exploited by capital, yet capitalists in that they dominate workers. Moreover, concrete social formations rarely comprise a single mode of production, so that capitalist societies, for example, will typically contain certain non-capitalist forms of production relations. Most obviously they inherit the legacy of simple commodity production in which direct producers own and control only their own productive means (including their own labour power). These are the *petit bourgeoisie* or own account workers more common to feudal societies. Certain class locations in fact interpenetrate both modes of production and so constitute contradictory locations between them. The most important of these define small employers, on the one hand, and semi-autonomous employees on the other. The former are simultaneously *petit bourgeois* and capitalist in that they are self-employed direct producers but also employers and therefore exploiters of labour. Semi-autonomous employees are non-owners of

23

Table 2.3 *Distribution of respondents into Wright class categories*

Capitalist mode of production		*Simple commodity production*

Bourgeoisie

Small employers

Managers and supervisors   Petit bourgeoisie

Semi-autonomous employees

Proletariat

[classes/*contradictory locations within class relations*]

Class		*N*	%
Bourgeoisie		26	2.0
Small employers		59	4.5
Petit bourgeoisie		79	6.0
	managers	163	12.4
Managers and supervisors	advisory managers	59	4.5
	supervisors	124	9.4
Semi-autonomous employees		153	11.6
Workers		652	49.6
		1315	100.0

productive means but still exercise considerable control over their own activities within production. Employed professionals are the example most often cited by Wright.[33]

This framework can be criticized for being static, mechanical, crudely deterministic, and (in common with those proffered by most other structuralists) devoid of human agency.[34] Again, however, it is Wright's operationalization of class relationships, rather than their theoretical rationale as such that is the focus of attention here. Wright argues that the relational properties of exploitation and domination which underpin his schema can be tapped by means of information about ownership of productive means, the degree of autonomy exercised by individuals at work, and their involvement in decision-making and supervision of other employees (Table 2.4). These translate into concrete activities such as participation in decisions dealing with budgets and investment, the ability to design and execute work-tasks, possession of authority to impose sanctions upon subordinates, and so forth.

Of course, given the location of our own project in Wright's international network of comparative studies, our interviewers fielded questions about precisely these activities, and in sufficient depth as would enable us to conduct a class analysis in terms of Wright's categories. In addition, however, the

Table 2.4 *Overall logic of the Wright's class categories*

Type of class location	Class location	Capitalist Mode of Production				Simple commodity production	
		Relations of Appropriation			Domination		
		Ownership relation	Exchange relation	Real exercise of effective property	Authority relations	Ownership relations	Domination relations
Basic class location	Bourgeoisie	Owns means of production	Buys labour power	Directly makes core decisions over allocation of resources and use of means of production	Directly controls the authority hierarchy		
Contradictory location within the capitalist mode of production	Managers	Does not own means of production	Sells labour power	Directly involved in at least some core decisions	Dominant and subordinate		
	Supervisors	"	"	Excluded from all decisions over the workplace	Dominant and subordinate		
Basic class location	Workers	"	"	"	Subordinate		
Contradictory location between capitalist production and simple commodity production	Semi-autonomous employees	"	"	"	"	Non-owner of means of production	Substantial direction within the labour process (unity of conception and execution)
Basic class location	Petty bourgeoisie					Owns means of production and directly uses them without employing labour power	Complete self-direction within the labour process
Contradictory location between capitalist and simple commodity production	Small employers	Owns means of production	Buys limited amounts of labour	Makes core decisions	Controls authority structure	Owns means of production and directly uses them within the labour process and employs some wage labour	

Reproduced by permission from Wright *et al.* (1982: 713).

British team routinely gathered information about occupation and employment status in a form that replicated the Oxford study of career and intergenerational mobility. This somewhat eclectic strategy is easily explained. Since we do not hold with essentialist definitions of class the most important question is, in our view, an empirical one. Which conception of social class best illuminates the nature of collective action, shared life-style and beliefs, and patterns of association? We reasoned that, if it were possible to fit our data to class schemata as diverse as those of the Marxist Erik Wright, at one extreme, and the Registrar-General's empiricist life-style and prestige groupings at the other – embracing John Goldthorpe's neo-Weberian occupational class schema *en route* – then we would be able to provide a systematic comparison of the utility of these approaches in practice rather than merely in logic. In any case, as has been demonstrated above, the major traditions of class theory are sufficiently ambiguous as to make any appeal to first principles wholly inconclusive in the attempt to apportion relative merits.

This is not to suggest that we are total relativists where social class is concerned. Our own conception of class (see Chapter 9 below) is itself theoretically derived. Rather, our objection is to protracted disputes conducted almost exclusively in theoretical terms, where the issues involved are at least in part resolvable in practice on empirical grounds. The so-called boundary debate in class analysis offers a good example of this. Goldthorpe and Wright have each intervened in the discussion, both at the levels of theory and evidence, and in so doing have attracted loud responses couched almost entirely in terms of theoretical critique. Our modest intention here is to offer a more systematic and empirical assessment of their alternative conceptions of the class structure and class processes in modern capitalist societies in order to complement the theoretical discussion already available.

III

What then are the implications of pursuing a class analysis of our data in terms of these contrasting approaches? It is now clear that the three schemes diverge, not only in their origins and logic, but also and perhaps most radically in the operational details of their implementation. Goldthorpe and Wright classify the self-employed separately whereas the Registrar-General does not. However, Goldthorpe's class I comprises respondents who, in Wright's terms, would be variously bourgeois, managerial, and semi-autonomous employees. The Wright schema alone separates out members of the bourgeoisie from relatively privileged employees. There is also considerable disagreement about the role and place of supervisors and managers. Wright places all supervisors in one class position. Indeed, in terms of his more general model, they appear in the same social class as do managers on the basis of their shared – contradictory – location within class relations. Goldthorpe, by comparison, allocates supervisors of manual and nonmanual employees to quite different social classes, alongside lower grade technicians on the one hand and members of the service class on the other, because of their (allegedly) distinct market and work situations. The logic of the Registrar-General's approach in similar, although in this case employers, managers, supervisors, other employees, and the self-employed in fact appear in most social classes on the supposition that they share a common life-style or are of similar social standing in the wider community.

Certain discrepancies are therefore to be expected in describing a population according to the three class models. An indication of the parameters of the dissimilarity can be gained by cross-classifying the Essex sample according to the different class algorithms (as in Table 2.5). Since the classifications are based on disparate criteria and contain non-comparable groupings (Wright's semi-autonomous employee category, for example, has no equivalent in the other schemes) it is difficult to express the extent of their incongruity in a single numerical index. Still, a cross-tabulation of the Goldthorpe and Wright schemata, for example, shows that 6 per cent of Wright's proletarians actually appear in Goldthorpe's service class. Fully two-third's of the latter's class III routine nonmanual employees are to be found among the former's workers. Wright's semi-autonomous employees in fact occur in Goldthorpe's service, intermediate, and working classes in a ratio of approximately 3:3:2. Fifteen per cent of his managers and supervisors are routine manual and nonmanual employees according to Goldthorpe's criteria. In short, there is some overlap, but also considerable disagreement between the two classifications.

As one would expect, there are relatively fewer discrepancies between the Registrar-General (RG) and Goldthorpe classes, and proportionately more between RG classes and those of Erik Wright. In the former case, RG classes 2, 3N and 3M present the greatest number of anomalies in Goldthorpe's terms. Intermediate occupations are spread across four Goldthorpe classes; less than half of those in skilled manual occupations are to be found in the corresponding Goldthorpe class; while 74 per cent of all skilled nonmanual respondents emerge in Goldthorpe's routine nonmanual category. Professional, semi-skilled, and unskilled occupations correspond, on the whole, to the appropriate Goldthorpe classes I and VII. This correspondence largely disappears in the comparison of RG and Wright class allocations. Almost every RG occupation is to be found in every Wright class. Conversely, Wright's workers, semi-autonomous employees, and managers/supervisors appear in every RG social class. The two schemes are simply incommensurable.

All of this would be of merely esoteric interest, of course, were it not for the fact that the allocation of individuals to class places has significant effects on putative patterns of class formation, social mobility, class behaviour and class consciousness. Routine white-collar employees, for example, can plausibly be classified either as 'proletarians' or as members of a 'new middle class'. For this reason they are theoretically crucial to the various contrasting models of 'late capitalist' and 'post-industrial' society which are currently available. Do these workers enjoy the relative privileges of more obviously semi-autonomous employees or are their market and work situations largely

Table 2.5 *Cross-classification of respondents into Registrar-General, Goldthorpe, and Wright class categories*

A – Goldthorpe by Wright

		Bourge-oisie	Small employers	Petit bourge-oisie	Wright Managers and super-visors	Semi-auto-nomous employers	Workers	Total
	I	1.4 (18)	0.5 (7)	0.3 (4)	6.1 (80)	0.5 (7)	0.5 (7)	9.4 (123)
	II	0.5 (6)	0.5 (6)	0.5 (7)	10.0 (132)	3.9 (51)	2.5 (33)	17.9 (235)
	III	0.0 (0)	0.0 (0)	0.0 (0)	2.4 (31)	4.1 (54)	13.0 (171)	19.5 (256)
Goldthorpe	IV	0.2 (2)	3.4 (45)	5.2 (68)	0.0 (0)	0.0 (0)	0.0 (0)	8.7 (115)
	V	0.0 (0)	0.0 (0)	0.0 (0)	6.4 (84)	0.4 (5)	1.4 (18)	8.1 (107)
	VI	0.0 (0)	0.0 (0)	0.0 (0)	0.6 (8)	1.2 (16)	10.7 (141)	12.5 (165)
	VII	0.0 (0)	0.1 (1)	0.0 (0)	0.8 (11)	1.5 (20)	21.4 (282)	23.9 (314)
Total		2.0 (26)	4.5 (59)	6.0 (79)	26.3 (346)	11.6 (153)	49.6 (652)	100.0 (1315)

B – RG by Goldthorpe

		I	II	III	Goldthorpe IV	V	VI	VII	Total
	1	3.7 (48)	0.0 (0)	0.0 (0)	0.0 (0)	0.0 (0)	0.0 (0)	0.0 (0)	3.7 (48)
	2	5.2 (68)	13.6 (179)	2.6 (34)	3.5 (46)	0.0 (0)	0.0 (0)	0.0 (0)	24.9 (327)
RG	3N	0.0 (0)	4.0 (53)	16.5 (217)	1.2 (16)	0.5 (7)	0.0 (0)	0.1 (1)	22.4 (294)
	3M	0.2 (3)	0.2 (3)	0.2 (3)	3.0 (39)	6.8 (89)	12.2 (161)	4.6 (60)	27.2 (358)
	4	0.0 (0)	0.0 (0)	0.2 (2)	0.8 (11)	0.5 (6)	0.3 (4)	14.4 (189)	16.1 (212)
	5	0.0 (0)	0.0 (0)	0.0 (0)	0.2 (3)	0.0 (0)	0.0 (0)	4.9 (64)	5.1 (67)
	6	0.3 (4)	0.0 (0)	0.0 (0)	0.0 (0)	0.4 (5)	0.0 (0)	0.0 (0)	0.7 (9)
Total		9.4 (123)	17.9 (235)	19.5 (256)	8.7 (115)	8.1 (107)	12.5 (165)	23.9 (314)	100.0 (1315) •

C – RG by Wright

		Bourge-oisie	Small employers	Petit bourge-oisie	Wright Managers and super-visors	Semi-auto-nomous employees	Workers	Total
	1	0.4 (5)	0.4 (5)	0.2 (3)	2.1 (27)	0.3 (4)	0.3 (4)	3.7 (48)
	2	1.4 (18)	2.0 (26)	2.2 (29)	12.0 (158)	4.0 (53)	3.3 (43)	24.9 (327)
RG	3N	0.0 (0)	0.7 (9)	0.8 (10)	4.5 (59)	4.0 (52)	12.5 (164)	22.4 (294)
	3M	0.2 (3)	1.1 (14)	2.1 (27)	6.6 (87)	1.7 (22)	15.6 (205)	27.2 (358)
	4	0.0 (0)	0.3 (4)	0.6 (8)	0.5 (6)	1.6 (21)	13.2 (173)	16.1 (212)
	5	0.0 (0)	0.1 (1)	0.2 (2)	0.1 (1)	0.1 (1)	4.7 (62)	5.1 (67)
	6	0.0 (0)	0.0 (0)	0.0 (0)	0.6 (8)	0.0 (0)	0.1 (1)	0.7 (9)
Total		2.0 (26)	4.5 (59)	6.0 (79)	26.3 (346)	11.6 (153)	49.6 (652)	100.0 (1315)

Note: i Figures in brackets are raw numbers.

ii In this and some subsequent tables percentages may not add up exactly because of rounding.

indistinguishable from those of unskilled manual labourers? Are they normatively distinct from the credentialled middle class? Our analysis is clearly not an exercise in taxonomy for its own sake. Substantive conclusions about social processes such as embourgeoisement or proletarianization may be significantly affected by the choice of a particular class schema as the basis for any analysis. It is for this reason, then, that the present text has not only examined the construction of three contrasting frameworks for class analysis but will also investigate their comparative utility for explaining observed differences in the patterning of life-chances, social behaviour, and social consciousness. Our class analysis will therefore proceed, rather unusually, by fielding not one but three social class schemata. To what extent do the different frameworks illuminate data on inequality and schism in modern Britain? Indeed can any class analysis shed light upon our findings? These questions are the leitmotiv of the following chapters.

Notes

1 Crompton and Gubbay (1977; 2).
2 Calvert (1982).
3 Abercrombie and Urry (1983; 89, 152).
4 On this issue see Marshall (1982).
5 On the European tradition see Giddens (1973). American sociologists have tended to equate social class with prestige or life-style – Lloyd Warner's *Yankee City* volumes are a good example – this being an approach favoured in Britain mainly by officialdom in the shape of the Registrar-General (see Page, 1969; Warner *et al.*, 1960; Szreter, 1984).
6 Compare Runciman (1983) and Nef (1934). Of course the capitalist market neither extended across nor integrated the political territories and social structures of the Roman Empire or seventeenth-century England. Rightly, therefore, these societies are not conventionally described as capitalist, whereas this label can aptly be applied to industrialized West European states, in which the market mechanism acts as the primary means of system integration (see Polanyi, 1957; 1977). This is not to deny that market economies tend to exert a destabilizing influence on the societies within which they operate. 'System integration' via the capitalist market is rarely associated with 'social integration' in the sense of social or value consensus (see Lockwood, 1964).
7 Garnsey (1981: 348). See also Clarke (1982) for a detailed exposition of this argument.
8 The significance of the infamous unwritten 52nd chapter of the third volume of *Capital* is not that Marx had yet to express himself fully upon the subject of 'Classes' but that, in addressing himself directly to this topic, he might have provided clarification of his already extensive expositions upon the theme.
9 Marx (1973: 67–8), Marx and Engels (1970a: 52–3).
10 Compare Marx and Engels (1970a: 43), Marx (1970a: 208), and Marx (1972: 885–6).
11 Marx and Engels (1970b: 38–42), Marx (1970b: 312–507). On this point see also Garnsey (1981: 348) and Rattansi (1982).
12 Compare Braverman (1974), Stone (1974), Edwards (1979), Marglin (1974), and Friedman (1977).
13 Compare, for example, Marx (1970c: 181–2; 1970d: 170–1; 1972: 791–2, 818–19; and 1970e: 28). See also Ossowski (1963: 86) and Wesolowski (1979: 18–29).
14 Compare Cutler *et al.* (1977) and Cohen (1978), Althusser (1977) and Thompson (1978).
15 Weber (1968: 302). Weber's account of social classes, like that of Marx, is both ambiguous and unsystematic. In particular there are a number of possible inconsistencies between his earlier and later treatments of the subject (compare Weber, 1968: 926–39, 302–7). What follows is one interpretation of these texts rather than close scrutiny of their nuances. For further details and an alternative reading see Barbalet (1980).
16 Compare Weber (1968: 927–8) and Marx (1970b: 175–6).
17 Lazonick (1979: 257). See also Rubery (1978), Elger (1982), Littler and Salaman (1982).

18 Garnsey (1981: 347) is therefore correct when she claims that Weber's account of the division of labour 'is an account of the social relations which it engenders and does not provide the basis for a theory of economic and social development. In this he differs from the classical political economists and Marx'. Weber did not subscribe to a theory of history – far less an economic and deterministic one. However she is wrong to imply (pp. 346, 348) that Weber merely followed the marginalists in taking the organization of work (hence the occupational structure) as given, as the outcome of 'the prevailing state of technology'. Indeed he explicitly denies this. Although he does not develop a systematic theory of the technical division of labour ('It is out of the question here to undertake to develop even the most modest outline of a theory of the evolution of the technology and economics of tools and machinery'), Weber is quite unambiguous in attributing a significant role to market forces in capitalist societies, by way of explaining both the application of changed technology and the social organization of labour. Neither are simple residual categories in the manner of marginalist economics. Moreover, neither technology itself nor the division of labour are neutral, since both are socially constructed and negotiated. They are not the outcome of mere 'economic' calculations (Weber, 1968: 44–6, 67, 121, 128, 129, 141).

19 Weber (1968: 928–32).

20 See OPCS (1970: x; 1980: xi) and Brewer (1986).

21 Marsh (1986).

22 Szreter (1984).

23 OPCS (1980: vi, xi).

24 Leete and Fox (1977), OPCS (1985: 13). The recoding of occupational data from the Nuffield Mobility Study and British General Election Study of 1983, undertaken by Goldthorpe and Payne (1986b) for their report on intergenerational mobility in England and Wales since 1972, also suggests that coding of occupational data is reasonably reliable so long as coders are given sufficient information by respondents. The authors required the translation of survey material coded to the 1970 OPCS system into the categories of the 1980 system, for the Nuffield data, and vice versa for that of the BGES. In this fairly extensive exercise a better than 90 per cent agreement was obtained between two sets of coders working independently on the same (very full) occupational information. In only 3 per cent of cases would a different allocation of social classes have resulted from coding disagreements.

25 Hindess (1973).

26 Goldthorpe and Hope (1974).

27 Goldthorpe (1980: 39). In fact the concepts 'market situation' and 'work situation' were claimed by their author to be Marxian in provenance. David Lockwood, in his study of clerical workers, defined 'class position' as including the following factors.

First, 'market situation', that is to say the economic position narrowly conceived, consisting of source and size of income, degree of job-security, and opportunity for upward occupational mobility. Secondly, 'work situation', the set of social relationships in which the individual is involved at work by virtue of his position in the division of labour. And finally, 'status situation', or the position of the individual in the hierarchy of prestige in the society at large . . . 'Market situation' and 'work situation' comprise what Marx essentially understood as 'class position'; 'status situation' derives from another branch of social stratification theory (Lockwood, 1958; 15–16).

The issue of whether or not 'market situation' and 'work situation' accurately depict Marx's concept of class location need not be pursued here. (Most Marxists would, in fact, deny this.) Whatever the intellectual origins of the schema, it has subsequently been used by Lockwood and Goldthorpe as the basis for a sustained critique of Marxist (and other non-Marxist) theories of class, and is now generally acknowledged to be a defining characteristic of contemporary 'neo-Weberian' class analysis (see Goldthorpe et al., 1969; Abercrombie and Urry, 1983: 15–48; Crompton and Gubbay, 1977: 20–40).

28 Goldthorpe (1983: 467).

29 Weber (1968: 302).

30 See, for example, Barbalet (1980) and Penn (1981).

31 For example, see Binns (1977).

32 See Wright (1980b).

33 Wright (1979).

34 For example, see Lockwood (1981), Holmwood and Stewart (1983) and, more generally, Parkin (1979).

3 Constructing the Wright classes

Before proceeding to our class analysis proper there is one preliminary complication that must be dealt with. Having intitiated an international project in order to test the worth of his theory of contradictory class locations, Erik Wright subsequently revised his whole class scheme, and indeed abandoned his initial formulation altogether. By that time many national surveys, the American and British studies among them, had already been fielded. Understandably, a number of confusions have been occasioned by this shift, not the least of which concerns the status now to be accorded the very ideas which prompted the project in the first place. How seriously should we take the original class model?

It is therefore necessary, at this juncture, to introduce yet another framework for class analysis – the revised Wright schema. Moreover, in order to comprehend Wright's intellectual journeying, rather more must be made of the *theory* of social class than has thus far been the case. Wright's autocritique raises, we believe, acute problems for his Marxism. The twist in the story, as we read it, is that his new class schema, though Marxist in disposition, is more often than not justified by reference to orthodox Weberian arguments about the nature of class processes. Wright himself would of course deny this. Weberian treatments of social class are given typically short shrift in even his most recent writings.[1] Of course it could be argued that these genealogical issues are of secondary importance to the concerns of the present volume since here, as before, it is the empirical application of the schema that is the primary focus of our interest. However, it is important, in this particular context, that at least the essentials of Wright's theoretical reasoning be laid bare, since his new approach, as we shall see, is sometimes constrained by the practicalities of research in ways that in fact compromise his entire intellectual project as a whole.

I

Wright's revised framework has the same starting point as his previous one: the need for Marxist theory to come to terms with the 'middle classes' since, as Wright euphemistically puts it, 'it is no longer assumed that history will eliminate the conceptual problem'. His subsequent argument is based on a distinction between, on the one hand, class analyses which focus on class structure and those which focus on class formation; and, on the other, between the different levels of abstraction used in class analysis of whatever kind. His definitions of class structure and class formation are themselves instructive. Class structure is defined as a 'structure of social relations into which individuals (or, in some cases, families) enter which determine their class interests'; class formation refers to 'the formation of organized collectivities within that class structure on the basis of the interests shaped by that class structure'.[2] Class structure deals with relations between classes while class formation addresses relations within classes. The levels of abstraction used in class analysis are the familiar trinity of mode of production, social formation, and conjuncture. Within all the possible forms of analysis available on these bases, Marx himself concentrated on class structure within the pure capitalist mode of production, on class alliances in the social formation, and on concrete class organizations in the specific conjuncture. Neo-Marxism has attempted to fill in the gaps, by theorizing the social formation and the conjuncture, and by examining how class structure translates into the formation of collective actors. As a result of these theoretical and empirical endeavours, neo-Marxists such as Wright seemingly now agree with non-Marxists that class formation is not 'given' by the structure, since there is a 'complex and contingent . . . relationship between class structure and class formation'.[3]

How then can Wright produce a theory 'at the middle level of abstraction' which is capable of 'specifying the variability of the concrete' yet remains consistent with the general theory of modes of production? Clearly, the first task must be to identify the irreducible elements of Marx's abstract theory of class, since any more concrete statement would need to be compatible with these. Wright identifies six such elements: the primacy of class structure over other class processes such as class formation, class consciousness, and class struggle; the idea of class structure as the central organizing principle of societies; the notion that class is a relational concept and not a gradational one; that the social relations which define classes are intrinsically antagonistic; that exploitation is the objective basis of antagonistic interests; and that exploitation is itself firmly based in the social relations of production. From these axioms one can arrive at the proposition that certain positions in the structure are simultaneously in two classes and so constitute contradictory locations within class relations. As we have seen it was this concept which Wright operationalized for his initial empirical work.

Wright now offers several criticisms of his original attempt at middle-range theorizing, although in effect, as he notes, they are all a part of the same general problem. For those of us who believed that a major weakness of the original model was that it was too economistic, Wright on the contrary believes it was not economistic enough. The concept of contradictory locations embraced by his first model of class structure was, in his view, underpinned by a theory of domination rather than one of exploitation. ('Who is *subordinate* to whom?' rather than 'Who *exploits* whom?' in the hierarchies of decision-making and supervision at work.) This results in class being merely one element, rather than the central element, in social stratification. Hence Wright's self-appointed task is to return exploitation to centre-stage. This he proposes to do by way of an adaptation of the work of one of the leading rational choice Marxists, John Roemer, using the latter's insights on exploitation to transform the earlier concept of contradictory locations. Unfortunately (for this would have eased considerably the task of exposition), Wright does not simply adopt Roemer's rational choice model as it stands, for unlike Roemer he is not prepared to abandon all aspects of the labour theory of value in favour of a game-theoretic view of exploitation.[4] Moreover, since the structure of Wright's new schema emerges squarely from his differences with Roemer, it is necessary to unravel the thread of Wright's class theory back to Roemer himself in order to grasp the logic underpinning the revised class framework.

II

Roemer, in common with other Marxist theorists, sites exploitation in the interrelationship between different sources of income. His particular interpretation of these relationships is, however, at odds with that proffered within classical Marxism.[5] Roemer treats the organization of production as a game. His strategy is to ask whether particular players in the game would be better off if they were to withdraw from one game in favour of another. Hence, exploitation is a situation in which a coalition of actors have a hypothetically feasible alternative where they would be better off (and their complement, the exploiting coalition, would be worse off), if the former withdrew from the game. Four such situations of exploitation are identified; feudal, capitalist, socialist and status. Each is defined in terms of a withdrawal rule. Under feudalism, peasants would be better off, and lords worse off, if the former withdrew with their personal assets, that is, were freed from feudal obligations. This rule specifies whether or not feudal exploitation exists. Capitalist exploitation exists in a situation where capitalists would be worse off, and workers better off, if the latter withdrew with their per capita share of society's productive assets. Under socialism, exploitation exists where a 'coalition' would be better off, and its 'complement' worse off, if the former left the game with its per capita share of inalienable assets, for example its skills. Finally, status exploitation exists where a coalition would be better off, and its complement worse off, if the former exempted itself from the dues to status. Here Roemer is thinking of exploitation through state bureaucracy.

What does this game-theoretic version of exploitation offer a more orthodox Marxist such as Wright in his attempt to rework the concept of contradictory locations in class structures? One obvious attraction is that Roemer's view of exploitation is materially grounded in property relations:

The asset–exploitation nexus depends in each case upon the capacity of asset holders to deprive others of equal access to that asset. . . . On the one hand, inequalities of assets are sufficient to account for transfers of surplus labour; on the other hand, different forms of asset inequality specify different systems of exploitation. Classes are then defined as positions within the social relations of production derived from the property relations which determine the patterns of exploitation.[6]

This argument presents a challenge to any definition of class based on domination within production – such as was implicit in Wright's original model. For Roemer, domination is subordinate to exploitation, so that (to quote Wright) 'domination *within* the production process or within the labour process does not enter into the definition of class relations'. This is an argument that Wright now accepts; domination is relevant to aspects of class formation but 'the *basis* of the capital–labour relation should be identified with the relations of effective control (i.e. real economic ownership) over productive assets as such'.[7]

However, Wright has some difficulties in accepting Roemer's argument *in toto*, because of the way in which the latter completely abandons the labour theory of value. According to Wright, Roemer's theory 'allows us to assess inequalities that are the result of causal interconnections between actors [but] lacks the additional force of the view that the inequalities in question are produced by real transfers from one actor to another'.[8] In other words Roemer has mistaken simple economic oppression for exploitation. The former produces a class concept which defines a set of objective material interests but does not make clear how 'the welfare of the exploiting class *depends upon the work* of the exploited class'. Whereas for Roemer it is the withdrawal rules which define exploitation, for Wright exploitation is a combination of economic oppression with appropriation.

Wright is critical of Roemer's concept of feudal exploitation in particular. Roemer includes only two types of productive asset within his general framework; namely, physical or alienable assets, and skill or inalienable assets. Wright wishes to include labour power as a productive asset too. In capitalism, each person owns one unit of labour power, but under feudalism, serfs have less than one unit and lords have more than one, because of the existence of corvée labour. Hence, for Wright, the withdrawal rule for feudal exploitation involves leaving the game with one's unit of labour power rather than with one's personal assets; it is not physical assets *per se* which are unequally distributed in feudal societies but rather labour power. This reformulation then allows Wright to produce a symmetrical analysis in which feudal exploitation derives from unequal distribution of assets in labour power and leads to the class relation between lords and serfs; capitalist exploitation is based on the unequal distribution of alienable assets and produces the class relation between bourgeoisie and proletariat; and socialist exploitation is based on the unequal distribution of inalienable assets (skills) and results in the class relation between experts and workers. In this recasting of feudal exploitation, therefore, Wright has removed the non-materialist basis of Roemer's withdrawal rule (freedom from obligations of personal bondage) and has replaced it with a materialist one (labour power as a productive asset).

He proceeds in similar fashion when dealing with the concept of status exploitation. Marxists are, as a general rule, uncomfortable with the concept of status – and Wright is no exception. He argues that status 'has no necessary relationship to production at all' and is therefore inadmissible in any Marxist account of class. His economistic solution to the problem of the Roemerian concept of status exploitation is to replace it with one of organizational exploitation. That is, he takes organization to be a particular type of productive asset, and so arrives at the view that each type of class structure is precisely typified by the principal asset which is unequally distributed: under feudalism it is labour power; under capitalism, the means of production; under statism, organization; and, under socialism, skills.

In this manner Wright is able to produce a typology of assets, forms of exploitation and class structures by which feudalism, capitalism, statism and socialism can be defined in terms of the principal asset that is unequally distributed, the mechanism of exploitation involved, and the polarized class system which results. In the abstract, and with the modifications described above, Wright follows Roemer – the four forms of exploitation correspond to four modes of production. However, in order to deal with the 'variability of the concrete', Wright abandons the idea of a simple association between forms of exploitation and modes of production. Just as the *petit bourgeoisie* were introduced into his earlier model as a class of a subsidiary mode of production to that of capitalism, so Wright now claims that the principal asset which is unequally distributed within any particular mode of production is not the only asset which is so distributed, but merely the prime basis of exploitation. In other words, within any given system, assets other than the primary one may be the basis of exploitation. For example, in capitalism the principal asset exploited by capitalists is ownership of the means of production, and this is the defining feature of the system. However capitalists may also exploit workers through their control of organizational assets. Thus it makes sense to produce a class typology which incorporates all the assets which are unequally distributed in the four modes of production earlier identified. As Wright observes, he is not concerned with delineating abstract mode of production concepts, but rather the actual class structure of contemporary capitalism, especially the various non-polarized positions:

Since concrete societies are rarely, if ever, characterized by a single mode of production, the actual class structures of given societies will be characterized by complex patterns of exploitation relations. There will therefore tend to be some positions which are exploiting along one dimension of exploitation relations, while on another are exploited. Highly skilled wage earners (e.g. professionals) in capitalism are a good example: they are capitalistically exploited because they lack assets in capital and yet are skill-exploiters. Such positions are what are typically referred to as the 'new middle class' of a given class system.[9]

In this way Wright not only modifies Roemer's analysis but also shifts the central focus from a concern for determining the characteristics of different modes of production to the idea that several exploitation processes operate simultaneously within real capitalist societies.[10] And so the result of this extended exercise in conceptual excavation is the twelve-class model illustrated in Table 3.1. (The percentages are those for the resulting 'class map' of Britain derived from our sample.) The typology is in two segments; one for owners of the means of production and one for non-owners. Within the latter,

locations are distinguished by the two subordinate relations of exploitation characteristic of capitalist society – organization assets and skill/credential assets. It is thus possible to distinguish within this framework a whole terrain of class-locations in capitalist *society* that are distinct from the polarized classes of the capitalist *mode of production*; expert managers, non-managerial experts, non-expert managers, etc.[11]

Table 3.1 *Distribution of respondents into revised Wright class categories*
Assets in the means of production

Owners	Non-owners (wage labourers)				
1 Bourgeoisie	4 Expert managers	7 Semi-credentialled managers	10 Uncredentialled managers	+ Managers	
2.0% (26)	5.6% (74)	7.9% (104)	3.2% (42)		
2 Small employers	5 Expert supervisors	8 Semi-credentialled supervisors	11 Uncredentialled supervisors	>0 Supervisors	**Organization assets**
4.5% (59)	2.2% (29)	3.8% (50)	3.4% (45)		
3 Petit bourgeoisie	6 Expert non-managers	9 Semi-credentialled workers	12 Proletarians	– Non-management	
6.0% (79)	4.1% (54)	14.4% (189)	42.9% (564)		
	+ Experts	>0 Skilled employees	– Non-skilled		
		Skill/credential assets			

Thus has Wright reconceptualized the basis of the various contradictory locations within class relations. The heterogeneous middle classes

will typically hold contradictory interests with respect to the primary forms of class struggle in capitalist society, the struggle between labour and capital. On the one hand, they are like workers in being excluded from ownership of the means of production; on the other, they have interests opposed to workers because of their effective control of organization and skill assets.[12]

There are now no less than eight such locations; that is, cells 4 to 11 in Table 3.1. Naturally, these are now to be termed 'contradictory locations within exploitation relations', so as to reflect the putatively materialist basis of the typology. Cells 9 and 11 are 'marginal working-class' positions, since their incumbents have very limited control over organization or skill assets, while those in other contradictory locations are more obviously of the 'new middle class'.

Of course, after all this theoretical work Wright faces considerable difficulties in operationalizing these new class structure variables, for he has to find measures for the three forms of asset which define the model using a research instrument which was designed with his earlier scheme in mind. Table 3.2 shows how this is achieved (and can be compared with Table 2.4

Table 3.2 *Overall logic of Wright's revised class categories*

I Assets in the means of production

	Self-employed	*Number of employees*
1 Bourgeoisie	Yes	10 or more
2 Small employers	Yes	2–10
3 Petty bourgeoisie	Yes	0–1
4 Wage-earner	No	

II Assets in organizational control

	Directly involved in making policy decisions for the organization	*Supervisor with real authority over sub-ordinates*
1 Managers	Yes	Yes
2 Supervisors	No	Yes
3 Non-management	No	No

Note: The actual criteria used were somewhat more complex than indicated here, since a variety of other criteria were used to deal with certain kinds of problematic cases (eg. a respondent who claims to directly make policy decisions and yet does not have real authority over subordinates).

III Assets in scarce skills/talent

	Occupation	*Education credential*	*Job autonomy*
1 Experts	Professionals Professors		
	Managers Technicians	B.A. or more B.A. or more	
2 Marginal	School teachers Craftworkers		
	Managers Technicians	less than B.A. less than B.A.	
	Sales Clerical	B.A. or more B.A. or more	Autonomous Autonomous
3 Uncredentialled	Sales Clerical	less than B.A. *or* Non-autonomous less than B.A. *or* Non-autonomous	
	Manual non-crafts		

Reproduced by permission from Wright (1985, p. 150). Note that Wright elaborates on the operational criteria for Assets II and III in a very full appendix on variable construction. For full details see Wright (1985, pp. 303–17).

which gives the corresponding information for the original class framework). Measuring assets in the means of production poses least problems since this simply involves making a distinction between owners and non-owners and then subdividing the former. Owners are differentiated (in what Wright admits is a crude way) in terms of numbers of employees: capitalists are owners with ten or more employees; small employers have from two to ten employees; and the *petit bourgeoisie* have one employee or none. Employees are then differentiated according to each of the other assets. Organizational assets are defined in terms of an individual's relation to supervision and decision-making in his or her organization. Three categories emerge from this: managers, defined as people who have direct involvement in decision-making and real authority over subordinates; supervisors, who lack decision-making powers, but do have real authority over others; and non-managers, who have neither supervisory nor decision-making powers. Finally, skill/credential assets are defined. This dimension causes Wright some problems, since a credential means nothing unless it is exploited; as Wright notes, a Ph.D. in chemistry is not exploiting his or her credentials if employed on an assembly line. Simply to measure credentials would therefore be inadequate; they must be matched to jobs. For this reason Wright includes job traits in the operationalization of this asset. This is done in terms of both an aggregated occupational variable (derived from the official American coding of occupations) and, for certain occupations, a measure of job autonomy. The three categories of skills/credentials produced by Wright are those for 'experts', 'skilled employees', and the 'non-skilled'. The experts include all professionals, together with managers and technicians holding a college degree; skilled employees embrace teachers, craftworkers, managers and technicians without degrees, and sales and clerical workers with both degrees and high autonomy; the non-skilled are all other sales and clerical workers and all manual and service workers.

Finally, having gone to such trouble to distinguish the various contradictory locations indicated in Table 3.1, Wright proceeds in his subsequent class analysis to collapse the full typology in diverse ways. Most commonly he combines cells 1, 2, and 3 ('self-employed'), 4 and 7 ('credentialled managers'), 5 and 8 ('credentialled supervisors'), 6 and 9 ('credentialled employees'), 10 and 11 ('uncredentialled managers and supervisors'), leaving cell 12 ('workers') by itself. For some other purposes he combines cells 4, 5, and 6 ('experts'), 7, 8, 10 and 11 ('non-expert managers and supervisors'), leaving cell 9 as 'skilled workers'. Occasionally employers (cells 1 and 2) are distinguished from the *petit bourgeoisie* (cell 3), managers (cells 4, 7 and 10), supervisors (cells 5, 8, 11), expert non-managers, skilled workers and workers. In order to simplify matters we shall employ only the first of these in our own analyses – the simple six-category model distinguishing the polarized capitalist and proletarian classes from the contradictory locations of credentialled managers, supervisors, and employees, and uncredentialled managers and supervisors. On rare occasions, where numbers permit, the full twelve-class schema will be displayed.

III

These, then, are the most salient aspects of Wright's lengthy introduction to his new taxonomy. While it may not be thought necessary for the primary purposes of this volume to follow the details of the autocritique, nevertheless in fairness in Wright we cannot simply proceed to a comparison of his new model with other schemes, such as those of John Goldthorpe and the Registrar-General. Wright has obviously reconstituted his class categories for what he feels are sound theoretical reasons. Since he has taken the trouble to rework his entire theory of class, and is convinced of the superiority of the new framework, it is not unreasonable to expect colleagues who are collaborating in the international project organized under his auspices to give serious consideration to his arguments. Furthermore, those who are interested sufficiently in that project may want to consult the full interview schedule in order to investigate more closely the precise construction of the rather complex variables used in defining the class categories, and this will require some understanding of the theory itself. That schedule, it must be remembered, was designed to operationalize the original class schema. As a result, some of the measurements for factors that are salient only within the revised framework (skill/credential assets for example) are not as satisfactory as they might be, though Wright himself seems not to be fully aware of the extent to which this is in fact the case.

There are two additional reasons why we in particular felt it important to look at the gestation of Wright's revised framework. The first is that we are not convinced a priori of its superiority to his original schema. We can see weaknesses in both models so, unlike Wright himself, we intend a thorough empirical investigation of each in order to determine their comparative utility in a systematic class analysis. This will now proceed, therefore, with *four* class categorizations: official, sociological, earlier Marxist and later Marxist. Second, in so far as Wright has repaired certain theoretical deficiencies in his initial position, the reformulation of the argument makes it harder rather than easier to pursue a class analysis in his own terms. For example, his new theory admits to the importance of class formation and therefore social mobility in class analysis, a revision that we would consider to be an improvement upon the earlier rigidly structuralist approach. Unfortunately, however, Wright himself cannot explore this phenomenon empirically without recourse to the categories of 'bourgeois' sociology and economics – categories he has earlier rejected as wholly inadequate to the study of social class.

It is worth considering the last objection in more detail – and this we propose to do in what remains of the chapter. Our reservations about the new schema, and corresponding reluctance to use its appearance alone as sufficient grounds for abandoning the old, are methodological, theoretical, and substantive in tenor. The first of these can be stated briefly and is best understood with reference to the idea of contradictory class locations. Wright states that he reformulated his theory of class in order to remedy four perceived weaknesses in this central concept: it rests almost exclusively on relations of domination rather than those of exploitation; fails to grasp the complexity of class relations in post-capitalist (that is state socialist) societies; suggests (wrongly) that small employers and semi-autonomous employees have internally inconsistent interests analogous to those of managers and supervisors; and, finally, depends upon a defining element of 'autonomy' which is, in fact, an unstable factor in many work situations and so generates anomalies in its research application. Wright claims that his reworking of the concept rectifies these problems. In our view he simply redescribes them. His new taxonomy eliminates the troublesome category of 'contradictory locations between modes of production', and with it the semi-autonomous employees, who are redistributed into the now exploitation-centred categories of expert non-manager, semi-credentialled worker, and proletarian (see Table 3.3). However, in operationalizing the new class categories Wright must still utilize a research instrument that was designed in respect of the problematic earlier scheme, and so he incorporates precisely the same problems about autonomy in the workplace into his study. A glance at the American interview schedule (Wright reproduces the relevant section in *Classes*) will reveal the weakness which generated the empirical anomalies in the original model. It is quite possible that an office cleaner, having considerable scope as to when and how he or she goes about the appointed overall tasks, will be, in the final analysis, more autonomous than an airline pilot. The latter must follow a strictly defined routine and will appear as having been almost totally deskilled since, for a large part of the time, the task of flying the plane is actually performed by a machine. The cleaner, on the other hand, can start at one end of the building or the other; decide to polish one day and vacuum the next; or, indeed, decide not to polish at all. Now Wright is correct in his observation that a proletarian pilot and semi-autonomous cleaner make little intuitive sense. However, his operationalization of the skill/credential assets dimension of his new schema depends in part on the same questions about autonomy, and the same coding exercise, as did his measurement of autonomy *tout court* in the old. He now uses autonomy 'as a criterion for *skill* assets . . . for those occupational titles, such as sales or clerical jobs, which are particularly diffuse in the real skill content of the job', on the (highly implausible) grounds that 'the degree of conceptual autonomy in the job is likely to be a good indicator of the skill assets attached to the job'.[13] The airline pilot/school cleaner example suggests that this is not in fact the case. Nevertheless it is autonomy scores that finally determine whether or not particular sales and clerical workers are categorized as 'skilled employees' or 'non-skilled'. In other words, Wright has relabelled the boxes in his schema, and constructed them according to a different blueprint, but in some cases at least they are fabricated out of the same problematic materials as before.

Wright himself is not unaware of the many objections that can be raised against the autonomy variable. In his defence, he can legitimately claim that it enters into the construction of the skill asset dimension of his scheme in a fairly narrow way; that is, it applies to only a small proportion of total

Table 3.3 Wright I (original) classes by Wright II (revised) classes

Wright II classes	Wright I classes						
	Bourgeoisie	Small employers	Petit bourgeoisie	Managers and supervisors	Semi-autonomous employees	Workers	Total
Bourgeoisie	2.0 (26)	0.0 (0)	0.0 (0)	0.0 (0)	0.0 (0)	0.0 (0)	2.0 (26)
Small employers	0.0 (0)	4.5 (59)	0.0 (0)	0.0 (0)	0.0 (0)	0.0 (0)	4.5 (59)
Petit bourgeoisie	0.0 (0)	0.0 (0)	6.0 (79)	0.0 (0)	0.0 (0)	0.0 (0)	6.0 (79)
Expert managers	0.0 (0)	0.0 (0)	0.0 (0)	5.6 (74)	0.0 (0)	0.0 (0)	5.6 (74)
Expert supervisors	0.0 (0)	0.0 (0)	0.0 (0)	2.2 (29)	0.0 (0)	0.0 (0)	2.2 (29)
Expert non-managers	0.0 (0)	0.0 (0)	0.0 (0)	0.1 (1)	2.1 (27)	2.0 (26)	4.1 (54)
Semi credentialled managers	0.0 (0)	0.0 (0)	0.0 (0)	7.9 (104)	0.0 (0)	0.0 (0)	7.9 (104)
Semi credentialled supervisors	0.0 (0)	0.0 (0)	0.0 (0)	3.8 (50)	0.0 (0)	0.0 (0)	3.8 (50)
Semi credentialled workers	0.0 (0)	0.0 (0)	0.0 (0)	0.1 (1)	4.1 (54)	10.2 (134)	14.4 (189)
Uncredentialled managers	0.0 (0)	0.0 (0)	0.0 (0)	3.2 (42)	0.0 (0)	0.0 (0)	3.2 (42)
Uncredentialled supervisors	0.0 (0)	0.0 (0)	0.0 (0)	3.4 (45)	0.0 (0)	0.0 (0)	3.4 (45)
Proletarians	0.0 (0)	0.0 (0)	0.0 (0)	0.0 (0)	5.5 (72)	37.4 (492)	42.9 (564)
Total	2.0 (26)	4.5 (59)	6.0 (79)	26.3 (346)	11.6 (153)	49.6 (652)	100.0 (1315)

respondents. In the British case these represent 29 per cent of routine clerical and sales workers – or 6 per cent of the class sample as a whole. However, this is a crucial 6 per cent, since it is precisely these categories of employees which are centrally contested in the debate about putative processes of pro- letarianization in class structures. Moreover, this item offers simply one instance among many in which Wright is forced into rather unsatisfactory, sometimes simply *ad hoc* solutions to substantive coding decisions. Another example, taken again from his discussion of assets in credentials, concerns the coding of schoolteachers who, for reasons that are simply never disclosed, are automatically to be given 'skilled employee' status on the basis of their occupational title alone.[14] It is not clear to us why this group cannot equally plausibly be assigned to the category of 'expert'. Ultimately, of course, it is these sorts of coding decisions that determine the allocation of respondents to class locations.

The coding of occupations itself introduces similar methodological problems into the equation. Before receiving from Wright the necessary details for constructing the aggregated occupational variable that comprises the major component of the skill/credential assets dimension of his schema, we attempted to use the OPCS definition of socio-economic group as a proxy, since Wright's variable distinguishes apparently similar groups of occupations to those identified in the SEGs. The former requires the grouping of professional occupations together, craftworkers together, clerical workers, and so on. Similarly, socio-economic group has categories for employed professionals, skilled workers, and junior nonmanual workers.[15] With some careful recoding of our data it appeared we could approximate the American variable. Indeed, we believed that in some respects SEG, in combination with our details of respondents' credentials, would produce a credential assets variable which allowed for finer distinctions than the American equivalent. Table 3.4 shows the effects of coding occupations to one rather than the other scheme. There is a marked difference in the resulting class maps of Britain according to which collapsed occupational variable is used. There are in fact discrepancies across all categories of non-owners. These are substantial in the cases of cells 9 and 12. Is it merely coincidence that Wright's measure produces a larger working class?

At the very least Table 3.4 highlights the difficulties of assuming, as Wright seems to have done, that any occupational coding will be relatively neutral in its effects when applied to the derivation of a sociological model of class. There would appear to be no simple solutions to this problem, given that all official measures of occupation have their own difficulties, but Wright's approach does seem somewhat cavalier – especially in the context of an international comparative class analysis. When discussing the details of variable construction in an appendix to *Classes* he notes that 'the coding of occupational title . . . [is] entirely conventional and straightforward and [does] not require any specific commentary'.[16] This is hardly a satisfactory treatment unless it is also shown that there are no problems with the official American coding of occupations which might affect the production of a

Table 3.4 *Distribution of respondents into Wright II (revised) classes according to (1) socio-economic group and (2) American occupational variable (%)*

Wright II (revised) classes	(1) Socio-economic group	(2) American occupational variable	(Difference)
Bourgeoisie	2.0	2.0	(0.0)
Small employers	4.5	4.5	(0.0)
Petit bourgeoisie	6.0	6.0	(0.0)
Expert managers	5.2	5.6	(+0.4)
Expert supervisors	1.6	2.2	(+0.6)
Expert non-managers	2.1	4.1	(+2.0)
Semi-credentialled managers	8.7	7.9	(−0.8)
Semi-credentialled supervisors	4.3	3.8	(−0.5)
Semi-credentialled workers	22.4	14.4	(−8.0)
Uncredentialled managers	2.9	3.2	(+0.3)
Uncredentialled supervisors	3.5	3.4	(−0.1)
Proletarians	36.9	42.9	(+6.0)
Total	100.0	100.0	

sociological model of class. By comparison, John Goldthorpe felt able to use the British scheme in his model only after a prolonged study of the problem of occupational coding, and by combining occupational title with a measure of employment status. Thus it is not occupational title which determines a person's Goldthorpe class, but it is occupational title (along with qualifications, and in some cases job autonomy) which specifies one dimension of Wright's model. Yet it is Wright who has criticized Goldthorpe for the latter's inexplicit theorization of his class model and over-reliance on occupational coding to operationalize it.

Beyond this, of course, there is the more fundamental issue raised by the introduction of occupational titles into the algorithms for generating social classes. Was not Wright's whole intellectual enterprise launched on a critique of precisely this practice? Occupations, if Wright's research agenda is to be believed, map 'only' the technical relations of production in societies: social classes are defined by 'more fundamental' social relations of production.[17] Since the object of the exercise is to demonstrate the analytical superiority of the latter over the former it is, to say the least, undesirable that Wright should have to depend on occupational codings as a central element in his definition of class itself.

IV

Discussion of occupational coding brings us to some of the broader theoretical problems associated with Wright's new schema. He has effectively rejected a wholly structural account of class since he now wishes to raise the issue of class formation and hence the questions of process and agency. Indeed it is precisely these aspects of the new framework which seem to us to be an improvement on the old. However, the attempt to incorporate these newer elements to the general theory produces considerable strains in Wright's argument, and ultimately carries heavy costs for the integrity of his project as a whole.

Consider, for example, Wright's stated preference for a trajectory view of class over his earlier strictly positional approach. Wright now concedes that class is a 'probabilistic' concept, so that 'a full account of class structure . . . has to include some kind of recognition of these probabilistic trajectories'. Thus, for example, 'proletarianized white-collar jobs that are really pre-managerial jobs should therefore not be considered in the same location within class relations as proletarianized jobs which are not part of such career trajectories'.[18] Clerical workers, in other words, are a disparate group of elderly and lately promoted shop-floor workers with no prospects of future advancement in the managerial hierarchy; young secretaries with minimal such prospects; and young credentialled managerial trainees gaining 'shop-floor experience' in the early stages of a career that will almost certainly take them into the middle and upper levels of the relevant bureaucratic structures. All clerical workers, therefore, are not necessarily in the same social class. Of course this is an argument that has long been used against Marxists by (among others) Stewart, Prandy, and Blackburn – indeed the example quoted by Wright is their very example.[19] Similarly, on the question of agency, Wright again gives ground to his non-Marxist critics and brings his analysis very close to theirs. Thus his statement that attitudes cannot be regarded as merely epiphenomenal, since they have real consequences for class action, sounds very like a restatement of the neo-Weberian theory of action used in much British social stratification research.

Class location is a basic determinant of the matrix of objective possibilities faced by individuals, the real alternatives people face in making decisions. At one level this concerns what Weber referred to as the individual's 'life chances', the overall trajectory of possibilities individuals face over the life cycle. In a more mundane way it concerns the daily choices people face about what to do and how to do it.

The objective alternatives faced by individuals, however, are not directly transformed into actual choices or practices. Those objective alternatives must be perceived, the consequences (both material and normative) of different choices assessed, and a specific alternative chosen in light of such assessments. . . . [Hence] subjectivity *mediates* the ways in which the objective conditions of class locations are translated into the active choices of class actions. While the objective social context of choice is clearly important in this explanation, I would argue that the subjective mediation of choices . . . is an essential part of the process as well.[20]

These arguments – which we would wholeheartedly endorse – quite properly open up for discussion the issue of how far individuals do in fact share common interests and engage in collective action along class or any other lines. However they sit somewhat uneasily alongside Wright's fundamental conception of class structure and class formation. Indeed, class structure is defined in terms of what needs to be demonstrated, if Wright is to follow the logic of his own arguments; that is, 'a structure of social relations into which individuals . . . enter which determine their class interests'. This, surely, begs the question. Whether class interests can ever be said to be determined by a structure of positions in an unmediated way is highly dubious. To define the class structure in terms of people's supposed real interests is to ignore precisely the kinds of questions which Wright now wishes to open up for empirical examination.

Similarly his definition of class formation is at odds with his subsequent comments concerning the relative openness of social processes. For Wright, as we have seen, class formation is 'the formation of organized collectivities within [the] class structure on the basis of the interests shaped by that class structure'. How can this be consistent with a trajectory view of class? Surely the precise purpose of such a view is to ask whether or not, in the particular empirical instance, classes have in fact formed as identifiable social collectivities. Wright's implicit model of class structure → class interests → class formation is too crude to bear the weight of his own insights. As Goldthorpe has argued, class formation must be shown to exist at the demographic level before it can be expected to exist in any socio-cultural sense, or provide a basis for collective action. To produce a model of class structure consistent with a set of theoretical propositions is only the first step in the process. It is for this reason, as Goldthorpe observes, that 'little value can attach to attempts, such as those of structural Marxists, to treat problems of class formation and class action without reference to the extent of class mobility'.[21] We would argue, therefore, that Wright is only partially facing up to the problematic issues concerning classes as collectivities. In particular he fails to square his structural map with his preference for a trajectory view. Certainly he appears to be aware of some of the problems. How else could he acknowledge that

the process of class formation is decisively shaped by a variety of institutional mechanisms that are themselves 'relatively autonomous' from the class structure and which determine the ways in which class structures are translated into collective actors with specific ideologies and strategies?[22]

In other words, it is not class structure alone which determines people's interests, nor is it the only factor affecting class formation. To recognize this is, of course, to strip Wright's account of its distinctively Marxist tenor – which is presumably why Wright does not pursue the point further.

There are also practical problems associated with the attempt to introduce 'class trajectories' into Wright's framework. It will be clear from the interview schedule for the British project that several pages of questions are required in order to collect information sufficient to place each respondent into the appropriate Wright class. Suppose, therefore, that Wright wishes to address the topic of intergenerational mobility. It is simply impractical to collect the necessary information about the immediate work situations of parents from each respondent to the study. In any case, it is unrealistic to assume that he or she will possess detailed knowledge of the specific decision-making and supervisory responsibilities, degree of job autonomy, and educational credentials associated with the appropriate parental jobs. The best one might hope for is an occupational title, together with a short description of the sort of work involved, and an indication of employment status – whether the parent in question was a manager, supervisor, employee, or was self-employed. This, in fact, is Wright's own strategy. His 'class biography' variables – which specify the class of the respondent's parents and of his or her three closest friends or relatives – are constructed from information about the occupation and employment status of the individuals concerned.[23] This is an uncontroversial solution to a common problem in studying social mobility and social networks – but in this particular case it does tend, yet again, to undermine the logic of Wright's whole enterprise which is, of course, to demonstrate the superiority of class frameworks based on social relations of production over those which rest on occupational and employment status categories. So, not only is Wright introducing inconsistencies of principle into his theoretical reasoning by acknowledging the importance of process to the explanation of class phenomena, but he is also, quite clearly, undermining the practical utility of his approach to class analysis.

Wright's revisions to his class framework come into direct conflict with his Marxism in other ways as well. For example, it will be seen from Table 3.1 that Wright's new middle classes are differentiated internally according to the organizational assets and skill/credential assets they possess, though they share the common feature of non-ownership of the means of production. This latter attribute obviously characterizes the proletariat as well, but they are correspondingly 'negatively privileged' with regard to organizational and skill/credential assets. In this way, Wright not only specifies a variety of contradictory locations within exploitation relations, but also concludes that some contradictory locations are more important than others. Within capitalism, for example, managers and state bureaucrats occupy the principal contradictory location by virtue of the fact that 'they embody a principle of class organisation which is quite distinct from capitalism and which potentially poses an alternative to capitalist relations'. State managers in particular are singled out. In a statement calculated to give a whole new meaning to the phrase 'the managerial revolution', Wright observes an important consequence of his new scheme for conceptualizing the middle class, namely

that it is no longer axiomatic that the proletariat is the unique, or perhaps even universally the central, rival to the capitalist class for class power in a capitalist society. That classical Marxist assumption depended upon the thesis that there were no other classes within capitalism that could be viewed as the 'bearers' of a historical alternative to capitalism. Socialism (as the transition to communism) was the only possible future to capitalism. What [Table 3.1] suggests is that there are other class forces within capitalism that have the potential to pose an alternative to capitalism.[24]

This sort of heresy so emasculates the Marxist theory of history that, taken together with Wright's other concessions to his critics, one is left wondering as to what, precisely, is any longer distinctively Marxist about his account.

Certainly, Wright's discovery of the importance of credentials and organizational position to any understanding of modern stratification systems provides yet another illustration of the way in which his concessions to reality are consistent with distinctively non-Marxist accounts of social class, and so casts severe doubts upon the supposedly Marxist rationale for the new class framework. After all, it was Weber who originally investigated the coincidence of these two factors in his writings on bureaucracy, and it is Goldthorpe, and Stewart, Prandy, and Blackburn who have developed this approach more recently.[25] Not only did Weber refer to the 'bureaucratization of capitalism, with its demand for expertly trained technicians, clerks etc.', but he also noted that

if we hear from all sides demands for the introduction of regulated curricula culminating in specialized examinations, the reason behind this is, of course, not a suddenly awakened 'thirst for education', but rather the desire to limit the supply of candidates for these positions and to monopolize them for the holders of educational patents'.[26]

Indeed we are tempted to go further in our comparison of Wright and Weber. Surely Wright's use of credential and organizational assets to differentiate among the propertyless is not so different from Weber's view that the propertyless are distinguished 'according to the kind of services that can be offered in the market' and 'that the kind of chance in the *market* is the decisive moment which presents a common condition for the individual's fate'.[27] Or, to put the matter more bluntly, organization assets and credential assets are aspects of work situation and market situation respectively.

Wright himself is not unaware of this development in his thinking and thus takes considerable pains to distinguish his account from those of Weberian class theorists which, to us at least, it so closely resembles. For example, in examining the relationship between his approach and various alternative class theories, he explicitly addresses the charge that the former has come very close to what he himself had previously regarded as 'neo-Weberianism'. In many respects, of course, it has. Indeed Wright hardly bothers to contest the fact that there are similarities between aspects of his framework and that of the self-confessed 'bourgeois' sociologist Frank Parkin. In his search for a way out of his embarrassment he concludes that Weber makes the 'mistake' of viewing production from the vantage point of the market because he fails to make the distinction between a mode of production and a social formation. This error stems from the fact that Weber and his followers resolutely refuse 'to treat historical development as a trajectory of qualitatively distinct forms of class structure'. This is indeed true. However, by not accepting the historicism of Marx, Weberians avoid the kind of problem Wright has to face when, later in the argument, he confronts his general framework with the Marxist theory of history and has to proceed upon yet another rewrite of what the latter means. We are told that it is a 'probabilistic statement', 'a sequence of historical possibilities', and that 'the actual transition from one form [of society] to another . . . may depend upon a whole range of contingent factors that are exogenous to the theory'. This leads Wright to challenge three traditional theses of historical materialism; that 'socialism is the immanent future to capitalism' (it could as easily be statism); that the proletariat is 'the only bearer of a revolutionary mission within capitalism' (there might be a 'managerial revolution' instead); and that socialist societies will be free of economic exploitation (in fact skill and credential assets might continue to be exploited). Despite such revisionism he tries to rescue the theory of history from these not inconsiderable problems by asserting that history remains progressive, so that while 'capitalism may no longer be thought of as the last antagonistic form of society in the trajectory of human development (nevertheless) the progressive character to the trajectory is retained'.[28] One can but wonder yet again as to what, if anything, is left of the original edifice, for if the Marxist theory of history means nothing more than that history is 'progressive', how then does it differ from the Whig theory?

V

Of course the fact that Wright blurs the distinction between Weberian and Marxist accounts of class processes, both in his theory and his method, need in no way affect the utility of his substantive analysis. As we observed in the previous chapter, the differences between the two approaches are sometimes difficult to see, no less so in the case of the founding fathers themselves than in that of their acolytes. Granted, it would be surprising were Wright's theoretical and methodological difficulties to have *no* adverse effects on the coherence of his empirical findings. We have suggested that, in certain key areas (such as the measurement of skill assets and charting of class biographies), his analysis is in fact suspect simply on these grounds alone. But there are other rather more concrete problems in applying Wright's Marxist categories to the analysis of social classes in contemporary capitalism.

Consider, for example, Table 3.5. This shows the distribution of respondents in the revised Wright categories against that for the seven principal Goldthorpe classes. This can be compared with Table 2.5A – the corresponding cross-tabulation for the original Wright model. It is clear that the removal of the problematic semi-autonomous employee category has eliminated some of the anomalies between the two classifications. But they are by no means yet coterminous. Twelve per cent of expert managers and one-third of semi-credentialled managers fall outside the Goldthorpe service class. Significant numbers of semi-credentialled and uncredentialled supervisors appear in both service (I and II) and intermediate (V) locations. Semi-credentialled workers – 29 per cent of whom were semi-autonomous employees in the earlier model – are spread across all the Goldthorpe class categories containing employees. Wright's proletariat is still substantially split by Goldthorpe's unskilled manual/routine nonmanual distinction. In fact the proportion of proletarians

Table 3.5 Wright II (revised) classes by Goldthorpe classes

		I	II	III	IV	V	VI	VII	Total
						Goldthorpe			
Wright	B	1.4 (18)	0.5 (6)	0.0 (0)	0.2 (2)	0.0 (0)	0.0 (0)	0.0 (0)	2.0 (26)
	SE	0.5 (7)	0.5 (6)	0.0 (0)	3.4 (45)	0.0 (0)	0.0 (0)	0.1 (1)	4.5 (59)
	PB	0.3 (4)	0.5 (7)	0.0 (0)	5.2 (68)	0.0 (0)	0.0 (0)	0.0 (0)	6.0 (79)
	EM	2.7 (35)	2.3 (30)	0.5 (7)	0.0 (0)	0.2 (2)	0.0 (0)	0.0 (0)	5.6 (74)
	ES	0.9 (12)	0.8 (11)	0.5 (6)	0.0 (0)	0.0 (0)	0.0 (0)	0.0 (0)	2.2 (29)
	ENM	0.8 (10)	1.9 (25)	1.4 (19)	0.0 (0)	0.0 (0)	0.0 (0)	0.0 (0)	4.1 (54)
	SCM	1.9 (25)	3.4 (45)	0.4 (5)	0.0 (0)	1.9 (25)	0.2 (3)	0.1 (1)	7.9 (104)
	SCS	0.5 (7)	1.4 (18)	0.1 (1)	0.0 (0)	1.7 (23)	0.1 (1)	0.0 (0)	3.8 (50)
	SCW	0.3 (4)	4.0 (52)	0.5 (7)	0.0 (0)	1.5 (20)	7.8 (102)	0.3 (4)	14.4 (189)
	UM	0.0 (0)	1.1 (14)	0.6 (8)	0.0 (0)	1.1 (15)	0.2 (3)	0.2 (2)	3.2 (42)
	US	0.0 (0)	1.1 (14)	0.3 (4)	0.0 (0)	1.4 (19)	0.0 (0)	0.6 (8)	3.4 (45)
	P	0.1 (1)	0.5 (7)	15.1 (199)	0.0 (0)	0.2 (3)	4.3 (56)	22.7 (298)	42.9 (564)
Total		9.4 (123)	17.9 (235)	19.5 (256)	8.7 (115)	8.1 (107)	12.5 (165)	23.9 (314)	100.0 (1315)

Key: B=Bourgeoisie; SE=Small employers; PB=Petit bourgeoisie; EM=Expert managers; ENM=Expert non-managers; SCM=Semi-credentialled managers; SCS=Semi-credentialled supervisors; ES=Expert supervisors; SCW=Semi-credentialled workers; UM=Uncredentialled managers; US=Uncredentialled supervisors; P=Proletarians.

in Goldthorpe class III has increased from about one-quarter, in the old scheme, to just over one-third in the new. The Goldthorpe class positions of Wright's 'capitalist' classes (bourgeoisie, small employers, *petit bourgeoisie*) are, of course, unaltered between the two models since these categories are operationalized according to the same criteria as before.

What is the significance of these discrepancies? This question can be addressed in different ways. Each model claims to shed light on the process of demographic class formation – the allocation of people to places over time. We can, therefore, legitimately explore the implications of the different class maps that are produced by Goldthorpe and Wright for arguments about class biographies and social mobility. Wright's analysis suggests that there are many managers and supervisors in the structure. Is it really the case that quite so many British workers have been upwardly mobile into these privileged locations? There are also large numbers of proletarians: in fact they constitute almost 50 per cent of the class sample, using the old definition, and 43 per cent according to the new. How plausible is this claim? These issues will be addressed in Chapters 4 and 5 in the context of our wider discussion of demographic class formation.

The discrepancies between the two models will also have implications for our conclusions about socio-political class formation. As Wright himself states, 'all other things being equal, all units . . . within a given class should be more like each other than like units in other classes *with respect to whatever it is that class is meant to explain.*'[29] Both he and Goldthorpe claim that their class analyses illuminate the study not only of life-chances, but also of life-styles, socio-political orientations, and collective action. Is this in fact the case? And, if so, which is the more robust of the approaches? These issues are addressed in Chapters 6 to 9 of this book.

However, before moving on to consider differences between the models in terms of their research implications for rather complex arguments about demographic and socio-political class formation, one can more straightforwardly investigate the coherence of the class categories with reference to the objective criteria that allegedly define their common attributes. That is to say we can simply unpack the observed discrepancies themselves. For example, if certain members of Goldthorpe's service class are among Wright's proletariat, then who are these people and why does this anomaly occur?

Wright's explicitly problematic category of semi-autonomous employees offers a convenient starting point for this simple though, in our view, illuminating exercise. From Table 2.5A it will be seen that Goldthorpe would classify fifty-eight of these employees as service class and another thirty-six as working class. If we then identify these ninety-four respondents, and record for each their occupation and its gross annual wage, we can see why Goldthorpe would want to challenge the integrity of Wright's category. (See Table 3.6 which also gives basic demographic and socio-political details to help complete the picture.) Those semi-autonomous employees who are in Goldthorpe's service class are a predictable mixture of teachers, computer programmers, social workers, and the like. Working-class respondents comprise an equally unsurprising group of coalminers, motor mechanics, process workers, and so forth. Yet all ninety-four individuals appear in the same (semi-autonomous employee) category, in Wright's terms, because they are non-owners of capital and non-managers, yet claim to have high autonomy in carrying out their work. Because of respondents' varying perceptions of what constitutes 'autonomy of conception and execution in the work task', this particular class category embraces everyone from lawyers and doctors, on the one hand, to hospital orderlies and fork lift truck drivers, on the other. And, sure enough, there are a number of cleaners, caretakers, and domestic helpers in the group.

The observed disparity in wages – within Goldthorpe classes and even particular occupations – is, of course, to be expected since there are no controls in this table for age, position within the hierarchy of an employing organization, or for hours worked. Many of the females earning less than £2800 per annum (as domestic helpers, teachers, hairdressers or whatever) are part-time employees. Some of the professionals in classes I and II are starting out on company careers while others are in promoted positions. This aspect of the table illustrates forcefully the importance of taking *process* into account in any systematic class analysis. Individuals shape different sorts of career mobility trajectories through the structure. Credentialled men doing routine clerical work typically end up in managerial jobs. Uncredentialled women doing the same initial work typically do not enjoy such promotion. Indeed it may be the case that credentialled women are promoted in different measure to credentialled men.[30] For this reason the calculation of mobility chances will clearly be central to arguments about processes such as proletarianization and embourgeoisement.

There are, therefore, good grounds for questioning the coherence of the category of semi-autonomous employees. Indeed the demographic problems of this class location are to a considerable extent reflected in the socio-political inclinations of its incumbents. Over 60 per cent of those whom Goldthorpe would call service class identified themselves as middle or upper class; whereas, conversely, fully three-quarters of semi-autonomous employees who appear in Goldthorpe's working class claimed working-class identities. Voting intentions are less obviously structured by the service class/working class split, though the Conservatives have a majority among the former group, while Labour enjoys predominance among the latter. There is a clear suggestion here that the category of 'semi-autonomous employees' is rather heterogeneous with respect to a number of items that class might be expected to explain.

Other anomalies between the Goldthorpe and original Wright classifications can be unpacked in similar fashion. The 6 per cent of Wright's proletarians who appear in Goldthorpe's service class include a lawyer, investment broker, aeronautical engineer, and chartered accountant, a couple of electrical engineers, some senior clerical workers, several schoolteachers, two draughtsmen, one lecturer in higher education, a medical radiographer, two physiotherapists, and an environmental health officer (but no airline pilot).

Table 3.6 *Selected characteristics of Wright semi-autonomous employees who are in Goldthorpe service class or working class*

A – in Goldthorpe service class

Occupation	Sex	Age	Gross annual wage	Self-assigned class	Voting intention
Class I					
Design and development engineer	M	27	*	Middle	Alliance
Lawyer	F	36	£7,000–8,999	Middle	Conservative
Quantity surveyor	M	27	*	Middle	Conservative
Buyer (retail trade)	F	35	£7,000–8,999	Working	*
Doctor	F	33	£18,000–24,999	Middle	Would not vote
Design and development engineer	M	40	£5,000–6,999	Working	Alliance
Office manager	M	42	£15,000–17,999	Middle	*
Class II					
Teacher	M	51	£10,000–11,999	Working	Labour
Draughtsman	M	60	£5,000–6,999	Working	Labour
Teacher	F	53	£2,800–3,999	Middle	*
Teacher	F	46	£9,000–9,999	Working	Alliance
Teacher	F	40	£9,000–9,999	Middle	Alliance
Welfare worker	F	25	£5,000–6,999	Middle	Labour
Welfare worker	F	26	£7,000–8,999	Middle	*
Teacher	F	48	£7,000–8,999	Middle	Conservative
Physiotherapist	M	53	£7,000–8,999	Middle	Alliance
Town planner	M	40	£10,000–11,999	Middle	Conservative
Computer programmer	M	32	£12,000–14,999	Middle	Alliance
Computer programmer	M	23	£5,000–6,999	Middle	Conservative
Taxation expert	F	31	< £2,800	Working	Labour
Teacher	F	36	£5,000–6,999	Middle	*
Teacher	F	30	£5,000–6,999	Working	Labour
Teacher	F	26	*	Working	Labour
Teacher	F	52	£4,000–4,999	Middle	Labour
Teacher	M	31	£2,800–3,999	Working	Labour
Teacher	F	42	£5,000–6,999	Middle	Conservative
Buyer	M	18	*	Don't know	Conservative
Commercial artist	M	36	£7,000–8,999	Working	Conservative
Professional administrator	M	21	*	Don't know	Labour
Vocational/industrial trainer	F	58	£4,000–4,999	Middle	*
Nurse administrator	F	54	£9,000–9,999	Working	Labour
Computer programmer	M	40	£9,000–9,999	Don't know	Conservative
Librarian	M	62	£12,000–14,999	Working	Conservative
Teacher	M	40	> £25,000	Don't know	*
Teacher in higher education	F	55	< £2,800	Working	Labour
Valuer	M	29	£10,000–11,999	Working	Labour
Teacher	F	54	*	Middle	Conservative
Policeman	M	25	£7,000–8,999	Middle	Conservative
Professional in health/ education	F	25	£7,000–8,999	Middle	Conservative
Computer programmer	M	26	*	Middle	Alliance
Computer programmer	M	40	£7,000–8,999	Middle	Conservative
Policeman	M	52	*	Middle	*
Teacher	F	48	< £2,800	Middle	Conservative
Teacher in higher education	F	56	£4,000–4,999	Middle	Conservative

Teacher	F	28	£5,000–6,999	Middle	Alliance
Computer programmer	M	26	£7,000–8,999	Middle	Conservative
Office manager	M	39	£7,000–8,999	*	Alliance
Teacher	M	61	£10,000–11,999	Middle	Conservative
Commercial artist	M	38	£9,000–9,999	Working	Labour
Writer	F	24	£9,000–9,999	Middle	Conservative
Sales manager	F	17	*	Working	Alliance
Scientist/engineer	M	47	£18,000–24,999	Middle	Alliance
Advertising executive	M	36	£12,000–14,999	Middle	Conservative
Teacher	F	31	£9,000–9,999	Don't know	Labour
Vocational/industrial trainer	F	41	£7,000–8,999	Middle	Alliance
Draughtsman	M	24	£9,000–9,999	Working	Labour
Medical technician	F	25	£5,000–6,999	Middle	Alliance
Teacher	F	26	£5,000–6,999	Middle	Alliance

B – in Goldthorpe working class

Class VI

Coalminer	M	42	£7,000–8,999	Working	Labour
Sheet metal worker	M	19	£5,000–6,999	Working	Would not vote
Fitter/machinist	M	27	£5,000–6,999	Middle	Labour
Carpenter	M	64	*	Working	Labour
Motor mechanic	M	31	£7,000–8,999	Working	Alliance
Toolmaker	M	26	£9,000–9,999	Working	Conservative
Motor mechanic	M	20	£5,000–6,999	Working	Conservative
Carpenter	M	34	£4,000–4,999	*	Alliance
Cook	M	22	£2,800–3,999	Working	*
Hairdresser	F	33	< £2,800	Middle	Alliance
Coalminer	M	45	£9,000–9,999	Working	Labour
Hairdresser	F	17	< £2,800	Middle	*
Fitter/machinist	M	59	£9,000–9,999	Working	Labour
Electrical fitter	M	62	£10,000–11,999	Working	Labour
Electrical fitter	M	51	£12,000–14,999	Working	*
Process worker	M	32	£7,000–8,999	Middle	*

Class VII

Domestic helper	F	41	< £2,800	Working	Labour
Fork lift truck driver	M	50	*	Working	Conservative
Domestic helper	F	59	< £2,800	Working	*
Storekeeper	M	27	£2,800–3,999	Working	Conservative
Service worker	M	45	£12,000–14,999	Middle	Alliance
Caretaker	F	59	< £2,800	Working	Would not vote
Domestic helper	F	39	< £2,800	Middle	Conservative
Cleaner	F	56	< £2,800	Working	Would not vote
Pavior/kerb layer	M	62	*	Working	Conservative
Process worker	M	26	£4,000–4,999	Working	Would not vote
Painter/assembler	M	22	£4,000–4,999	Working	Labour
Painter/assembler	M	62	£7,000–8,999	Working	Labour
Domestic helper	F	51	< £2,800	Working	Labour
Van roundsman	M	51	£7,000–8,999	Working	*
Service worker	F	48	£4,000–4,999	Working	*
Hospital orderly	F	54	< £2,800	Middle	Conservative
Hospital orderly	F	32	< £2,800	Working	Labour
Inspector/viewer	M	37	£7,000–8,999	Working	Conservative
Domestic helper	F	44	< £2,800	Don't know	Labour
Hospital orderly	F	41	< £2,800	Working	Labour

Note: * indicates missing data (respondent refused to answer question).

This group of assorted professionals, senior administrators, and engineers are clearly out of place among the proletariat, but have nevertheless been allocated to working-class locations on the grounds that they are not property-owners or managers, and perceive their autonomy at work to be extremely limited. Some routine clerical workers think they are largely self-directed, so emerge as semi-autonomous employees, while others are convinced that they perform mundane tasks and are therefore classified as proletarians. This is apparently true of many other occupational groups as well – and as a result we find semi-autonomous office cleaners and proletarian investment brokers emerging from Wright's original class categories.

Does his revised framework eliminate these sorts of discrepancies? We observed from Table 3.3 that the old semi-autonomous category of employees has been redistributed into the proletarian, semi-credentialled worker, and expert non-managerial locations of the new schema. Cross-tabulating these against the Goldthorpe classes we can see (from Table 3.5) that some anomalies have been removed but that others remain. Two-thirds of expert non-managers appear in Goldthorpe's service class but the remainder are given routine nonmanual (class III) locations; semi-credentialled workers appear in all Goldthorpe classes except that for the self-employed; and there are still some rogue 'service-class proletarians'. As before one can examine these anomalies at the level of individual cases. It would be tedious to replicate the detailed analysis shown in Table 3.6 for all such instances. We shall therefore confine ourselves to the discussion of general tendencies and in this way attempt to paint a reasonably complete picture of the overall pattern of responses.

The most extreme discrepancy can be dealt with most concisely. 'Proletarians' appearing in Goldthorpe's service class are a buying and purchasing officer, investment broker, retail-trade supervisor, secretarial supervisor, hospital matron, and two clerical supervisors. Though engaged in highly paid and relatively secure professional and supervisory work, these eight individuals nevertheless appear among Wright's working class since they are non-owners of capital and non-managers engaged in clerical, sales, and white-collar service occupations, and possess low educational credentials or claim little autonomy in their work (see Table 3.2 which explains the logic of this classification). These few anomalies aside, however, the major difference between Wright's proletariat and Goldthorpe's working class is, as we have observed throughout, that the former embraces routine nonmanual workers whereas, in the Goldthorpe schema, this group is systematically allocated to a class location distinct from that of skilled and unskilled manual workers. Since this particular 'boundary debate' is central to arguments about proletarianization we shall be looking at the relevant Goldthorpe and Wright classes in more detail in due course. The issues of demographic and socio-political class formation that are involved here are best resolved on empirical rather than theoretical grounds.

The other 'basic' class within Wright's typology – those who own the means of production – are, as one would expect, to be found in Goldthorpe classes I,

II, and IV. Goldthorpe, like Wright, reserves a distinct class location for the own-account workers of the *petit bourgeoisie*, but merges larger proprietors into his service class, on the pragmatic grounds that a national random sample survey is not an appropriate research instrument for investigating 'the bourgeoisie'. Only a small proportion of 'top people' are selected into such studies. Moreover, the distinction between employee, self-employed, and employer is at this level rather ambiguous, as in the cases of working proprietors, company directors, and managers holding sizeable ownership assets. Sometimes the distinction is artificially introduced simply for income tax or national insurance purposes. So, Goldthorpe argues, it makes little practical sense to distinguish the classic bourgeoisie from others having a high, secure, and steadily rising income, who exercise discretion or authority at work.[31] Here again our data suggest that it is Goldthorpe who has the better of the argument. Most of Wright's small employers would seem to be barely distinguishable from his *petit bourgeoisie*, in that both groups comprise essentially own-account workers employing limited assistance on a variable and *ad hoc* basis. It makes little theoretical sense to place a small shopkeeper employing two counter assistants in one social class and a shopkeeper employing but one in another. Yet this practice is actually forced by Wright's categories. Moreover, turning to the twenty-six members of the 'bourgeoisie' who did emerge from our relatively small-scale survey, one can indeed ask whether or not it makes practical sense in a class analysis to distinguish a category which comprises but 2 per cent of the employed population.

Table 3.7 *Selected characteristics of Wright capitalist class*

Case	Goldthorpe class	Biographical details
1	I	Male; aged 62; self-employed; partner in small coal-mine; raised capital for his partnership from a bank loan; spends approximately half of his time on managerial work; employs 25–50 persons; about 20 per cent of his annual income of £15,000–£17,999 comes from second job as a shepherd; former coalminer and long-distance lorry driver.
2	II	Female; aged 27; self-employed; part-owner of three residential homes for the elderly employing 10–24 people in all; raised her share of initial capital from bank loan; five other members of her family are partners or employees; spends about half of her work time in managerial duties; has a short career history in hotel and restaurant management; her annual income varies.
3	II	Male; aged 60; employee; part-owner and manager of a market research company which was originally a family concern and is now part of a larger multinational corporation; initial capital investment in company was from own savings; spends about three-quarters of his time managing the 51–100 employees of the company; would not declare details of his annual income.
4	I	Male; aged 46; self-employed partner in an engineering consultancy; raised capital for his partnership from savings

55

Table 3.7 (*cont.*)

Case	Goldthorpe class	Biographical details
		after having worked his way up in the company from the shop-floor; spends about three-quarters of his time on management tasks; company retains 501–1000 employees; his gross annual income is £18,000–£24,000.
5	II	Female; aged 50; partner in an automobile filling station and repair shop; employee who does accounts for the business which employs 10–24 people including three other members of her family; husband built and sold a house to raise his and her shares of the initial capital to start the business; her income varies with annual profits.
6	I	Male; aged 45; part-owner of a small specialist transport company; 201–500 employees; the business was a family concern, now part of a larger company; he spends all of his working time on managerial concerns; was formerly a shop assistant and inspector of telephone equipment; bought into family business using a bank loan; his gross annual income exceeds £25,000.
7	I	Male; aged 33; junior partner in an insurance company for whom he acts as a loss adjuster; spends about one-quarter of his time on management tasks; self-employed; the company has between 51 and 100 employees; he bought his partnership using his own resources; formerly a quantity surveyor, his father was a television engineer, his mother a machinist in a factory; his gross annual income exceeds £25,000.
8	II	Male; aged 41; part-owner and chairman of a company dealing in raw material for textile industry, with minor interest in paper industry, employing 25–50 people in total; he inherited his financial interest in this long-established family firm and has never been employed elsewhere; spends all his time in management; no details of annual income given.
9	I	Male; aged 51; partner and joint managing director of a family firm specializing in the repair of electrical motors which he inherited and now operates with his brother; spends about half of his time on managerial duties; employs 25–50 people; his gross annual income is in the range £10,000–£11,999.
10	IV	Male; aged 60; partner in a family grocery store employing 10–24 people including four family members; self-employed; spends about one-quarter of his time on managerial tasks and the rest dealing directly with customers; formerly a clerk in a coal-mine and self-employed dairy roundman, he raised his share of the start-up capital from his own resources; his declared gross annual income varies between £5,000 and £6,999.
11	I	Male; aged 54; partner in a company manufacturing specialist machine tools; he runs the design side of the business and spends about three-quarters of his time on management tasks; this is a first-generation family business involving others within his family; his share of initial capital came from his own resources; formerly employed in the design of machine tools for other companies, his own now retains 51–100 employees, giving him a gross annual income of £12,000–£14,999.

56

Table 3.7 *(cont.)*

Case	Goldthorpe class	Biographical details
12	I	Male; aged 47; partner and sales director in a company manufacturing ironmongery and having 201–500 employees; this is a subsidiary of a large multinational company having up to 10,000 employees; formerly a draughtsman, he did not buy an interest in the company, but was given shares on achieving a directorship; he earns more than £25,000 per annum.
13	II	Male; aged 45; manager doing all the clerical work in a small engineering company; worked his way up from shop-floor in the company and now has shares in it, purchased using a bank loan together with his own resources; the company employs between 51 and 100 people and earns him an annual salary in excess of £25,000.
14	I	Male; aged 39; junior partner in a firm of quantity surveyors; spends little or no time in managing the company which has between 51 and 100 employees; self-employed, he worked his way up through the company, was offered a partnership, and used a bank loan to buy his small share; no details of annual income given.
15	I	Male; aged 44; managing director of a leather goods manufacturer operating on two sites; his company was formerly owned by his father, was taken over and expanded as part of a larger business, and he stayed on as managing director; he retains an ownership interest inherited through the family, employs 201–500 people in the leather factories, and earns £18,000–£24,999 per annum.
16	I	Male; aged 52; self-employed; used his own resources to set up a coal merchant and road haulage business jointly with his relatives; spends all of his working time on management matters ('doing the books'); employs 25–50 people; was formerly a salesman of agricultural machinery and self-employed lorry driver; no details of income were obtained.
17	II	Male; aged 55; manager in a hotel owned jointly with four other family members; used his own resources for his share of start-up capital; formerly a trainee waiter and self-employed restaurateur; spends about half of his time on management matters and the other half 'doing whatever needs done'; 10–24 employees; income not declared.
18	I	Male; aged 37; self-employed chartered accountant with junior partnership in company having 10–24 employees; spends about one-quarter of his time on managerial matters; started work as an articled clerk with the firm and used bank loan to buy a partnership when it was offered; annual income of between £18,000 and £24,999.
19	IV	Male; aged 32; self-employed sole proprietor of a small bakery employing 10–24 people; bank loan provided start-up capital; also assists father who is a farmer; annual income of £18,000–£24,999.
20	I	Male; aged 57; self-employed partner in an estate agency having 10–24 employees; spends little or none of his time on managing the business; started work as a junior office clerk and

Table 3.7 (*cont.*)

Case	Goldthorpe class	Biographical details
		was an estate agent employee before leaving to set up own business using a bank loan; father was a taxi-driver and mother a milk roundswoman; he earns £10,000–£11,999 annually.
21	I	Male; aged 55; self-employed; part-owner, director, and chairman of a small building construction company employing 25–50 people; spends all of his time in management; set up the firm with another member of his family both using their own resources; his father was a timber merchant; no details of income available.
22	I	Female; aged 48; self-employed; partner in family real estate firm established by her father; spends all of her working time 'looking after the finances'; the company has 25–50 employees; no details of income available.
23	I	Male; aged 47; self-employed accountant in business with one other family member; worked as an accountant for other companies before using bank loan to set up in business for himself; employs 25–50 people and spends half his time on managerial business; his income exceeds £25,000.
24	I	Male; aged 44; financial director of a company involved in the leisure industry; the company employs between 1,000 and 10,000 persons and has subsiduaries; formerly a financial consultant, he bought shares in this company when offered a directorship, using his own resources to purchase these; spends about three-quarters of his time at work on managerial matters; his father was a foreman steel worker and his own wife is a teacher; no details of income were obtained.
25	I	Male; aged 36; partner in a small roofing contractors; spends all of his time on the managerial side 'doing everything administrative'; used his own resources for his share of the start-up capital; formerly a wood-cutter and foreman roofer, he now employs 25–50 people, and earns £18,000–£24,999 per annum; his father was a self-employed woodcutter.
26	I	Male; aged 38; self-employed solicitor in a partnership employing 10–24 people; he used a bank loan to establish the business and devotes almost none of his time to management; no income details available; his father was a van driver and his mother a cleaner.

Certainly there are no solid empirical grounds on which to isolate the twenty-six individuals concerned. It will be seen from Table 3.7 that several of the so-called bourgeoisie are in fact simply senior executives holding shares in a company as part of their overall remuneration. These are clearly salaried employees rather than capitalists, in any meaningful sense of that term, and their salaries would appear to be commensurable with those earned by other top employees. Cases 12, 14, and 18 are typical of this group. The first of these is sales director of a company that manufactures ironmongery. The company retains between 200 and 500 employees but is itself part of a larger multinational organization. The respondent started his career as a draughtsman, worked his way up through the company to board level, and at this point was given shares as part of his promotion settlement. There would seem to be little theoretical or empirical sense in distinguishing these sorts of individuals from other top employees in Goldthorpe's class I, or in Wright's various managerial categories, simply on the grounds that they possess shares in their employing organization. Similarly, there is often very little separating the classic bourgeoisie that are supposed to be embraced by this group, from the more humble own-account workers of Goldthorpe class IV. Case 10, for example, is that of a self-employed proprietor of a large grocery store. He spends about one-quarter of his time actually managing the business and the rest in dealing directly with customers. Formerly a clerk in a coal-mine and then a self-employed dairy roundsman, he now employs between ten and twenty-five people, four of whom are family members also having a financial interest in the business. Cases 2, 5, 17 and 19 are similar, comprising part-proprietors of a residential home for the elderly, an automobile repair business, a hotel, and a family bakery respectively. There would seem to be little here to distinguish these individuals from own-account workers generally – other than the fact that they employ ten or more people.

Perhaps our only genuinely capitalist respondents, in the classic Marxist sense of that term as intended by Wright, are cases 3, 4, 6, 22, and 26 – though even these are problematic in different ways. In case 4, for example, that of the consulting engineer for an electrical supply company, the respondent used his savings to buy himself a partnership in the business, so in this respect is part-owner of a firm having over 500 employees, but did so only after having worked his way up from the shop-floor of the company. Is his situation with regard to the 'ownership and non-ownership of productive assets' really any different from that of the 'top employees' whom we looked at above? He is essentially a highly paid employee having a limited proprietory interest in a company over which he exercises shared managerial authority. Indeed, what is striking about our allegedly bourgeois group as a whole is that it contains none of those whom we know, from detailed research elsewhere, actually shape the capitalist contours of modern Britain, by manipulating huge sums of money in and out of financial and industrial markets.[32] There are, for example, no managers of pension funds among the twenty-six. Nor are there any executors of unit trusts, top bank managers, or directors of insurance companies. The fact is that Wright's operational definition of the bourgeoisie is derived from a nineteenth-century conception of family proprietorship which is wholly inadequate to the study of class processes in a late twentieth-century capitalist economy. Goldthorpe's notion of a 'service class', though less tidy as a concept since it embraces both nominal employers and employees, seems much closer to the reality of modern corporate Britain. It is certainly a more practical proposition in survey research of the type in which both he and Wright are engaged.

Finally, there are the contradictory class locations themselves, the various categories of credentialled and uncredentialled managers, supervisors, and workers. Of these, Wright's semi-credentialled workers offer the greatest number of inter-scheme divergencies, with approximately 30 per cent of this group appearing in Goldthorpe's service class, 15 per cent in his intermediate class, and the rest among his workers. Since there are 189 respondents in this category it is impractical to give details of every individual case. In any event it is unnecessary to do so since the parameters of the discrepancy, together with the reason for its occurrence, are readily apparent from a consideration of the polar instances alone. There are four semi-credentialled workers in Goldthorpe class I and four in class VII. The latter group are all employees – two roofer/glaziers, a metal worker, and a slinger. They are allocated semi-credentialled worker status because they are non-managerial and non-supervisory wage-earners but are judged to be 'skilled' on the credential assets dimension of Wright's typology since they are 'craftworkers'. The class I group comprise two quantity surveyors, both employees, and two buying and purchasing officers of managerial standing in establishments employing more than twenty-five persons. These are senior white-collar workers. But they are non-management (according to their pattern of responses to the decision-making and authority items), technical and managerial wage-earners (according to their *Wright* occupational coding), so also are semi-credentialled employees because they too are 'skilled' – in this case by virtue of their managerial and technical occupational codes and low educational qualifications. Had they, in fact, been highly qualified, they would have become 'experts' in terms of skill assets, and so been moved to the expert non-managerial class location. (Here again Table 3.2 makes the sequence of these coding decisions clear.) It is not difficult to see why Goldthorpe, looking at market situations and work situations, would want to place Wright's semi-credentialled workers in a variety of class locations. Conversely, since these workers arrive in the same Wright class for quite different reasons (in some cases because of formal qualifications held and in others on the basis of *occupational* title alone), one can be legitimately sceptical about the homogeneity of respondents in certain of Wright's contradictory class locations; homogeneity, that is, with respect to the very features that allegedly circumscribe social class locations themselves. The managerial and supervisory categories raise similar doubts, but these are probably best raised in the context of a discussion about social mobility into these positions, so will be dealt with in the following chapter.

Prima facie, therefore, the class schema proposed by John Goldthorpe seem to be more robust than those of Erik Wright. But this is a tentative (and perhaps controversial) claim which must be further explored by examining the patterns of demographic class formation in modern Britain. These are the subject of the following two chapters. The issues here are those of social mobility and class biographies. We shall focus in particular on two of the central themes in recent discussions; namely, those of women in class analysis, and of proletarianization in the class structure. Which conception of social class sheds most light on these subjects, and why?

Notes

1 See, for example, Wright (1985: 106–8).
2 Wright (1985: 9–10).
3 Wright (1985: 14).
4 For a critical appraisal of game-theoretical Marxism see Lash and Urry (1984).
5 In fact Roemer has produced two models of exploitation. The first was based on a labour transfer approach but he found that he had to make too many simplifying assumptions for such a model to work. He therefore developed the game-theoretic approach in order to overcome the problems which arise when the simplifying assumptions are relaxed. It is this second version of exploitation which Wright finds attractive (though in need of modification) because 'it allows for a particularly elegant way of characterizing the different mechanisms of exploitation in different types of class structures' (Wright, 1985: 68).
6 Wright (1985: 72).
7 Wright (1985: 72).
8 Wright (1985: 74).
9 Wright (1985: 87).
10 Indeed, when all Wright's amendments to the original theory are taken together, they seriously undermine Roemer's project. Certainly it is not clear to us why, in order to produce a theory based on exploitation, Wright needs Roemer's work at all. After all, exploitation as conceptualized within the labour theory of value (in the manner in which Wright wishes to use it) has a long if suspect pedigree. Why introduce a new and controversial version of the concept simply in order to reject its novel elements in favour of some more orthodox version?
11 Wright (1985: 87).
12 Wright (1985: 87).
13 Wright (1985: 314).
14 Forced coding of particular occupations in this way may simply be the result of common-sense reasoning on Wright's part – but it does constitute ethnocentrism in a comparative analysis since it unproblematically equates the content of jobs across countries.
15 The categories of socio-economic group are given in Table A.3 of the Appendix to this volume and can be compared with those for the collapsed American occupational variable which are as follows: physicians and dentists; other medical; accountants, auditors, actuaries; elementary and secondary teachers; university teachers, social scientists, librarians; mathematicians, engineers, scientists, architects; technicians; public advisory; judges and lawyers; creative and entertainment; managers and administrators in public sector; corporate managers; other managers; secretaries; other clerical; sales; foremen; crafts; government protective workers; transportation; operatives except transport; labourers except farm; farm labourers and foremen; white-collar services; skilled manual services; unskilled services; farmers.
16 Wright (1985: 314). Wright's confidence is not justified by our own experience in translating British occupational data into the American classification. We experienced considerable practical difficulties in doing this because of the different conventions of the two schemes.
17 See, for example, Wright (1980b).
18 Wright (1985: 185–6).
19 See Stewart et al. (1980).
20 Wright (1985: 144–5).
21 Goldthorpe (1983b: 20).
22 Wright (1985: 14).
23 Wright (1985: 319–22).
24 Wright (1985: 89).
25 Goldthorpe (1982), Stewart et al. (1980).
26 Weber (1968: 999–1000).
27 Weber (1968: 927–8).
28 Wright (1985: 114–18).
29 Wright (1985: 137).
30 See, for example, Crompton and Sanderson (1986).
31 Goldthorpe (1980: 39–40). Wright himself is alert to the conceptual problems involved here. In *Classes* he concedes that

the data used in this study . . . cannot rigorously distinguish all of these categories. In particular, the only data available to distinguish small employers from proper capitalists is the number of employees of the respondent, and this is at best a weak indicator, since it does not really measure the amount of capital owned by the capitalist' (p. 151).

However, if the British sample is anything to go by, his faith that the 'rather arbitrary convention' of defining all employers of more than ten people as 'fully-fledged capitalists' provides an effective solution to this problem would seem to be misplaced.

32 See, for example, Scott (1979).

4 Class formation and social mobility

Currently the most controversial demographic issue in class analysis stems, ironically enough, from an aspect of research strategy that is common to all three approaches featured in this study. It is clear that, in each case, only those individuals who are in formal employment can be allocated directly to a particular class location. Some 30 per cent of our sample lack precisely this qualification. At the time of our survey these individuals were either unemployed or engaged full time in domestic labour.[1]

The difficulties this raises for class analysis are conceptual as well as practical. How long must an individual take 'between jobs' before he or she becomes 'unemployed'? At what point does an 'unemployed married woman' become a 'housewife' – and so lose her unemployed status? These taxonomic problems, together with their associated theoretical implications, have been discussed at length elsewhere. The arguments need not be rehearsed here.[2] It is the practical problems that they raise for the conduct of class analysis that are of immediate interest. These are obvious enough. Does an individual losing his or her job thereby 'lose' an associated class position? Do married women who keep house have a class affiliation of their own – or can they be assumed simply to share the class positions of their spouses? In short, if the unit of class analysis is the individual, and class locations are to be allocated in practice according to some combination of occupational or employment related attributes, what treatment is to be accorded individuals who are not engaged in paid labour at the time of study? Are they somehow detached from the class structure? Might it not be the case, therefore, that the most appropriate unit for class analysis is the nuclear family rather than (as we have taken it to be thus far) the particular individual? But if this alternative strategy is to be pursued, how is a putative 'head of family' to be identified, since many households will contain more than one individual who is formally occupied?

These are large and complex issues and they are currently receiving close attention in a number of quarters.[3] Our interest here is more specific and concerns the extent to which the different class frameworks with which we are particularly concerned resolve these problems. Two questions arise at this juncture and these form the subject of the present chapter. First, do the class schemes of the Registrar-General, John Goldthorpe, and Erik Wright converge in their assumptions about domestic labour and unemployment, despite otherwise distinct operational definitions of class affiliation? Second, and following on from this, what are the implications of pursuing these particular strategies (convergent or otherwise) in a class analysis of the Essex data? Fortunately, from our point of view, Goldthorpe and Wright have written at some length about the issues surrounding the selection of units for class analysis, particularly in reference to the relationship between class inequality and the sexual division of labour. However, in focusing our attention on this problem we must also consider broader questions of class formation and social mobility, since these are central to the arguments of both authors in justifying the unit of their respective class analyses.

I

Early statements about the implications of sex differences for class analysis tended to be programmatic and sometimes deliberately polemical.[4] However, the more recent exchange between John Goldthorpe and his critics in the pages of the journal *Sociology* identified concrete problems of integrating women into class theory, and so moved discussion on to much firmer ground. The principal point of contention that emerged among the protagonists concerned the fundamental issue of the unit of the class analysis itself. Are social class locations most appropriately attributed to families, according to the labour market position of the 'head of household'; to individuals, as individuals, each according to his or her own position in the market; or by some composite measure that takes account of the possibly different market and work situations of the man and woman who make up a particular family grouping? All three strategies were championed during the course of the debate.[5]

Goldthorpe himself, in the article that initiated the controversy, offers a sophisticated defence of orthodox class analysis against the charge of intellectual sexism. Drawing on data collected for the Oxford Mobility Study in the early 1970s he attempts to show that the increased participation of women (especially married women) in paid labour over recent years carries fewer implications for theorists of social stratification than feminists have generally supposed. Women's paid employment is often part time or, if undertaken on a full-time basis, more intermittent and limited than that of men since it is generally interrupted by motherhood. Discontinuity aside, the family can still be seen as the basic unit of stratification, since the Oxford data at least suggest that, in important ways, married women's employment is affected by the class experiences of their conjugal partners. Indeed the duration and timing of a wife's employment is itself conditioned by the class position and mobility experience of her husband.

The mobility data also cast doubt on the thesis that there exist in Britain large numbers of 'cross-class families' which conventional class theory can no longer ignore. Goldthorpe's argument here is that wives' conditions of employment will either be the same as, or inferior to, those of their husbands, since (as the evidence produced by feminists themselves shows) women in lower-level nonmanual occupations are less favourably treated than even many manual-labouring males, notably in terms of pay, guarantees of security, access to fringe benefits and promotion. If the wife of a manual worker is employed either in secretarial duties or as a shop assistant, as is often the case, it is by no means apparent to Goldthorpe that a cross-class family is thereby created. Although the husband is involved in manual work, and his partner in nonmanual, both are engaged in the exchange of labour power for wages under similar, that is relatively unfavourable, conditions of employment.

For Goldthorpe, then, the conjugal family remains the unit of class fate, class formation, and class action. A range of women's life-chances are (apparently) mediated by their husbands' class positions and, since women from families in different class situations will tend to make correspondingly different social demands, class cleavages will continue to run between but not through families.

This conclusion is keenly contested by Anthony Heath and Nicky Britten who are convinced that class analysts simply cannot ignore the growth of paid employment among married women. Rather than continue to treat the family as a unit, the class position of which derives from the location within the occupational division of labour of a putative head of household, they propose instead a joint classification which takes explicit cognizance of the wife's labour market participation. Drawing on data from a wide range of official statistics to make their case, Heath and Britten maintain that across a range of attributes including fertility and voting behaviour, more of the variance within and between conjugal families can be accounted for using a joint classification than if households are indexed simply according to the husband's employment alone. Women's jobs, they emphasize, 'do make a difference' and 'have explanatory power for class and family behaviour over and above that attributable to their husbands' class positions'.[6] Similarly, the shape of women's involvement in the labour market is allegedly conditioned to a greater extent by a woman's own qualifications and job history, than by her husband's class position or career.

Moreover, the critique continues, since the market and work situations of women in many occupations (notably office and sales jobs) are inferior to those of similarly placed men, women tend to develop distinctive career paths within 'semi-professional', 'office' and 'proletarian' labour markets, such that mobility between, say, sales and secretarial jobs is very infrequent. It is certainly less common than Goldthorpe suggests – which obviates his claim that the joint classification strategy yields huge amounts of artefactual social mobility among female respondents crossing and recrossing a nominal manual/nonmanual class boundary. Heath and Britten maintain that, Goldthorpe to the contrary, their data show semi-professional, office, and sales work to be so different from each other that women have strong commitments to one or another type. These then form the basis for distinctive patterns of class behaviour – notably in respect of family size and party identification. Cross-class families, for example, where the husband holds a blue-collar job and the wife a white-collar one, tend to exhibit different fertility and voting patterns to those of homogeneous blue-collar families with whom they are conventionally grouped.

The Heath and Britten revisions of the conventional approach are perhaps more radical than at first appears to be the case. Not only do women's jobs make a difference to the explained variance in observed class attributes; they are also sufficiently distinct in market, work, and typical career trajectory terms as to cast doubts on all occupational classifications that were originally devised with men in mind – Goldthorpe's own class schema included.

Many of the objections to Goldthorpe's strategy documented by Heath and Britten are also voiced by Michelle Stanworth. However, while the former retain the family as the unit of analysis but classify its location according to the employment and occupational statuses of both conjugal partners, Stanworth proposes a wholly individual approach to the problem of assigning class membership.

Stanworth in fact challenges all three of Goldthorpe's principal claims: namely that, within families, husbands have the major commitment to labour market participation; that wives' employment is conditioned by husbands' class positions; and that contemporary marriages are largely homogeneous in social class terms. She argues that Goldthorpe has chosen simply to ignore accumulated evidence about the ways in which the class fates of both married women and men are mediated by family structures. Women's earnings, for example, may have affected class formation, inequality, and action in numerous ways ranging from expanding home-ownership among the working class to reconciling intergenerationally stable proletarian men to class immobility. The orthodox approach also ignores the financial insecurity of wives that ensues from their dependence on the marital partner. This dependence is alleviated only by the woman's employment which then has a more pronounced impact on her life-chances (she has access to resources for expenditure on her own needs) than does any change in her husband's class position. Similarly, the early return of professional and managerial wives to employment after childbirth, facilitated according to Goldthorpe by the managerial husband's ability to purchase alternative childcare services, can as easily be seen as a consequence of the relatively well-paid, satisfying and flexible jobs held by the wives themselves. In any case, Stanworth's understanding of the evidence available is that the vast majority of women in fact share a proletarian class experience by virtue of the subordinate nature of their own occupations, so that the extent of cross-class discrepancy within marriages will be far greater than Goldthorpe would have us believe.

Many of Stanworth's criticisms hinge on the inferences one is prepared to draw from Goldthorpe's particular statistics. They raise specific points of interpretation that are internal to the debate and these cannot be pursued here. Nevertheless, the general direction of her arguments is clear and is towards the conclusion that women's restricted employment opportunities are a consequence of the operation of the class system itself, rather than the outcome of negotiations within individual marriages which, because of conventions about family responsibilities, place women in subordinate positions to their husbands.

While Goldthorpe's approach discourages further investigation of the impact of wives' . . . employment on the 'class situation' of families, both approaches foreclose avenues of research (the operation of the labour market *vis-à-vis* women; the processes which shape interrelationships between women's and men's class positions; the significance of unpaid work and of the informal economy; the relationships within the class system between individuals, households and families) which are far too important to be ignored. Thus the problems raised by a serious consideration of women's relation to the class structure require much more radical re-working of the categories of class analysis than either Goldthorpe's position or that of the cross-class theorists allows.[7]

Unfortunately, Stanworth's own approach is much less developed than those of her adversaries, so we are left only to reflect on this ambitious programme for study and on how her resolutely individual strategy might possibly be translated into investigative practice. Indeed comparative assessment of the different strategies on offer is rendered generally difficult by the fact that two of the three positions under discussion are not fully formulated. We simply do not know whether Stanworth would assign a typist married to a salaried professional to the same class position as a typist married to a manual wage-worker. Nor is it clear how she would explain such findings as those relating to the political partisanship of married women in clerical jobs (which Stanworth would regard as proletarian). In 1979, for example, clerical women married to industrial workers gave Labour a 6 percentage point advantage over the Conservatives, while among those married to professionals and managers the Tories held a 45 percentage point lead over Labour.

Similarly, whatever the merits of joint classification in distinguishing the class position of families in which the woman is in paid employment from those in which she undertakes no paid labour (holding husband's class position constant), this strategy does tend to generate rates of class mobility that are spuriously high and so creates a problem which as yet Heath and Britten have been unable to resolve. For example, an 'everyday working-class family' as depicted by Goldthorpe, in which a male who is throughout a manual wage-earner marries a shop assistant, who then leaves employment during early motherhood, returns some years later but to factory work, stops temporarily to have a third child, then takes up part-time factory employment before returning full time to saleswork, will have been class mobile, according to Heath and Britten, no less than five times in some twenty or so years.

On the other hand, as Goldthorpe's own data confirm, some professional and managerial women are married to manual labouring men, and it is by no means clear how he would assign class membership to these families if the wife's career is significantly interrupted by motherhood. In some places he states clearly that his *revised* conventional approach locates whole families in the class structure according to the social class of 'the family member who has the fullest commitment to participation in the labour market'. Elsewhere, however, his argument amounts to a defence of the *standard* application of conventional class analysis in which the class positions of married women are derived from those of their husbands.[8] Since there are no explicit operational procedures given for determining commitment to labour market participation, it is unclear in the case of the particular service-class women mentioned above, for example, whether or not motherhood renders a commitment to the labour market on their part necessarily inferior to that shown by their permanently employed husbands. Are such families therefore 'working class'?

II

Our own view is that the participants in this particular controversy were to a considerable extent talking past each other's positions. This raises the intriguing possibility that Goldthorpe and Stanworth may both be correct. Certainly there is more at issue here than the straightforward question of which might be the most appropriate unit for study. It is the very definition of class analysis itself – its rationale and objectives – that is implicitly being contested. The unit of and scope for the enterprise are two separate, though related, issues and our data bear on both in equal measure.

These show, first of all, that cross-class families occur in sufficient numbers as to constitute a genuine problem in pursuing a class analysis. Table 4.1 gives the figures for cohabiting respondents in our sample, where both partners are gainfully employed according to Goldthorpe class categories. The issue for class analysts is clear. Significant proportions of respondents in all class categories are permanently co-resident with partners who are in paid employment and, of these, many are in what can only be described as cross-class families. In fact, if we collapse this table over sex (as in Table 4.2A), and then about its diagonal (see Table 4.2B), to calculate the proportions of couples living as married in each of the possible class pairings where both partners are gainfully employed, we can see that fully half of these conjugal units in our sample are cross-class families, using the three-category version of Goldthorpe's class schema.

It is true, as Goldthorpe claims, that women typically will either share the class positions of their spouses or are to be found in relatively lower class positions. Among all respondents in service-class (I and II) locations, for example, 47 per cent (170 from a total of 358) live with employed partners. Of the 101 men in this category, half are married to service-class women, while half live with intermediate-class (III, IV, V) or working-class (VI and VII) partners. Among service-class women these proportions are 64 per cent and 36 per cent; and, of course, there are more service-class men than service-class women in the population as a whole. (Some 65 per cent of service-class respondents in our sample were males.) Similarly, 32 per cent of routine white-collar (class III) female respondents have service-class husbands, as compared with 1 per cent of class III male respondents having service-class

Table 4.1 *Distribution of cohabiting men and women, where both partners are gainfully employed, by Goldthorpe social class of both partners*

A – Class distribution of men's partners

| | | | | | Wife's class | | | | | |
		I	II	III	IV	V	VI	VII	Total	
	I	4.3	39.1	43.5	0.0	2.2	4.3	6.5	100	(46)
	II	5.5	50.9	29.1	1.8	0.0	1.8	10.9	100	(55)
	III	0.0	8.3	50.0	8.3	0.0	16.7	16.7	100	(12)
Husband's	IV	2.4	24.4	29.3	24.4	4.9	2.4	12.2	100	(41)
class	V	3.3	16.7	26.7	0.0	3.3	10.0	40.0	100	(30)
	VI	2.0	2.0	42.9	0.0	2.0	6.1	44.9	100	(49)
	VII	0.0	11.9	40.3	3.0	3.0	9.0	32.8	100	(67)

(N = 300)

B – Class distribution of women's partners

| | | | | | Husband's class | | | | | |
		I	II	III	IV	V	VI	VII	Total	
	I	50.0	25.0	8.3	0.0	0.0	0.0	16.7	100	(12)
	II	24.6	36.8	5.3	8.8	8.8	8.8	7.0	100	(57)
	III	9.8	23.5	9.8	9.8	17.6	11.8	17.6	100	(102)
Wife's	IV	25.0	10.0	5.0	60.0	0.0	0.0	0.0	100	(20)
class	V	7.1	14.3	7.1	21.4	7.1	14.3	28.6	100	(14)
	VI	0.0	9.1	9.1	0.0	18.2	45.5	18.2	100	(11)
	VII	2.7	6.8	4.1	9.6	17.8	27.4	31.5	100	(73)

(N = 289)

Note: i   This table includes all couples married or living as married.
ii   If all presently unemployed, retired, and houseworking spouses having a recent work history (that is, formal employment at any time in the past five years) are included in this calculation, then the total numbers rise from 589 to 765 couples. However the marginal percentages for both versions of the table are nearly identical and the differences within the cells are insignificant. By restricting this part of our analysis to those couples in which both partners are at present gainfully employed we are in no way distorting the picture of class homogeneity and heterogeneity.

wives. Translating this into couples, we can see that the female class III/male class I or II pairing comprises some 12 per cent of cohabiting employed couples, whereas the male class III/female class I or II combination constitutes barely 1 per cent. In other words, and as the data in Tables 4.1 and 4.2 confirm, in a 'cross-class' couple it is more commonly the man who has the higher social class standing. Still, the fact remains that some working-class men are married to service-class women (these are 4 per cent of cohabiting employed couples in our sample), and they constitute a clear anomaly within the conventional view – especially if the female interrupts her career for childrearing purposes. This conclusion is confirmed even when intergenerational social mobility is taken into account (as in Table 4.3). Service-class men with

Table 4.2 *Proportions of cohabiting couples, of which both partners are gainfully employed, by Goldthorpe social class pairings*

A – Goldthorpe seven-category scheme

		I	II	III	Wife's class IV	V	VI	VII	Total
	I	1.4 (8)	5.4 (32)	5.0 (30)	0.9 (5)	0.3 (2)	0.3 (2)	0.8 (5)	(84)
	II	1.0 (6)	8.3 (49)	6.8 (40)	0.5 (3)	0.3 (2)	0.3 (2)	1.9 (11)	(113)
Husband's	III	0.2 (1)	0.7 (4)	2.7 (16)	0.3 (2)	0.2 (1)	0.5 (3)	0.8 (5)	(32)
class	IV	0.2 (1)	2.5 (15)	3.7 (22)	3.7 (22)	0.8 (5)	0.2 (1)	2.0 (12)	(78)
	V	0.2 (1)	1.7 (10)	4.4 (26)	0.0 (0)	0.3 (2)	0.8 (5)	4.2 (25)	(69)
	VI	0.2 (1)	1.0 (6)	5.6 (33)	0.0 (0)	0.5 (3)	1.4 (8)	7.1 (42)	(93)
	VII	0.3 (2)	2.0 (12)	7.6 (45)	0.3 (2)	1.0 (6)	1.4 (8)	7.6 (45)	(120)
Total		(20)	(128)	(212)	(34)	(21)	(29)	(145)	(589)

B – Goldthorpe three-category scheme

		N	%	Cumulative frequency (%)
Class	Service–Service	95	16	
homogeneous	Intermediate–Intermediate	96	16	
	Working–Working	103	18	50
Cross-class	Service–Intermediate	114	19	
	Intermediate–Working	140	24	
	Working–Service	41	7	100
Total		589	100	100

service-class backgrounds are less likely to be found with working-class wives than are men upwardly mobile into service-class positions. But even men intergenerationally stable within the working class are sometimes married to service-class partners. Is the class location of such families to be considered identical to that of conjugal units comprising working-class men with intermediate-class or working-class partners; or, indeed, with partners who are not in paid employment at all?[9]

Of course the mere existence of cross-class families – in whatever numbers and however these are defined – would carry few implications for class analysis if, as Goldthorpe maintains, the typically intermittent and more limited labour market participation of most women means that their life-chances and demands are class conditioned rather than class conditioning; that is, if the class behaviour of wives is a function of their husbands' class positions, rather than their own occupational experiences. In fact there is some evidence to suggest that this might be the case. Table 4.4, for example, shows that voting intentions among married women in employment depend

Table 4.3 *Type of employment of wives of men with differing class mobility experience**

| Subsample of men | Class of wife's employment | | | |
	I + II	*III-V*	*VI + VII*	*Total*
Stable in service class	68	32	0	100 (25)
Stable in intermediate class	23	54	23	100 (26)
Stable in working class	9	53	38	100 (58)
Upwardly mobile, working to intermediate	16	55	29	100 (31)
Upwardly mobile, intermediate to service	53	34	13	100 (32)
Upwardly mobile, working to service	44	35	21	100 (34)
Downwardly mobile, service to intermediate	30	40	30	100 (10)
Downwardly mobile, intermediate to working	6	41	53	100 (34)
Downwardly mobile, service to working	18	45	36	100 (11)

(N = 261)

*Comparing current Goldthorpe class with Goldthorpe class of the chief childhood supporter when he or she was at the same age as the respondent is now.

Note: Again, as with Tables 4.1 and 4.2, the proportions within the cells remain constant even if spouses' work histories are taken into account. (To do so raises the total in the subsample from 261 to 346.)

Table 4.4 *Interrelationship between vote and class*

A – Wife's voting intention, wife's class, husband's class

Model	df	Y^2	Difference			Y^2/df	p
1 [FV] [FM] [VM]	12	19.1	⇒FVM	12	19.1	1.6	0.10
2 [FM] [VM]	18	29.5	⇒FV	6	10.4	1.7	>0.10
3 [FM] [V]	24	64.1	⇒VM	6	34.6	5.8	<0.0005
4 [VM] [F]	22	99.3	⇒FM	4	69.7	17.4	<0.0005

Key: F = Wife's social class (Goldthorpe three-category scheme);
V = Wife's voting intention (Conservative, Labour, Alliance, Would not vote/don't know);
M = Husband's social class (Goldthorpe three-category scheme).

B – Husband's voting intention, husband's class, wife's class

Model	df	Y^2	Difference			Y^2/df	p
1 [MV] [MF] [VF]	12	12.4	⇒MVF	12	12.4	1.0	>0.5
2 [MV] [MF]	18	24.9	⇒VF	6	12.5	2.1	0.10
3 [MV] [F]	22	79.8	⇒MF	4	54.9	13.7	<0.0005
4 [MF] [V]	24	72.0	⇒MV	6	47.2	7.9	<0.0005

Key: M = Husband's social class (Goldthorpe three-category scheme);
V = Husband's voting intention (Conservative, Labour, Alliance, Would not vote/don't know);
F = Wife's social class (Goldthorpe three-category scheme).

mostly on their husbands' jobs. There is, as one would expect, a strong association between the social class locations of husbands and those of wives (Table 4.4A, parameter FM). A significant association between wife's vote and husband's class is also observed (VM). Perhaps surprisingly, however, a woman's own occupation contributes no extra useful information once the social class of her husband is determined. (The change in Y^2 to change in df ratio for the parameter FV is close to one.) The relationship between a wife's class and her own vote is much less important than that between her vote and the class of her husband. Moreover, as the bottom half of the table shows, this pattern of relationships is not evident where husbands' votes are concerned. There is a much stronger association between a man's vote and his own class (MV) than between his vote and the social class of his wife (VF). These results are also obtained when voting data are modelled using the full seven-category version of the Goldthorpe class scheme. Partisanship clearly runs between rather than through families.

On the other hand, there is no evidence that the character of a married woman's work is more powerfully conditioned by her derived class than by her own credentials. In fact the opposite is true (see Table 4.5A). As one would expect, there are positive associations between a woman's class and her qualifications (QF), between husband's class and wife's qualifications (QM), and between the class positions of conjugal partners (FM). Omitting any of these relationships leads to a significant worsening of the fitted model. However, the strongest observed association is between a wife's class and her own credentials, rather than between the class positions of spouses. (The ratio of change in Y^2/df is much stronger for the former relationship than for the latter.) Similar findings are obtained if one looks at the cohabiting male respondents in our sample (as in Table 4.5B). These results are quite inconsistent with Goldthorpe's argument that the social class positions of most wives are indirectly determined and, as it were, 'derived' from the male 'family head'. On the contrary, they suggest that the appropriate unit for demographic class analysis is the individual rather than the family. The class locations of married women (and behind this their class trajectories) are more importantly conditioned by their own attributes (in this case their formal qualifications) than by the class of the male 'head' of the family unit to which they are attached.

Goldthorpe is therefore vindicated only in part by the data here on offer. Married women's class fates are no more (or no less) mediated by the conjugal family than are those of married men. But there are, it seems, good reasons for believing that conjugal families rather than individuals may be the unit of class action – at least in so far as this is expressed in voting intentions. This is why John Goldthorpe judges the nuclear family to be the most appropriate unit for conducting a class analysis. However, we are not convinced by this argument, since there are as good grounds for pursuing Stanworth's (admittedly sketchy) remarks about the articulation of sex with class structures as there are Goldthorpe's observations about the dependence of women upon men within nuclear families. Principal among these is the fact

Table 4.5 *Interrelationship between educational qualifications and class*

A – Wife's qualifications, wife's class, husband's class

Model		df	Y^2	Difference			Y^2/df	p
1	[QF] [QM] [FM]	8	11.1	⇒QFM	8	11.1	1.4	>0.20
2	[QF] [QM]	12	43.5	⇒FM	4	32.4	8.1	<0.0005
3	[QF] [FM]	12	32.5	⇒QM	4	21.4	5.4	<0.0005
4	[QM] [FM]	12	89.3	⇒QF	4	78.2	19.6	<0.0005

Key: Q = Wife's educational qualifications (low, medium, high*);
F = Wife's social class (Goldthorpe three-category scheme);
M = Husband's social class (Goldthorpe three-category scheme).

B – Husband's qualifications, husband's class, wife's class

Model		df	Y^2	Difference			Y^2/df	p
1	[QM] [QF] [MF]	6	5.1	⇒QMF	6	5.1	0.9	>0.50
2	[QM] [QF]	10	20.8	⇒MF	4	15.7	3.9	<0.005
3	[QM] [MF]	10	32.4	⇒QF	4	27.2	6.8	<0.0005
4	[QF] [MF]	9	145.2	⇒QM	3	140.1	46.7	<0.0005

Key: Q = Husband's educational qualifications (low, medium, high)*;
M = Husband's social class (Goldthorpe three-category scheme);
F = Wife's social class (Goldthorpe three-category scheme).

*   low: holds no formal qualifications; CSE Grades 2–5; or job training (e.g. HGV driving licence) only.

medium: holds CSE Grade 1; GCE O or A level or Scottish equivalents; Overseas School Leaving Certificate; ONC, OND, City and Guilds; HNC, HND, City and Guilds, RSA, clerical or commercial; or full apprenticeship qualification.

high: holds teacher training qualification; nursing qualifications; other technical or business qualifications; professional qualification; degree or higher degree; or other vocational qualification equivalent to a degree.

that, as it seems to us, class systems are structured by sex in ways that clearly affect the distribution of life-chances, class formation, and class action among both women and men alike. In other words, while it may be true that, at the level of individual families, women's class experiences are (in some part) dependent upon those of their husbands, it is also the case that the mobility chances of men are dependent on a pronounced degree of sexual differentiation in the social division of labour, that is at the level of the class structure as a whole. Classes and class phenomena are conditioned by the peculiar pattern of women's participation (however intermittent) in the market for paid labour. This raises an important point of principle about the objectives or parameters of class analysis itself. It is on this point that we part company with John Goldthorpe.

Consider the following findings from our survey. Women are, as one would expect, unevenly distributed across the various social classes (see Table 4.6). If one allocates respondents to classes on the basis of their own occupations

Table 4.6 *Distribution of respondents by Goldthorpe social class and sex*

Count Row % Column % Total	Sex		
	Male	*Female*	*Total*
Class			
I	101 82.1 13.1 7.7	22 17.9 4.0 1.7	123 9.4
II	132 56.2 17.1 10.0	103 43.8 18.9 7.8	235 17.9
IIIa	44 22.2 5.7 3.3	154 77.8 28.3 11.7	198 15.1
IIIb	2 3.4 0.3 0.2	56 96.6 10.3 4.3	58 4.4
IVa	40 85.1 5.2 3.0	7 14.9 1.3 0.5	47 3.6
IVb	40 67.8 5.2 3.0	19 32.2 3.5 1.4	59 4.5
IVc	10 90.9 1.3 0.8	1 9.1 0.2 0.1	11 0.8
V	87 82.1 11.3 6.6	19 17.9 3.5 1.4	106 8.1
VI	134 81.2 17.4 10.2	31 18.8 5.7 2.4	165 12.5
VIIa	176 57.5 22.8 13.4	130 42.5 23.9 9.9	306 23.3
VIIb	5 71.4 0.6 0.4	2 28.6 0.4 0.2	7 0.5
Total	771 58.6	544 41.4	1315 100.0

then, among employed men and women in our sample, 13 per cent of men will be found in class I as against 4 per cent of women; 6 per cent of men are in class IIIa (routine nonmanual employees in administration and commerce) as compared with 28 per cent of women; less than 1 per cent of men are in personal service work (class IIIb) whereas 10 per cent of women are so engaged; and 17 per cent of males are in skilled manual work (class VI) as compared with 6 per cent of females. Or, reading across the rows of the same table, men comprise 82 per cent of class I, 77 per cent of own account workers, 82 per cent of all manual supervisors and lower-grade technicians, and a similar percentage of skilled manual workers; whereas, conversely, 82 per cent of all routine nonmanual employees and personal service workers will be found to be women. Given this degree of class segmentation by sex one can feasibly claim that the distribution of male life-chances is conditioned by the highly particular location of women within the overall structure. Or again, reasoning counterfactually, there would be many fewer service-class men if the distribution of routine nonmanual tasks were more evenly divided between the sexes rather than, as at present, being largely the responsibility of women.

Of course Goldthorpe would rightly maintain that a satisfactory class analysis must take seriously the issues of process and continuity as well as those of differentiation as such. Tables 4.7 and 4.8 therefore chart the mobility experiences of married men and women by contrasting their own present social class with that of their chief childhood supporter when he or she was at the same age as the respondent is now. Table 4.7 is a class composition table, showing inflow mobility matrices for men and women, hence the class origins of the respondents within each social class. Table 4.8, on the other hand, presents the same data but in outflow terms. This gives a picture of class distribution since it shows the amount and pattern of mobility experienced by men and women from the various class origins.

The results of these analyses require some interpretation but the overall pattern seems clear. Put simply, women's mobility chances are worse than those of men, notably where access to service-class locations is concerned. For example, of those men presently in top service-class (I) locations, 26 per cent are from service-class origins, 40 per cent from intermediate-class origins, while 34 per cent have been recruited from working-class backgrounds. The corresponding percentages for women are 40, 30, and 30. In other words proportionately more men than women are likely to be upwardly mobile into the service class from other class locations. Among male respondents in class III (routine white-collar) locations however, 21 per cent hail from service-class origins, 26 per cent from intermediate-class origins, and 53 per cent from working-class origins, as compared to figures of 14, 37, and 49 per cent respectively for class III females. In this case, proportionately more men than women have been downwardly mobile from service-class origins and upwardly mobile from working-class origins into class III destinations, though the differences are not particularly marked. Sex differentiation is, however, more apparent when we turn to consider outflow patterns. Among men from

Table 4.7 *Class composition by sex and class of chief childhood supporter at same age as respondent – Goldthorpe class categories*

		Males						
					Class of respondent			
		I	II	III	IV	V	VI	VII
	I	14.1	13.8	15.8	4.1	3.0	4.6	2.1
	II	12.0	19.3	5.3	8.2	1.5	6.4	3.4
Class of	III	8.7	6.4	0.0	2.7	4.5	9.2	1.4
chief	IV	14.1	12.8	13.2	35.6	13.6	9.2	9.0
childhood	V	17.4	19.3	13.2	11.0	22.7	13.8	21.4
supporter	VI	13.0	16.5	34.2	12.3	30.3	29.4	24.1
	VII	20.7	11.9	18.4	26.0	24.2	27.5	38.6
	Total	100.0	100.0	100.0	100.0	100.0	100.0	100.0
		(92)	(109)	(38)	(73)	(66)	(109)	(145)

(N = 632)

		Females						
					Class of respondent			
		I	II	III	IV	V	VI	VII
	I	20.0	8.9	8.6	4.3	0.0	0.0	2.1
	II	20.1	13.3	5.6	0.0	0.0	0.0	3.2
Class of	III	5.0	10.0	5.6	4.3	0.0	4.8	3.2
chief	IV	25.0	15.6	10.5	21.7	13.3	4.8	11.7
childhood	V	0.0	24.4	21.0	21.7	6.7	23.8	13.8
supporter	VI	20.0	18.9	30.2	13.0	40.0	42.9	24.5
	VII	10.0	8.9	18.5	34.8	40.0	23.8	41.5
	Total	100.0	100.0	100.0	100.0	100.0	100.0	100.0
		(20)	(90)	(162)	(23)	(15)	(21)	(94)

(N = 425)

social class I origins, 28 per cent are themselves in class I locations, with 32 per cent in class II and only 13 per cent engaged in routine nonmanual tasks. Only 14 per cent of women from class I backgrounds have made it into class I occupations, with 28 per cent in class II, and a significant 48 per cent in class III. In fact, among men from all service-class (I and II) backgrounds, 60 per cent are themselves in service-class locations, with only 8 per cent in routine nonmanual occupations. Only 49 per cent of women from service-class origins are presently in these occupations whereas 40 per cent are to be found in the routine nonmanual category. Twenty-one per cent of men from working-class backgrounds are currently in service-class occupations. Only 15 per cent of women from similar origins are so located.

These tables demonstrate the pronounced effects of sex upon patterns of social mobility. Whatever their class origin, women are far more likely than men from similar backgrounds to arrive at class III destinations, whereas men are more likely to arrive at service-class or working-class positions. Men are also more likely than women to be mobile into self-employment (class IV) or supervisory (class V) positions and again this is true across all class backgrounds. Within classes, those women who are mobile into the service class are more likely than corresponding men to be found in its cadet or subaltern level (class II), while men are more likely than women to arrive at skilled working-class rather than unskilled working-class destinations.

These findings are scarcely surprising given the extent of sex segregation in the occupational division of labour that was observed above. However our data also suggest that there are some rather less obvious sex differences in the structuring of social classes. These can be seen in Table 4.9. This table contrasts the market situations (columns 1 and 2) and work situations (columns 3 to 5) of men and women in the various Goldthorpe class locations. In the top half of the table all employees are included. Part B shows the figures for those in full-time employment only. Respondents were asked to report on their gross pay, location within recognized career or promotion ladders, autonomy, decision-making, and supervisory responsibilities at

Table 4.8 *Class distribution of respondents by sex and class of chief childhood supporter at same age as respondent – Goldthorpe class categories*

| | | Males | | | | | | | |
| | | Class of respondent | | | | | | | |
		I	*II*	*III*	*IV*	*V*	*VI*	*VII*	*Total*
	I	27.7	31.9	12.8	6.4	4.3	10.6	6.4	100.0 (47)
	II	20.8	39.6	3.8	11.3	1.9	13.2	9.4	100.0 (53)
Class of	III	25.0	21.9	0.0	6.3	9.4	31.3	6.3	100.0 (32)
chief	IV	14.4	15.6	5.6	28.9	10.0	11.1	14.4	100.0 (90)
childhood	V	14.4	18.9	4.5	7.2	13.5	13.5	27.9	100.0 (111)
supporter	VI	8.0	12.4	9.5	6.6	14.6	23.4	25.5	100.0 (139)
	VII	11.9	8.1	4.4	11.9	10.0	18.8	35.0	100.0 (160)

(N = 632)

| | | Females | | | | | | | |
| | | Class of respondent | | | | | | | |
		I	*II*	*III*	*IV*	*V*	*VI*	*VII*	*Total*
	I	13.8	27.6	48.3	3.4	0.0	0.0	6.9	100.0 (29)
	II	14.3	42.9	32.1	0.0	0.0	0.0	10.7	100.0 (28)
Class of	III	4.2	37.5	37.5	4.2	0.0	4.2	12.5	100.0 (24)
chief	IV	9.1	25.5	30.9	9.1	3.6	1.8	20.0	100.0 (55)
childhood	V	0.0	27.5	42.5	6.3	1.3	6.3	16.3	100.0 (80)
supporter	VI	3.6	15.3	44.1	2.7	5.4	8.1	20.7	100.0 (111)
	VII	2.0	8.2	30.6	8.2	6.1	5.1	39.8	100.0 (98)

(n = 425)

Table 4.9 *Market and work situations of women and men in Goldthorpe social classes*

A – All employees

			Wage (£ mean)	Career (% affirmative)	Autonomy (mean score)	Decision-making (mean score)	Supervision (mean score)
	I	M	14,130	80	5.1	3.6	4.6
		F	9,357	77	4.6	2.1	3.0
	II	M	10,956	75	4.4	2.5	3.1
		F	6,259	66	3.8	1.5	2.3
	III	M	7,238	60	3.4	0.7	0.3
Social		F	4,135	35	2.6	0.3	0.3
class	V	M	8,469	72	3.0	1.6	3.2
		F	3,314	47	3.0	1.0	2.7
	VI	M	7,022	36	1.8	0.4	0.1
		F	4,132	35	1.5	0.3	0.1
	VII	M	6,485	25	1.8	0.2	0.2
		F	3,081	8	1.7	0.1	0.0

B – Full-time employees (30 or more hours per week) only

			Wage (£ mean)	Career (% affirmative)	Autonomy (mean score)	Decision-making (mean score)	Supervision (mean score)
	I	M	14,130	80	5.1	3.7	4.5
		F	9,357	77	4.7	2.2	3.0
	II	M	11,017	75	4.4	2.4	3.1
		F	7,011	72	3.8	1.5	2.5
	III	M	7,238	60	3.5	0.7	0.4
Social		F	4,859	43	2.7	0.4	0.4
class	V	M	8,567	72	3.0	1.6	3.3
		F	3,611	56	3.5	1.3	2.8
	VI	M	7,024	36	1.9	0.4	0.2
		F	4,395	35	1.7	0.3	0.1
	VII	M	6,604	26	1.9	0.2	0.2
		F	4,558	11	1.4	0.0	0.0

Note: i Autonomy, decision-making, and supervision means are calculated from each of six items. See interview schedule, Qs. 55(a), 56(a,b,c,e,g,); 62(a), 63(a), 64(a), 65(a), 66(a), 67(a); 58(a,b,c,d,), 59(a), 60(a). Low = 0, High = 6.
ii Class IV (the self-employed) are excluded because they were not asked the relevant questions, it being assumed that their employment was not part of an established career ladder, and that as own account workers their autonomy, decision-making, and (if helpers were employed) supervisory responsibilities could plausibly be taken to be high. In fact this assumption may be questionable in some instances, since those defined as 'self-employed' in official statistics include homeworkers, outworkers, and freelances who may be working in a variety of employment situations. On this point see Dale (1986).

work. Men score higher than women on almost all items within every social class location. At each occupational level men receive higher incomes; have greater (perceived) chances of economic advancement; and tend to exercise more autonomy, authority, and control in performing their work-tasks and roles.

Some of the individual figures are as significant as the uniformity of the overall pattern. Most importantly, perhaps, they show that, among employees in routine nonmanual occupations, 60 per cent of men are in a recognized career or promotion ladder as compared with 35 per cent of all women. Class III males also enjoy salaries that are not far short of twice those of comparable females. Since these employees are crucially located on the interface between the (conventionally defined) working and middle classes, the different market situations (and to a lesser extent work situations) of men and women in this class suggest that debates about class boundaries must perforce consider sex differentiation seriously, notably, for example, where the issues of proletarianization are concerned. As one would expect, the differences between the sexes are diminished somewhat when part-time workers are excluded, since proportionately more of these are female. Nevertheless these differences do persist even among exclusively full-time employees.

This variation in mobility, work situations, and market situations according to sex is not difficult to explain. It is the effect of differential social constraints imposed on men's and women's participation in the labour market. Table 4.10 shows that, in every class location, household and family responsibilities affect women more forcefully than men. Domestic obligations more often require wives to change jobs or cease paid employment, and more frequently prevent them from looking for paid labour, from changing jobs, and from accepting either a full-time job or promotion. Again some of the individual scores in the table are particularly striking. To take but one that seems especially relevant to the present context, no more than 1 per cent of the men in any class category had ever been required to leave paid employment because of domestic responsibilities, whereas 36 per cent of service-class, 41 per cent of intermediate-class, and 47 per cent of working-class women had experienced at least one such interruption to their work careers. Whether this

Table 4.10 *Constraints imposed by domestic responsibilities on men and women in Goldthorpe classes*

Household and family responsibilities		I	II	III	IV	V	VI	VII	Total
					Social Class				
Prevented looking for	M	10 (10)	8 (10)	4 (2)	3 (3)	3 (3)	5 (6)	5 (9)	6 (43)
a job	F	41 (9)	36 (37)	37 (77)	7 (2)	42 (8)	39 (12)	51 (67)	39 (212)
Prevented accepting	M	6 (6)	6 (8)	2 (1)	1 (1)	6 (5)	4 (5)	5 (9)	5 (35)
full-time job	F	36 (8)	39 (40)	40 (83)	19 (5)	53 (10)	39 (12)	46 (61)	40 (219)
Prevented accepting	M	9 (9)	9 (12)	4 (2)	3 (3)	9 (8)	2 (3)	3 (6)	6 (43)
promotion	F	9 (2)	15 (15)	19 (39)	4 (1)	16 (3)	7 (2)	20 (26)	16 (88)
Prevented change of	M	13 (13)	12 (16)	7 (3)	1 (1)	13 (11)	6 (8)	4 (7)	8 (59)
job	F	14 (3)	14 (14)	14 (30)	11 (3)	21 (4)	3 (1)	24 (31)	16 (86)
Required change of	M	9 (9)	9 (12)	9 (4)	16 (14)	15 (13)	14 (18)	14 (25)	12 (95)
job	F	32 (7)	17 (17)	14 (30)	15 (4)	16 (3)	7 (2)	14 (18)	15 (81)
Required leaving	M	1 (1)	1 (1)	0 (0)	0 (0)	0 (0)	1 (1)	1 (1)	1 (4)
paid employment	F	36 (8)	36 (37)	41 (87)	26 (7)	53 (10)	32 (10)	51 (66)	42 (225)

Note: Percentages in this table are the percentages of those in each class (controlling for sex) stating that household responsibilities had either prevented or required them to take the actions listed. Figures in brackets give the count of respondents in each category.

is evidence of women's lesser commitment to paid labour or of male dominance within nuclear families is actually beside the point. Either way the fact remains that men's labour market participation, hence patterns of class formation and the distribution of male life-chances, are forcefully conditioned by the impact of sex differentiation throughout the class structure as a whole.

But to what extent is sexual differentiation the result of direct sex discrimination rather than merely an outcome of social conventions about the division of domestic and family responsibilities? Of course, feminists might want to argue that these conventions themselves discriminate against women, but that is not the point at issue. The issue is, rather, one of determining the extent to which occupational outcomes reflect meritocratic rather than discriminatory criteria. One way of approaching this is to inspect the relationship between educational attainment and occupational achievement. We have already observed (Table 4.5) that men's and women's class destinations are more powerfully conditioned by their own credentials than by the occupational experience of their conjugal partners. However, comparing model 4 in the top half of this table with the same model in the bottom half, we see that the association between qualifications and class is much stronger for husbands than it is for wives. (The own class/own qualification parameter yields a Y^2/df ratio of 19.6 for women as compared to 46.7 for men.) Table 4.11 reports some of the data that generate this finding. Two conclusions stand out from this table. From the column percentages it will be seen that men receive greater returns on their credentials, in terms of life-chances, than do women. For example, of males with low formal qualifications, 12 per cent are in service-class (I and II) locations. Twenty-five per cent of males with medium educational attainment are also in this class, as are 91 per cent of those possessing high credentials. Among females, by comparison, the equivalent proportions are 6 per cent, 21 per cent, and 62 per cent. No less than 32 per cent of highly qualified women, and 54 per cent of those with medium level credentials, are likely to be found in class III (routine nonmanual) occupations. Only 2 per cent and 8 per cent respectively of comparably qualified men are so situated. In other words, more men than women will get into service-class positions at every level of educational attainment, while many well-qualified women find themselves trapped in routine nonmanual employment.

The row percentages of this table tell a similar story and show that women are more likely than men to require credentials if they aspire to relatively privileged social class positions. Among class I men, for example, 13 per cent have low educational qualifications, 29 per cent are of medium educational attainment, while 47 per cent possess high credentials. The comparable proportions among class I women are 5, 27, and 68 per cent respectively. Thirty-two per cent of class III women are highly qualified as compared with 2 per cent of class III men. The higher the social class the more likely it is that proportionately more women than men will be better qualified.

Table 4.11 *Goldthorpe social classes by educational qualifications and sex*

		Males				Females			
Count Row % Column % Total		Qualifications*				Qualifications*			
		Low	Medium	High	Row total	Low	Medium	High	Row total
	I	13	29	59	101	1	6	15	22
		12.9	28.7	58.4		4.5	27.3	68.2	
		4.0	9.0	47.2		0.4	2.9	13.6	
		1.7	3.8	7.7	13.1	0.2	1.1	2.8	4.0
	II	25	52	55	132	12	38	53	103
		18.9	39.4	41.7		11.7	36.9	51.5	
		7.7	16.1	44.0		5.3	18.4	48.2	
		3.2	6.7	7.1	17.1	2.2	7.0	9.7	18.9
	III	18	25	3	46	64	111	35	210
		39.1	54.3	6.5		30.5	52.9	16.7	
		5.6	7.8	2.4		28.1	53.9	31.8	
		2.3	3.2	0.4	6.0	11.8	20.4	6.4	38.6
Social class	IV	38	47	3	88	12	11	4	27
		43.2	53.4	3.4		44.4	40.7	14.8	
		11.7	14.6	2.4		5.3	5.3	3.6	
		4.9	6.1	0.4	11.4	2.2	2.0	0.7	5.0
	V	38	50	0	88	15	4	0	19
		43.2	56.8	0.0		78.9	21.1	0.0	
		11.7	15.5	0.0		6.6	1.9	0.0	
		4.9	6.5	0.0	11.4	2.8	0.7	0.0	3.5
	VI	60	71	3	134	24	7	0	31
		44.8	53.0	2.2		77.4	22.6	0.0	
		18.5	22.0	2.4		10.5	3.4	0.0	
		7.8	9.2	0.4	17.4	4.4	1.3	0.0	5.7
	VII	132	48	2	182	100	29	3	132
		72.5	26.4	1.1		75.8	22.0	2.3	
		40.7	14.9	1.6		43.9	14.1	2.7	
		17.1	6.2	0.3	23.6	18.4	5.3	0.6	24.3
	Total	324	322	125	771	228	206	110	544
		42.0	41.8	16.2	100.0	41.9	37.9	20.2	100.0

*For details on the composition of qualification categories see Table 4.5.

III

What, then, are the implications of these findings for the debate between John Goldthorpe and his critics and, more generally, for arguments about the significance of sex differences for class analysis? It seems clear to us that Goldthorpe has been subjected to much unwarranted criticism – probably as a result of his claim to champion the 'conventional' view. This is in fact a misnomer since, as he makes clear from the outset, the orthodoxy maintains, not only that it is the family rather than the individual which forms the basic unit of social stratification, but also that particular families are allocated a class standing by reference to the occupational grade of the *male* head of household. This position, adhered to by mainstream American theorists, finds its rationale in functionalist arguments about the necessary separation of roles within the family, where social system imperatives invest instrumental leadership in the husband/father, and expressive leadership in the wife/mother. Goldthorpe supports the convention whereby the position of the family as a whole within the class system derives from the 'family head', that is the member who has the greatest commitment to, and continuity in, labour market participation, but willingly concedes that this person may or may not be a male. Of course he also claims that, empirically, it is predominantly husbands who are in such positions, arguing here from a premiss and evidence that are widely accepted by, among others (one assumes), most feminists; namely, that women are oppressed by the structure of nuclear families, and so placed in subordinate and disadvantaged positions relative to men. Goldthorpe's (qualified) support for Robert Erikson's related strategy of assigning a class position to family units on the basis of 'dominance' and 'worktime' criteria (that is, according to the occupational category that will have greatest impact on the life-chances, ideology, and behaviour of family members, with full-time employment ranking higher than part-time), confirms that his is a position rooted firmly in theoretical reasoning and empirical observation rather than, as some critics would have it, the mere conventions of intellectual sexism.

Nevertheless Goldthorpe's 'revised conventional' approach to class analysis is not without its difficulties. These can be traced to his concept of class formation. In fact he uses this term to describe two quite distinct processes: demographic class formation and socio-political class formation. The former charts the association of individuals with particular sets of structural positions over time; that is, the degree to which classes are self-recruiting, such that 'members possess a relatively high degree of homogeneity in their social backgrounds and patterns of life experience'. The latter, by contrast, refers to class 'pushfulness' – pursuit by class members of their 'industrial and political interests by means of their own organizations'.[10] Class analysts are quite properly concerned with both processes (however they are labelled). The former bears directly on questions of inequality and opportunity. The latter is central to the explanation of social schism. Of course Goldthorpe argues that demographic maturity enhances socio-political maturity (and, as we shall see in Chapter 9 below, there is some evidence to support his view). However his interest in demographic class formation is of a particularly limited kind and restricts the scope of his enterprise unduly. It is this issue that lies at the centre of the controversy between Goldthorpe and his critics.

The problem here is that Goldthorpe's arguments take the occupational division of labour as given for the purposes of class analysis. This, indeed, is the gist of Stanworth's otherwise obscure objections to his defence of the conventional view. In short both she and we disagree with Goldthorpe about the scope of class analysis itself. This is not merely semantic quibbling. It affects the questions which class analysis addresses and therefore, in some form, the findings which it derives. Of course there is much in Goldthorpe's approach with which we would agree, in particular his insistence that 'structure' does not consist of a static categorization of positions, but the formation of career-like trajectories through the set of positions. In this sense we accept that social mobility is central to class analysis by virtue of the role it plays in demographic class formation.[11] Moreover, as our data have shown, the distribution of people to places across time is forcefully conditioned by gender, so that the career trajectories (and thereby life-chances) of men are inexplicable without reference to the highly particularistic ways in which, and conditions under which, women also participate in paid employment. Quite simply, and for familiar reasons that are documented both here and elsewhere, a man's absolute mobility chances are greater than those of a comparable woman; he will benefit from better returns on his formal qualifications; and within every class location will find his market and work situations superior to those of occupationally similar females. Goldthorpe himself would not wish to deny this. Indeed he argues explicitly that

the long-term change in the occupational distribution of males, and especially the growing proportion found in professional, administrative, and managerial positions, which emerges as the key dynamic element in mobility over the period we have studied, cannot be understood other than in relation to the trend and character of female employment.[12]

The structure of occupational opportunities into which it is possible for women to be mobile is different from that available to men. In other words the sexually segregated social division of labour systematically disadvantages women in mobility terms.

Goldthorpe would seem, however, to wish to regard such sexual segregation (among the many other factors which influence the structure of class positions) as beyond the legitimate concerns of class analysis. We find this unwarrantably conservative. He and we obviously agree that class analysts should inquire whether classes have formed as relatively stable collectivities (demographic class formation). Additionally, we would both examine the degree to which these collectivities are differentiated to form a basis for social solidarity and conflict, and to form collective identities, behaviour, and beliefs in general (socio-political class formation). But Goldthorpe's concern for demographic class formation is exhausted by its relationship to socio-political issues. He is interested in the former because, and only in so far as, it affects the latter. Presumably, however, an interest in demographic class formation embraces the study of the various mechanisms that generate and stabilize the demographic collectivities themselves. Not to ask how it is that places become available in the structure across time is to assume (wrongly) that class processes are wholly independent of the social division of labour – which can therefore be ignored in analyses of class formation. In other words, if one accepts Goldthorpe's dynamic conception of structure, and in consequence the premiss that demographic class formation is integral to descriptions of structure itself, then the manner in which the class structure is (at least in part) constituted through relations between the sexes is also, in our view, intrinsic to class analysis. Class structures, and the market processes behind them, are (to use the current terminology) 'gendered'.[13] It is not 'social actors' that are distributed via the market through the places of the structure: it is men and women. Their differing experiences are interdependent, so that the distribution and situations of men are powerfully influenced by those of women, as well as vice versa. The fact that women are routinely constrained in this way serves only to highlight the obverse side of the structure; namely, that the collective effect of women's employment on the occupational system would seem to be one of privileging men.

Of course Goldthorpe can rightly point to the extent to which a woman's broad social consciousness is typically conditioned – perhaps strongly so – by the class position of her husband. Goldthorpe's data suggest this; our own, admittedly limited evidence tends to confirm it, at least in respect of voting intentions; and, as Goldthorpe points out in reply to his critics, a great deal of feminist research into power and subordination within nuclear families is entirely supportive of such a conclusion. Furthermore, when viewed from Goldthorpe's perspective, the claim by Heath and Britten that 'women make a difference' since the explained variance in particular aspects of social behaviour is increased by the inclusion of women's occupations into regression analyses is in fact uncontroversial, and leaves the conventional approach wholly unscathed. Class analysts do not claim that social class accounts for all socio-cultural patterning – only that, in empirical investigations, its explanatory power is considerable. The addition of variables that are independent of class position (such as race or region) will almost certainly explain variance over and above that attributable to class as such. However, women also make a difference to precisely those aspects of social structure that John Goldthorpe considers to be the first concern of class analysis, namely those pertaining to questions of demographic class formation. People are distributed to places through time according to processes that are powerfully shaped by gender. The structuring of opportunities itself is therefore a legitimate part of the subject matter for a class analysis concerned with demographic as well as socio-political class formation.

There is, then, no reason why class analysis should not begin, as Goldthorpe proposes, 'with a structure of positions, associated with a specific historical form of the division of labour'. However, the further stipulation that 'it is . . . in no way the aim of class analysis to account . . . for a structure of class positions',[14] rules out an interest both in the determinants of demographic class formation and in its subsequent impact on the structuring of positions. Since the findings of class analysis in general, and of students of social mobility in particular, can shed light on both processes (while not claiming to explain either in its entirety) it seems reasonable to conclude that class analysis should embrace not only the issues addressed by Goldthorpe, but also those raised by his critics.

IV

So, to return to the *raison d'être* of the controversy, what is the proper unit for class analysis? We have argued that, in large part, this depends on how one defines the objectives and parameters of the enterprise itself. Goldthorpe's emphasis on the family as the unit of investigation is consistent with his conception of class analysis. We feel, however, that this is unduly narrow in scope and that, whatever the problems of complexity and tractability, class analysis must integrate the study of the distribution of people into positions with the study of the determinants of these positions themselves. We recognize the significance of Stanworth's observation that individuals enter the market as individuals. In so doing women are constrained by the sexual division of labour: into part-time employment, less skilled jobs, and so forth. But they continue (for the most part) to live in families, and this too has consequences for their life-chances and social actions (including, as we have seen, their voting behaviour). In challenging Goldthorpe on this point his critics are caught in the dilemma of seeming to argue that the family is oppressive yet that its oppression is insufficiently substantial to support the logic of conventional class analysis. Social classes comprise neither families nor individuals but individuals in families. It is for this reason, therefore, that the study of class is properly conducted at different levels of analysis. In this way the collective effects of women's limited access to economic and political power on the reproduction of positions within the structure can be explained, as well as the complex determination of life-chances accruing to individuals in conjugal units.[15] That there is no all embracing schema which captures the complexity of both processes perhaps need not worry us unduly. This is, after all, simply one more instance of sociological theory lagging some way behind the reality it addresses.

Meanwhile our analysis of the Essex data has necessarily been shaped (if only in part) by the assumptions about the unit and scope of class analysis that are built into Goldthorpe's class algorithm. Only those among our sample who are in employment, or have recently been so, appear in Goldthorpe class locations. Men and women not in paid employment (including those who are married to employed spouses) are omitted throughout. This is not to argue that unemployed men and women are somehow outside the class structure. Goldthorpe himself views structure as a series of trajectories and almost all our respondents have a work-history or, if they have never been formally occupied, a class background. However, we have not reallocated the 'long-term unemployed' (both men and women) to Goldthorpe classes on this basis since his class analysis rests on a work-centred theory of stratification describing market and work situations, and it seems incongruous to investigate the current socio-political proclivities of respondents exclusively by reference to (perhaps) long-since changed work circumstances. Were we to do so, critics of class analysis might reasonably criticize us for stacking the evidence in Goldthorpe's favour, though Goldthorpe himself would disagree on the (remarkably unconventional) grounds that those outside formal employment are not unaffected by class processes.[16] However the obverse is also true. If the analyses in subsequent chapters determine that there exist strong Goldthorpe class effects in the structuring of identities, beliefs, and voting intentions, then our conclusions may safely be claimed to underrepresent rather than exaggerate these, since they will have been identified via classes comprising individuals presently in employment – according to a class framework designed to allocate men only to demographic classes on the basis of previous as well as present occupations.

The last-mentioned claim points to the one significant difference between 'Essex' Goldthorpe classes and their 'Oxford' counterparts. Our strategy throughout has been to place respondents into Goldthorpe classes on the basis of their own occupations. We have not followed John Goldthorpe's practice of allocating families to classes according to the occupation of the (usually male) 'head of household' since, in our view, this practice gives a misleading picture of the class structure. This can be demonstrated by comparing three sets of figures for Goldthorpe classes; those for our sample as a whole; for males only within the sample; and the percentages obtained if all female respondents in our study are 'reclassified' and given the class position of their male cohabitees (Table 4.12). The effect of the last mentioned strategy is to convert the social class position of most of the females in the sample into that of their husbands – or, in other words, to sample only males. This 'male only' strategy corresponds to that pursued by Goldthorpe and his colleagues in their study of social mobility in England and Wales. (The figures for the Oxford study have been included in the table to facilitate comparison.) It can be seen from the comparative statistics that the manufactured 'male only' figures are very similar to those for the actual males

Table 4.12 *Relative sizes of Goldthorpe classes for men and women (%)*

| | | | Sex | | |
| | | | Essex data | | Oxford data |
		men and women	men	'male only'	male only
	I	9.4	13.1	13.8	13.6
	II	17.9	17.1	16.6	11.5
Social	III	19.5	6.0	5.7	9.2
class	IV	8.7	11.4	12.0	9.4
	V	8.1	11.4	12.1	11.6
	VI	12.5	17.4	17.5	21.2
	VII	23.9	23.6	22.4	21.8
	Total	100.0	100.0	100.0	100.0

within our own sample. However, both are quite dissimilar from the Essex totals for men and women together, since a concentration on males only tends to inflate the proportions within classes I, IV, V, and VI, while decreasing (rather spectacularly) the relative importance of class III. These differences are entirely what one would expect given the sexual segregation of occupations and observed variation in absolute mobility rates. They suggest that our 'individualistic' strategy for the allocation of employed persons to Goldthorpe classes yields a more accurate class map of modern Britain than can be produced by sampling 'heads of households'. John Goldthorpe would doubtless disagree with this particular usage of his class categories, but it is one we are prepared to defend on grounds that he himself occupies in respect of the jobless; namely, that employed women are not outside the class structure – even if they are typically found in class locations that are relatively disprivileged when compared to those of their husbands. Whether or not cross-class families differ significantly in terms of life-style and social consciousness from class homogeneous families, as Heath and Britten claim, is of course an empirical issue. This is also true of their thesis about men's and women's allegedly different career paths. Both will be investigated further in the following chapter.

V

Finally, however, we should turn to consider the manner in which alternative class frameworks approach the issues raised by the gender and class debate. How do Erik Wright and the Registrar-General view housewives and the unemployed? Fortunately our observations can be brief since all of the class schemata in which we are interested are here indistinguishable for practical purposes of analysis. The Registrar-General's classes are identified in occupational and employment status terms so are constructed by a procedure wholly analogous to that practised by Goldthorpe. They will thus come to comprise individuals presently (or recently) in employment and so exclude housewives and the long-term unemployed. Interestingly enough, Erik Wright arrives at precisely the same operational strategy for a Marxist class analysis, despite the fact that he starts from quite different theoretical premises. Clearly, unemployment and domestic labour are not embraced by the structural criteria for class that were outlined in Chapters 2 or 3, since these positions are not directly defined by the social relations of production. Yet Wright also insists that those outside formal employment are nevertheless affected by class processes. In an attempt to resolve this dilemma he introduces the distinction between 'fundamental' and 'immediate' class interests.

Immediate class interests are those constituted within a given structure of social relations whereas fundamental interests call into question the structure of social relations itself.

Struggles for wages, better living conditions, better education opportunities and so forth all constitute struggles for objectives defined within the basic structure of capitalism. Struggles for socialism, on the other hand, challenge the premises of capitalist relations and reflect the fundamental interests of the working class.[17]

Demands for higher wages are evidence of a correct but incomplete understanding of capitalist society on the part of the workers since these 'fail to grasp the possibility of transcending the entire system of capitalist exploitation through socialism'. Wishful thinking leads Wright to conclude that the pursuit of fundamental interests will displace more immediate concerns in a revolutionary situation. (This could hardly be otherwise, since the fundamental interest of the proletariat in socialism is taken by Wright to be a distinguishing characteristic of the revolution itself, so that in its absence, by definition, there cannot be a revolutionary situation.)

However, the putative political significance of this distinction aside, it also serves to resolve for Wright the issues arising out of domestic labour and unemployment since the class location of people in such circumstances 'is determined by their relations to the fundamental interests of classes defined within the social relations of production'. Housewives, in other words, share the same class interests as their husbands. Of course they may have different interests as women but this does not affect their class proclivities. Wright concludes, in a paragraph that might equally have been penned by John Goldthorpe, that

This treatment of the class location of housewives is sometimes viewed as sexist, since it assigns the class position of the housewife on the basis of the class location of the husband. If we treat the family as the essential unit of analysis, and ask: how is the family articulated with production relations, then it is clear that the class location of the housewife is not defined via her husband but via the family unit of which they both are a part. It is, indeed, a reflection of the sexism of capitalist society that the division of labour within such a family unit often sends the man out to work and leaves the woman in the home. But it is not sexist to identify the class location of the woman in terms of the way in which the family is inserted into capitalist relations of production. The only way of identifying how the family is so inserted is then to examine the class location of the husband.[18]

In principle, therefore, Wright treats the nuclear family as the unit of his class analysis. In practice, however, he samples individuals and allocates both male and female respondents to class categories in accordance with their own social relations of production. The few housewives in his American survey (those in households where no employed person was available for interview instead) are omitted from the subsequent analysis.[19]

Similarly, Wright (like Goldthorpe) sees the unemployed as 'tied to trajectories of class positions', acknowledging here and elsewhere the general importance of mobility processes to the study of class formation.[20] However, it is unlikely that respondents will be able reliably to recall precise details about the extent of autonomy, supervisory responsibilities, and decision-making that were associated with all previously experienced work situations. Moreover, it makes little theoretical sense to relate an individual's present socio-political inclinations to his or her earlier (perhaps much earlier) circumstances, given the resolutely structural nature of Wright's theory. Realizing this himself perhaps, Wright utilized in his national survey of the class structure of the United States, a sampling procedure which systematically selected employed respondents before those unemployed in any household. The few unemployed respondents who were contacted and answered questions other than those pertaining to present employment have been ignored in Wright's analyses to date.[21]

In any case, even if it could be agreed that domestic labourers and the unemployed of both sexes were not problematic to Wright's account of class structure – that is, they could simply be excluded from the analysis, for what were commonly taken to be sound theoretical reasons – nevertheless, those women actually appearing in social classes by virtue of their own employment would raise another more serious problem for his models. That problem is precisely one of social mobility and is all too evident in the figures given in Table 4.13. These show, in the case of the original Wright classes, that the majority of employers, managers, supervisors, and workers are men, while women are predominant only among semi-autonomous employees. Reading the data the other way round, in terms of the class distribution within sexes, almost 60 per cent of all employed females are in the worker category. About 60 per cent of men, on the other hand, are to be found in the more privileged bourgeois, managerial, and semi-autonomous locations. Or, looking at the revised class categories, 47 per cent of men are in the capitalist and managerial classes (another 3 per cent are expert non-managers), while almost 60 per cent of women are proletarians. Of course, it is difficult to draw a direct comparison between these findings and those reported in Table 4.6, given the incommensurability of the Goldthorpe and Wright categories. One aspect of the figures that surely does merit comment, however, is that they imply a degree of openness in the class structure that is entirely implausible given what is generally known about patterns of social mobility among males in Britain. (Compare, for example, the outflow percentages reported in Table 4.8.) It is indeed ironic that an analysis conducted according to explicitly Marxist principles should suggest that class processes in this particular capitalist society are so obviously tenuous.

It is not difficult to ascertain how so much apparent upward mobility among men is built into Wright's map of the present class structure. It is an artefactual consequence of his operational procedures for distributing respondents to class locations. This becomes apparent from an investigation of the 'supervisors' and 'managers' who appear as anomalies in the cross-tabulation of Wright against Goldthorpe class categories (see Table 3.5 in the previous chapter). For example, those in the expert managerial class could plausibly be in Goldthorpe's service class (I and II) or supervisory class V, but should not appear in his routine clerical, sales, or personal service class III. From the table it will be seen that seven employees have been so classified. There is a clear disagreement between the two schemes here. Which offers the more plausible picture with respect to these cases? In fact it transpires that all seven respondents are nurses. Following Erik Wright's class algorithms, they emerge as 'experts' on account of their occupational coding, since 'medical and paramedical staff other than physicians and dentists' are coded as professionals (and therefore experts in terms of their skill assets). Wright is quite unambiguous about this. Registered nurses, so categorized according to

Table 4.13 *Distribution of respondents by Wright social class and sex*

A – Wright I (original) classes

Count Row % Column % Total		Sex		
		Male	*Female*	*Total*
	Bourgeoisie	23 88.5 3.0 1.7	3 11.5 0.6 0.2	26 2.0
	Small employers	50 84.7 6.5 3.8	9 15.3 1.7 0.7	59 4.5
	Petit bourgeoisie	54 68.4 7.0 4.1	25 31.6 4.6 1.9	79 6.0
Social class	Managers	117 71.8 15.2 8.9	46 28.2 8.5 3.5	163 12.4
	Advisory managers	44 74.6 5.7 3.3	15 25.4 2.8 1.1	59 4.5
	Supervisors	78 62.9 10.1 5.9	46 37.1 8.5 3.5	124 9.4
	Semi-autonomous employees	70 45.8 9.1 5.3	83 54.2 15.3 6.3	153 11.6
	Workers	335 51.4 43.5 25.5	317 48.6 58.3 24.1	652 49.6
	Total	771 58.6	544 41.4	1315 100.0

B – Wright II (revised) classes

Count Row % Column % Total		Sex		
		Male	*Female*	*Total*
	Bourgeoisie	23 88.5 3.0 1.7	3 11.5 0.6 0.2	26 2.0
	Small employers	50 84.7 6.5 3.8	9 15.3 1.7 0.7	59 4.5
	Petit bourgeoisie	54 68.4 7.0 4.1	25 31.6 4.6 1.9	79 6.0
	Expert managers	53 71.6 6.9 4.0	21 28.4 3.9 1.6	74 5.6
Social class	Expert supervisors	15 51.7 1.9 1.1	14 48.3 2.6 1.1	29 2.2
	Expert non-managers	20 37.0 2.6 1.5	34 63.0 6.3 2.6	54 4.1
	Semi-credentialled managers	89 85.6 11.5 6.8	15 14.4 2.8 1.1	104 7.9
	Semi-credentialled supervisors	39 78.0 5.1 3.0	11 22.0 2.0 0.8	50 3.8
	Semi-credentialled workers	139 73.5 18.0 10.6	50 26.5 9.2 3.8	189 14.4
	Uncredentialled managers	18 42.9 2.3 1.4	24 57.1 4.4 1.8	42 3.2
	Uncredentialled supervisors	24 53.3 3.1 1.8	21 46.7 3.9 1.6	45 3.4

91

Table 4.13 (*cont.*)

B – Wright II (revised) classes

Count Row % Column % Total	Sex		
	Male	*Female*	*Total*
Proletarians	247	317	564
	43.8	56.2	
	32.0	58.3	
	18.8	24.1	42.9
Total	771	544	1315
	58.6	41.4	100.0

the 1970 Census codes for classifying American occupations, become experts on this basis alone.[22] This group of (expert) state registered nurses are also 'managers', because they participate directly in any one of the decision-making items about which they were asked, and claim authority over subordinates.[23] In this way seven of Goldthorpe's 'rank-and-file personal service employees' become 'expert managers' in Wright's class map. But there is one further complication. From Table 3.5 it will be seen that there are also six anomalous cases of Goldthorpe routine nonmanual class III employees who appear in Wright's 'expert supervisor' category. On inspection it transpires that these individuals too are all nurses. As before, they are experts by occupational title, though in this case they are supervisors rather than managers because they claim only involvement in the supervision of subordinates and not responsibilities for decision-making.

It is difficult to follow exactly the lengthy sequence of taxonomic steps being traced here without consulting the interview schedule, extensive codebook, and published work from Wright's international project. The coding procedures are indeed complex. However, the two principal points at issue are not at all obscure, and the example provided by the nurses offers forceful and concise illustration of these. First, nurses are given 'expert' standing in the skill assets dimension of Wright's classification simply on the basis of their *occupational* title alone, so demonstrating the significance of our earlier observation that occupational coding is not sociologically neutral in the way that Wright effectively assumes. The fact that he accords registered nurses the status of experts (alongside, in the same occupational category, chiropractors, optometrists, pharmacists, podiatrists, veterinarians, dieticians, and therapists), may be testimony to a substantial difference in the social standing of nurses in the United States as compared to the United Kingdom, to the difficulties of doing serious comparative work using occupational classifications, or simply to Wright's personal ethnocentrism. Goldthorpe could properly claim that, in Britain at least, the market and work situations of veterinarians and nurses are radically different. Nor are they the same for nurses and lawyers, or accountants, or doctors, or university lecturers – yet, according to Wright, all of these are professional occupations and therefore possessed of high (expert) skill assets.

Second, nurses emerge as 'managers' or 'supervisors' because of their reported supervisory and decision-making responsibilities, as indicated at questions 57 to 68 of the British interview schedule. Wright's intention here is laudable. He has attempted to derive a measure of actual social relationships at the point of production by questioning people directly about their decision-making and supervisory activities. His is a more obviously sociological approach than that pursued by John Goldthorpe, since the putative 'work situation' of respondents in the latter's class schema is determined by the official coding of employment status, and Goldthorpe's own perception of the authority and autonomy involved in these statuses. Yet the manner in which interviewees have answered Wright's questions has created the anomaly of (at least some) Goldthorpe employees appearing among Wright's managers and supervisors. The problem here would seem to be that Wright's class algorithm in practice contains a very weak criterion for distinguishing managers and supervisors from other employees; namely, that one needs only to be involved directly in making any *one* of the decisions mentioned in the interview, to be considered some kind of manager, or be involved in the limited supervision of a single subordinate, in order to emerge as a supervisor. In fact respondents need only offer advice to others who then make decisions, rather than participate directly in the decision-making process itself, to be considered managers according to Wright's criteria.[24] Since the range of possible involvement includes participation in fairly low level decisions concerning changes in 'the service delivered by the organization', in the routine 'pace or amount of work performed', and in 'methods or procedures', it is not difficult to see how some nurses can claim to be 'managers'. Similarly, fairly routine supervision of the specific tasks, tools, and pace of work pursued by very few subordinates qualifies one as a 'supervisor'. Of course, it could reasonably be claimed that these criteria were in fact robust if they separated out senior nursing officers and ward sisters, from staff nurses on the one hand, and ordinary nurses on the other. However our data show that this is not what happens. The anomalous expert managers and expert supervisors we have been discussing are all unelevated state registered nurses. Even so, they do sometimes offer advice about changes in procedures to their superiors, and are often involved in the routine supervision of nursing auxiliaries and other ward orderlies. As a result they appear, alongside senior nursing staff, as possessed of considerable organizational assets; that is, of effective control over the co-ordination and integration of the division of labour.

As it happens all of these nurses are women. However, the other obvious discrepancies between the managerial and supervisory categories of the Wright and Goldthorpe schema involve mostly men, and they arise for similar reasons. For example, there are three Goldthorpe class VI skilled manual workers who are each classified as 'semi-credentialled managers' in the Wright scheme – two fitters working underground for British Coal, and a manufacturing jeweller. They are 'semi-credentialled' because they are 'craftworkers'. However, since each has at least one assistant over whom supervision on at least one item is claimed, and since each also claims to be a decision-maker or adviser, they also attain managerial status. Ultimately, for this group, it is their claim to decision-making, combined with their status as craftworkers, which accounts for their allocation to the semi-credentialled manager category. Elsewhere, however, there are people who have been allocated to one of Wright's supervisory classes solely on the basis of having a 'mate' whom they 'supervise'. These include nearly all of the Goldthorpe class VII unskilled workers who appear in Wright's scheme as 'uncredentialled supervisors'. The classic example here is that of the heavy goods vehicle driver who 'supervises his mate'. Goldthorpe routine white-collar workers whom Wright regards as uncredentialled supervisors emerge via the same logic: the 'senior sales assistant' who 'keeps an eye' on her colleagues on the shop-floor (for example by directing them to customers) becomes a 'supervisor' for this reason alone.

It would be tedious to multiply examples of the way in which Wright's framework creates artificially high numbers of managers and supervisors and so gives the appearance of large-scale social mobility among males in modern Britain. A complete listing of discrepant cases between the Goldthorpe and Wright schemes confirms that many of the latter's managerial and supervisory respondents are, in fact, routine manual and nonmanual employees who offer occasional advice to their superiors or perform nominal supervisory tasks in respect of very limited numbers of subordinates. They include school caretakers who 'supervise' assistant caretakers; experienced secretaries who 'supervise' the activities of a couple of junior or temporary typists; and chefs in small restaurants who 'make decisions' about 'services and products' (menus) and supervise someone to prepare raw materials for them. An agricultural contract worker who operates a mechanical digger to erect fences and lay drains, and has a labouring assistant whose tasks he 'supervises', may strictly speaking be involved in the 'task supervision of subordinates' but surely has not experienced upward social mobility in any meaningful sociological sense. It is more plausible to classify him as a semi-skilled or unskilled manual employee (Goldthorpe class VII), alongside his mate, than as an uncredentialled supervisor – his designated Wright class location.

There is more than one irony in all of this. So often, in the classification of skill assets, it is Wright rather than Goldthorpe who is a prisoner of occupational coding. Nurses are 'experts' yet schoolteachers are automatically given 'marginal' skill assets. Moreover, Wright – a Marxist – employs measures of organizational control that take no account of the context of that control, and so creates implausibly high numbers of managers and supervisors. The irony here is compounded by the fact that this seemingly frequent upward mobility among men has been generated by a class framework that emerged in the context of arguments about proletarianization (rather than embourgeoisement) in the class structure. Wright himself has argued that there is 'a strong and consistent proletarianization process' in contemporary capitalism.[25] On the face of it his own class schema would seem to suggest otherwise – that is, unless it is overwhelmingly females who are subject to this effect, since (as we have seen), almost 60 per cent of women are in this class and they make up 56 per cent of its complement. Given the rather radical disjuncture between our data and Wright's own arguments it is appropriate to consider this question of proletarianization in more detail. For this reason we take it to be our second major theme, alongside that of gender, in the discussion of demographic class formation. It is the principal subject of the following chapter.

Notes

1 Respondents in the sample were engaged in the following economic activities: in work full time 56.2 per cent; in work part time 13.2 per cent; waiting to start a job already obtained 0.5 per cent; out of work as temporarily sick 0.7 per cent; permanently sick or disabled 2.4 per cent; retired 2.7 per cent; unemployed/looking for work 8.8 per cent; keeping house 15.2 per cent; other 0.5 per cent (N = 1770). From the filters in our interview schedule (see Appendix, section 5) it will be seen that we have adopted the practice of treating those respondents unemployed for less than one year as if they were still in work, for certain interview purposes, and in particular questioned them about the social relations of production in their last employment. The 'long-term unemployed', those out of work for one year or more, were not asked questions 38–94.
2 See, for example, Marshall (1984).
3 Sinfield (1981) reviews the questions raised by unemployment generally while those arising out of domestic labour and women's employment have been surveyed by Dex (1985).
4 An example is Hartmann (1979).
5 See Goldthorpe (1983a), Stanworth (1984), Heath and Britten (1984), Erikson (1984), Goldthorpe (1984a), Dale et al. (1985), Goldthorpe and Payne (1986b).
6 Heath and Britten (1984: 489). See also Britten and Heath (1983).
7 Stanworth (1984: 165).
8 See Goldthorpe and Payne (1986b: 535, 548–9).
9 The proportions of homogeneous and cross-class marriages were also calculated according to RG class categories, and the results obtained were somewhat different from those reported for the Goldthorpe classes, with 67 per cent of employed cohabiting couples in class homogeneous households (taking RG classes 1–3N as nonmanual and 3M–5 as manual). However this improvement is an artefact of the more crude manual/nonmanual classification utilized. Even this simple dichotomy, however, still places well over 30 per cent of households into the cross-class category. (As with Goldthorpe classes this figure is unaffected if spouses' work histories are taken into account.) It is impossible to make this calculation for Wright categories on the basis of our data, since several pages of questions are required in order to collect information sufficient to place each respondent into the appropriate Wright class, and it proved simply impractical to collect this information for spouses as well. We would not assume respondents themselves to be reliable sources of such detailed information about their spouses' immediate work situations; nor, because of resource constraints, could we interview spouses in all two-adult households. Wright himself faced the same problem in studying the United States and was forced to adopt the (in our view wholly unsatisfactory) solution of allocating spouses to a social class according to very crude employment status categories. Of course, this goes against the logic of his own argument, since he seeks to demonstrate the superiority of class frameworks based on social relations of production over occupational and employment status categories. Yet, in effect, he is here cross-classifying 'social class' against what he elsewhere dismisses as 'occupation'. (See Wright, 1985: 225–32.)
10 Goldthorpe (1978: 206).
11 This common interest in demographic class formation separates both Goldthorpe and ourselves from the tradition of class analysis which concentrates exclusively on socio-political class formation. Phenomenological, culturalist, and Marxist writers have all addressed the problem of class membership in this way. I. C. Jarvie (1972: 120), for example, defines a social class as

a quasi-grouping of people whose links are that they *think* they have similar interests, and who share common *beliefs* about the system of social class, their own position in that system, and similar dispositions as to the behaviour appropriate to their position in that system.

This is close to Edward Thompson's (1965: 85) conclusion that

class is a social and cultural formation . . . which cannot be defined abstractly, or in isolation, but only in terms of relationships with other classes . . . a class [is] a very loosely defined body of people who share the same categories of interests, social experiences, traditions and value system . . . class itself is not a thing. it is a happening.

Or, in the aphorism of Nicos Poulantzas (1978: 14), 'social classes do not firstly exist as such, and only then enter into a class struggle. Social classes coincide with class practices, i.e. the class struggle'. What these writers have in common is a definition of class solely in dispositional terms: classes are groups of people who behave and act in 'class ways'. This stratagem solves almost all problems of class analysis by fiat since demographic and sociopolitical class formations are synonymous. Almost any form of mass action of a vaguely redistributive nature becomes equivalent to class action. The unit of class analysis is the class itself – and mature classes are finally constituted in the revolution. All that remains on the agenda of class analysis is to await the eventual convergence of theory and action – and, in the meanwhile, to speculate about the distance between classes and class demands as presently observed and classes as these will emerge under revolutionary conditions (see Lockwood, 1981). For a similar critique as applied to certain forms of closure theory, see Murphy (1986).

12 Goldthorpe (1980: 295, 58–62).
13 For further discussion and evidence on this point see Scott (1986).
14 Goldthorpe (1983a: 467).
15 At least one group of participants in the debate itself seemed to be moving towards the same conclusion. Dale and her co-authors (1985: 387–8) argue that

all those, both men and women, who have a direct relationship to the labour market can be allocated an occupational position. It is not, however, possible to extend this class position to encompass all members of the family. Because occupational class, in this sense, depends upon the market power which an occupation can command, it must be an attribute of an individual. Nevertheless, the role of unwaged labour in the home should not be ignored, although it does not have a *direct* relationship to the labour market. Therefore the relationship of the individual to the labour market cannot be used to predict life-style and life-chances, for they depend upon the inputs and demands of all family members, whether or not directly involved in the economic sphere. It is clear from patterns of consumption of private housing, health care and education that there is no close identification between these and occupational class, although there will undoubtedly be a two-way effect between the occupation of an individual and the patterns of consumption of the family.

16 Goldthorpe and Payne (1986a: 15–18) have argued that there are also good empirical grounds for including the unemployed in class mobility tables. (That is, that nothing is gained by allocating the jobless to a distinctive position of their own, as opposed to a class according to their last employment.) They find that trends in class distribution since 1972 stand unchanged even when unemployment is regarded as a separate mobility status. Nevertheless, in the interests of theoretical consistency and of pursuing a direct comparison with the Wright class frameworks we have omitted the unemployed from our own Goldthorpe class categories, since they must necessarily be omitted from those of Erik Wright. We will be reporting in detail on the unemployed respondents in our sample, as well as those who stated that they were keeping house, in a separate publication. See also Marshall *et al.* (1988).
17 Wright (1979: 90).
18 Wright (1979: 92).
19 In his later work Wright somewhat revises his theoretical reasoning but still arrives at the same conclusions. In *Classes* he argues that, since 'whatever directionality historical development has is the result of the development of the productive forces, . . . then . . . property relations . . . define the basic terrain of interests with respect to historical development.' From this premiss, and viewing the situation of housewives from the game-theoretic perspective, he can conclude

first, working-class housewives have no organization assets or credential assets, and at most extremely limited assets in the means of production (household appliances). Secondly, like workers, they would be better off and capitalists worse off if they withdrew along with their husbands from the capitalist game with their per capita share of capital assets. Their exploitation-interests *with respect to capitalism*, therefore, do not differ from those of their spouses (Wright, 1985: 97, 128).

20 See, for example, Wright (1985: 199–200; 1979: 93).
21 See Wright *et al.* (1982), Wright (1985).
22 See Wright (1985: 150).
23 See Wright (1985: 309–10).
24 See Wright (1985: 310).
25 Wright and Singelmann (1982).

5 The structure of class processes

If gender is presently the most controversial topic in class analysis then that of proletarianization follows not far behind. Indeed, the two issues are often intertwined, since it has commonly been argued that it is women more frequently than men who are subject to the process of proletarianization itself. It is therefore scarcely surprising to find that both John Goldthorpe and Erik Wright have written at some length about this particular aspect of class analysis.

The latter's argument is relatively straightforward. From US census and other survey materials Wright concludes that there is marked evidence of proletarianization within the different sectors of the American economy. However, economic liberals have failed to detect the relevant shifts in the composition of classes, because the proletarianization process is obscured by a counteracting tendency in the industry shift effect. The distinction between industry shift effects and class composition shift effects was expounded in Chapter 1. Briefly, Wright's argument is that there has been a marked expansion of 'working-class locations' within economic sectors, though this has been more than offset by the relatively more rapid expansion of those sectors that were proportionately less proletarianized to begin with. In simple terms, within given economic sectors there was 'a systematic tendency for those positions with relatively little control over their labor processes to expand during the 1960s and for those positions with high levels of autonomy to decline',[1] but this tendency was masked by the tremendous growth of the state (and therefore of semi-autonomous employment) during the same period. Wright speculates that this effective proletarianization of the class structure will become increasingly apparent as fiscal crisis adds a decline in state employment to that induced in the transformative industries by competition from abroad. Be this as it may, Wright's American class project offers data that are taken by him to be consistent with this general interpretation, since they suggest that proletarians constitute by far the largest class in the American labour force.[2]

Goldthorpe, on the other hand, argues against the proletarianization thesis. His interpretation of European and American census statistics is that they 'flatly contradict . . . the Marxist "labour process" theory of class structural change which claims a necessary "degrading" of work and a progressive proletarianization of the work-force under capitalism'. In Britain and the United States alike the census data for the period since 1945 show that it is professional, administrative, and managerial occupations that are in expansion, with the greatest decline being evident in manual (especially unskilled) labour. Goldthorpe is dismissive of the attempt by Wright (and others) to sustain the thesis of proletarianization by recourse to the argument about counterbalancing shift effects. In his view, the growth of 'service-class' occupations during the post-war period cannot simply be seen as a result of the increasing importance of the services sector within the economy, since official statistics even for the 'recessionary' 1970s suggest otherwise. During this particular period, which saw an accelerated relative decline of manufacturing, it was still the case that professional, managerial, and administrative occupations continued to expand, and manual ones to shrink, even when all inter-industry shifts were allowed for. In other words, 'the major trends apparent in census data were generated not only by industrial and sectoral changes in employment but also by the (net) effects of technological, organisational and other changes determining the occupational "mix" within production units'.[3] Goldthorpe argues further that some of the major exponents of labour process theory have lately been forced to concede this point – thus seriously undermining the argument in favour of proletarianization. A few have shifted their ground by making the additional and rather different claim that the expansion of administrative and professional positions is more apparent than real because most of these involve the performance of increasingly routinized and therefore degraded labour. Again, however, Goldthorpe can find no systematic evidence in favour of this claim, for particular case-studies of occupational degrading (in terms of skill and job content) can readily be offset against others reporting occupational upgrading, and in any case are themselves not inconsistent with the claim that the *net* result of organizational and technological changes over the whole economy is one of increasing both skill levels and the proportion of the work-force in service-class conditions of employment.

This last point raises more general issues about the way in which the debate as a whole has been pursued. Goldthorpe's contention is that the argument about proletarianization is an argument about class structures as a whole. Since, in his view, macro-sociological issues of this kind can be resolved only on the basis of macro-sociological data, then particular case-studies that report degrading or upgrading of labour are of little value for or against the thesis of proletarianization as such. The fact that other contributors to the discussion have taken such case-studies to be the very means of settling its principal issues[4] suggests that the various interested parties have rather different conceptions of what the thesis itself proposes. Indeed, it is clear from the extant literature that what has come to be known as the 'labour process debate' has ranged far beyond the territory of the original argument, as reported in Braverman's *Labour and Monopoly Capital*, since this stated simply that the imperatives of capitalist production compelled those who managed industry to fragment and deskill work in line with Taylorist principles, so as to increase output and maintain control over labour. In fact we have identified no less than four different interpretations of this so-called proletarianization thesis in the current literature. First, there are those like

99

Erik Wright who have taken the argument to be one about the relative proportions of class locations within class structures, and in particular the tendency for the working class to expand in relationship to the numbers in capitalist and contradictory class locations. The debate here hinges about the proletarianization of places within the structure. By comparison, others such as John Goldthorpe have referred their discussion to data concerning trajectories through the class structure, attempting to calculate the likelihood of those from particular class backgrounds being 'proletarianized' by downward social mobility during the course of their employed lives. For these authors it is people rather than places in the structure that constitute the subjects of the process at issue. Somewhat different again is the interpretation of Crompton and others who have concentrated their attention on the proletarianization of particular sorts of jobs. Their argument is that seemingly non-proletarian places in the structure (such as those occupied by routine white-collar workers) have often been so deskilled, in terms of job content and the routinization of tasks, that they are similar or even identical to those occupied by the manual working class. Finally, we can distinguish arguments about proletarianization in its socio-political sense, that is the extent to which certain groups within the labour force come to identify themselves as working class, or as allies of the working class, and so to share its cultural and ideological proclivities. This usage is often implicit in arguments about locations, people, and jobs (as in Crompton's account), is sometimes explicit in these arguments (as in Wright's own texts), and occasionally itself constitutes the explanandum of a study in which objective proletarianization (of jobs, locations, or people) is scarcely an issue (as in the work of Richard Edwards).[5]

In all four cases the argument has been complicated by the question of gender. As we have seen, women occupy particular class locations, and so constitute a disproportionately large number of routine white-collar workers or non-managerial employees. It has often been suggested therefore, that women's class trajectories will be different from those of men, with women experiencing 'blocked mobility' and consequently greater chances of being trapped in proletarian class positions. Moreover, so the argument continues, females perform tasks which, whatever their nominal class affiliation, are more likely to have been routinized and deskilled than those typically undertaken by males. This sex differentiation in the proletarian work-force generates a sectionalism which divides men and women and inhibits the development of (transsexual) 'working-class consciousness'.

The literature generated by these interrelated discussions has reached enormous proportions and we could not hope to review it systematically as a prelude to our own contribution. Nor is it possible, within the space available, to pursue the issues that separate Goldthorpe and Wright with reference to their contradictory interpretations of census materials pertaining to supposed trends in the occupational structure.[6] We propose, instead, to explore the four dimensions of the proletarianization thesis identified above with reference to the data from the Essex national sample survey. There are good grounds for our particularism in this matter since this study offers the possibility of exploring these different issues within a single data set. This opportunity has not been available to others before us, who have necessarily had recourse to official statistics on the *occupational* structure, social surveys dealing with the narrow concerns of class mobility, or case-studies of deskilling in particular jobs. By comparison, our macro-sociological data on class locations, mobility trajectories, occupational deskilling, and socio-political class formation can bear on the various arguments in a more rigorous way since they are standardized on a representative sample of individuals in the British class structure.

I

It is convenient to begin our analysis by investigating further the issues of social mobility that were raised in the previous chapter, since one of our principal findings is directly relevant to the present discussion. We established that there was considerable upward mobility into professional, administrative, and managerial positions. Although Wright tends to exaggerate the numbers involved, there is no doubting that members of Goldthorpe's service class have been recruited from throughout the class structure, so that, for example, fully one-third of Goldthorpe class I and II respondents in our sample come from class VI and VII backgrounds. In fact, the changes in the shape of that structure apparent from a comparison of the distribution of origins and destinations suggest that the manual working class (classes VI and VII) has shrunk from 48 per cent to 35 per cent of the employed population, comparing the chief childhood supporters of our respondents to their sons and daughters. Over the same transition the service class has grown to comprise 29 per cent rather than 15 per cent of the labour force.

These figures are obtained by comparing the marginal percentages for Tables 4.7 and 4.8 in the previous chapter. They are reproduced in Table 5.1. There is no evidence here to support the thesis of proletarianization in the class structure. The proportions in classes I, II, and III have increased while those in V, VI, and VII have decreased – a clear shift away from manual labour towards both routine and specialized white-collar work. Nevertheless, we have seen that Erik Wright attempts to substantiate precisely this thesis, particularly by reference to his finding that some 40 per cent of American workers are proletarians. Indeed if, as Wright maintains, there are 'good reasons' for adding to this those with marginal control over organization and skill assets – uncredentialled supervisors and semi-credentialled workers and supervisors – then 'the working class becomes a clear majority' (66 per cent of those employed) in the United States. The British data are rather similar, with almost 43 per cent of the work-force in proletarian positions, and another 22 per cent in the marginal categories.[7] However, we have also seen that Wright's class categories are of suspect reliability, both in their original and revised forms. For example, significant numbers in his managerial and

Table 5.1 *Distribution of respondents and of respondents' chief childhood supporters (at same age as respondents) by Goldthorpe class and sex*

Class	Male		Female		All	
	CCS	Resp.	CCS	Resp.	CCS	Resp.
I	7.4	14.6	6.8	4.7	7.2	10.6
II	8.4	17.2	6.6	21.2	7.7	18.8
III	5.1	6.0	5.6	38.1	5.3	18.9
IV	14.2	11.6	12.9	5.4	13.7	9.1
V	17.6	10.4	18.8	3.5	18.1	7.7
VI	22.0	17.2	26.1	4.9	23.6	12.3
VII	25.3	22.9	23.1	22.1	24.4	22.6
Total	100.0	100.0	100.0	100.0	100.0	100.0

N = 1057 (632 males, 425 females)

Δs for chief childhood supporters' and respondents' distributions:

    All, 28.1
    Males, 17.0
    Females, 47.0

supervisory categories have decision-making responsibilities that are so limited, and perform such minimal supervisory functions, that their conditions of employment are effectively rendered indistinguishable from those of ordinary workers, with whom they can more properly be grouped. (These are the coal-mining fitters, heavy goods vehicle drivers, sales assistants, and the like, who were discussed in Chapter 4.) On the face of it, of course, this would seem to increase the numbers in routine employment and so provide substantive evidence in favour of the proletarianization thesis. However, a glance back at the cross-tabulation of Goldthorpe against Wright schemata in Table 3.5 confirms that there is a corresponding movement in the other direction elsewhere, with for example 35 per cent of Wright's proletarians being found in Goldthorpe class III, 31 per cent of uncredentialled supervisors in Goldthorpe class II, and a quarter of all semi-credentialled workers in service-class (I and II) locations.

We have already examined the anomalous category of 'service-class proletarians' and found it to contain some rather unlikely members of the proletariat: accountants, lawyers, investment brokers and the like. Similarly, the 'service-class semi-credentialled workers' include an environmental health officer, therapist, two computer programmers, two executive officers in the civil service, several quantity surveyors, some policemen, draughtsmen, and large numbers of teachers and social workers. This group of employees would hardly seem to be part of – or even marginal to – the 'working class'. So there is no prima facie reason to suppose that Wright's enforced proletarianiz-ation of large numbers of Goldthorpe's service-class and routine white-collar employees is any more plausible than his seeming embourgeoisement of equally large numbers of Goldthorpe's working class. Both processes would appear to be artefacts of Wright's classificatory system itself. Here, as elsewhere, it is the Goldthorpe class categories which are seemingly the more robust.

However the argument about proletarian places in the structure is only in part an empirical one. Wright could legitimately claim that some so-called service-class respondents are performing routine, degraded, and in that sense proletarianized labour. They have no managerial or supervisory responsibilities, only modest educational credentials, and lack autonomy in carrying out their work – which is why they appear as proletarians or semi-credentialled workers in his schema. Goldthorpe would consider such factors to be largely irrelevant to the class-placement of these individuals. In some cases they have been given the title 'manager' or 'supervisor' by an employing organization, all have fairly secure employment, good promotion prospects, incremental incomes, and enjoy relatively favourable conditions of work. For Goldthorpe, it is not one's *functions* in employment that are significant to the determination of life-chances and the formation of social consciousness; rather it is one's *conditions* of employment. It is for this prior theoretical reason that he distinguishes, for example, routine white-collar employees from rank-and-file manual workers. And it is the inclusion of this category of employees as a separate grouping in his class schema that constitutes the major point of disagreement between himself and Wright, at least in so far as arguments about proletarianization in class structures are concerned. These routine nonmanual workers may or may not have been deskilled and may or may not share the socio-political proclivities of their manual labouring counterparts. In fact both of these issues – which were referred to earlier as the proletarianization of tasks and of social consciousness respectively – will be pursued below. However, at this juncture it is necessary to look more closely at the simple demographic characteristics of this crucial routine nonmanual category, particularly in comparison to those of the conventionally defined manual working class. From the discussion in earlier chapters it will be remembered that 56 per cent of British proletarians (in Wright's terms) are women. Indeed 58 per cent of all female employees in the British sample are to be found in this class category. (Wright's own findings for the United States are similar.) By comparison, 82 per cent of Goldthorpe class III respondents are also found to be women, indeed they are precisely those respondents about whom Goldthorpe and Wright most obviously disagree as regards their putative class position. The data in Table 5.2 confirm that by far the largest 'anomalous' outflow from Wright's proletariat is into Goldthorpe's class III and that most of the discrepant cases are female. Are these women 'proletarian' or are they not? This brings the issue of sex differentiation in class processes firmly to centre-stage in the discussion of proletarianization.

II

It has been clear throughout our analysis that intergenerational mobility

Table 5.2 *Goldthorpe class distribution of Wright proletariat, by sex*

		Wright proletariat (revised definition)			
		Male		*Female*	
	I	0.0	(1)	0.0	(0)
	II	0.8	(2)	1.6	(5)
	IIIa	13.4	(33)	35.3	(112)
	IIIb	0.8	(2)	16.4	(52)
	IVa	0.0	(0)	0.0	(0)
Goldthorpe class	IVb	0.0	(0)	0.0	(0)
	IVc	0.4	(1)	0.0	(0)
	V	0.4	(1)	0.6	(2)
	VI	15.8	(39)	5.4	(17)
	VIIa	66.8	(165)	40.4	(128)
	VIIb	1.2	(3)	0.3	(1)
	Total	100.0	(247)	100.0	(317)

patterns for men and women are rather different. Looking back at Table 5.1, for example, we can see the familiar picture of class segmentation by sex. Proportionately more women than men will arrive at class II or class III destinations, while the opposite is true in the case of classes I, IV, V, and VI. The effect of sex on the transition from origins to destinations is reflected in the observed dissimilarity index (Δ) of 47 for women as compared to 17 for men: the class distribution of female respondents is more different from that of their chief childhood supporters than is the class distribution of men compared to their childhood supporters. How does this finding about mobility patterns bear on arguments about proletarianization? If, as seems to be the case, there is no obvious net expansion of working-class places in the structure as a whole, might it not be possible nevertheless that specific groups within the employed population (in this case females) have trajectories through that structure which effectively proletarianize the individuals involved, either in an absolute sense (they are downwardly mobile into the working class) or in comparison to the mobility trajectories typical of some other groups (that is, males) with whom they are in competition for class places? Is it perhaps true, as Michelle Stanworth and others claim, that women are as a whole proletarianized because their relative mobility chances are different from those found among men?[8]

The data in Table 5.3 suggest that this is not in fact the case. They express the overall mobility trends evident in Table 4.8 as a series of odds ratios. (In addition, however, mobility trajectories have been broken down into three transitions; from class or origin to class position on entry into employment; from class of origin to present class position; and career mobility from the respondent's first full-time job to his or her present job.) The figures in the

Table 5.3 *Relative mobility chances in terms of odds ratios, by Goldthorpe class and sex*

(a) Transition from class of origin to class position on entry into employment

Pairs of origin classes 'in competition'	Pairs of destination classes 'competed for'					
	Men			Women		
	S vs I	*S vs W*	*I vs W*	*S vs I*	*S vs W*	*I vs W*
S vs I	2.02	4.13	2.05	2.43	4.63	1.90
S vs W	1.95	7.76	4.09	3.84	14.07	3.63
I vs W	0.96	1.88	2.00	1.58	3.04	1.91

(b) Transition from class of origin to present class position

Pairs of origin classes 'in competition'	Pairs of destination classes 'competed for'					
	Men			Women		
	S vs I	*S vs W*	*I vs W*	*S vs I*	*S vs W*	*I vs W*
S vs I	2.75	3.09	1.12	1.67	3.75	2.23
S vs W	4.00	7.35	1.82	3.77	12.95	3.43
I vs W	1.47	2.37	1.62	2.23	3.45	1.54

(c) Transition from class on entry into employment to present class position

Pairs of origin classes 'in competition'	Pairs of destination classes 'competed for'					
	Men			Women		
	S vs I	*S vs W*	*I vs W*	*S vs I*	*S vs W*	*I vs W*
S vs I	2.39	8.71	3.64	4.31	10.96	2.51
S vs W	6.08	41.68	7.01	6.04	50.00	8.15
I vs W	2.54	4.79	1.93	1.40	4.56	3.25

Key: S = Service (classes I and II);
I = Intermediate (classes III, IV, and V);
W = Working (classes VI and VII).

table are an indication of the relative chances of getting to alternative class destinations. They are the outcome, as it were, of a competition between individuals of different class origins to achieve or avoid one rather than another destination in the overall structure. Where such competitions are perfectly equal – in other words the odds for the particular movement in question are even – then the ratio will be 1:1 (or simply 1). In fact, if we examine transition 'a' for men from service-class and working-class backgrounds competing for service-class rather than working-class destinations, we can see that the odds ratio here is 7:76 (to 1). That is a measure of the advantage held by the former over the latter in this particular competition. However the corresponding figure for women is 14:07. This suggests that daughters from service-class origins are more likely, as compared to daughters from working-class backgrounds, to arrive at service-class destinations than are service-class sons as compared to working-class sons. Or, to put the matter another way, among men the chances of someone starting in the service class being found in the service class, rather than in the working class, are almost eight times greater than the same chances for someone starting in the working class – while for women they are more than fourteen times greater. There is a greater inequality of class among women, in this particular case, than among men. Women, no less than men, are divided by the forces making for class inequalities in mobility chances.

Now John Goldthorpe, unlike Michelle Stanworth, maintains that the pattern of relative rates, or 'social fluidity', that underlies women's inter-generational class mobility (when women are allocated to class positions by their own employment) is more or less indistinguishable from that underlying men's mobility.[9] The odds ratios noted above tend to confirm his argument. Overall patterns among men and women are not dissimilar although there are differences in the relative odds pertaining to particular transitions. But for the full intergenerational trajectory ('b') from class of origin to present class these differences are fairly small. In any case they may be insignificant since odds ratios are particularly sensitive to the effects of sampling error. Moreover, looking both down and across the three sets of comparative odds, it is rather difficult to determine whether or not any systematic changes are evident in the pattern of relative chances. A more reliable and perspicuous approach to the problem of allowing for structural changes in the investigation of mobility trends, and so measuring the degree of openness or fluidity that prevails net of all marginal effects, is to fit multiplicative or loglinear models to the observed mobility matrices. These allow us to compare the expected cell frequencies resulting from a given model with those actually observed for the real world. By moving through a hierarchy of models embracing independence, two-way association, three-way association and so on between variables, and testing at each stage the goodness of fit between the cell frequencies obtained from the model and those actually observed, we can determine whether significant improvements are gained by allowing for more complex associations between the variables involved. In this way we can determine the model that best fits – or predicts – the observed values.[10]

Goldthorpe himself applies to mobility data for men and women a model which hypothesizes that the relative rates for the sexes are the same. This 'common social fluidity' model confirms that, for data from the 1983 British General Election Study, sexual differences in absolute mobility rates are almost entirely attributable to differences in the marginal distributions of the matrices for men and women. That is, that an association exists between sex and the distribution of class destinations, and between class of origin and class of destination, but that this latter association does not itself vary with sex. This model allows for structural change (the distribution of destinations being different from that of origins), and for imperfect mobility (inequality of relative mobility chances), but requires that the pattern of these unequal chances are expressed in odds ratios should be the same for both sexes. In fact our own data suggest that the links between class of origin (O), class on first

106

entry into full-time employment (F), present class (D) and sex (S) are of precisely this order. The relative rates for intergenerational mobility among men and women are indeed the same.

We can demonstrate this in a two-stage analysis. Looking first at the relationship between O, F and S, we can fit the model [OS][OF][SF]. This is the most complicated model that is possible, except for the one that includes OFS itself, and the fit is shown in Table 5.4. We can see that, while there are strong OF and SF associations, the OFS interaction is not significant and can be set to zero. Fitting the two simpler models [OS][OF] and [OS][SF], which omit respectively the effects of sex and class of origin upon class of first job, we see that it is sex that has the greatest effect upon destination (since the ratio of change in Y^2 to change in df is 97 as compared to 29). The differences between the social class patterns for men and women, comparing class on entry into employment and class of origin, are therefore wholly accounted for by the independent influences of sex and class background. In other words, fitting a common social fluidity model to the transition from class of origin to class on entry to employment, we observe that the relative mobility regimes for men and women are the same. We can then extend the analysis to include present social class. The corresponding model is [OFS][OD][FD][SD]. It will be seen from the results reported in Table 5.5 that the effects of O, F and S on

Table 5.4 *Interrelationship between class on entry into employment, class of origin, and sex*

Model	df	Y^2	Difference			Y^2/df	p
1 [OS] [OF] [SF]	4	2.7	⇒ OFS		2.7	0.7	>0.50
2 [OS] [OF]	6	197.2	⇒ SF	2	194.5	97.3	<0.0005
3 [OS] [SF]	8	118.0	⇒ OF	4	115.3	28.8	<0.0005

Key: O = Class of origin (chief childhood supporter, Goldthorpe three-category scheme);
F = Class of respondent on entry into employment (Goldthorpe three-category scheme);
S = Sex.

Table 5.5 *Interrelationship between present class, class on entry into employment, class of origin, and sex*

Model	df	Y^2	Difference			Y^2/df	p
1 [OFS] [FDS] [OD]	20	22.4					
2 [OFS] [OD] [FD] [SD]	24	24.4	⇒ FDS	4	2.0	0.5	>0.70
3 [OFS] [OD] [FD]	26	43.1	⇒ SD	2	18.7	9.3	<0.0005
4 [OFS] [OD] [SD]	28	177.8	⇒ FD	4	153.4	38.4	<0.0005
5 [OFS] [FD] [SD]	28	60.0	⇒ OD	4	35.6	8.9	<0.0005

Key: O = Class of origin (chief childhood supporter, Goldthorpe three-category scheme);
F = Class of respondent on entry into employment (Goldthorpe three-category scheme);
D = Present class (Goldthorpe three-category scheme);
S = Sex.

D are still independent of each other. There is no indication of any three-way interactions since even the most important of these [FDS – Model 1) is not significant (the change in Y^2/df ratio is less than 1). However each of OD, FD and SD certainly are important, and of these FD is obviously the most significant.

The implication of these data seems clear enough. The pattern of relative rates that underlies women's intergenerational mobility, as defined according to their own employment and that of chief childhood supporters, is the same as that underlying men's mobility. Goldthorpe's common social fluidity model clearly fits[11] and Stanworth's speculations about the proletarianization of women are shown to be correspondingly unwarranted – at least in so far as relative mobility chances are concerned.

Of course common social fluidity – the fact that men's and women's mobility regimes are similar – has to be set against the absolute differences for the sexes observed in Table 4.8. The class distributions of males and females are very different. Common social fluidity is conditional upon unequal opportunity. A simple comparison between men's and women's absolute mobility rates shows that females are at a clear disadvantage in both intergenerational and career transitions. Tables 5.6 and 5.7 make the trends in class distribution (Table 4.8) rather more apparent by collapsing the Goldthorpe class schema to its three-category version and distinguishing intergenerational from career mobility. As one would expect, the social classes of males and females on first entry into employment are quite different, as will be seen from Table 5.6. In the transition from origins to first job, sex affects principally the likelihood of arriving at working-class, as opposed to intermediate-class destinations. Irrespective of class origins, proportionately more women arrive at the latter than the former, while the opposite is true for men. (Obviously, as is also apparent from this table, service-class parents give rise to a disproportionately large number of service-

Table 5.6 *Class on entry into employment by class of origin and sex (Goldthorpe class categories)*

			Service	Intermediate	Working	Total	
				Class on entry			
	Service	Male	41	28	31	100	(105)
		Female	38	52	10	100	(98)
		All	39	39	21	100	(203)
	Intermediate	Male	18	25	57	100	(261)
Class of		Female	18	60	22	100	(223)
origin		All	18	41	41	100	(484)
	Working	Male	12	16	72	100	(348)
		Female	10	53	37	100	(304)
		All	11	33	56	100	(562)
		All	18	37	45	100	(1339)

Table 5.7 *Present class by class on entry into employment by class of origin and sex (Goldthorpe class categories)*

A – Class of origin = service

			Present Class				
			Service	Intermediate	Working	Total	
Class at entry	Service	Male	84	13	3	100	(31)
		Female	77	15	8	100	(13)
	Intermediate	Male	50	33	17	100	(24)
		Female	33	52	14	100	(21)
	Working	Male	37	17	47	100	(30)
		Female	0	80	20	100	(5)
		All	53	27	19	100	(124)

B – Class of origin = intermediate

			Present class				
			Service	Intermediate	Working	Total	
Class at entry	Service	Male	67	26	7	100	(31)
		Female	65	25	10	100	(20)
	Intermediate	Male	42	29	29	100	(45)
		Female	24	59	18	100	(80)
	Working	Male	20	36	44	100	(111)
		Female	23	35	42	100	(26)
		All	32	39	29	100	(313)

C – Class of origin = working

			Present class				
			Service	Intermediate	Working	Total	
Class at entry	Service	Male	64	29	7	100	(28)
		Female	43	57	0	100	(14)
	Intermediate	Male	33	43	24	100	(42)
		Female	12	52	37	100	(101)
	Working	Male	10	28	62	100	(173)
		Female	5	41	54	100	(59)
		All	17	38	45	100	(417)
		All	28	37	35	100	(854)

class offspring of both sexes.) If we then extend the analysis to include worklife mobility (as in Table 5.7), we can see that there are, still, rather less presently working-class respondents in the female proportions than in those for males (20 to 47, 42 to 44, and 54 to 62), with rather more women again in the intermediate category. Moreover, proportionately fewer women than men are upwardly mobile into service-class locations during the course of their occupational careers, though women from service-class and intermediate-class origins fare almost as well as men providing their class at entry was itself service. Note also the general effect of class of origin. Eighty-four per cent of males from service-class origins whose own initial social class was service are currently in service-class locations, as compared to 64 per cent for those initially in the service class, but from working-class origins. (The proportions for female respondents are 77 per cent and 43 per cent.) We can conclude that, after taking account of social class at time of first employment, sex continues to have implications for class destination. Its general effect, after taking account of class of origin and class at first entry into employment, is that males have a better chance of being in the service class rather than the intermediate class and females vice versa.

Perhaps the most straightforward way to represent these various relationships is diagramatically, as in Table 5.8, where the number of heads on the arrows gives an idea of the magnitude of the effects involved. In substantive terms, and to confirm our earlier observations, the association between sex, class background, and class destinations can conveniently be described as one, not of women being proletarianized, but of their relative 'bunching up' into intermediate-class positions while men are distributed towards the working-class and service-class 'ends' of the class structure.

Table 5.8 *Relationship between class of origin, class destination, and sex*

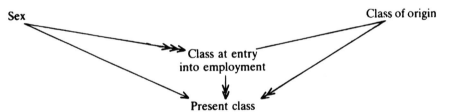

Two conclusions then follow from this comparison of absolute against relative mobility rates for men and women. First, as was already suggested, social fluidity among men and women is virtually the same. This result is also obtained when the full seven-category class schema is used in the model.[12] Thus, for example, it is not true that daughters from class I and II backgrounds are less likely as compared with other women to arrive at class I and II destinations than are class I and II sons as compared with other men, so it does not follow that women are 'united in adversity' in having relative mobility chances that are more equal among them than are those found among men. Goldthorpe expresses this conclusion most forcefully in the observation that

even if the argument were to be accepted that the majority of employed women are engaged in 'proletarian' work, it would still be important to note that women of all class origins are *not* equally likely to share in this fate. Although women overall confront at any one time a less favourable set of employment opportunities than do men, the forces making for class inequalities in mobility chances are not annulled among women. On the contrary, they appear to operate in a way that is quite blind to gender; hence women are divided by these inequalities to much the same degree and on much the same pattern as men.[13]

This means that, given the good fit of the common social fluidity model to the data on class mobility, the distinctive pattern of women's class destinations (their bunching up into routine nonmanual work and into the lower echelons of the service class) results from a sex segregation in employment which persists to the general disadvantage of women. This, as Goldthorpe himself points out, is scarcely a novel finding.

Second, however, we would conclude from the foregoing analysis that relative rates tell only a part of the story – and in no way justify John Goldthorpe's subsequent conclusion that the 'conventional' approach to the location of women within class structures is justified. It will be remembered from the previous chapter that this approach starts from the assumption that it is the family, rather than the individual, which forms the basic unit of social stratification, Goldthorpe defends this strategy on the grounds that

if the individual approach is taken differences in absolute mobility rates between women and men do clearly appear, and on the lines that exponents of this approach would anticipate; in particular, women more often than men display downward mobility from their class origins. However, when women are thus allocated to class positions by reference to their own employment, in the same way as men, it further turns out that the pattern of their relative mobility chances is more or less indistinguishable from that of men. The implication of this is, then,·that the differences shown up in absolute rates must be seen as the result not of endogenous mobility processes *per se*, which would appear essentially invariant to gender, but rather of differing marginal distributions in the mobility table reflecting, most obviously, the degree of sex segregation in the occupational division of labour.[14]

He then denies that the evidence of sex segregation obvious in the absolute figures

can properly be translated into an argument concerning class mobility; for example, to the effect that, when the individual approach to the class location of women is adopted, a strong and hitherto neglected tendency for downward class mobility is revealed – with the accompanying subcultural and socio-political shifts that might be expected.[15]

Our objection to this line of reasoning was spelled out in the previous chapter and hinges on the definition of class analysis itself. Goldthorpe's interest in women's class mobility is restricted by his insistence that any sex effects must have clear and observable consequences for socio-political class formation – as the above quotation makes clear. Yet women's participation in paid labour has obvious and rather marked consequences for the distribution of men in the structure, that is for demographic class formation itself, which Goldthorpe admits as the first concern for class analysts. Excluding women from the field of study results in a loss of information that is clearly important – even from the restricted point of view of understanding mobility among men – so why exclude them? Moreover, the observation that relative mobility chances among women are similar to those found among men means simply that, in comparison to other women, women from (let us say) working-class origins have the same chances (calculated in terms of odds ratios) of achieving service-class destinations as men from working-class origins have of achieving service-class destinations, in comparison to other men. This does not mean that the chances of working-class women reaching service-class destinations are the same as those for men. It is one thing to conclude that, since relative mobility rates for men and women are the same, changes in structural mobility (in the structure of objective mobility opportunities) must account for all changes in total observed mobility. But it is quite another to deduce that, under these circumstances, 'to concentrate attention on the experience of males is unlikely to bring one to very misleading conclusions'.[16] In fact, as we have shown, this strategy generates a misleading 'map' of the class structure of modern Britain; paints a distorted picture of typical mobility trajectories through that structure; and forces one to exclude from consideration those sex-related factors that help explain the observed demographic characteristics of both men's and women's mobility. It is rather as if one had looked at social mobility in the Republic of South Africa and found that the chances of a white man from a service-class background reaching a service-class rather than a working-class destination, as compared to those of a white man from a working-class background reaching a service-class rather than a working-class destination, were the same as those for black men in the service class and working class making the same transitions – and concluded, on this basis alone, that blacks could safely be excluded from any investigation into social mobility in South Africa since the study of whites alone would yield a comprehensive, intelligible account of class processes in that society, and one which was unlikely to lead to any 'very misleading conclusions'. Can class analysis sensibly exist in the sort of conceptual vacuum that prevents its practitioners engaging with crucial factors (such as gender and race) which are interwoven with class in the real world? Should we really be *that* limited in our aspirations? We think not.

Finally, however, before leaving the subject of relative mobility and turning to that of the routinization of tasks, we should investigate the evidence (if any) for proletarianization that may be evident in changes to the mobility chances of people from particular class backgrounds across birth cohorts, that is to say across time. This can be examined by fitting to the data in Table 5.9 that same model of common (or, more accurately in this context, constant) social fluidity that was utilized above with respect to the class distributions of men and women. In this case the model postulates an association between cohort and the distribution of class origins, cohort and the distribution of class destinations, and class of origin and class destination, but hypothesizes also that the pattern of unequal chances between classes evident in the last-mentioned of these should be the same from one cohort to another. In fact, inspection of the cross-tabulated data themselves suggests that relative mobility rates have not altered over the period covered by our study, and fitting the model simply confirms this (see Table 5.10). Moreover,

Table 5.9 *Class distribution of respondents by class of chief childhood supporter and age-groups (Goldthorpe class categories)*

Age-group 44–64		Service	Respondent's class Intermediate	Working	Total	
	Service	63.0	22.2	14.8	100	(54)
CCSs class	Intermediate	33.5	36.5	30.0	100	(170)
	Working	19.1	36.4	44.5	100	(209)

N = 433

Age-group 23–43		Service	Respondent's class Intermediate	Working	Total	
	Service	60.2	23.9	15.9	100	(88)
CCSs class	Intermediate	35.8	39.6	24.6	100	(187)
	Working	20.3	35.9	43.7	100	(231)

N = 506

Note: It is necessary to set the lower age limit for the younger of our cohorts at 23 years in order to avoid introducing a distorting effect from differential educational take-up rates into the mobility tables. Although the lower limit of our sample is set at age 16, the sample itself excludes those in full-time education, and since proportionately more of those staying on at school go into further and higher education, and subsequently achieve service-class occupations, this will tend artificially to deflate the numbers who are upwardly mobile, or who are retained in the service class, while increasing (no less artificially) the proportion who seemingly stay in the working class. Nevertheless, it is worth noting that the results in the bottom half of the following table (Table 5.10B) show that fitting the model of constant social fluidity to a cohort analysis that includes the whole sample does not alter the outcome. Relative mobility rates are the same for the age-groups 16–31, 32–47, and 48–64.

as a check on the robustness of our findings, we tested the model of constant relative rates against both a simple two-cohort and a more elaborate three-cohort breakdown of our basic mobility data, thus allowing for the possibility not only of a linear, but of a curvilinear trend in mobility patterns. As will be seen from the results reported, the model fits the data rather well, since there is no evidence of systematic variation in the association between origins and destinations across cohorts (that is no significant ODC interaction) in either case. Although there are weak (though statistically significant) associations between cohort and either the distribution of origins or of destinations in the models, reflecting a certain amount of change in the occupational structure, by far the largest and most significant association is that between origins and destinations themselves. However, this does not itself vary across cohorts, no matter whether one anticipates a linear or curvilinear trend.

Granted, this sort of birth cohort analysis is not the most reliable method of investigating historical trends (period effects) in mobility, since the results are confounded by the effects of age and cohort. In other words, the data may be difficult to interpret because observed changes in the mobility of respondents in a particular cohort may be attributable

Table 5.10 *Interrelationship between class of origin, class destination, and age-group*

A – Cohorts aged 23–43, 44–64

Model	df	Y^2	Difference			Y^2/df	p
1 [DO] [C]	8	6.0					
2 [D] [O] [C]	12	103.1	⇒ DO	4	97.2	24.3	<0.0005
3 [DO] [DC]	6	4.6	⇒ DC	2	1.3	0.7	>0.5
4 [DO] [OC]	6	1.5	⇒ OC	2	4.5	2.2	>0.1

B – Cohorts aged 16–31, 32–47, 48–64

Model	df	Y^2	Difference			Y^2/df	p
1 [OD] [OC] [DC]	8	11.8	⇒ ODC	8	11.8	1.5	>0.15
2 [OD] [DC]	12	18.3	⇒ OC	4	6.5	1.6	>0.15
3 [OD] [C]	16	29.2	⇒ DC	4	10.9	2.7	<0.05
4 [DC[[O]	16	115.7	⇒ OD	4	97.4	24.4	<0.0005

Key: O = Class of origin (chief childhood supporter, Goldthorpe three-category scheme);
D = Present class (Goldthorpe three-category scheme);
C = Age-group.

to their having been born at around the same point in historical time; or to their having lived for a similar number of years; or to their cohort membership *per se*, which places them in a certain relationship with the members of other cohorts which at any one time exist within the total work-force or population.[17]

We have tried to meet this problem by comparing each respondent's present class with that for his or her chief childhood supporter when he or she was at the same age as the respondent is now. (It will be remembered that this was also the procedure adopted in generating the basic intergenerational mobility data discussed in the previous chapter.) To a limited extent this eliminates age (or life cycle) influences by standardizing the effect of intragenerational (career) mobility. (Goldthorpe, by comparison, indexes class origin by father's occupation at respondent's age 14). These difficulties aside, however, our findings are unlikely to be seriously misleading since they are quite consistent with those obtained elsewhere from more extensive studies of mobility in Britain conducted at different times during the past fifteen years.[18]

It would seem to be the case, therefore, that relative mobility rates have remained unaltered over time. (Naturally, in fitting this model of constant social fluidity, it is unnecessary to distinguish male and female respondents since we have previously established that the relative class mobility rates for the sexes are the same.) We can conclude, therefore, that there is no obvious proletarianization process at work in the class structure as a whole. We have observed that there is a net decline in the proportion of working-class places in the structure; that relative mobility rates between the classes, or chances of intergenerational mobility, have not altered to any appreciable degree, at least over the last quarter of a century or so, a period spanning the years both of post-1945 economic expansion and post-1973 economic recession;[19] and, finally, that the relative mobility rates for men and women are the same, though there are clear differences in absolute (percentage inflow and outflow) rates of class mobility between the sexes, the result of a marked sex segregation in the occupational division of labour. It is therefore appropriate, at this juncture, to shift from a consideration of proportionate class sizes and the comparison of class trajectories to an inspection instead of the characteristics of particular occupational locations within the structure itself. Are certain types of work (and therefore specific class locations) proletarianized in the sense that the tasks typically associated with them have been deskilled and degraded? For example, is it the case, as Crompton and others have claimed, that the routine white-collar (class III) occupations typically filled by women are indistinguishable, in all significant respects, from those of the manual workers who constitute the proletariat *strictu sensu*?

III

The data here are perhaps harder to interpret than those pertaining to class structure and social mobility. Three aspects of our material are particularly problematic. First, we are dependent on our respondents' own reports about their work situations, and do not have access to descriptions based on direct observations. In consequence, second, it will be difficult to place our data regarding the nature of work into its situational contexts. Finally, we can say understandably little about the labour *process*, given the synchronic nature of our study. These are all unavoidable drawbacks of the sample survey method of sociological research. Nevertheless, we do possess a considerable amount of information about the jobs performed by our interviewees and this can be brought to bear on arguments about the deskilling of work, making due allowance for the above-mentioned shortcomings in the data.

In considering this particular version of the proletarianization thesis we face the obvious difficulty that there is no commonly acknowledged definition of 'skill'. The Registrar-General's class categories offer a convenient example of the problem. Purportedly constructed in such a way as to bring together 'people with similar levels of occupational skill', they are in fact (as was observed in Chapter 2) nothing more than a classification by fiat, since the central concept of occupational skills is left unexplained by the OPCS. It is not even clear whether the skills in question are an attribute of the jobs themselves or of the individuals who come to perform them. The categories probably reflect nothing more than the preconceptions of the Registrar-General's staff. Why, for example, is nursing (class 2) 'more skilled' than secretarial work (class 3N)? Is it because the occupational tasks associated with nursing require greater manual or mental dexterity than those performed by secretaries?; because nurses typically exercise more control over their daily activities and therefore enjoy more autonomy at work?; because they are

115

required to undertake a more thorough and extensive training?; or, perhaps, is it simply the case that nurses have been more successful than have secretaries in creating and defending a 'skilled work' status for themselves?

The sociological literature about the labour process confirms that all four usages of the term – skill as technique, as autonomy, as credentials, and as social status – are in wide circulation.[20] We shall say nothing more about the last two of these on this particular occasion, partly because our survey data will necessarily shed little light on the social processes by which skilled status is 'negotiated' in terms of (for example) strategies of exclusionary closure about some specific credential requirements, but also because it is the first two senses of the term which are crucial to the theoretical formulation of the Wright class schema. Deskilling, for Wright, means the routinization, regulation, and fragmenting of tasks, such that there is a loss of real autonomy in the labour process.[21] Items 55 and 56 in the British interview schedule are his attempt to operationalize Braverman's fundamental idea that work is deskilled via a separation of conception from execution; that is, thought (knowledge or skill) is disassociated from action (the labour process), so that workers are reduced to performing 'simplified job tasks governed by simplified instructions . . . unthinkingly and without comprehension of the underlying reasoning or data'.[22] Skill as complexity and skill as freedom are – for Braverman and Wright at least – central to the thesis that work is being proletarianized through the deskilling of tasks. We, however, can find no evidence in the British data to substantiate this claim.

To what extent have our employed respondents been deskilled in the technicist sense? That is, has the combination of tasks they are required to perform been changed, so as to decrease their ability to manipulate objects and tools? They themselves seem widely disposed to argue that this is not in fact the case – as can be seen from the results displayed in Table 5.11. Asked to report on whether their present jobs required more, less, or about the same amount of skill as when they first started to do them, more than 96 per cent of all employees claimed that their work had not been visibly deskilled. Looking at the row percentages in the table, we can see that, among men, the few who did suggest that their jobs now required less skill were concentrated in the manual working classes, while among women they were more equally divided between manual (Goldthorpe classes VI and VII) and routine nonmanual (class III) locations. There is also a clear class effect in the results. Men and women in higher social classes are significantly more likely than those in lower classes to report that their jobs now involve more skills than were previously required. These sex and class differences are interesting and worthy of note – but are scarcely surprising. Nor do they provide any evidence to substantiate the thesis of labour being deskilled. Rather, the two most important aspects of the findings from our point of view are the facts that fewer than 4 per cent of all respondents perceived any deskilling of their work to have taken place, and that the theoretically crucial class IIIa women show no signs of having been systematically proletarianized in such terms. Indeed, looking down the columns of the table, we can see that these routine white-collar (clerical and

Table 5.11 *Deskilling (job technique) by Goldthorpe class and sex (% by row and column)*

Row % Column % (Job requires)	I	II	IIIa	IIIb	Males Class V	VI	VII	Total
More skill	14	25	8	0	15	19	19	100
	79	81	68	0	76	59	46	65
Less skill	5	5	0	0	15	40	35	100
	2	1	0	0	4	6	4	3
Same skill	7	11	7	1	8	24	42	100
	19	18	32	100	20	35	50	32
Total	100	100	100	100	100	100	100	100

(N = 568)

Row % Column % (Job requires)	I	II	IIIa	IIIb	Females Class V	VI	VII	Total
More skill	7	28	39	6	4	5	11	100
	94	79	66	31	56	54	24	55
Less skill	0	13	33	13	0	7	34	100
	0	2	4	4	0	4	5	3
Same skill	1	9	23	16	3	5	43	100
	6	19	30	65	44	42	71	42
Total	100	100	100	100	100	100	100	100

(n = 443)

Note: The self-employed were not asked this question so are excluded from the table.

secretarial) female employees make generally similar claims about skill to those put forward by their male counterparts. In the case of both sexes the distribution of responses is distinct from that of service-class and working-class respondents – and in precisely the manner that would have been predicted from the Goldthorpe class categories. Class IIIa is situated 'somewhere between' (as it were) classes I and II and classes VI and VII in terms of the extent to which its members see themselves as being subject to processes of technical deskilling. There is no evidence here that routine clerical work is being degraded.

On the other hand, class IIIb women (personal service workers) do stand out in this table, since their pattern of responses is more like that of unskilled manual than of routine nonmanual interviewees. This suggests perhaps that the work situation of shop assistants, receptionists, check-out and wrap operators, and the like, is similar to that of the manual working class – rather than of routine administrative employees. The findings reported in Table 5.12

Table 5.12 *Deskilling (job autonomy) by Goldthorpe class and sex (% by column)*

A – Job allows respondent to design and plan important aspects of the work? (Q55a)

	I	*II*	*IIIa*	Males Class *IIIb*	*V*	*VI*	*VII*
Yes	74	71	41	0	49	22	17
No	26	29	59	100	51	78	83
Total	(73)	(118)	(44)	(2)	(87)	(134)	(181)

	I	*II*	*IIIa*	Females Class *IIIb*	*V*	*VI*	*VII*
Yes	74	58	30	20	39	16	9
No	26	42	70	80	61	84	91
Total	(19)	(97)	(154)	(56)	(18)	(31)	(131)

B – Job requires respondent to design work or he/she does so by own initiative? (Q55b)

	I	*II*	*IIIa*	Males Class *IIIb*	*V*	*VI*	*VII*
Requires	79	77	72	0	49	59	35
own initiative	21	23	28	0	51	41	65
Total	(53)	(83)	(18)	(0)	(41)	(29)	(31)

	I	*II*	*IIIa*	Females Class *IIIb*	*V*	*VI*	*VII*
Requires	64	70	51	36	43	80	50
own initiative	36	30	49	64	57	20	50
Total	(14)	(56)	(45)	(11)	(7)	(5)	(12)

C – Respondent decides day to day tasks? (Q56a)

	I	*II*	*IIIa*	Males Class *IIIb*	*V*	*VI*	*VII*
Yes	90	74	46	50	50	21	18
No	10	26	54	50	50	79	82
Total	(72)	(117)	(44)	(2)	(86)	(132)	(180)

	I	II	IIIa	Females Class IIIb	V	VI	VII
Yes	84	78	45	41	67	10	27
No	16	22	55	59	33	90	73
Total	(19)	(95)	(152)	(56)	(18)	(31)	(131)

D – Respondent decides amount and pace of work? (Q56b)

	I	II	IIIa	Males Class IIIb	V	VI	VII
Yes	95	86	82	0	67	51	48
No	5	14	18	100	33	49	52
Total	(73)	(117)	(44)	(2)	(87)	(133)	(181)

	I	II	IIIa	Females Class IIIb	V	VI	VII
Yes	84	81	73	54	83	48	43
No	16	19	27	46	17	52	57
Total	(19)	(97)	(154)	(56)	(18)	(31)	(129)

E – Respondent decides start and quit times? (Q56c)

	I	II	IIIa	Males Class IIIb	V	VI	VII
Yes	71	50	50	0	25	12	18
No	29	50	50	100	75	88	82
Total	(73)	(119)	(44)	(2)	(87)	(133)	(181)

	I	II	IIIa	Females Class IIIb	V	VI	VII
Yes	74	29	33	4	22	10	16
No	26	71	67	96	78	90	84
Total	(19)	(97)	(153)	(54)	(18)	(31)	(129)

Table 5.12 (*cont.*)

F – Respondent can reduce work pace? (Q56e)

	I	II	IIIa	Males Class IIIb	V	VI	VII
Yes	77	73	77	0	56	56	52
No	23	27	23	100	44	44	48
Total	(73)	(119)	(44)	(2)	(87)	(133)	(181)

	I	II	IIIa	Females Class IIIb	V	VI	VII
Yes	68	53	59	41	50	39	40
No	32	47	41	59	50	61	60
Total	(19)	(97)	(154)	(56)	(18)	(31)	(129)

G – Respondent can initiate new tasks on job? (Q56g)

	I	II	IIIa	Males Class IIIb	V	VI	VII
Yes	81	72	52	100	54	22	33
No	19	28	48	0	46	78	77
Total	(73)	(119)	(44)	(2)	(87)	(132)	(181)

	I	II	IIIa	Females Class IIIb	V	VI	VII
Yes	61	70	44	37	39	26	27
No	39	30	56	63	61	74	73
Total	(18)	(97)	(154)	(56)	(18)	(31)	(131)

tend, on the whole, to confirm that this is indeed the case. Here we shift from considering skill as occupational technique to an investigation of skill as autonomy at work. (These data relate to Questions 55 and 56 in the British interview schedule.) In general terms the same class and sex effects can be observed in this table as in the previous one. Routine clerical employees of both sexes apparently enjoy a 'guaranteed autonomy' that is significantly greater than that experienced by members of the manual working class, since they are more likely to be trusted or encouraged to self-direction in their labour, though somewhat less so than are members of the service class. Sales and service workers, by comparison, are more likely to find themselves in circumstances similar to those of manual employees generally. For example, class III employees as a whole are less likely to claim that they are 'allowed to design and plan important aspects of their own work' than are those in class I and II occupations, though more likely to do so than those in class VI and VII jobs. However, within class III itself, the situation of clerical employees is more like that of the service class, while that of personal service workers is more like the working class, and (of course) the majority of personal service workers are women. Among those claiming to design important aspects of their work, service-class and class IIIa respondents are more likely to report that such self-direction is actually required of them, whereas working-class and class IIIb respondents will more typically state that they have undertaken this on their own initiative. Continuing down the table, we see that routine clerical employees of both sexes are more likely than their working-class counterparts but less likely than those in the service class to decide on the specific day-to-day tasks that will be undertaken, on the amount of work performed and pace at which it is completed, and on the times at which the working day starts and finishes. This situation also prevails with respect to the ability to slow down the pace of work and introduce into it a new task or assignment on one's own initiative. In fact class IIIa men and women offer responses that are very similar to those observed among class V (supervisors of manual workers) – which is, again, consistent with the logic of Goldthorpe's class scheme, since both classes are grouped together as locations 'intermediate' between the working and service classes.

Where the scheme breaks down, however, is in its treatment of sales and service workers. This largely female group is more or less indistinguishable from the working class as conventionally defined. They are, on the whole, significantly less likely to be in positions of trust, positions which give individuals control over their labour such that it is to an appreciable degree self-directing, than are those involved in routine clerical tasks. These personal service workers would seem, instead, to have more in common (in terms of job autonomy at least) with members of the skilled and unskilled working classes. For women in these occupations class III may be a proletarian – rather than an intermediate – class location.[23]

Naturally, a definitive answer to the question of job techniques and job autonomy could be provided only by systematic and direct observation over a prolonged period of time, since (as was suggested above) there are acknowledged problems in establishing the context of our survey data and so determining their reliability. We are not convinced that these questions on autonomy are sufficiently reliable as to provide by themselves an adequate operational criterion for a class categorization. Nor is Erik Wright himself any longer possessed of this opinion. Indeed, it was for this reason above all others that he revised his original class schema, and as our analysis of the 'semi-autonomous employee' category in Chapter 3 has already shown he was well advised to do so. However we are impressed by the extent to which our results all tend to point in the same direction. We can find no evidence that routine clerical employees – male or female – constitute, as some have claimed, a white-collar proletariat. Their occupational tasks have not been deskilled. Nor are these jobs typically degraded since the autonomy profile for this class is quite unlike that found among the manual working classes. Sales and rank-and-file service employment, on the other hand, more often offers proletarian conditions of work to those – mostly women – who undertake it. Few report a deskilling of sales and service tasks as such, but this group of employees are no more likely to experience autonomy and self-direction in their work than are their manual working-class peers, and in that sense their jobs are routinized and degraded.

Finally, bearing in mind the possibility that Goldthorpe's class IIIb may be a proletarian rather than an intermediate-class position, we can look at the career paths of men and women separately in order to determine the likelihood of females being 'proletarianized' over the course of their working lives. We have already observed (Table 5.5) that relative class mobility chances across work careers are the same for both sexes. That is to say, using the original Goldthorpe class categories, there is no evidence that the chances of mobility between class of first job and of present job vary with sex. (The FDS interaction in Table 5.5 is not significant.) However, as was found to be the case with intergenerational mobility, social fluidity tells only a part of the story. Sex segregation in the occupational division of labour has a marked effect on absolute mobility rates. For example, the data in Table 5.7 show that proportionately fewer women than men will be upwardly mobile from working-class and intermediate-class to service-class positions during the course of their working lives, while proportionately fewer men are downwardly mobile from service-class to intermediate-class locations. Indeed, it will be remembered from the discussion in the previous chapter that Heath and Britten (among others) have argued that these dissimilarities in career trajectories indicate differences in the labour market behaviour of women as compared to men, with the former having distinctive commitments to particular kinds of work. More specifically, Heath and Britten want to distinguish sales, personal service, and manual jobs from office and semi-professional employment. The first of these comprises 'the unskilled labour market of casual, low paid work (the secondary labour market as it is often called)', in which 'there are no clear distinctions in recruitment patterns between sales, personal service and manual work', and within which they expect to find 'a high degree of circulation'.[24] While we cannot give detailed consideration to the question of labour markets as such at this stage in our discussion (though we will be pursuing this topic in later publications), it is worth noting the implications of this argument for the question which has thus far formed the leitmotiv of our text, namely that of assigning class membership. Heath and Britten maintain that, unlike men, women move only infrequently between office or semi-professional work, on the one hand, and sales, personal service, or manual work on the other. Consequently, the method of 'joint classification' of households to classes that these authors advocate ('adding' women's employment to that of their partners in order to derive a composite measure of class standing) will not generate artefactually high rates of social mobility, since women rarely move between one type of work and another.

What then are the implications of our data on career mobility, for the debate about proletarianization in general, and the exchange between Heath and Britten and Goldthorpe in particular? These data are presented in Table 5.13 which, in the light of our earlier findings about job autonomy, treats

Table 5.13 *Career paths of men and women by Goldthorpe class (collapsed)*

A – Job 1 to job 2

						Males				
				Job 2						
		P	C	S	W	SE	Total	⇨	same	different
	P	78	5	0	13	4	(55)	⇨	78	22
	C	55	20	0	25	0	(40)	⇨	20	80
Job 1	S	36	14	14	36	0	(14)	⇨	50	50
	W	13	5	1	77	4	(277)	⇨	78	22
	SE	0	0	0	67	33	(3)	⇨	33	67

(n = 389)

						Females				
				Job 2						
		P	C	S	W	SE	Total	⇨	same	different
	P	65	5	10	20	0	(20)	⇨	65	35
	C	20	53	10	16	1	(83)	⇨	53	47
Job 1	S	5	32	22	38	3	(37)	⇨	60	40
	W	10	9	14	67	0	(58)	⇨	81	19
	SE	0	0	0	0	0	(0)	⇨	0	0

(n = 198)

B – Job 2 to job 3

						Males				
				Job 3						
		P	C	S	W	SE	Total	⇨	same	different
	P	77	6	2	12	3	(117)	⇨	77	23
	C	16	52	6	10	16	(31)	⇨	52	48
Job 2	S	20	0	0	80	0	(5)	⇨	80	20
	W	5	2	1	88	4	(299)	⇨	89	11
	SE	25	6	0	56	13	(16)	⇨	13	87

(n = 468)

Table 5.13   (*cont.*)

				Females					
				Job 3					
		P	*C*	*S*	*W*	*SE*	*Total*	⇨	*same*	*different*
	P	62	23	**5**	**8**	**2**	(60)	⇨	*62*	*38*
	C	**23**	60	**3**	**12**	**2**	(97)	⇨	*60*	*40*
Job 2	S	**9**	**30**	25	**34**	**2**	(44)	⇨	*59*	*41*
	W	**3**	**10**	**6**	77	**4**	(121)	⇨	*83*	*17*
	SE	**0**	**0**	**0**	**33**	67	(3)	⇨	*67*	*33*

(n = 325)

C – Job 3 to job 4

				Males					
				Job 4					
		P	*C*	*S*	*W*	*SE*	*Total*	⇨	*same*	*different*
	P	75	**3**	**0**	**13**	**9**	(128)	⇨	*75*	*25*
	C	**44**	37	**0**	**12**	**7**	(41)	⇨	*37*	*63*
Job 3	S	**33**	**0**	0	**67**	**0**	(9)	⇨	*67*	*33*
	W	**9**	**2**	0	77	**12**	(290)	⇨	*77*	*33*
	SE	**22**	**11**	**0**	**37**	30	(27)	⇨	*30*	*70*

(N = 495)

				Females					
				Job 4					
		P	*C*	*S*	*W*	*SE*	*Total*	⇨	*same*	*different*
	P	60	**25**	**5**	**9**	**1**	(65)	⇨	*60*	*40*
	C	**18**	48	**11**	**19**	**4**	(90)	⇨	*48*	*52*
Job 3	S	**0**	**15**	37	**41**	**7**	(27)	⇨	*78*	*22*
	W	**8**	**15**	**7**	63	**7**	(109)	⇨	*70*	*30*
	SE	**11**	**33**	**0**	**45**	11	(9)	⇨	*11*	*89*

(n = 300)

Note: i   P = professional, managerial, higher administrative (Goldthorpe classes I and II;
C = routine clerical and administrative (Goldthorpe class IIIa); S = Sales and service (Goldthorpe class IIIb); W = manual workers and their immediate supervisors (Goldthorpe classes V, VI, VII); SE = self-employed (Goldthorpe class IV).
ii   Job 1 = first full-time job; Job 2 = penultimate job; Job 3 = last job; Job 4 = present job.
iii   Bold figures denote movements across class boundaries.
iv   Same = percentage retained within category; Different = percentage outflow to different class category.

routine administrative and personal service employees (Goldthorpe classes IIIa and IIIb) separately. It must be conceded at the outset that this does not give information about continuous and discrete work-histories. The unit of analysis here is the job shift rather than the individual career. For example, the first part of the table shows the transition between the distribution of first jobs and penultimate jobs for men and women, Part B the transition from penultimate to last jobs, and so on. It is not possible from this information to isolate those individuals who move away from then back to particular class locations. It is also the case that only those among our respondents who have had four or more jobs will appear in the table. The penultimate, last, and present jobs are a true sequence while, for some respondents at least, one or more jobs may have intervened between first job and penultimate job. Nevertheless, an analysis at the level of job shifts is sufficient for our present purposes, since it shows clearly that semi-professional, clerical, and personal service together with manual employment are not the discrete categories that Heath and Britten would have us believe. Moreover, even if personal service occupations (Goldthorpe class IIIb) are considered alongside manual employment as being distinctively working class, there is no evidence to suggest that women as a whole, including those in routine clerical work (the theoretically crucial class IIIa), are subject to some wholesale process of proletarianization.

If we consider first the question of women moving across the different categories, it will be seen that, for example, 35 per cent of those in the service-class (here called professional employment, in line with the terminology adopted by Heath and Britten) shift to clerical or proletarian work between jobs 1 and 2, 46 per cent of those in clerical employment move to professional or proletarian (sales or manual) locations, while 37 per cent of personal service workers and 19 per cent of manual workers switch to clerical or professional jobs. Similar figures pertain to these particular class movements in the transitions between jobs 2 and 3, and 3 and 4. They offer scant support to the claim made by Heath and Britten that semi-professional, office, and sales jobs for women constitute three separate labour markets between which females do not move to any great extent. Of course there are differences between the career trajectories for males and females. These are much as one would expect from our observations elsewhere: proportionately fewer women are upwardly mobile into the service class from either clerical or proletarian occupations; and proportionately fewer service-class men are downwardly mobile into any other form of employment. However, significant numbers of women in routine clerical jobs are upwardly mobile into professional occupations during their working lives, with 20 per cent making this movement between job 1 and job 2, 23 per cent between jobs 2 and 3, and 18 per cent between jobs 3 and 4. And, moreover, around 50 per cent or more of women in clerical employment actually retain their occupational standing in each of the three job-shifts under consideration. In short, women (like men) move between proletarian (manual or sales), office, and professional occupations with a frequency that causes grave problems for the 'joint classification' approach to class analysis. If the class standings of both partners in a nuclear household are to be taken into account then this will generate a profusion of household types, and such high rates of social mobility, that the classes so distinguished are, as Goldthorpe rightly claims, 'collectivities of a quite insubstantial kind'. However, this does not mean that women are as a whole proletarianized, since it is not the case that their relative mobility rates are different from those found among men. Nor are women engaged in routine clerical work in particular significantly more likely than similarly placed men to be downwardly mobile into sales or manual occupations. In our view, therefore, it could be argued that women in routine clerical work were especially vulnerable to 'proletarianization' if, and only if, there was good evidence that the work done by this group was characteristically 'working class' in terms of the 'job autonomy' offered by the associated tasks. But, as we have seen, there is nothing in our data to suggest that it is in fact the case that the work situations of women in routine nonmanual and routine manual employment are uniformly proletarian.

IV

Of course all of these data – about places in the structure and trajectories through it – pertain only to the notion of proletarianization in its objective sense. That is to say, they bear directly on arguments about the relative size of the working class, about the likelihood of specific types of persons being found in working-class locations, and about the actual content of particular sorts of jobs which might or might not be considered legitimately 'proletarian' in terms of the opportunities they offer for self-determination. However, there is also an important subjective dimension to the proletarianization thesis, since its proponents commonly assume that any section of the labour force which is proletarianized by its conditions or functions in employment provides a probable ally for the manual working class in the struggle against capitalist relations of production. Some contributors to the debate have been more deterministic than others in 'reading off' ideological and political predispositions from the demonstration (more commonly theoretical than empirical) of common economic interests.[25] We do not intend to review the details of these arguments here. The complexities of the 'relatively autonomous' relationship between the economic, political, and cultural dimensions of class have been fully explored by others better qualified than we to unravel the labyrinthine theoretical reasoning that this has often involved.[26] Our own contribution to this aspect of the debate about deskilling is considerably more modest; namely, to ask whether or not our data show any actual evidence of the processes putatively at work, that is of 'proletarianized' white-collar workers aligning themselves politically or culturally alongside the manual working class.

For the purposes of this discussion, we can simply suspend judgement as to the realities of the objective conditions of labour which are experienced by routine white-collar employees and others, and look instead at the observed socio-political proclivities of those who are allegedly the most likely candidates for deskilling. For example, is it the case that routine clerical employees identify with the manual working class, or support its political and industrial organizations? Are they as likely to vote Labour or belong to a recognized trade union? As before, we accept that our survey items provide a far from exhaustive coverage of these issues, but such data as we can field point uniformly towards the same conclusion: routine clerical employees are no more proletarian by temperament than they are by class location.

For example, if we consider class self-identification as a simple (though perhaps rather crucial) indicator of what we might call 'cultural' proletarianization, then the evidence is that routine clerical employees will more probably describe themselves as 'middle class' than 'working class', if they are males, and are almost as likely to do so if they are females (see Table 5.14).

Table 5.14 *Self-assigned class by Goldthorpe class and sex (% by column)*

		Males Goldthorpe class							
		I	*II*	*IIIa*	*IIIb*	*IV*	*V*	*VI*	*VII*
Self-assigned	Middle	79	68	59	50	49	27	22	21
class	Working	21	32	41	50	51	73	78	79
	Total	(90)	(117)	(39)	(2)	(79)	(79)	(122)	

		Females Goldthorpe class							
		I	*II*	*IIIa*	*IIIb*	*IV*	*V*	*VI*	*VII*
Self-assigned	Middle	75	59	47	51	58	26	33	30
class	Working	25	41	53	49	42	74	67	70
	Total	(20)	(97)	(144)	(55)	(26)	(19)	(27)	(123)

Whatever their sex they are somewhat less likely to claim middle-class affiliation than are members of the service class – but considerably more likely to do so than those in the working class. Interestingly enough, however, women in personal service work (class IIIb) are, if anything, more likely to see themselves as members of the middle class than are their routine clerical (class IIIa) sisters. (The figures for men can hardly be considered reliable since they are based on the perceptions of but two respondents.) This confirms our suspicion that the work and market situations of these employees deserve closer inspection, since our earlier findings suggest that routine clerical and service employees may be differently placed in these regards, yet they appear here to display similar profiles in terms of their class identities. In 'reconstructing' the Goldthorpe categories, and proposing our own alternatives to them, we shall pay particular attention to these matters. There are no obvious sex differences elsewhere in the table, other than a slight tendency for men in the higher classes to be more inclined to describe themselves as middle class than are similarly placed women, while the opposite is true at the other end of the class structure.

Trade union membership, as one would expect, does vary considerably between the sexes (see Table 5.15). It has long been recognized that women generally are less likely than men to belong to a union and our data confirm that this is the case across all class categories. (The single exception is that of class I women, and this is explained by the fact that proportionately more of these are in public sector and administrative occupations – teaching, social work, local government, and the like – than is the case among class I men, relatively larger numbers of whom are in managerial and proprietorial positions and in the private sector generally.) Again, however, the figures for union membership by class show no evidence of class III men or women being 'proletarianized' in the sense that they are as likely to belong to a trades union organization as are their working-class counterparts. Respondents who were not presently members of a union were then asked if they had ever belonged to one. Once more, class III employees of both sexes were less likely than those in the working class to have belonged at any time to a union, though in the case of women the distinction between those in routine clerical and sales work re-emerges in the data (Table 5.16). Some 42 per cent of female sales and service employees (as compared to 28 per cent of those in routine administration) had formerly been members of a union organization.

Table 5.15 *Current trades union membership by Goldthorpe class and sex (% by column)*

| | | Males Goldthorpe class | | | | | | |
		I	*II*	*IIIa*	*IIIb*	*V*	*VI*	*VII*
Union membership	Member	33	48	48	0	56	61	62
	Non-member	67	52	52	100	44	39	39
	Total	(75)	(119)	(44)	(2)	(87)	(134)	(181)
		Females Goldthorpe class						
		I	*II*	*IIIa*	*IIIb*	*V*	*VI*	*VII*
Union membership	Member	63	46	36	11	37	58	34
	Non-member	37	54	64	89	63	42	66
	Total	(19)	(97)	(154)	(56)	(19)	(31)	(131)

Note: The self-employed were not asked this question and so are excluded from the table.

Table 5.16 *Previous trades union membership (among current non-members) by Goldthorpe class and sex (% by column)*

		Males Goldthorpe class						
		I	*II*	*IIIa*	*IIIb*	*V*	*VI*	*VII*
Previous union	Yes	36	35	39	0	66	50	54
membership	No	64	65	61	100	34	50	46
	Total	(50)	(62)	(23)	(2)	(38)	(52)	(69)
		Females Goldthorpe class						
		I	*II*	*IIIa*	*IIIb*	*V*	*VI*	*VII*
Previous union	Yes	29	35	28	42	42	46	43
membership	No	71	65	72	58	58	54	57
	Total	(7)	(52)	(98)	(50)	(12)	(13)	(87)

Note: The self-employed were not asked this question and so are excluded from the table.

However, from the point of view of those who subscribe to the thesis of proletarianization, a more important index of socio-political inclinations is probably provided by voting behaviour – in the British case by support for the Labour Party. In fact class III males are, as a class category, to be found precisely where the Goldthorpe scheme would place them in the political spectrum: they are significantly less likely to vote Labour, and more likely to vote Conservative, than are men in the working class – but not as much as are men in classes I and II (see Table 5.17). Over 50 per cent of class I and II males in our sample intend to vote Conservative whereas around 20 per cent will vote for the Labour Party. These proportions are more or less reversed among working-class men. Class III men fall neatly between these groups; some 40 per cent stated they would vote Conservative as compared with 30 per cent or so who would support Labour.

Among women, on the other hand, the pattern of class voting seems to be seriously disrupted. In general terms, there is a tendency for those in the higher class categories to vote Conservative while those lower down vote Labour, but this relationship is not nearly as strong as the class/vote association found among men. Even so, the figures do show that class III women are not obviously proletarian by political preference, since their voting profile (especially for those in clerical work) is considerably more like that found among service-class women than among those in the working class. However, we can shed further light on the question of party preferences among females in particular, and confirm that our overall findings about the politics of proletarianization are generally robust, by looking again at the question of cross-class families. It will be remembered, from the previous

Table 5.17 *Vote by Goldthorpe class and sex (% by column)*

		|	||	|||a	|||b	IV	V	VI	VII
					Males Goldthorpe class				
	Con.	53	50	38	50	53	38	18	23
	Lab.	20	53	28	0	17	38	64	53
Voting intention	All.	21	21	26	0	19	19	11	16
	WNV	6	6	8	50	11	5	7	8
	Total	(86)	(116)	(39)	(2)	(80)	(82)	(115)	(156)
					Females Goldthorpe class				
	Con.	50	42	43	36	63	35	27	28
	Lab.	5	24	25	30	4	24	50	48
Voting intention	All.	30	26	20	17	21	29	15	17
	WNV	15	8	12	17	12	12	8	7
	Total	(20)	(92)	(122)	(47)	(24)	(17)	(26)	(110)

Key: Con. = Conservative; Lab. = Labour; All. = Social Democratic, Liberal, Alliance; WNV = Would not vote.

chapter, that Britten and Heath claim voting patterns among these families to be significantly different from those of homogeneous blue-collar couples. This is consistent with Wright's claim that 'class formation will be facilitated to the extent that families are class homogeneous and retarded to the extent that they are heterogeneous'.[27] As far as the issue of proletarianization is concerned, therefore, the crucial question is whether or not couples having one partner in working-class and one in intermediate-class employment are noticeably different from those where both partners are in one class location or the other. Our data suggest that the two familial types are indeed generally different: that the former of the two pairings therefore constitutes a 'cross-class' family; that the socio-political make-up of these cross-class families places them somewhere between homogeneous working-class and inter-mediate-class groupings; and, therefore, that intermediate-class men and women show no signs of socio-political 'proletarianization'.

Tables 5.18 to 5.22 show that there is no obvious correspondence between the working and intermediate classes in terms of class identity, perceptions of distributional justice, or voting behaviour. Each of these tables shows the distribution of each individual's responses by his or her 'family type' across a number of items indicative of class-cultural and political proclivities. The pattern for class-homogeneous groupings (where both partners in a family are in service-class, intermediate-class, or working-class locations) can be compared with that for the various cross-class marriages (service/working,

Table 5.18 *Class identity by family type of respondent (% by row)*

Respondent thinks of self as belonging to a social class		Male respondents			Female respondents		
		Yes	No	(N)	Yes	No	(N)
Family type:	S–S	61	39	(61)	58	42	(52)
Class	I–I	68	32	(57)	58	42	(62)
homogeneous	W–W	60	40	(72)	62	38	(71)
Respondent in	S–I	48	52	(56)	47	53	(17)
higher class	S–W	75	25	(16)	67	33	(12)
than spouse	I–W	74	26	(34)	60	40	(50)
Respondent in	W–S	73	27	(15)	55	45	(11)
lower class	W–I	69	31	(68)	59	41	(32)
than spouse	I–S	50	50	(24)	70	30	(53)
Respondent	U–U	60	40	(15)	75	25	(8)
unemployed or	U–S	100	0	(1)	57	43	(54)
keeping house	U–I	33	67	(3)	62	38	(61)
	U–W	75	25	(12)	54	46	(79)

intermediate/working, and so forth). For the sake of making the comparison complete we have included in the tables those among our respondents who were at the time of interview either unemployed or keeping house. The 'U–U' family pairing is a partnership in which two adults in a household are married (or living as married) and neither is in formal employment. (For the purposes of this analysis we make no distinction between respondents who described themselves as 'unemployed' and those who stated that they were 'keeping house'.) The figures for male and female respondents are given separately in each case. Looking at Table 5.18, for example, we can see that neither men nor women in cross-class families show any signs of being generally 'confused'

Table 5.19 *Self-assigned class by family type of respondent (% by row)*

Self-assigned class		Male respondents			Female respondents		
		Middle	Working	(N)	Middle	Working	(N)
Family type:	S–S	89	11	(56)	79	21	(48)
Class	I–I	44	56	(50)	49	51	(59)
homogeneous	W–W	14	86	(69)	25	75	(64)
Respondent in	S–I	68	32	(50)	44	56	(16)
higher class	S–W	40	60	(15)	25	75	(12)
than spouse	I–W	30	70	(33)	33	67	(49)
Respondent in	W–S	33	67	(15)	54	46	(11)
lower class	W–I	25	75	(64)	37	63	(30)
than spouse	I–S	62	38	(21)	45	55	(51)
Respondent	U–U	8	92	(12)	14	86	(7)
unemployed or	U–S	0	100	(1)	75	25	(48)
keeping house	U–I	33	67	(3)	42	58	(45)
	U–W	0	100	(10)	26	74	(74)

Table 5.20 *Perceptions of class structure by family type of respondent (% by row)*

		Male respondents			Female respondents		
British class structure has		*Changed*	*Stayed same*	*(N)*	*Changed*	*Stayed same*	*(N)*
Family type:	S–S	71	29	(61)	81	19	(52)
Class	I–I	55	45	(56)	57	43	(61)
homogeneous	W–W	37	63	(71)	34	62	(68)
Respondent in	S–I	54	46	(56)	65	35	(17)
higher class	S–W	38	62	(16)	58	42	(12)
than spouse	I–W	44	56	(34)	35	65	(49)
Respondent in	W–S	27	73	(15)	60	40	(10)
lower class	W–I	42	58	(66)	39	61	(31)
than spouse	I–S	76	24	(25)	56	44	(52)
Respondent	U–U	29	71	(14)	14	86	(7)
unemployed or	U–S	100	0	(1)	64	36	(52)
keeping house	U–I	0	100	(2)	52	48	(60)
	U–W	17	83	(12)	41	59	(76)

or 'ambivalent' about their class identity.[28] Asked whether or not they thought of themselves as belonging to any particular social class, individuals in the various cross-class combinations were not significantly less likely to answer in the affirmative than were those in the class-homogeneous categories. Nor is the pattern for male and female respondents appreciably different, except in so far as women in cross-class marriages are generally somewhat less inclined than are similarly placed men to make a claim to class belonging, a fact which tends to suggest that in such households it may be the

Table 5.21 *Perceptions of distributional justice by family type of respondent (% by row)*

		Male respondents			Female respondents		
Distribution of wealth in UK is		*Fair*	*Unfair*	*(N)*	*Fair*	*Unfair*	*(N)*
Family type:	S–S	32	68	(59)	30	70	(50)
Class	I–I	39	61	(57)	37	63	(60)
homogeneous	W–W	24	76	(72)	13	87	(68)
Respondent in	S–I	34	66	(56)	29	71	(17)
higher class	S–W	40	60	(15)	17	83	(12)
than spouse	I–W	36	64	(33)	14	86	(50)
Respondent in	W–S	20	80	(15)	20	80	(10)
lower class	W–I	26	74	(66)	25	75	(32)
than spouse	I–S	20	80	(25)	31	69	(52)
Respondent	U–U	29	71	(14)	0	100	(7)
unemployed or	U–S	0	100	(1)	38	62	(53)
keeping house	U–I	33	67	(3)	31	69	(59)
	U–W	8	92	(12)	13	87	(75)

Table 5.22 *Vote by family type of respondent (% by row)*

Voting intention		Male respondents					Female respondents				
		Con.	Lab.	All.	WNV	(N)	Con.	Lab.	All.	WNV	(N)
Family type:	S–S	36	24	35	5	(55)	47	15	27	11	(45)
Class	I–I	46	29	21	4	(52)	44	16	23	17	(52)
homogeneous	W–W	18	57	15	10	(60)	21	58	18	3	(61)
Respondent in	S–I	62	16	12	10	(50)	38	31	31	0	(16)
higher class	S–W	44	37	19	0	(16)	30	20	40	10	(10)
than spouse	I–W	50	19	22	9	(32)	26	49	15	10	(39)
Respondent in	W–S	14	64	22	0	(14)	27	36	37	0	(11)
lower class	W–I	24	56	15	5	(59)	42	37	8	13	(24)
than spouse	I–S	43	22	35	0	(23)	62	18	18	2	(45)
Respondent	U–U	7	73	7	13	(15)	14	57	0	29	(7)
unemployed or	U–S	0	0	100	0	(1)	56	16	22	6	(50)
keeping house	U–I	0	0	33	67	(3)	44	33	15	7	(54)
	U–W	0	80	10	10	(10)	25	52	14	9	(73)

Key: Con. = Conservative; Lab. = Labour; All. = SDP, Liberal, Alliance; WNV = Would not vote.

occupation of the male that is important for the attribution of class identities.

This suspicion was confirmed when respondents were next asked which particular class they felt they belonged to. There are clear class and sex effects in their responses (see Table 5.19). Cross-class couples, where one partner is in an intermediate-class location, are less likely than class-homogeneous service-class couples or working-class couples to identify themselves as middle class and working class respectively. Moreover, women living in cross-class family units are noticeably more likely to take their class identities from their husbands, than vice versa.

For example, among men in class-homogeneous families, 89 per cent of those in the service class, 44 per cent in the intermediate class, and 14 per cent among the working class described themselves as middle class. (Among similarly placed female interviewees the corresponding percentages were 79, 49, and 25.) If we then look at men in the various cross-class households, the data show that intermediate-class men married to working-class women are more likely than working-class men married to working-class women to place themselves in the middle class, though not as likely to do so as intermediate-class men married to intermediate-class women. These cross-class households are, as one would expect, 'half-way between' class-homogeneous inter-mediate-class and working-class units. Rather significantly, from our point of view, this same effect is observable even where one finds working-class men married to intermediate-class women; 25 per cent of men in such households claim to be middle class, as compared to 14 per cent of men in class homogeneous working-class households.

However, if we compare the pattern of responses for males and females in our sample, some rather interesting differences between the sexes also emerge. The same general class effects are apparent among women placing

133

themselves in class terms as have been observed among men: those in cross-class families show a pattern of responses which places each of the various types 'between' the relevant class-homogeneous categories. But the evidence suggests also that women tend, on the whole, to be more influenced by their husbands' class positions in the matter of describing their own class situations, than are men by the class locations of their wives. Only 44 per cent of service-class women married to intermediate-class husbands will describe themselves as middle class. Among service-class husbands married to intermediate-class wives this figure rises to 68 per cent. Twenty-five per cent of service-class wives married to working-class husbands will make this same claim – whereas 40 per cent of service-class husbands married to working-class wives will do so. Sixty-seven per cent of working-class husbands will claim affiliation to the working class even when they are married to service-class wives. When the sexes are reversed only 46 per cent of women will make such a claim.

Looking through the data on perceptions of class inequality, assessments of distributional justice, and at patterns of voting among the various family types, the same general pattern emerges in each case. Respondents were asked (Question 25) whether it was still the case that a dominant class controlled economic and political affairs, leaving a lower class with no say in such matters, or whether things had changed. They were also asked whether or not they thought the distribution of wealth and income in Britain was fair and (as was noted above) how they intended to vote at the next general election (Questions 15 and 21). In most cases the distributions for cross-class couples are different from those for the class-homogeneous couples who are, as it were, on 'either side' of them. In some cases the differences are not large – but the overall shape is unmistakeable. For example, if we concentrate on the intermediate-class/working-class combinations that are central to the debate about the alleged proletarianization of routine clerical and personal service employment, we can see that intermediate-class and working-class men who marry across this class boundary give a pattern of responses on the attitudinal items which places both groups between those for men in class-homogeneous intermediate-class and working-class households.

This pattern is also evident among comparable women. However, spouse's class has a more marked effect on the assessment of class and income inequalities when the spouse is a man, with the result that men in cross-class marriages tend to give responses which are more like those among class-homogeneous families than are those for women in cross-class as opposed to class-homogeneous families. For example, intermediate-class women married to working-class men are almost as likely to claim that the distribution of wealth is unfair as are working-class women married to working-class men, whereas working-class women married to intermediate-class men are noticeably less likely to do so. Conversely, the judgements of men in the corresponding situations do not seem to be susceptible to the class of their partners to nearly the same degree, with intermediate-class and working-class men tending towards their class-homogeneous counterparts rather than their cross-class wives in the pattern of their assessments.

Putting these observations together we can therefore conclude that intermediate-class women (routine clerical and service workers) are not uniformly proletarianized. Even those families in which such women are themselves married to working-class men tend to show a different pattern of responses to items measuring important socio-political characteristics. Moreover, and rather crucially, to the extent that these women do show evidence of proletarianization in their ideological make-up, their judgements would seem to be related to the class position of their husbands, rather than of their own employment. This means that, as far as the arguments about socio-political proletarianization are concerned, intermediate-class women are not all of a piece: they will tend towards those socio-political attributes that are characteristic of the classes of their husbands. Intermediate-class women married to service-class men are much more likely than those married to working-class men to claim middle-class identities, to assert that the distribution of wealth in Britain is fair, and to judge the class structure as having changed in the direction of equality. There is no evidence here that women in routine clerical and sales jobs are subject to some universal process of socio-political proletarianization.

Finally, returning to the question of voting intentions, we can see that the data in Table 5.22 substantiate this general claim. Men and women in class-homogeneous service-class families are most likely to vote Conservative, while those in class-homogeneous working-class families are most likely to vote Labour. However, the distribution of votes by party among intermediate-class women married to service-class men is rather similar to that among service-class women married to service-class men, while among intermediate-class women married to working-class men the distribution is more like that for women in homogeneous working-class families. In other words, inter-mediate-class women show no signs of being uniformly proletarianized where voting behaviour is concerned, since they tend to vote Conservative or Labour according to whether or not their husbands are found in service-class or working-class occupations. This 'class effect of husbands' can also be seen in the voting intentions of service-class and working-class wives. The impact of wives' employment on husbands' votes is, however, much less pronounced. For example, more than 55 per cent of cohabiting working-class men will vote Labour irrespective of the class position of their partners, while the proportion of intermediate-class men voting for the Conservative and Labour Parties does not vary much between those married to service-class wives, or to working-class wives, and those in class-homogeneous family groupings. (Among men in I–I families, 46 per cent vote Conservative and 29 per cent Labour, as compared with 43 and 22 per cent, and 50 and 19 per cent, for those in I–S and I–W families respectively.)

Of course, in a table as complicated as this it can sometimes be difficult to see the wood for the trees, which is why these data were earlier modelled in a loglinear analysis of voting intentions and social class among employed husbands and wives (see Table 4.4 above). It is worth restating the conclusion that was reached on the basis of that analysis; namely, that the relationship between a wife's class and her own vote is much less important than that between her vote and the class of her husband, whereas in considering the votes of husbands this situation is reversed. On that occasion these data were taken as evidence that political partisanship runs between rather than through families. Here, we can draw an additional though complementary conclusion, which is that they offer substantial proof that the thesis of socio-political proletarianization among women employed in routine clerical and sales work is mistaken. It is not the putatively deskilled nature of this work which best explains the voting intentions of those women who undertake it: it is, rather, the class situation of their husbands. Or, more generally, we can say that our results contain no evidence to support the thesis that routine clerical and sales workers are proletarian by temperament.[29]

V

What then remains of the thesis that the class structure of modern Britain is subject to a process of systematic proletarianization? We can find no evidence that the proportion of working-class locations in the structure is expanding; indeed, on the contrary, our data suggest that the numbers employed in specialized and routine nonmanual activities continue to grow at the expense of 'traditional' (manual) working-class occupations. There is nothing in our data to suggest that some particular sections of the labour force are nevertheless proletarianized by virtue of having greatly reduced mobility chances relative to other sections. The relative mobility regimes for the sexes and for particular cohorts are the same – these examples being highlighted since the 'post-affluence' work-force in general, and women in particular, are the two groups to which this argument has most commonly (and seemingly erroneously) been applied. Moreover, routine clerical jobs seem not to have been 'deskilled' to an extent that is typical of manual employment, irrespective of whether these jobs are held by men or women. (However, we did find some evidence to suggest that women engaged in rank-and-file service employment may perform routinized tasks that render their work situations more or less indistinguishable from those typical of manual employees, and we intend to pursue this matter further in subsequent publications.) Finally, having examined some of the principal socio-political characteristics of different groups of workers, we are led to conclude that intermediate-class employees are different from their working-class peers. Families having one partner in each class can legitimately be described as cross-class. Such families display a pattern of socio-political characteristics that locates them firmly between class-homogeneous intermediate-class and working-class types – they are not uniformly 'proletarianized'.

So, to return to the initial claim made by Britten and Heath and endorsed by Erik Wright, cross-class families are indeed characteristically different from their homogeneous blue-collar and white-collar counterparts. It seems generally to be the case, as Wright maintains, that such heterogeneity inhibits the development of a clear-cut 'class consciousness'. Ironically, however, this finding actually undermines Wright's own arguments about proletarianization, since the persistent differences between the family types suggest that the class situation of intermediate-class respondents remains distinct from that of their working-class spouses. The former have not been proletarianized by their conditions of employment. Where, as in the case of voting, cross-class families less obviously form a distinct grouping within the class structure, the data still cannot be shackled to the proletarianization cause, since the most obvious subjects of the process (intermediate-class women) tend to display the ideological characteristics appropriate to their husbands' rather than their own class location. The 'proletarianization' of some intermediate-class women (that is, those married to workers, and who tend to vote Labour) is therefore counterbalanced by the 'embourgeoisement' of others (intermediate-class women married to service-class husbands and voting Conservative). It would seem to be the case, therefore, that John Goldthorpe's conclusions about proletarianization more accurately portray the structure of class processes, as this is reflected in our data at least, than do those arrived at by Erik Wright.

Placing these findings alongside those reported in earlier chapters, we can now draw some fairly firm conclusions about the strengths and weaknesses of class analysis in general, and the class schemata of Goldthorpe and Wright in particular. Our first observation is that class still matters – in a demographic sense at least. As a measure of its importance we would cite the odds ratios calculated for the transitions from origins to destinations; namely, that among men for example, the chances of someone from service-class origins securing service-class rather than working-class employment for himself are more than seven times greater than those for someone arriving at service-class employment rather than working-class employment from a working-class background. Among corresponding women the chances are thirteen times greater. Of course this does not mean that the British class structure is entirely 'closed' to social mobility. Our basic mobility data suggest that perhaps as many as one-third of those presently in the service class have arrived there from working-class origins. However, these data also show that this upward mobility is not the result of changes in relative mobility rates, since these are unaltered between successive cohorts entering formal employment. There have been no changes in social 'fluidity' – that is, in the direction of greater equality of opportunity – during the period covered by our mobility tables. It should be noted that this straddles the so-called years of affluence, the 1950s and 1960s, as well as the more recent recessionary 1970s and 1980s. The implication is obvious. Such upward mobility as has existed is the result of changes in the *shape* (rather than the *openness*) of the class structure. The growth of the service class and contraction of the working class reflects the transformation in the occupational division of labour in Britain since the war – the decline of manufacturing and manual labouring together with the expansion of the services sector and of professional, administrative, and managerial jobs – it does not signify a reduction in the

137

inequalities of class life-chances. More 'room at the top' has not been accompanied by greater equality in the opportunities offered to get there. Economic development has not brought a more egalitarian society; nor, for that matter, has economic recession. The classes are not now 'more equal in their misery' since there are no signs that the most privileged groups are somehow less able than before to use their resources to preserve their advantages and avoid downward mobility. In the light of these findings we would wholeheartedly endorse John Goldthorpe's radical (though it seems to us incontrovertible) conclusion that the post-war project of creating in Britain a more open society, through economic expansion, educational reform, and egalitarian social policies, has signally failed to secure its objective.

Our second observation is that women are generally disadvantaged when compared to men. This finding will probably surprise no-one. We have shown, for example, that the objective mobility opportunities available to women are different from those available to men. Again, however, this reflects a feature of the occupational division of labour – in this case the sex segmentation of jobs – and is not indicative of differential class fluidity between men and women. Women are no less divided by class differences than are men. (It is not the case, for example, that they are uniformly proletarianized.) However, common social fluidity occurs in the context of different male and female occupational class structures, with women tending to be underrepresented in the more privileged class locations and over-represented among those with fewer advantages. Moreover, the market situation and work situation of women within each of the Goldthorpe classes is typically inferior to that of class-comparable men, despite the fact that women at almost all levels in the structure are proportionately at least as well qualified as are men. The class structure is obviously 'gendered'.

Class analysts need to take this into account in theorizing and operationalizing their various notions of social class. Here we disagree with John Goldthorpe, because we find an inconsistency in his position. On the one hand, he argues that a cohort analysis of trends in social mobility confirms unchanging relative mobility rates, but significant changes in absolute rates. That is, the structure is changing, but the extent to which it is open is not. From this finding he draws a number of interesting conclusions about the nature of class inequality in Britain over the years, the effectiveness or otherwise of egalitarian social policies, and the accuracy and inaccuracy with which liberal and Marxist theorists have predicted the arrival of 'post-industrial' and 'late capitalist' societies. (His participation in the debate about proletarianization is one example of this. The expansion of the service class, and of nonmanual work generally, constitutes good evidence against certain Marxist theories of the development of capitalism.) Note that both absolute and relative rates are taken on board in the argument against deskilling. Elsewhere, on the other hand, finding that an analysis of social mobility by sex also confirms unchanging (common) relative rates though obviously different absolute rates, Goldthorpe concludes that common social fluidity constitutes a sufficient defence of the 'conventional' approach to class analysis. In other words, the absolute differences between the sexes are deemed to be largely irrelevant to the interests of the class analyst, and common relative rates are used in defence of the strategy of sampling only the (invariably male) 'head of household'.

We believe that these two positions cannot easily be reconciled. Most of what Goldthorpe finds interesting about social mobility over the years lies in the observed differences (or in the relationship) between absolute and relative rates. Yet, in looking at mobility between the sexes, he seems prepared to argue that the obvious differences in absolute rates are inconsequential from the point of view of 'class analysis' since relative rates for men and women are the same. The relationship between relative and absolute mobility, which constitutes the centre of attention in studying males, is simply defined as external to the concerns of class analysis when Goldthorpe turns his attention to look at the mobility experiences of females. Or, to put the matter somewhat differently, changes in the occupational division of labour over time are crucial to the explanation of patterns of class mobility among men, yet differences in the occupational division of labour between the sexes are irrelevant to the explanation of class mobility among women. We are not convinced that both arguments can be correct. Consequently, therefore, in our own study we have sampled both men and women and then allocated each to social classes by reference to their own employment.

Finally, however, we have been led again and again to the conclusion that, whatever its weaknesses in relation to the class allocation of women, the Goldthorpe class scheme is generally more robust than either of the Marxist alternatives offered by our colleague Erik Wright. There are several points we would wish to make here. One is that the Wright classifications are not generally reliable in terms of what they themselves purport to be measuring. There are too many instances of managers who are not really managers, supervisors who are not really supervisors, and workers who are not really workers. The categories are extremely heterogeneous – even in their own terms. Moreover, such is the complexity of their construction that it is highly unlikely one could devise a research instrument to facilitate the study of processual aspects of class, since informants will simply be unable to provide reliable and detailed information about their previous experiences to the extent required by Wright's class algorithm. The important point here is that Wright himself recognizes class processes as central to the concerns and explanations of class analysis – but he has constructed a set of class categories which by their very nature systematically obstruct the study of career and intergenerational mobility. On practical grounds alone his schemes are of doubtful value. Nor is it clear that Wright's class algorithms generate meaningful categories – irrespective of the reliability with which they operationalize the theory. We have seen, for example, that they generate maps of the class structure which are highly implausible. These tend to suggest erroneous conclusions about processes such as social mobility itself. Thus, for example, Wright's frameworks would lead one to believe that the

139

process of proletarianization was well established in the British class structure – when, in truth, there is scant evidence to support this thesis.

So, in considering the twin objectives that we set ourselves at the outset of our study, we would argue, first, that British society has been structured by social class to an important degree throughout the post-war period; and, second, that there are good grounds for studying the nature of class processes from a neo-Weberian rather than a neo-Marxist perspective. This is not to suggest that inequality in Britain can be reduced to class differences. It would be foolish to deny the effects of, for example, race and locality. Rather, it is simply to claim that, despite the much vaunted restructuring of capital and labour occasioned by the recent economic recession, distributional inequalities are still in large measure inequalities of social class. Of course the demographic importance of class – its significance for the differential structuring of life-chances – provides few if any clues as to its importance in the socio-political sphere. Class can structure people's lives in the manner and to the extent we have observed, yet they themselves might attach no particular importance to this, nor even be aware that class operates to this effect. Is it the case, therefore, as a number of recent commentators have argued, that class is of comparatively little importance in structuring social and political life in this country? Have class awareness and class politics been replaced by new forms of sectionalism: by the privatism of individuals and families, the fatalistic acceptance of social inequality, and by a collective instrumentalism which reflects, for example, sectoral production and consumption cleavages rather than the development of a 'class consciousness'? In the following chapters it is these questions about the nature of social identities and social consciousness that are to the fore.

Notes

1 Wright and Singelmann (1982: 198).
2 See Wright (1985: 195, 285).
3 Goldthorpe and Payne (1986a: 19).
4 See, for example, Crompton and Jones (1984).
5 Crompton (1979), Wright (1985), Edwards (1979).
6 For overviews of the literature arising out of the 'labour process debate' see Thompson (1983), who writes from a viewpoint that is sympathetic to the notion of proletarianization, and the more sceptical account in Salaman (1986). In the matter of the interpretation of official statistics, Goldthorpe seems for the moment to have the better of the argument, because the most recent publication by Joachim Singelmann (a leading exponent of shift-share analysis and originally an enthusiast with Wright on behalf of the proletarianization thesis) suggests that the evidence does indeed run contrary to Wright's conclusions. That is, the increase in professionals, managers and administrators is not simply the consequence of a growth in the service sector (within which these sorts of occupations have been relatively more numerous) and decline in the manufacturing sector (in which manual occupations are more typical), since such upgrading persists when these inter-industry shifts are allowed for. They are therefore the result, not of fairly transient industry shift effects, but of class composition shifts – the actual occupational mix occurring at the level of production units. (Compare Singelmann and Browning, 1980; Wright and Singelmann, 1982; and Singelmann and Tienda, 1985.) For a detailed critique of Braverman, and an interpretation of American census materials that supports Goldthorpe's general position by charting a growth in 'skilled' occupations since the Second World War, see Penn (1982; 1986).

7 See Wright (1985; 194, 285), and Tables 3.1 and 2.3 above.
8 See Stanworth (1984: 164), Heath (1981: 123–8).
9 See Goldthorpe and Payne (1986b).
10 On the distinction between absolute and relative mobility in general, and the techniques of odds ratios and loglinear modelling in this particular context, see Goldthorpe (1980: 68–93) and Heath (1981: 255–69). For an introduction to the principles behind the loglinear techniques used in the present volume see Upton (1978).
11 Our own common social fluidity model is not identical in substance to that fitted by Goldthorpe, though it is formally equivalent in hypothesizing that there is common social fluidity across the male and female portions of the labour force. He measures intergenerational mobility in the single transition from class of origin to class of destination, whereas we break this down into separate transitions from class of origin to class on first entry into employment, and class on first entry to present class.
12 For example, the data for the basic transition from class of origin to present class (Table 4.8) yield the following results, where (as before) O = class of origin, D = present class, and S = sex.

Model	df	y^2	Difference			y^2/df	p
1 [OD][OS][DS]	36	39.6	⇒ ODS			1.1	> 0.30
2 [OD][DS]	42	44.0	⇒ OS	6	4.4	0.7	> 0.60
3 [DS][OS]	72	220.6	⇒ OD	36	180.9	5.0	< 0.0005
4 [OD][OS]	42	271.9	⇒ DS	6	232.3	38.7	< 0.0005

Again, both class of origin and sex have a significant association with class of destination (of these sex is the more important), but the association between class of origin and class of destination does not itself vary with sex (the ODS interaction is insignificant).
13 Goldthorpe and Payne (1986b: 542).
14 Goldthorpe and Payne (1986b: 548–9).
15 Goldthorpe and Payne (1986b: 543).
16 Goldthorpe (1980: 288).
17 Goldthorpe (1980: 68).
18 See, for example, Goldthorpe (1980), Goldthorpe and Payne (1986a), Erikson et al. (1982).
19 It should be noted that this finding is consistent with Goldthorpe's own and that his mobility data go back as far as the 1920s. The year 1973 is significant as that in which a renewal of the Arab–Israeli conflict led to a dramatic increase in the price of oil and an international economic crisis that marked the end – in Britain at least – of the post-war years of industrial expansion and relative affluence.
20 See, for example, the papers in Wood (1982).
21 This is, in fact, probably also the most common interpretation of 'deskilling' encountered throughout the labour process debate as a whole. (See, for example, Blackburn and Mann, 1979: 291–2, and Crompton and Jones, 1984: 57–60).
22 Braverman (1974: 118). On this point generally see Braverman (1974; 112–20) and Wright (1979: 64–7).
23 This reclassification raises broader issues about the construction of the Goldthorpe schema as a whole, and also suggests that it might profitably be reworked somewhat, particularly to take account of differences between the market situations and work situations of the sexes. We intend to pursue this issue fully in a subsequent publication, but for some important initial clarification, see the Coda to this volume (pp. 305–9).
24 Heath and Britten (1984: 482). On this point generally compare Heath and Britten (1984: 481–6) and Goldthorpe (1984a: 496–7).
25 See, for example, the range of positions represented in the papers collected in Hunt (1977).
26 See, as examples, Parkin (1979) and Lockwood (1981).
27 Heath and Britten (1984: 475), Wright (1985: 225).
28 This is at odds with the claim made by McRae (1986: 191–2, 197) that those in cross-class marriages will be significantly more likely than those in class-homogeneous marriages to show signs of confusion about their self-placement in the class structure.
29 In view of our earlier findings it would obviously have been desirable, in analysing cross-class marriages generally, to have separated out routine clerical employees from those in sales and service occupations. Unfortunately, because of the relatively small numbers in our sample, it

141

was not possible to distinguish class IIIa women from their class IIIb sisters reliably throughout the analysis. However, we did calculate the voting and class self-placement figures to allow for this distinction, and although the numbers mean that we cannot place much weight on the findings, there is nothing in them to suggest that women in either group are evidently proletarian by socio-political inclination. Females in both clerical and sales employment tend to vote according to their husbands', rather than their own class location, and both groups are similarly affected by the class of their spouses when assigning themselves to particular social classes.

6 The moral order of a capitalist society

It is appropriate, against the background of criticism that has recently been directed towards class analysis, to report first on our findings about social identity in general and class awareness in particular. We find that class is still the most common source of social identity and retains its salience as such. It is true that the collectivism of our respondents can most appropriately be characterized as instrumental. To that extent it reflects the pursuit of self-interest rather than collective improvement. However, our data also suggest that such instrumentalism is an entirely pragmatic response to a distributional order and distributional mechanisms that are perceived to be unjust, but are accepted as largely unalterable facts of life. This general perspective may be summarized as one of 'realism', 'resignation', 'cynicism', or – as we would prefer to describe it – 'informed fatalism'.[1] Its origins lie in the evaluative rather than the cognitive sphere. People are often aware of alternatives but they are, on the whole, resigned to the fact that they can do little or nothing to help achieve these. Our findings suggest, then, that contemporary British society lacks a moral order, and that its cohesion is rooted more in resignation and routine than consensus and approval.

I

There is no obvious lack of class awareness among the population of modern Britain as a whole. Sixty per cent of our sample claimed that they thought of themselves as belonging to one particular social class and well over 90 per cent could place themselves in a specific class category (see Table 6.1). The proportions who refused to do so, or stated that they did not know to which class they belonged, were very small.[2] Almost three-quarters (73 per cent) of the respondents felt class to be an inevitable feature of modern society; 52 per cent thought that there were *important* issues causing conflict between social classes (only 37 per cent actually disagreed with this); and, perhaps most strikingly of all, half of the sample agreed with a question (Question 25a) which was formulated so as to invite respondents to disagree with the judgement that today, as in the past, there is a dominant class which largely controls the economic and political system, and a lower class which has no control over economic and political affairs (48 per cent thought things had changed and 2 per cent were unsure). Note that the question explicitly posits the extreme case of *no* control over public affairs by the lower class – since its

Table 6.1 *Self-assigned class*

Class	N	%	Cumulative adjusted %
Upper	4	0.2	
Upper middle	53	3.0	
Middle	419	23.7	
Lower middle	208	11.8	42 Middle
Upper working	197	11.1	
Working	665	37.6	
Lower working	74	4.2	58 Working
(Refused)	50	2.8	
(Don't know)	100	5.6	
Total	1770	100.0	100

purpose is to invite respondents to think about the ways in which the class structure *has* changed. Yet 50 per cent of respondents endorsed the picture of gross class inequalities. Those who contested it did so largely in reference to the extension of citizenship rights (Table 6.2). Sixty per cent of respondents disagreeing (43 per cent of responses) mentioned political citizenship, 19 per cent mentioned industrial citizenship, and 4 per cent citizenship in the form of the welfare state. Far fewer thought that class processes themselves had changed significantly; among those who thought the class structure had changed, only one-quarter justified this view on the grounds that the distribution of wealth had become more equal, or living standards more

Table 6.2 *Ways in which class processes have changed*

Change	N	% of responses	% of cases
Expansion of democracy	493	42.6	59.6
Distribution of wealth is fairer	208	18.0	25.2
Trades unions give working people a say	153	13.2	18.5
Social mobility more common	123	10.6	14.9
Expansion of the welfare state	36	3.1	4.4
Trades unions run the country	35	3.0	4.2
Pay in general has risen	13	1.1	1.6
Other	95	8.2	11.5
Total	1156	100.0	139.8

(Valid cases = 827)

Note: In reading this and all similar subsequent tables which report the figures for multiple-response items, it should be noted that the stated N (here 1156) relates to responses, and not respondents or cases (who actually number, in this instance, 827). Thus, to take the top line of the above table as an example, 'expansion of democracy' was mentioned 493 times. This figure constitutes 42.6 per cent of all responses. However, since some people nominated several items in reply to this question, 'expansion of democracy' was in fact mentioned by 59.6 per cent of those who answered it.

similar, while 15 per cent were prepared to argue that social mobility between classes was more common now than in the past. This is consistent with our finding elsewhere that, among those who were asked the question, 74 per cent thought that it was hard for a person to go from one social class to another with only 19 per cent prepared to state that this was easy.[3]

This evidence suggests that social identities are widely and easily constructed in class terms. They may also be defined according to other reference groups – this remains to be seen – but there would seem to be no grounds for claiming (as we originally envisaged) that social class is entirely opaque to the majority of individuals and therefore unavailable as a source of social identity. In conceptualizing who 'we' are a great many people have access to a world-view structured in social class terms.

Of course people's perceptions of what it is that constitutes social class may be quite divergent. For this reason we asked our respondents to describe the sorts of individuals whom they thought of as upper class, middle class, and working class. Their answers drew upon a great many criteria and our coding frame for these questions therefore runs to seventy categories. However it proved possible to devise generic codes for the data without doing an injustice to their detail. These are shown in Table 6.3, together with the distribution of the responses. (Note that the illustrations under each generic code are

Table 6.3 *Popular perceptions of social class*

				Characteristics of the upper, middle, and working classes (What sort of person do you think of as . . . class?)					
		Upper			Middle			Working	
Criterion	N	% Responses	% Cases	N	% Responses	% Cases	N	% Responses	% Cases
Market	470	14.0	27.2	380	12.3	22.4	601	19.8	34.9
Income	741	22.1	43.0	425	13.7	25.1	369	12.2	21.4
Status	1113	33.3	64.5	759	24.6	44.8	558	18.4	32.4
Education	216	6.5	12.5	89	2.9	5.3	56	1.8	3.2
Occupation	618	18.5	35.8	1257	40.7	74.2	1212	39.9	70.3
Political	131	3.9	7.6	24	0.8	1.4	7	0.2	0.4
Denied	42	1.3	2.4	101	3.3	6.0	170	5.6	9.9
Other	15	0.4	0.9	56	1.8	1.3	62	2.0	3.6
Total	3346	100.0	194.0	3091	100.0	182.6	3035	100.0	176.0
		(Valid cases = 1725)			(Valid cases = 1693)			(Valid cases = 1724)	

Key to criteria:

Market: class as relationship to the market or system of production (e.g. owners of land, the self-employed, those who have to work for a living).

Income: class as level of income (e.g. the very rich, the low paid, those dependent on welfare benefits).

Status: class as status (e.g. those with a particular life-style, the aristocracy, home-owners, respectable people).

Education: class as educational experience (e.g. public school educated, those with higher education, the uneducated).

Occupation: class as occupation or nature of employment (e.g. those working in particular industries or jobs, professionals, skilled workers).

Political: class as a political phenomenon (e.g. those voting for a particular party, politicians).

Denied: denial of social class (e.g. upper class no longer exists, everyone is middle class now, no difference between the middle and working classes).

examples only and do not exhaust the descriptions given to our coders.) There are several interesting features about this table. The largest overall category of responses consists of those who view class as a function of occupation or employment: classes are described as being 'professional people', 'office workers', 'the unemployed' or similar. Most commonly, the working class are identified as 'manual workers' or 'unskilled workers' (by 34 per cent and 15 per cent of individuals respectively), whereas the middle class are more frequently thought of as 'professional people' (by 35 per cent of respondents), 'managers' (11 per cent), 'business people' (8 per cent), and 'white-collar workers' generally (7 per cent). However, while occupational conceptions of the middle class and working class are shared by 74 per cent and 70 per cent of respondents respectively, only 36 per cent of our sample thought of the upper class in this way. In fact, the majority (65 per cent) conceived of the upper class in terms of social status; that is, as those having some sort of hereditary title – 'the aristocracy' – or living a 'hunting, fishing, and country house' (upper-class) life-style. A further 12 per cent described this class as being 'well educated' or, more specifically, as having gone through the public school system.

As one would expect, income is also a commonly utilized criterion of class, as indeed is relationship to the market or production system, in the sense that the upper and middle classes are often described as 'landowners' or 'owners of businesses' and the working class as those who 'have to work for wages' or who 'work for someone else'. For example, the upper class are pictured as having a private income (by 10 per cent of our sample), as landowners (by a further 9 per cent), and as business owners (by 7 per cent); the middle class are characterized as having 'good incomes' or 'high salaries' by 19 per cent of the sample and as owners of small businesses (or as self-employed) by another 8 per cent; whereas the working class are 'the workers' (mentioned by 28 per cent of respondents) and those on low incomes generally (16 per cent of respondents). However, the proportion of responses that conceptualized class as in any way a political phenomenon was tiny, with fewer than 8 per cent of those whom we interviewed identifying 'politicians' as being upper class. (The middle class and working class were described in political terms even less frequently.) On the other hand, fully one-quarter of all responses were rooted in the sphere of social status, both in its conventional and legal senses. Classes were described as groups sharing a particular life-style (such as 'prestigious' or 'rough') or as possessing hereditary titles (in the case of the upper class). Only 12 per cent of our sample associated home-ownership with the middle class and fewer still, a mere 8 per cent, characterized the working class as council tenants. A bare 3 per cent of responses denied the existence of classes, either outright, or implicitly in the form of the claim that 'we are all middle class (or working class) now'.

Finally, as the statistics for the distribution of cases suggest, most of our respondents in fact offered descriptions of the various classes which contained more than one item. This, together with the variation in the way that the three classes are described, offers an early clue that class is widely perceived to be a multifaceted or complex phenomenon – a point to which we shall return in due course.

Following upon our asking respondents to describe the characteristics of classes, we then attempted to tap their perceptions of the mechanisms by which classes were constituted; the 'causes', as it were, of class structure. The answers obtained reflect the extent to which this structure is seen as ubiquitous and largely unchanging (Table 6.4). No less than three-quarters of our sample stated that people were born into particular class groupings. Of course there is an obvious problem of interpretation here since allocation to classes 'by birth' could mean different things to different people. A good many interviewees may have had materialistic or even status factors in mind when answering in this way. In any event, far fewer respondents subscribed to either a meritocratic view of class processes (emphasizing hard work or education), or a crudely materialistic one, perceiving the determinants of class to be entirely reducible to income or possessions. We have already observed the consequences of these views of class processes and class characteristics for perceptions of social mobility: the great majority of people deem mobility between classes to be hard rather than easy. Class is more commonly taken to be an ascribed rather than an achieved characteristic.

It would seem, then, that people's perceptions of social class are sufficiently concrete to enable them to see this as a possible source of social identity. Classes are viewed largely as occupational, income or status groupings, or as categories having a specific relationship to the market or to production; people are born into these though to a lesser extent classes can also reflect meritocratic or material standing; and the class structure itself remains an obvious feature of life in late twentieth-century Britain.

Table 6.4 *Factors perceived as determining class membership*

Factor	N	% of responses	% of cases
Birth	1280	44.2	76.1
Hard work	403	13.9	24.0
Education	377	13.0	22.4
Job or work position	261	9.0	15.5
Income or standard of living	260	9.0	15.5
Status	66	2.3	3.9
Innate ability	57	2.0	3.4
Possessions	53	1.8	3.2
Luck	47	1.6	2.8
Personal qualities	35	1.2	2.1
Marriage	17	0.6	1.0
Other	42	1.4	2.5
Total	2898	100.0	172.4

(Valid cases = 1681)

II

One objection to these findings might be that they pertain only to cognition of class processes. In other words, while they suggest an awareness of or sensitivity to social class, they do not indicate the salience of class in the everyday lives of our respondents. People may understand social class but nevertheless ignore it in conducting their routine affairs.

This is a difficult criticism to meet as survey research is not the most appropriate vehicle for investigating the importance of different frames of reference in everyday life. Nevertheless, certain of our findings do bear more or less directly on this matter, and provide some guidance as to the relative salience of class and similar shared identities. Most obviously we asked respondents to suggest any other groups that they might identify with. Seventy-nine per cent could think of no such grouping. Of the 331 individuals (or 19 per cent) who did say they identified with some other group (2 per cent did not know), 64 per cent (209) claimed primary identification with the 'other' grouping, 6 per cent with their particular social class, 12 per cent with both equally, and 18 per cent stated that they did not normally think of themselves as members of either. Table 6.5 shows the reference groups that were nominated as sources of social identity other than that available from a sense of class belonging. The random sampling techniques we employed generated, as they should have, an overwhelmingly white group of respondents, but seventy-five individuals selected were black, brown or yellow-skinned, though only about half of these claimed an ethnic or racial identification. A perhaps surprisingly small number of women (only twenty in all) claimed a

Table 6.5 *Sources of social identity other than class*

Source	N	% of responses	% of cases
Business or professional group	85	23.9	26.8
Religious group	66	18.5	20.8
Ethnicity or race	41	11.5	12.9
Life-style grouping	24	6.7	7.6
Pressure group	22	6.2	6.9
Political party	20	5.6	6.3
Gender	20	5.6	6.3
Unemployment	16	4.5	5.0
Age group	14	3.9	4.4
The lower paid	13	3.7	4.1
Respectability	7	2.0	2.2
Trades unionism	5	1.4	1.6
The self-made	4	1.1	1.3
Others	19	5.3	6.0
Total	356	100.0	112.3

(Valid cases = 317)

feminine or feminist identity. Rather more respondents identified with a particular religious or occupational grouping.

But questioning people directly about their reference groups is a fairly blunt strategy for unearthing the subtleties of social identities. We therefore approached this problem more obliquely by exploring the nature of the boundaries between 'us' and 'them' that were erected by respondents at various points in the interview. For example, voters were asked what other kinds of people they thought voted for their chosen party, and *for the same reasons as themselves*. Again the many answers that were offered can be generically coded and these are shown in Table 6.6. It will be seen that 19 per cent of responses (and about a third of all respondents) mentioned particular social classes while 17 per cent or so were status related. The most widely utilized criteria, constituting some 30 per cent of the total responses to this question, were those pertaining to employment or work. Looking at the answers in more detail, we see that personal qualities ('respectable people', 'hard working people') and age groups ('the young', 'old people') are the most commonly cited referents among status-based answers, while those who nominated work groups as likely to vote for the same reasons as themselves often gave answers that were surrogates for social class itself (such as 'the working man' or 'business owners'). Fewer than 13 per cent of the work-oriented responses referred to others working in a particular industry or sector of the economy ('steel workers', 'public sector employees', or whatever).

These data seem to suggest two things. First, social class is by far the most common, and seemingly the most salient frame of reference employed in the construction of social identities. Moreover, and as a corollary of this, there is little initial evidence to suggest that sectoral cleavages ('we the employees of multinationals', 'we the public sector workers') are much to the fore in constructing such identities; nor, for that matter, are gender, feelings of locale or community, or consumption differences such as those associated with household tenure. This finding is reinforced by data on work-centred identities collected late in our interviews. Having deliberately let respondents 'go cold' on the subject of work we rather abruptly invited them, as a parting shot, to describe 'what they did for a living'. Their verbatim answers were coded according to the type of work-centred identities that they ascribed to themselves in this, as it were, unprompted or spontaneous manner. As will be seen from Table 6.7, over 50 per cent of the sample expressed a clear occupational identification, with another 7 per cent claiming a weak occupational referent. Company and industrial identities constituted just over 8 per cent of responses. Sectoral elements were negligible. It would seem, therefore, that production-based cleavages of a sectoral, industrial, or company nature are of no real significance to those in formal employment – at least in so far as the formation of social identities is concerned.

Table 6.6 *Others voting for same political party as respondent and for same reasons*

Social category (others voting same way are . . .)	N	% of responses	% of cases
A particular social class			
The working class	255	12.8	21.1
The middle class	104	5.2	8.6
The upper class	20	1.0	1.7
An employment or work related group			
Working people, the working man or woman	142	7.1	11.8
The self-employed, those in business	122	6.1	10.1
The unemployed	81	4.1	6.7
Those in a particular industry or economic sector	74	3.7	6.1
Those in a particular job (e.g. other teachers)	73	3.7	6.0
Other work related answers	93	4.7	7.7
A group defined by income			
The poor, those on low incomes	72	3.6	6.0
The well-off, those on high incomes	57	2.9	4.7
Other income related answers	21	1.1	1.7
A particular status grouping			
Personal qualities (e.g. ambitious/respectable people)	98	4.9	8.1
A particular age group	83	4.2	6.9
Tenure grouping (home owners or council tenants)	40	2.0	3.3
Those living 'round here' or in particular locale	28	1.4	2.3
Those in specific family situation (e.g. young parents)	23	1.2	1.9
An ethnic or racial group	20	1.0	1.7
Gender answers (other women or men)	12	0.6	1.0
Other status answers	23	1.2	1.9
A group defined by a political criterion			
Those fed up with Conservative and Labour parties	83	4.2	6.9
Those who have benefited from Conservative rule	43	2.2	3.6
Traditional supporters of this particular party	33	1.7	2.7
Those who have suffered under Conservative rule	27	1.4	2.2
Other political answers	99	5.0	8.2
Generalised answers			
(e.g. all sorts of people, ordinary people)	210	10.5	17.4
Other answers	62	3.1	5.1
Total	1998	100.0	165.4

(Valid cases = 1208)

Table 6.7 *Sources of work-centred social identities*

Referent of identity	N	%
Occupational (Nominates specific occupation e.g. 'I am a miner')	901	51.3
House or family (Women who answer 'housewife' or 'mother')	280	15.9
Unemployment (Answers in terms of being 'unwaged' or 'out of work')	165	9.4
Weak occupational (Nominates nature of work rather than specific occupation: 'I do a cleaning job')	129	7.3
Company or organization (e.g. 'I work for ICI', 'I work in a university')	75	4.3
Industry (Nominates industry worked for: e.g. 'I work in the oil industry')	73	4.2
Retirement (People who say they are 'retired')	36	2.0
Not specific (People who say 'I work for a living' or similar)	29	1.6
Self-employment (Direct reference to being 'self-employed')	16	0.9
Economic sector (Nominates sectoral location of job: e.g 'I'm in the public sector')	2	0.1
Other	52	3.0
Total	1758	100.0

III

Of course class identity is not class consciousness – in the sense that this term has conventionally been employed in the sociological literature. Among our respondents, social class was widely perceived as a potential source of social identity, and class or class-affiliated characteristics were generally more salient than possible alternative bases for such identities. Nevertheless, the people we interviewed were by no means nascent class activists, and possessed neither a common blueprint for some desired social order, nor the collective inclination to pursue clear class objectives. On the contrary, our findings suggest that the most visible forms of social conflict (including those shaped by feelings of common class identity) are sponsored by the desire for a redistribution of income and wealth within existing socio-political and economic arrangements. What sorts of evidence suggest this conclusion?

Consider, first of all, some data from the sphere of work itself. Almost two-thirds of our sample (63 per cent) agreed that the *main* social conflict in Britain today was between those who run industry and those who work for them. Some 24 per cent of respondents disagreed while 13 per cent felt that they didn't know. However, even among those who disagreed, almost 80 per cent subsequently stated that there were *some* important issues causing industrial conflict of the sort alluded to. Table 6.8 shows in some detail the sorts of issues that were perceived by both groups as generating industrial conflict. The most commonly cited were those rooted in poor industrial relations: lack of mutual understanding between workers and employers, unreasonable behaviour by unions or management, and so on. These were some 45 per cent of total responses among those who perceived industry as the main site of social conflict in Britain. Conflict about the distribution of rewards constituted another 31 per cent and working conditions approximately 15 per cent. (The proportions are very similar among those describing

151

Table 6.8 *Suggested reasons for industrial conflict*

Nature of reason	N	% responses	% cases
Distribution of rewards			
Pay or money when not further specified	227/59	14.1/13.8	21.8/20.3
Excessive wage demands by workers	152/30	9.4/ 7.0	14.6/10.3
Employers are overpaid or greedy	74/17	4.6/ 4.0	7.1/ 5.9
Distribution of profits	50/ 9	3.1/ 2.1	4.8/ 3.1
Working conditions			
Working conditions not elsewhere specified, including health and safety	73/22	4.5/ 5.2	7.0/ 7.6
Numbers employed, redundancies, job security	60/22	3.7/ 5.2	5.8/ 7.6
Hours of work	58/11	3.6/ 2.6	5.6/ 3.8
Decision-making process as it relates to how work gets done	53/12	3.3/ 2.8	5.1/ 4.1
Industrial relations			
Employers and employees mutual antipathy and unwillingness to compromise	225/61	13.9/14.3	21.6/21.0
Trade union militancy and strikes called by trades unions	201/70	12.5/16.4	19.3/24.1
Employers attitudes to workers, including unreasonable management	157/35	9.7/ 8.2	15.1/12.1
Bad management, including lack of expertise and failure to invest	63/12	3.9/ 2.8	6.0/ 4.1
Workers attitudes to employers, including laziness	60/11	3.7/ 2.6	5.8/ 3.8
Workers or trades unions fear of new technology or change in general	19/10	1.2/ 2.3	1.8/ 3.4
Weak management which gives in to unions too easily	3/ 4	0.2/ 0.9	0.3/ 1.4
Power structure			
Distribution of power in the workplace	27/ 1	1.7/ 0.2	2.6/ 0.3
The capitalist system itself	3/ 0	0.2/ 0.0	0.3/ 0.0
Other answers	108/41	6.7/ 9.6	10.4/14.1
Total	1613/427	100/100	154.8/147.2

(Valid cases = 1042/290)

Note: In this table, the first figure in each column gives the distribution of responses for those who agreed that the main conflicts in Britain are between those who run industry and those who work for them, showing the issues that were nominated as causing this conflict. The second set of figures shows the distribution of responses across the same issues, as these were nominated by respondents who disagreed with the initial proposition that the main conflicts in Britain were within industry, but who subsequently agreed that there were nevertheless important conflicts in this sphere. (See Qs 7 to 9 in the interview schedule.)

industry as a secondary such site.) The most widespread perception of industrial conflict, then, is that it stems from unreasonable behaviour on the part of one or both sides of industry, or is explicitly about the distribution of monetary rewards. The obvious point to be made here, of course, is that industrial conflict is not commonly seen to be part of an explicit class struggle. The question of power in or control over the workplace was rarely mentioned. Capitalism was nominated as an issue on only three occasions.

Most people, in fact, saw the two sides of industry as sharing a number of interests in common. Sixty per cent of our sample thought this was the case, while 36 per cent could see no common interests between employers and employees, with 4 per cent unsure. In many cases this common concern was seen to originate in the simple economic interest of most people in constructing a better life for themselves and their children. But the majority of responses go beyond this and indicate a measure of identification with the particular objectives of the employing organization itself (Table 6.9). These include its profitability, expansion and survival, as well as greater productivity and the preservation of jobs. As we shall see below, there is an apparently widespread preference for greater social justice in the distribution of income and wealth accruing from industry, but it is clear from these data that this is premised on an acceptance of, or at least resignation to, the capitalist mode of production itself. Distributional justice is not commonly held to be incompatible with modern capitalism.

More generally, in the context of questioning respondents about social class, our interviewers inquired of those who thought there were important issues causing conflict between the classes as to the precise nature of the schisms in question. In the great majority of cases class conflict was perceived as distributional conflict: class actors contested the allocation of monetary rewards because they were envious of those whose share was relatively larger and life-style correspondingly more comfortable. (The figures are given in Table 6.10.) Perhaps the centrality given to money in these answers is not surprising since the dictates of living in a modern market society ensure that most people are interested in the size of their incomes. Money is the generalized medium of exchange in capitalist societies so people will tend to think – and to answer sociologists' queries – in monetary terms. This is an important issue and it will be pursued further in the following chapter. For the moment, however, the obvious point to be made in respect of these findings is that, even among those who acknowledge class conflict to be an important

Table 6.9 *Suggested common interests of those who run industry and those who work for them*

Perceived common interest	N	% of responses	% of cases
Greater prosperity or higher living standards for all	250	20.7	28.5
Profitability of the enterprise (which is in everyone's interest)	218	18.1	24.8
Survival of the company or industry	187	15.5	21.3
Safeguarding or preserving jobs is in everyone's interest	137	11.4	15.6
Greater productivity (which is in everyone's interest)	113	9.4	12.9
Expansion or improvement of the firm and its market position	86	7.1	9.8
Company policy (all have interests in how the company is run)	70	5.8	8.0
Pride in the firm or the quality of its products	48	4.0	5.5
The good of the country (all working for the national interest)	25	2.1	2.8
Government policy (all have interest in how this affects enterprise)	5	0.4	0.6
Other	66	5.5	7.5
Total	1205	100.0	137.2

(Valid cases = 878)

Table 6.10 *Issues perceived as causing class conflict*

Nature of issue	N	% of responses	% of cases
Money generally (including envy of a particular life-style)	687	64.8	77.5
Lack of understanding or communication, ignorance	87	8.2	9.8
Public versus private services (in health, education, etc.)	73	6.9	8.2
Employment versus unemployment	59	5.6	6.7
General political issues	57	5.4	6.4
Race	17	1.6	1.9
Management versus union conflict	12	1.1	1.4
Other	68	6.4	7.7
Total	1060	100.0	119.6

(Valid cases = 886)

source of schism in contemporary Britain, this conflict is (here as elsewhere) only rarely perceived as being rooted in the economic system as such, or as having an overt political dimension. A simple point, granted, but one that is central to debates about the 'moral order' (or lack of it) underpinning capitalist societies today, and to arguments about the demise of social class, as we shall see shortly.

This equation of class conflict with a struggle about the distribution of income or wealth was common even among that 30 per cent of our sample (47 per cent of those in formal employment) who were members of trades unions. The most frequently cited reason for belonging to a union was employment in a closed shop. But instrumental reasons also featured prominently: union membership helped in the fight for higher pay or was an insurance policy against future contingencies such as plant closure (Table 6.11). A principled commitment to trades unionism was expressed by only 26 per cent of union members – and some of these cited additional self-interested reasons for

Table 6.11 *Reasons for trades union membership*

Membership due to	N	% of responses	% of cases
Closed shop	214	31.5	40.7
Safeguard in case of future problems	164	24.2	31.2
Belief in trades unions	137	20.2	26.0
Fight for higher pay or better conditions	113	16.6	21.5
Union fringe benefits (cheap insurance, etc.)	20	2.9	3.8
Pressure from workmates	11	1.6	2.1
Family tradition	2	0.3	0.4
Other reason	18	2.7	3.4
Total	679	100.0	129.1

(Valid cases = 526)

joining. This pattern of responses was carried forward into expressed preferences for the directions in which unions ought to exert themselves (Table 6.12). Resisting plant closures and increasing pay were the most commonly nominated concerns and by a large margin. More altruistic inclinations – such as the prevention of discrimination at work or reduction in the gap between rich and poor – were rarely offered as a principal concern of unions. The pursuit of industrial democracy fared somewhat better, and was nominated by 13 per cent of respondents as being the most important issue for unions today, but this was still some way behind pay (30 per cent) and plant closures (36 per cent).

Table 6.12 *Issues on which unions should concentrate*

Issue	N	%
Fighting against plant closures or redundancy	272	35.9
Raising pay levels	227	29.9
Getting a greater say for workers in management	99	13.1
Improving health and safety at work	91	12.0
Reducing the gap between the rich and the poor	57	7.5
Preventing racial or sexual discrimination at work	12	1.6
Total	758	100.0

It is also interesting to note the more general and evidently widespread perception of Britain as a society characterized by social conflict. The people in our sample, at least, were clearly of the view that social order rested on something other than social consensus. Sixty-two per cent of those we interviewed were convinced that, as well as conflicts in industry, there were additional important conflicts in Britain today. (Twenty-four per cent could see no such conflicts while 14 per cent were undecided.) Among the conflicts that were cited, those most commonly referred to centred about the issues of race, defence, and class itself, though a number of other divisions were quite widely identified (see Table 6.13). There is no evidence here that respondents see their own society as possessing some form of unified moral order.

In summary, then, our data suggest that contemporary Britain is still widely perceived among its population as being class structured, and that class is readily available as a source of social identity to most people. Indeed it is the most commonly cited such source and is more salient than other potential identities that have recently been suggested as transcending that of social class itself. Needless to say this does not mean that Britain is a nation of class warriors, resolutely pursuing a struggle to preserve or usurp power, in order to achieve specifically class objectives. The most common perception of class conflict is as a distributional struggle over the national income. This is true also of industrial conflict and of trades union activity. In other words there is considerable support for those who would argue that an instrumental

155

Table 6.13 *Perceptions of other important conflicts in Britain today*

Nature of conflict	N	% of responses	% of cases
Racial conflicts	382	21.6	35.4
Conflicts about defence	253	14.3	23.5
Class conflict	185	10.5	17.2
Political conflict	132	7.5	12.2
Conflicts over unemployment and lack of jobs	131	7.4	12.2
Conflicts about other government policies	131	7.4	12.2
Conflicts about law and order	127	7.2	11.8
General conflict caused by trade unions	65	3.7	6.0
Unions versus government conflicts	56	3.2	5.2
Conflicts in or over Northern Ireland	56	3.2	5.2
Religious conflicts	41	2.3	3.8
People versus government conflicts	35	2.0	3.2
Conflicts between age groups	33	1.9	3.1
Other answers	140	7.9	13.0
Total	1767	100.0	163.9

(Valid cases = 1078)

collectivism, in respect of class organizations, characterizes the British population in the mid 1980s. That is to say, the class struggle reflects the nature of the society in which we live, rather than the society we might aspire to achieve.

IV

Are these findings not paradoxical? On the one hand, there is considerable evidence that class awareness is rather widespread in British society, and that social class is the most readily available and commonly employed source for constructing social identities. On the other hand, however, there is nothing to suggest that individuals link this perception to a collectivism that leads them to demand improved life-chances for other members of the social class with which they identify. Most people pursue higher incomes, and would have class organizations pursue it, for strictly personal gain and apparently selfish reasons. What is it that explains this seeming inconsistency? Or, to put the matter another way, why does class awareness not foster class action; and, conversely, how is it that pecuniary and instrumental collectivism does not undermine the sense of class identities?

The answer seems to lie in the evaluative rather than the cognitive sphere. Thus far we have looked only at the latter: at perceptions of social hierarchy and the relative salience of various sources for the construction of social identities. In turning to the former we find a fairly widespread mood of what might be called 'informed fatalism', some might say simply 'realism', among the majority of our respondents. That is, they would endorse such redistributive efforts as were likely to result in a more just society, but judge these unlikely to be forthcoming given existing social, economic, and political arrangements. They do not approve of social injustice, can conceive both of a more just society and the means by which it might be achieved, but nevertheless have judged present arrangements to be largely unassailable, for the foreseeable future at least. Under these circumstances a self-interested and pragmatic collectivism is perfectly rational. These, at least, would seem to be the conclusions to be drawn from our data on economic and political change.

If we look, for example, at the answers that were given in response to questions about distributional justice, we find that a full 70 per cent of our sample (1241 individuals) thought that the distribution of income and wealth in Britain was unfair. (Twenty-seven per cent thought it fair and 3 per cent did not know.) Perceptions of the injustice itself clearly vary, as will be seen from Table 6.14, though one of the most striking features of this table is that it shows well over 80 per cent of all responses indicating a desire to redistribute wealth down the social hierarchy. Less than 10 per cent of the responses favoured redistribution 'upwards', as it were, by claiming that distributional

Table 6.14 *Perceptions of distributional injustice*

Reason why distribution of wealth and income is unfair	N	% of responses	% of cases
Distribution favours those at the top			
Gap between 'haves' and 'have nots' is too wide	728	36.3	60.1
Pay differentials are too wide	243	12.1	20.0
Too much poverty, wages too low, too many reduced to welfare	217	10.8	17.9
Some people acquire wealth too easily (unearned income, etc.)	164	8.2	13.5
The higher paid are not taxed severely enough	161	8.0	13.3
Welfare benefits are too low	90	4.5	7.4
The lower paid or working class are taxed too severely	28	1.4	2.3
Inequalities of opportunity (in education, for jobs, etc.)	21	1.0	1.7
Unequal regional distribution (of jobs, income, etc.)	21	1.0	1.7
Distribution favours those at the bottom			
There are too many scroungers around	108	5.4	8.9
Pay differentials are too narrow	40	2.0	3.3
The higher paid are taxed too severely	32	1.6	2.6
Other reasons			
Inequality of wealth and income is inevitable	39	1.9	3.2
Key groups of workers can hold the country to ransom	5	0.2	0.4
Other reasons	107	5.3	8.8
Total	2004	100.0	165.3

(Valid cases = 1212)

unfairness was a consequence of welfare state scrounging, insufficiently large pay differentials, or of the better off paying too much tax. Sixty per cent of those who answered the question thought that the gap between rich and poor was unacceptably wide; 20 per cent judged pay differentials to be too extreme; less than 6 per cent felt that the higher paid were taxed too severely or that pay differentials were not wide enough.

Moreover, 66 per cent of those who thought the distribution of wealth unfair (825 individuals) were convinced that something could be done to change matters, and made a concrete policy proposal to this end. Naturally, their suggestions tend to reflect the initial perceptions of distributional issues themselves, so that 44 per cent of those answering this question favoured increased taxes on the higher paid, 19 per cent supported lower taxes on the poorer members of society, 12 per cent wanted to 'stop scroungers', 11 per cent mentioned increased welfare payments, and 10 per cent nominated a general incomes policy. (The class distribution of these responses will be discussed in the following chapter.) Many among the 30 per cent (379 people) who thought nothing could be done to make the distribution of income and wealth more fair justified their assessment in more or less fatalistic terms: people are born unequal so that inequality is in 'human nature' (25 per cent of cases); there will always be greedy individuals in society (11 per cent); and, in any case, it seems that we cannot change 'the system' for inequality has always been with us, despite our best efforts to ameliorate it (50 per cent). The responses of the remainder show that respondents had not, in fact, judged redistributive justice to be impossible; rather, they argued that it was highly unlikely to be achieved because of, for example, the obvious lack of interest on the part of the present government in reducing inequalities (mentioned in 18 per cent of cases), the economic climate created by the present recession (4 per cent of cases), or the power of societal elites to resist pressures to social change (2 per cent). In other words, only a small minority (some 16 per cent or so) of our total sample could be identified as existential fatalists, at least as far as issues of redistributive justice were concerned, in that they judged these simply to be beyond human volition. It would seem, then, that the majority of people have not abandoned their concern for social justice or their belief that significant social change is possible.

This finding would seem to hold in respect of economic matters as well. Respondents were asked to say what they thought were the main reasons for Britain's economic problems in recent years. Again their answers were predictably diverse. Full details are given in Table 6.15. It would be unwise to read too much into these since, to some extent, they will reflect the relatively transient issues that are identified as such by the media and government at different times. Note, for example, how few people were prepared to nominate inflation as an economic issue of recent years. This mirrors the fact that, at the time of the survey, the Conservative government had long been relaying the message that its policies had overcome this problem. Nevertheless, making due allowance for the probable lack of salience of many issues to most of our sample (49 per cent of those who nominated a reason for Britain's

Table 6.15 *Perceptions of Britain's economic problems*

Reason for economic problems is	N	% of responses	% of cases
Economic reason			
The general world recession	335	12.3	21.4
New technology or automation displaces workers	137	5.0	8.8
Too many foreign imports	122	4.5	7.8
Lack of investment in industry in general	113	4.1	7.2
Inefficient or bad management	71	2.6	4.5
Unemployment is too widespread	64	2.3	4.1
Reliance on declining or uncompetitive industries	53	1.9	3.4
Lack of exports	47	1.7	3.0
Too much foreign aid given or too much investment abroad	33	1.2	2.1
International reasons (activities of multinational companies, workings of international finance system, etc.)	29	1.1	1.9
Poor industrial relations	26	1.0	1.7
Inflation too high	19	0.7	1.2
Other economic reasons	205	7.5	13.1
Political problems			
The present Conservative government and its policies	361	13.2	23.1
The political system itself (government activities in general, party bickering, vote catching, etc.)	262	9.6	16.7
Participation in the EEC	118	4.3	7.5
Other political reasons (including poor relations between government and industry or unions)	42	1.5	2.7
Distribution of rewards			
Trades unions too powerful or irresponsible	172	6.3	11.0
Working class or unionists are too greedy	79	2.9	5.0
Problems created by the welfare state (direct expense reduction of will to work, etc.)	45	1.6	2.9
Pay in general is too high	35	1.3	2.2
Upper classes or bosses are too greedy	12	0.4	0.8
National characteristics			
National or group characteristics evident in individual characteristics (apathy, lack of effort, etc.)	141	5.2	9.0
People in general are too greedy	104	3.8	6.6
Other reasons			
Demographic factors (ageing population, etc.)	52	1.9	3.3
Explicitly fatalistic answers ('It's just one of those things', something that can't be helped', etc.)	4	0.1	0.3
Other reasons	50	1.8	3.2
Total	2731	100.0	174.5

(Valid cases = 1565)

economic decline also stated that this had not affected them personally), it is interesting to note how few people proffered straightforwardly fatalistic reasons for economic difficulties. The world recession and international economic factors generally may reasonably be placed beyond the immediate control of government and the other major economic actors in Britain, as may such factors as national characteristics ('apathy'), universal greed, and the demographic profile of the society at present. But, taken as a whole, these are

159

a minority of answers and, if the single category of world recessionary factors are removed, they become a very small minority indeed.

Other political and economic reasons suggest remedial action to be possible. In fact, almost three-quarters (72 per cent) of those who identified reasons for the country's economic problems were convinced that something could be done to change things for the better, and made specific policy prescriptions to this end. Their detailed suggestions (Table 6.16) are not particularly important in themselves. (Though it is interesting to note how little support there was for authoritarian solutions such as reducing trades union power or repatriating 'immigrants'.) What is significant, however, is the large number of responses (some 44 per cent of the total) which explicitly referred to government action as a putative remedy. When solutions that clearly imply government action are taken into account (for example improvements in education and training for work) these rise to 64 per cent of the total. There is no evidence here of the sort of fatalism that would deem Britain's economic future to be beyond human volition. A minority see recession as world-wide, created by impersonal forces that are largely uncontrollable, and therefore as 'nobody's fault'. Some refer to population

Table 6.16 *Proposed solutions to Britain's economic problems*

Proposed solution	N	% of responses	% of cases
Change individual attitudes (to work or leisure)	200	15.9	19.7
Change the present government	171	13.6	16.8
Increase national self-sufficiency	129	10.2	12.7
Increase economic, political, or social consensus	99	7.9	9.7
Changes in the way governments spend their money	80	6.3	7.9
Less government or public spending	77	6.1	7.6
Government action to reduce trades union power	66	5.2	6.5
Greater government spending in industry generally	62	4.9	6.1
Improvements in education and training for work	56	4.4	5.5
Investment in industry generally	49	3.9	4.8
Policies of the present government will suffice	43	3.4	4.2
Lower the age of retirement	40	3.2	3.9
Investment in new industries or technology	34	2.7	3.3
Repatriate immigrants or halt immigration	26	2.1	2.6
Greater government spending in new industries or technologies	25	2.0	2.5
Greater government spending in established industries	19	1.5	1.9
Reduce costs for industry	16	1.3	1.6
Investment in established industries	13	1.0	1.3
Increase government participation in industrial relations	8	0.6	0.8
Other solutions	48	3.8	4.7
Total	1261	100.0	124.1

(Valid cases = 1016)

trends or deeply ingrained character 'defects' as the root of economic decline. But the majority retain the belief that economic change is not beyond us and that existing arrangements can be improved upon significantly.

How, then, has the desire for socio-economic change come to manifest itself in entirely instrumental ways? Why has class identity, and the belief that significant moves towards social justice and economic change are both desirable and possible, been so resolutely transmuted into an instrumental concern for personal welfare rather than a politics of protest and reform? Our respondents are clearly aware of social inequality and economic decline. They are, as it were, 'informed'. Nevertheless they are also more inclined to pursue self-interest than redistribution and reorganization since, as we shall now see, past experience has bred a cynicism towards the very socio-political agencies who would necessarily be involved in accomplishing the envisaged social changes. Thus, people are aware of social inequality, on the whole do not approve of it, and generally can conceptualize means by which it might be reduced. However, it seems, they also judge this outcome to be highly improbable given the present structures of government.

This becomes clear, for example, in those questions in the interview schedule dealing with government spending. Just over 61 per cent of our sample (N = 1081) lived in households that they said had been affected in some way by changes in government spending on one of seven items: the National Health Service, education, law and order, public transport, council housing, unemployment benefit, and supplementary benefit. Eighty-five per cent of those affected disapproved of what had befallen them. Yet only 26 per cent of these individuals (235 people) had taken any of the (often fairly minimal) protesting actions listed in Table 6.17. Only thirteen individuals had even bothered to change their vote as a result of their experience. Most people had simply accepted the change on the grounds that they, as individuals, could do little or nothing about the matter. There was, therefore, no point in attempting this (see Table 6.18).

This may be true of individuals but surely governments might be able to effect changes in 'the system'? As we have already seen, the popular perception is that they can. To this, however, must be added the rider that, in the eyes of a substantial minority of respondents, governments most probably would not. In principle they could: experience suggested they wouldn't. For example, 42 per cent of those we spoke to thought it made no difference which party ran the country, and many went on to justify this assessment in fairly cynical terms (Table 6.19). Most commonly it was argued that parties in power were 'all the same' so that 'each was as bad as the other'. It does not really matter whether these are judgements about the competence or the political will of the different parties. Both signify a disaffection from the present party politics that is all too evident in the predictably low numbers participating in the sorts of 'political' activities indicated in Table 6.20. Only thirty-eight of our sample of 1770 individuals claimed any involvement in party political pursuits.

This same disaffection is evident in our respondents' assessments of trades

Table 6.17 *Responses to cuts in government expenditure*

Response	N	% of responses	% of cases
Signed a petition	40	12.7	17.0
Written to MP or Councillor	34	10.8	14.5
Complained to or contacted another authority	33	10.4	14.0
Complained to or contacted a government department	32	10.1	13.6
Attended public meeting	31	9.8	13.2
Changed to private service (BUPA, private school, etc.)	26	8.2	11.1
Joined campaign or organization	23	7.3	9.8
Complained to or contacted council	22	7.0	9.4
Taken part in protest	18	5.7	7.7
Provided things privately	15	4.7	6.4
Changed vote	13	4.1	5.5
Participated in march or demonstration	12	3.8	5.1
Written to newspaper	8	2.5	3.4
Other	9	2.8	3.8
Total	316	100.0	134.5

(Valid cases = 235)

Table 6.18 *Reasons for accepting cuts in government expenditure*

Reason	N	% of responses	% of cases
There is nothing that can be done about it	170	22.1	25.7
Individuals can't do anything, only authorities can	144	18.7	21.8
Ordinary people can't change policy	131	17.0	19.8
No point – no one would take any notice of my protest	98	12.7	14.8
Don't know what to do	97	12.6	14.7
Can't be bothered, apathy	79	10.3	12.0
Change has not affected me badly enough	31	2.5	2.9
Other	19	4.0	4.7
Total	769	100.0	116.3

(Valid cases = 661)

unions. We have already observed that most union members justify their subscriptions in largely instrumental terms. Our interviewers also asked non-members for their views on the union movement. Forty-one per cent of the 615 employees in our sample who were not union members had at one time been so. Only twelve had renounced their membership because they were opposed to trades unions in principle. Most simply moved to a job where membership was not a requirement and so didn't bother renewing their subscriptions (see Table 6.21). Apathy and indifference rather than hostility

Table 6.19 *Stated reasons as to why it makes no difference which party runs the country*

Reason	N	% of responses	% of cases
When in power all parties are the same	261	27.3	36.4
One party is as bad as another	231	24.2	32.2
No party has all the answers	154	16.1	21.4
No party can do anything to solve the problems of the country	109	11.4	15.2
All politicians merely look after themselves	91	9.5	12.7
Each party just undoes what the previous government has done	52	5.4	7.2
No party keeps its promises	35	3.7	4.9
Civil service runs the country	15	1.6	2.1
Other reasons	8	0.8	1.1
Total	956	100.0	133.1

(Valid cases = 718)

Table 6.20 *Membership distribution of those actively involved in political associations*

Political association	N	% of responses	% of cases
PTA, school governors, or educational pressure group	111	24.8	35.5
Trade union	65	14.5	20.8
Business group or club	65	14.5	20.8
Environmental, conservationist, or civic amenity group	61	13.6	19.5
Resident, ratepayer, or tenant association	51	11.4	16.3
Political party	38	8.5	12.1
National pressure group (e.g. CND, Amnesty International)	24	5.4	7.7
Other public body	20	4.5	6.4
Other local pressure group	13	2.9	4.2
Total	448	100.0	143.1

(Valid cases = 313)

explains their defection. This is true also of those who had never at any time been union members. Only 15 per cent of non-unionists (fifty-two people) expressed any hostility towards the union movement itself. Rather, most individuals were in jobs which didn't require union membership, and they were otherwise indifferent towards it (Table 6.22).

Table 6.21 *Reasons for leaving trade union*

Reason	N	% of responses	% of cases
Moved to job where membership not needed	159	62.4	64.1
Family reasons	17	6.7	6.9
Became unemployed	16	6.3	6.5
Union was generally ineffective	13	5.1	5.2
Opposed (or became opposed) to unions in principle	12	4.7	4.8
Union did nothing for me	8	3.1	3.2
Union collapsed at place of employment	6	2.4	2.4
Promoted so left union	5	2.0	2.0
Union did not collect dues	3	1.2	1.2
Other reasons	16	6.3	6.5
Total	255	100.0	102.8

(Valid cases = 248)

Table 6.22 *Reasons for not joining trade union*

Reason	N	% of responses	% of cases
Never had a job which required membership	224	58.9	62.6
Disagree with unions in principle	52	13.7	14.5
Never got round to it, disinterest, apathy	43	11.3	12.0
Employer doesn't allow or doesn't recognize unions	28	7.4	7.8
Currently employed and previously employed on government schemes	10	2.6	2.8
Not worked long enough; not eligible to join union	4	1.1	1.1
Might damage my career prospects	3	0.8	0.8
Other reason	16	4.2	4.5
Total	380	100.0	106.1

(Valid cases = 358)

V

In summary, then, these data would seem to indicate that people are not generally fatalistic about what governments might achieve given sufficient political will and/or competence. However they do doubt whether these actually exist. Present party politics are an object of widespread cynicism. National governments comprise alternating and largely indistinguishable self-interested authorities, and experience suggests that they are unlikely to implement policies which would secure either a greater measure of social justice, or significant economic reforms. Ordinary people are so far removed from the *loci* of decision-making that they can exert little if any influence on policy formation or its execution. In this context there are strong pressures to adopt instrumental attitudes towards the distributive order, towards class organizations, and towards the political sphere generally. Instrumentalism is thus consistent with a form of fatalism. But it is not the fatalism of the naïve. This is, rather, a fatalism informed by an awareness of distributional inequality and social injustice. It is also resignation to the fact that little or nothing will be done to rectify matters. Class awareness and class identities, though well to the fore as sources of meaning that structure the world-views of the majority, are held in check as sponsors of collective action, apparently by a realistic appraisal of the likely outcome of class actions undertaken through the medium of a political party or trades union, at least as these are presently constituted.

Of course it must be conceded that we are here painting with a very broad brush. Our unit of analysis is nothing less than the sample as a whole since, thus far at least, our data have taken the form of simple frequencies. This rather simple analysis is sufficient to establish our general proposition that there is no commonly agreed moral order underpinning contemporary British capitalism. However, there are two obvious (and closely related) difficulties with our account. The first concerns our interpretation of the data. We have constructed an argument which could, at least in part, be an artefact of the frequency distributions themselves. Is it really the case, for example, that it is the same individuals who think both that the class structure has not changed over the years and that there is too little social justice? Are those who are fatalistic about Britain's economic problems similarly fatalistic about the structure of inequality? The issue here is that of the interconnectedness of the various perceptions and evaluations elicited by the questions in our survey. Our problem is one of describing and analysing the perhaps complex beliefs about society held by our respondents within the strict methodological constraints imposed by a highly structured interview schedule. Of course there are various scaling and factor analytic techniques that can be brought to bear on this problem. However, without wishing to engage in controversy about these matters, many such techniques confound more than they clarify findings such as our own. Multidimensional scaling techniques, for example, require data that are hierarchically ordered and simplified so that, often, one loses at the outset as much information as one gains in the subsequent analysis; and with factor analysis there is the ubiquitous problem of interpreting any underlying factors. It is for this reason that we have felt it necessary to include the basic information conveyed by the frequency distributions themselves. More sophisticated calculations are shown in subsequent chapters.

In any case the issues here are not simply methodological – and this brings us to our second point. Larger questions about the nature of 'social consciousness' in general, and about the social structuring of beliefs and values in particular, also intrude at this juncture. What social factors, if any, shape the perceptions, beliefs, and preferences evident in the above tables? For example, is there a simple correlation between material privilege and perceptions of social justice, with those in higher social classes more likely than the relatively impoverished to argue that the distribution of wealth is truly fair? Are they more likely to claim that the rich pay too much in taxes, that there is excessive scrounging off the welfare state, and that pay differentials are unduly narrow? Indeed, will a class analysis of these various attitudes suffice at all, or are they structured by alternative social attributes? In particular, are gender, sectoral cleavages, or some other sectional divisions more relevant to the explanation of solidarities and schisms than is social class itself? This brings us, almost inevitably, to the vexed question of 'class consciousness'.

Notes

1 The particular label applied here will inevitably (and wrongly in this case) be taken as indicative of the political preferences of its authors. For example, Marxists might reject the term 'realism' as applied to any world-view that implies acceptance of the existing order, preferring instead to describe this as 'pragmatism' – a less passive term which carries clear connotations of some future rebellion against the status quo. Our own terminology, which is intended to be politically neutral, is taken from Lockwood's discussion of Durkheimian theories of social order. Fatalism is a matter of degree, and can result from either 'physical or moral despotism'; that is, from force of circumstances such as the 'iron cage of bureaucracy' and 'fetishism of commodities', or the constraints imposed by a system of explicitly fatalistic beliefs such as those embraced by the Hindu doctrine of *karma-samsara-moksha*. In both cases however, 'what is especially conducive to a fatalistic attitude is not so much the degree of oppressive discipline involved, but rather the fact that social constraint is experienced as an external, inevitable and impersonal condition' (Lockwood, 1982: 103). From our point of view, the main advantage of the concept of fatalism is that it carries no implication that beliefs in the inevitability of social structures imply beliefs in their legitimacy, leaving this issue instead as a matter for empirical adjudication. As Lockwood points out, whether subordinate strata view their positions as legitimate rather than simply unalterable will depend on whether the social order in question is secured primarily by beliefs or by ritual, since fatalism grounded in a specifically fatalistic ideology (such as Hindu soteriology) engenders an ethical commitment – unlike the ritualized fatalism of the masses in societies in which 'the lower strata stand at such a great distance from the ideological centre that its constraint over them consists chiefly in its inscrutability'. The difference here is one between ethical and existential fatalism. It is, of course, in the latter sense that some commentators have characterized the social consciousness of workers in modern Britain as 'fatalistic'.
2 These percentages are somewhat different from those obtained by Runciman (1966) who asked similar questions of a comparable sample during the early 1960s. Eighty-three per cent of his respondents placed themselves in a particular social class, on first being invited to do so, and this rose to 99 per cent after a follow-up item that forced such an allocation. Crucially, however, Runciman's initial question asked 'What social class would you say you belonged to?', as compared with our own much less leading 'Do you think of yourself as belonging to any particular social class?'. Furthermore, whereas his follow-up forced respondents to choose between classes ('If you *had* to say middle or working class, which would you say?'), there was no follow-up in our interview to the straightforward invitation to nominate a particular class ('Suppose you were asked to say which class you belonged to, which would you say?'). It is, therefore, difficult to judge whether the differences between Runciman's findings and our own are evidence of a decline in class identities, or simply an artefact of the different questions themselves. Our own impression is that the latter is probably the case. However, the broader issue of the comparison between Runciman's general findings about perceptions of social justice and our own requires more thorough investigation, and for want of space here this will

be reported in a subsequent volume. One of the secondary objectives of our survey, as stated in the research proposal, was to 'replicate' Runciman's study of attitudes to social inequality, in the changed climate of the recessionary 1980s. However, this proved to be a far from straightforward exercise, due to problems that emerged only when the unpublished documentation for Runciman's study was consulted in detail. In due course these too will be described in detail.

3 Because of a filtering error in the interview schedule, 492 of the total sample of 1770 were not asked this question. Of the 1278 respondents who were, 940 thought social class mobility hard, 249 said it was easy, 58 did not know, and 31 refused to answer.

7 Making and unmaking class consciousness

It is a frequently voiced criticism of sociologists that they tend to project their own socio-political aspirations on to the subjects of their research. Too often they have indulged, as John Goldthorpe has so aptly described it, in 'wishful, rather than critical, thinking' – a 'tendency to assert that what was desired was already historically in train'. Most commonly this accusation has been levelled at those on the political left. In pursuit of their own goal of revolutionary socialism, so the argument goes, left-wing intellectuals focus their interpretive efforts almost exclusively on the consciousness and actions of the working class, since this is the most likely agency through which a unity of revolutionary theory and practice might be effected. Where, as has invariably proved to be the case, explicit support for socialism among proletarians is largely absent, a highly implausible degree of implicit 'resistance' to the individual and privatized concerns of a 'capitalist hegemony' has been read into the norms of working-class culture. Alternatively, there has been a retreat from empirical research altogether, in favour of speculative, usually highly abstract and often covertly historicist theorizing, in the attempt to demonstrate some objective or ultimate commitment to communal rather than personal concerns on the part of the proletariat.[1]

Our colleague Erik Wright, co-ordinator of the international project on class structure and class consciousness to which the present survey of social class relationships in Britain is affiliated, is (at least on the face of it) guilty of neither of these sins. Wright's analysis is Marxist – but it is not unduly abstract nor is it unwarrantably romantic. His is a detailed and well-documented empirical study of class processes in the United States and Sweden. It arrives at three conclusions which have important implications for the pursuit of socialist politics within the parameters of existing (as opposed to imaginary) class struggles. First, he suggests that socialism is not the only possible future to capitalism, and that a more realistic assessment would place radical democracy on the immediate political agenda. Since, according to Wright, socialism is a society 'within which control over capital assets and organizational assets are no longer significant sources of exploitation', then 'socialism *means* radical democratic control over the physical and organizational resources used in production'. The struggle for democracy and the struggle for socialism are two aspects of the same process, because 'without a redistribution of organization assets through a democratization of the process of control and co-ordination of production, organization-asset exploitation would continue and upon that exploitation a new structure of class relations would be built.'

More specifically, in the absence of radical democracy, the elimination of private ownership of capital assets results merely in statism – the replacement of the capitalist class with an exploiting hierarchy of bureaucrats and managers instead.[2]

Second, and as a consequence of posing radical democracy as an objective of socialist struggle, Wright reformulates the problem of securing the conditions for a revolutionary transformation in society, from one of encouraging class formation within and among the proletariat, to that of establishing strategic alliances between workers and other social classes under capitalism. This means forging a 'cohesive socialist coalition' of the working class, on the one hand, and incumbents of contradictory locations who 'are either directly threatened by socialism, or at least have relatively ambiguous material interests in a socialist transformation', on the other. This will be a difficult task, but since the class structures of 'actually existing capitalism' are not simply polarized between working class and bourgeoisie, Wright quite correctly reasons that a realistic socialist political strategy should reflect rather than ignore this fact.[3]

Finally, Wright stresses 'the importance of creating the political mediations which will make these alliances possible', and so points to the importance of the spheres of politics and ideology. He recognizes that cultural and political processes have consequences which cannot be explained materially. Or, to use his terminology, the effects of class structure are mediated by politics and ideology. 'Class relations may define the terrain upon which interests are formed and collective capacities forged, but the outcome of that process of class formation cannot be "read off" the class structure itself.' This means that reforms which take place within the existing society should not be dismissed merely as poor strategy on the part of the workers; they may help neutralize the effects of contradictory material interests, transform the conditions of subsequent struggle, enhance the potential for class alliances, and so expand the 'horizon of historical possibilities'.[4]

Of course this is scarcely news to non-Marxist sociologists – most of whom have always taken the realms of politics and ideology seriously. However, the fact that Wright himself is committed to an empirical analysis of socio-political class formation as a complement to his description of class structure, gives his account of class consciousness in Sweden and the United States a degree of concreteness that is unusual among the followers of Marx. 'Class consciousness' is measured using six Likert items which offer the choice of a pro-capitalist or pro-worker response: 'corporations benefit owners at the expense of workers and consumers'; 'it is possible for a modern society to run effectively without the profit motive'; 'if given the chance, the non-management employees at the place where you work could run things effectively without bosses'; 'during a strike, management should be prohibited by law from hiring workers to take the place of strikers'; and 'big corporations have too much power in American (or Swedish) society today'. (We discuss the slightly more complex sixth item separately in note 12 below.) The number of agree and disagree responses is then scaled, and the pattern of the variation in the mean scores for each class category is calculated and explored, mainly via the use of multiple regression techniques. Wright finds that the pattern of variation in consciousness across the matrix of class locations corresponds to theoretical expectations in terms of relations of exploitation. In other words, members of the bourgeoisie are least likely to endorse the working-class position on the various attitudinal items, while proletarians are least likely to express pro-capitalist sentiments. As one moves up the class structure from proletariat to expert managers, so the values on the scale become decreasingly pro-working class, and increasingly pro-capitalist class. Since this is as true for Sweden as it is for the United States, despite the differences between them in terms of state expansion, income inequality, welfare state programmes and so on, Wright suggests that his data support the thesis that it is the underlying structure of class relations which shapes the overall pattern of class consciousness in capitalist societies generally.

Not surprisingly, however, the degree of polarization evident in the two countries is somewhat different, since working-class consciousness also depends 'on the extent to which political parties and unions adopt strategies which help to crystallize workers' experiences in class terms'. Unlike the Democratic Party and trades unions in America, 'the Swedish Social Democratic Party and the associated Swedish labour movement have adopted strategies which reinforce certain aspects of working class consciousness rather than absorbing it into a solid bourgeois hegemony'.[5] Moreover, the fact that union membership acts as a significant intervening variable in different ways in the two countries, supports the idea that the shape as well as the degree of polarization is mediated by organizational and political factors. The possible class alliances suggested by the overall patterns of consciousness in the two countries is rather different. In Sweden, though not in the United States, the labour movement has been able to unionize the majority of managerial employees and so drive a wedge between them and upper-level managers. This raises the possibility of their entering into at least a passive coalition with workers. 'Above all', Wright concludes, 'the effectiveness of the Swedish labour movement in massively unionizing white-collar employees and even substantial segments of managerial employees, has heightened the degree of perceived community of interests among wage earners in different class positions.'[6]

As a result of the different political strategies and ideologies of parties and unions in Sweden and the United States, class has more ideological salience in the former country than in the latter; class location has a greater effect on class consciousness; classes are more polarized in ideological terms; and the working-class 'coalition for socialism' that can be constructed upon that ideological terrain is (at least potentially) much bigger.[7]

These are rather uncontentious conclusions – though it is perhaps surprising to find a Marxist arguing for them on the basis of a multiple regression analysis. They can be summarized, in Wright's own words, in the general observation that 'while the broadest contours of the two countries' class structures are shaped by the level of economic development and the fundamentally capitalist character of both societies, the variations in their class structures are certainly significantly affected by political processes'.[8] Again this suggestion will surprise few non-Marxist sociologists, since others have long argued to this effect, and in rather more detail than Wright himself.[9] However, Wright's particular view of class consciousness *is* controversial, mostly because of what it leaves unsaid about this troublesome concept. There are two omissions in particular which we wish to pursue. Both stem from the rather narrow selection of Likert items used in Wright's analysis.

Wright nowhere considers the question of whether or not his subjects have attitudes that are consistent. Does 'class consciousness' imply that one holds radical views, as it were, across the board; that those among Wright's respondents who thought that corporations were too powerful, were also convinced that workers could run industry without bosses, that management should not encourage strike-breaking, and that society could run without the profit motive? Or, more generally still, do people holding radical views on, say, income redistribution, also support moves towards greater equality between the sexes and races? This is a difficult issue since consistency and inconsistency can arise in different ways. If someone believed in immediate unilateral nuclear disarmament, but also that the present government should spend more rather than less on intercontinental ballistic missiles, then his or her views would be logically inconsistent. Then there is the separate issue of the technical consistency between means and ends. Someone might endorse the proposition that income should be redistributed in favour of the poorer sections of society, and on that basis be expected to favour lower taxes for those on low wages, since this is one means whereby income redistribution can be achieved. However, since there are other means towards the same end (profit-sharing schemes, statutory minimum wages, and so forth), it is possible for individuals to support income redistribution but oppose tax reforms on the grounds that there are better ways of achieving the goal. This sort of reasoning may not be immediately apparent from fixed-choice survey items, nor might that associated with the consistency between ends themselves. Is one to expect normative or even ideological consistency in people's attitudes? Will someone who favours more public spending on defence also support greater powers for the police and the return of capital punishment since each specific goal is consistent with the general principle of 'strengthening the forces of law and order'? And are these general principles and values commonly ordered into some coherent world-view or ideology? Are Christians regularly supportive of the values of peace, charity, and the like? Or, more immediately relevant to our concerns, are workers who support the extension of the right to strike and of industrial democracy also in favour of redistributive incomes policies, the curtailing of profits, and egalitarian social measures? And, if they are not, in what sense can they be said to be 'class conscious'?[10]

Wright himself is not unaware of this problem. For example, he states that his analysis

does not imply that all incumbents of a given location in the class structure will have the same consciousness, but simply that the probability of them having forms of consciousness consistent with the objective interests attached to that class location is higher than for incumbents of other class locations.[11]

However he does offer a peculiarly limited choice of Likert items to his respondents. All but one are concerned specifically with class relationships – between owners and workers, managers and striking workers – so it is hardly surprising that the issues of logical, technical, and normative consistency do not arise.

This brings us to our second objection to Wright's account of class consciousness. Since his attitudinal items are all set in the narrow context of class relationships themselves it is hardly surprising that the pattern of responses to them tends to take a generally class-determined form. Wright justifies his strategy on the grounds that a wider variety of attitude items, covering political issues, the normative concerns of equal opportunity, and social problems more generally, have only an indirect specific class content, so that it seems advisable to focus on those items with the most explicit class connotations. It is true, as he claims, that this approach minimizes the number of assumptions that need to be made about the content of class consciousness. However, it can also be argued that it prejudices the outcome of the investigation in favour of a specifically class analysis, since all of the Likert items have obvious class (as opposed to, say, status) referents. This, in turn, means that they can easily be aggregated into a 'class consciousness' scale, on the assumption that this variable possesses a continuous form, and is therefore amenable to analysis via multiple regression techniques. Furthermore, it thus resolves by fiat all issues about consistency and the overall shape of specific class ideologies, while simultaneously restricting the likelihood that other variables (such as sex and home-ownership) will better be able to explain the variance in the six attitudinal items. In short, Wright so oversimplifies the concept of class consciousness in his research that it would be surprising had his finding not supported a class perspective on the various attitudes under study.[12]

Our own approach, therefore, will be somewhat different. We will look at a wider range of attitudinal variables than is explored by Wright. Consistency between the suggested means and ends will be treated as an issue for empirical investigation, though it must be admitted we are constrained in the extent to which our data allow us to explore this. Various attitudinal items will then be examined so as to determine whether or not these are structured by social class itself, by class-related variables (such as income), or by attributes that might cross-cut class processes (such as home-ownership). This may give our findings about 'class consciousness' some relevance beyond the confines of the international project itself – which would surely not be expected were we simply to extend Wright's comparative investigation by replicating his rather narrow analysis in the British context.

I

It is particularly difficult to check for logical consistency in people's world-views – especially when the research instrument is a highly-structured questionnaire such as our own. Incongruent answers on logically-related matters might indeed be the result of genuine inconsistencies in a respondent's reasoning. However, they might equally well be due to measurement error, as for example when fixed-choice questions fail to allow for subtle distinctions made by interviewees. Respondents may be more sophisticated in their reasoning than can possibly become evident from the inevitably limited questioning that is possible in a formal and fairly brief interview. Seeming contradictions might therefore be an artefact of the interview situation itself.

Technical consistency is even harder to assess. The additional difficulties here stem from the fact that there are usually several alternative means to any given end. Consequently, people can make different assessments, not only of the likely effectiveness of particular means, but also of their respective desirability, since judgements about a means–end relationship often contain a normative as well as a technical dimension. Given the limitations of our survey methodology itself, and the implicit moral assumptions that are made by researchers and subjects alike in relating means to ends and ends to each other, one is highly unlikely to observe perfect consistency in these areas.

Our questionnaire offers clear examples of this. Interviewees were asked both whether they thought it should be left to market forces to revive the economy and whether they thought there should be increased government spending to revive the economy. These items would appear to be mutually exclusive: support for an unfettered market should preclude that for government intervention. Yet, as Table 7.1 makes clear, there are only 7 percentage points difference between supporters and opponents of market solutions in terms of their subsequent approval of increased government spending. Or, looking at this another way, only 56 per cent of those answering

Table 7.1 *Consistency of attitudes to economic recovery*

		Support for market forces as means of economic revival	
		Yes	*No*
Support for government intervention	Yes	37 (233)	30 (277)
as means of economic revival	No	63 (405)	70 (637)
	Total	100 (638)	100 (914)

(N = 1552)

both questions gave a consistent pair of answers, either by supporting the market and opposing government intervention, or vice versa. Of course, it could be the case that some of the 46 per cent remaining supported neither strategy, and favoured instead some third alternative about which we did not ask, but it seems hard to see what this might be, and in any case this does not alter the fact that about one-quarter of those answering the questions (405 individuals) supported *both* an untrammelled market and more government intervention in it. Perhaps these interviewees did not fully understand our rather clumsy questions? Perhaps rather formal survey interviews are misrepresentative because they do not offer respondents adequate time to express themselves fully? Or, is it simply the case that people can unconcernedly hold contradictory beliefs, even about something as apparently straightforward as the choice between two opposing economic principles?

The issue of technical consistency raises similar questions. Respondents were asked both whether or not they agreed with the policy of increasing income tax, in order to raise welfare benefits, and also if they themselves would be prepared to pay higher taxes for such a purpose. As can be seen from Table 7.2, there is in fact a rather strong association between support for the general principle of welfare state expansion, and willingness personally to contribute higher taxes towards this end. Supporters and opponents of expansion differ by 47 percentage points in their willingness to pay higher taxes themselves. Although this difference is still high by social science standards, no less than 30 per cent or so of the sample (501 people) offer 'inconsistent' answers. In this instance, however, the incongruence might be more apparent than real, since it is quite consistent for someone to approve of the general policy of increasing tax for specific purposes, but state additionally that he or she would not be prepared personally to participate in such a stratagem, if they happen also to be convinced that they are already paying too much in taxes, whereas others are paying too little. Without supplementary questioning we simply cannot say whether or not this is the case.

Similarly, the responses to pairs of questions about reductions in wage

Table 7.2 *General attitude to tax and welfare benefits by willingness to finance increased welfare benefits personally*

| | | General endorsement of increased taxes to support expansion of welfare | |
		Yes	*No*
Personal willingness to pay more tax	Yes	81 (405)	34 (404)
so as to increase welfare benefits	No	19 (97)	66 (780)
	Total	100 (502)	100 (1184)

(N = 1686)

differentials and the creation of jobs can also be compared, with a view to determining the extent of consistency in the views expressed. Twenty-five per cent of those who supported the general principle of incomes policies which would reduce wage differentials also stated that they personally would be prepared to take lower wage increases so as to allow the lower paid to catch up. Only 16 per cent of those opposed to the general principle were prepared to make the particular sacrifice (see Table 7.3). Although this represents a 9 percentage points difference between supporters and opponents of a more egalitarian incomes distribution the figures show only a 40 per cent concordance between the two sets of replies. A majority of those who answered hold seemingly inconsistent views, since they are opposed to the general principle of a redistributive incomes policy but are prepared, nevertheless, to forgo wage increases in support of such a policy; or, conversely, support the general policy but are not prepared to see their own wages held in check. Of course this finding is again open to alternative interpretations. It is quite possible, for example, that many among the latter group of respondents are not prepared to see their own wages held in check precisely because they feel that they themselves are among 'the low paid' and ought therefore to benefit from any generalized wages redistribution.

Table 7.3 *General attitude to incomes policies favouring the low paid by willingness to finance income redistribution personally*

		General endorsement of incomes policies to reduce wage differentials	
		Yes	*No*
Personal willingness to accept wage restraint so as to reduce differentials	Yes	25 (183)	16 (41)
	No	75 (543)	84 (207)
	Total	100 (726)	100 (248)

(n = 974)

Contextual circumstances might also explain the analogous incongruities between willingness to pay increased taxes and to restrict wage increases in order to create jobs for the unemployed. The choice here is between two alternative means to the same end and, as the figures in Table 7.4 show, support for one strategy by no means guarantees support for another – even when they are both seeking to achieve the same goal. In fact, in this particular case, the degree of concordance between the two views is almost 68 per cent, with a 39 percentage points difference between supporters and opponents of tax increases, in terms of their support for wages restraint. But the problems of interpretation remain. Why are some people unwilling to pay more in tax to create employment yet prepared to forgo wage increases towards the same

Table 7.4 *Support for tax increases to create jobs by support for wage restraint to create jobs*

| | | Support for tax increases | |
		Yes	No
Support for wage restraint	Yes	56 (314)	17 (70)
	No	44 (250)	83 (351)
	Total	100 (564)	100 (421)

(N = 985)

end? Policies of wage restraint, for some reason or reasons, simply enjoy more popular support than do those which propose increased taxation.

Given these difficulties of interpretation, where the issues of logical and technical consistency are concerned, it is more profitable, from our point of view at least, to explore the degree of normative or ideological congruence in the world-views of our respondents. To what extent are people's beliefs and values concordant? For example, are they consistently 'egalitarian' across a range of issues, regardless of whether the issues themselves are logically or technically related?

One way of approaching this problem is to examine the normative items in the questionnaire so as to see whether or not people linked together the various topics about which they were asked to express a preference concerning what ought to be done. Because of the constraints imposed by the length of the questionnaire, these items were restricted to policy prescriptions for market or interventionist strategies in a limited range of contexts, including those of income redistribution, equality between the sexes, and economic policy (see Question 12). A factor analysis of responses to this question suggests that items E, H, I and B are grouped together, with E forming the central question, as are items D and G, where D is the key question.[13] Between them these factors explain more than 87 per cent of the variance in the set as a whole. The underlying dimensions are not difficult to interpret. Items E, H, I and B deal with racial and sexual discrimination, the creation of jobs, and support for those on lower incomes. These can plausibly be said to relate to 'distributive justice', ranging from support for positive discrimination, a progressive incomes policy, and the redistribution of profits, at one pole, to that for non-intervention in any of these spheres, at the other. The second factor suggests a dimension of 'economic nationalism', with support for protectionism and government controls over multinational companies at one pole, and for an international free market at the other.

We can see the overall pattern of association in Table 7.5. Among those who supported the taxation of profits to create jobs, 60 per cent also favoured positive discrimination in favour of ethnic minorities, as compared with only 34 per cent of those who were opposed to the former policy. Supporters and opponents of job creation through the taxation of profits thus show a

Table 7.5 *Association between normative items*

A – Factor 1

| | Supporters of job creation from company profits | Distributive justice | | |
		Opponents of job creation from company profits	Difference (%)	Overall concordance (%)
Percentage supporting:				
Positive discrimination for ethnic minorities	60	34	26	63
Incomes policy favouring the low paid	85	65	20	61
Positive discrimination for women	81	64	17	60

B – Factor 2

| | Supporters of import controls | Economic nationalism | | |
		Opponents of import controls	Difference (%)	Overall concordance (%)
Percentage supporting:				
Policies to make multinational companies reinvest in Britain all profits made here	87	69	18	72

difference of 26 percentage points in their attitude towards racial inequalities. There are differences of 20 per cent and 17 per cent respectively in their attitudes towards progressive incomes policies and sexual discrimination. This suggests that people's attitudes to these particular topics are informed by more general values, in this case support for or opposition to greater egalitarianism in life-chances, especially with regard to disprivileged class and status groupings. Nevertheless, the concordance in attitudes is far from complete, as the final column in this table shows. On average almost 40 per cent of respondents gave 'inconsistent' responses for each pair of items. For example, though 63 per cent of the sample either supported both job creation through taxation of profits and positive discrimination for ethnic minorities or were opposed to both of these, 37 per cent favoured one policy but not the other. Looking down the table, the overall concordance figures are not particularly high, since 50 per cent means only that as many individuals do support any two policies as do not support such a pairing.

This type of analysis can be extended to other cognitive and evaluative issues. Those of fatalism and of class itself are particularly apposite since these were subjects of discussion in the previous chapter. Taking the latter subject first, the survey data allow us to inspect perceptions of class, in particular the extent to which people associate distributional injustice with specifically class inequalities, and perceive social classes themselves as having antagonistic relationships to each other. Factor analysis suggests that the key question here is the extent to which people see class inequalities as having declined or remained unchanged. However, while there is some association between people's perceptions of class inequalities and of income inequalities, the former are not significantly related to feelings of class belonging, to perceptions of class relationships as being conflictual, or even to the siting of major conflicts in the relationship between managers and workers (see Table 7.6). This suggests either that people tend not to construct their perceptions of Britain as a class-divided society into an all-embracing class-based interpretation of the society – an ideology of class; or that they hold complex and perhaps sophisticated views about the nature of class relationships – views which escape detection in a highly structured interview. Both might be true. However, the more important point as far as the present study is concerned, is the clear suggestion in these data that 'class consciousness' tends not to take the form of a coherent and comprehensive world-view.

Table 7.6 *Association between class items*

| | | Class structure has . . . | | |
	Stayed the same	*Changed*	*Difference (%)*	*Overall concordance (%)*
Percentage who also claim:				
Distribution of income is unfair	80	64	16	58
Strong class identification	62	57	5	53
Conflicts between managers and workers are important	74	70	4	52
Class conflict is important	56	62	(–6)	47

Note: Table comprises answers to Questions 25(a), 15, 32, 7 and 30(a).

Indeed the evidence suggests that few people subscribe to similarly uncomplicated or one-sided world-views rooted in any single principle of social organization. If we turn to the question of fatalism, for example, it was argued in the previous chapter that many people are pessimistic and cynical about the chances for substantial social change, given the present structure of party politics. Nevertheless, and contrary to the views advanced by some contemporary commentators, we could find little evidence of a widespread fatalism which would place significant socio-economic change entirely beyond human volition. Table 7.7 confirms that ours is indeed a sound analysis. Taking the issue of whether or not people think it is possible to resolve Britain's economic problems as the key question, we see that 'fatalism' in this regard is significantly associated with the view that nothing can be done to make the distribution of wealth fairer, and that it makes little difference which political party is in power. Of course the figures also show that 33 per cent and 41 per cent of respondents respectively do not extend their fatalism

Table 7.7 *Association between fatalism items*

| | Britain's economic problems . . . | | | |
	Can be resolved	Cannot be resolved	Difference (%)	Overall concordance (%)
Percentage who also claim:				
Inequalities of wealth and income cannot be erased	44	26	18	67
Makes no difference which party runs the country	53	39	14	59
Unemployment will never again fall below one million	87	86	1	32

Note: Table comprises answers to Questions 3(c), 16(b), 19 and 6(a).

about the economy to these other spheres. Moreover, there is no association between the principal item itself, and fatalistic attitudes towards unemployment. In short, people are no more wholeheartedly 'fatalistic' than they are wholeheartedly 'class conscious'. Perceptions of and judgements about society are not that neatly packaged.[14]

II

We can see, then, that there is never a perfect concordance in people's attitudes. Indeed, as one moves from logically and technically related items to questions of normative or ideological consistency, so the level of prima facie concordance drastically declines. It is against this background that our replication of Erik Wright's analysis of 'class consciousness' must be set. That is, there must be a clear realization that class consciousness is not mass consciousness; we do not expect to find every member of a particular class sharing the same beliefs, nor will those in particular subgroups display perfect consistency in their attitudes. There is a theoretical as well as an empirical point here for we think that Wright's conception of class consciousness is theoretically naive as well as empirically unconvincing. The larger matter of theory will be taken up in due course. For the moment we will focus simply on the factual comparison between Wright's mapping of class consciousness and our own. In order to facilitate this it is necessary to construct a class consciousness scale analogous to that devised by Wright. For reasons that have already been made clear the normative items in the British survey are not identical to those used in Sweden and the United States. Nevertheless, we can use questions pertaining to class identification and class inequality in particular, together with those relating to the distribution of rewards more generally, to construct such a scale. In this way we can score 'class consciousness', as did Wright, on a continuum ranging from pro-working class

179

to pro-capitalist, and explore the variation in the scores using the techniques of multiple regression.

Our 'class consciousness index' was created from six items: subjective class identification, the perception of persisting and gross class inequalities, support for market principles, support for incomes policies which favoured the lower paid, for tax increases in order to increase welfare benefits, and for taxes on profitable companies in order to maintain and create jobs. Each item contains a 'pro-working class' and 'pro-capitalist' option. Thus, for example, those who stated that they agreed with incomes policies which increased the wages of the low paid more than those of the higher paid are considered as having given a pro-working-class response. Those who disagree have endorsed the pro-capitalist option. For technical reasons the index itself has the range 3 (pro-working class on every item) to minus 3 (pro-capitalist on every item). Of the alternative class schemes, that of John Goldthorpe explains 12 per cent of the variation in the index of class consciousness thus created, while those of Erik Wright and the Registrar-General each explain only 8 or 9 per cent. In other words the Goldthorpe categories offer much the best framework for the analysis of class consciousness. Table 7.8 shows the percentage of those in each of the Goldthorpe classes who endorse the working-class option on the individual items.

Table 7.8 *Responses to individual items in the class consciousness scale by Goldthorpe class*

Class	% who take the *working-class* position on item:					
	(1)	(2)	(3)	(4)	(5)	(6)
I	22	35	63	56	24	24
II	36	37	63	63	26	34
III	50	42	59	76	27	55
IV	48	41	44	69	19	37
V	74	54	54	80	32	47
VI	76	57	63	81	34	65
VII	75	63	59	83	28	63

Key to items:
(1) Class identification (question 33);
(2) Perception that class inequalities are undiminished over time (question 25a);
(3) Support for market principles in running the economy (question 12a);
(4) Support for incomes policy to favour low-paid (question 12b);
(5) Support for taxes to finance increased welfare benefits (question 12c);
(6) Support for taxes on company profits in order to create jobs (question 12e).

Adopting the Goldthorpe class schema as a benchmark for further analysis, we find that the inclusion of Goldthorpe class of origin increases the total amount of variation explained (the adjusted R^2) to 18 per cent, while voting intention and union membership add further 1 per cent increments. On its own, class of origin explains 11 per cent of the variation (as compared to 12 per cent for present class). Thus, either Goldthorpe present class or

Goldthorpe class of origin provides a considerable explanation for class consciousness, as measured by our index of six items, with the former being slightly the more efficacious. By comparison, sectoral cleavages (as represented by housing tenure, dependency on welfare benefits, and production sectoral location) are more or less irrelevant as explanations of the variation in class consciousness, while sex, income, and educational attainment are wholly so. Nor is there any significant variation in consciousness scores from one cohort to another. Table 7.9 shows the mean scores for those variables which explain significant amounts of variation in the index: class, class of origin, voting intention and union membership. The 18 per cent of the variation explained by the two Goldthorpe class items taken together is highly significant and represents about 90 per cent of the total explanation possible with all four variables.

Table 7.9 *Mean scores on class consciousness index for principal explanatory items*

A – Goldthorpe class

I	II	III	IV	V	VI	VII
−0.73	−0.42	0.05	−0.35	0.42	0.80	0.68

B – Goldthorpe class of origin

I	II	III	IV	V	VI	VII
−0.72	−0.48	−0.30	−0.06	0.35	0.60	0.53

C – Voting intention

Conservative	Alliance	Would not vote	Labour
−0.61	0.21	0.51	1.03

D – Union membership

Union member	Non-member
0.44	0.01

These findings from our replication of Wright's analysis of class consciousness in the British context point to a number of important conclusions. First, to the extent that class consciousness can be tapped by a series of attitudinal items pertaining to distributional mechanisms and injustices, then the sociological class framework devised by John Goldthorpe proves to be analytically superior to the commonsensical approach of the Registrar-General and the neo-Marxist schemes of Erik Wright in the matter of explaining variations in such consciousness. This reinforces our earlier finding that the Goldthorpe class framework was more useful in the analysis of class structure and class mobility than were the other class frameworks we considered. The categories of this schema are simply more robust than those devised by Erik Wright or the Office of Population Censuses and Surveys.

Second, we can find no evidence to suggest that social solidarities and schisms (as measured by the items in our index) are structured by sectoral cleavages, rather than the more longstanding differences associated with social class. The variation in the index scores is not related to housing tenure, production sectoral locations, dependence on welfare benefits, sex, income, or level of educational attainment. Our results here seem particularly convincing since, unlike Wright, we have not selected for inclusion in our index only those attitudinal items which are themselves set in the context of class relationships. In fact two of the items in our scale refer explicitly to social class. But the other four allude no more to class differences than to those associated with sectoral production and consumption cleavages, income, and political partisanship. Despite this, class is by far the most important factor in explaining the variation in the items included in the index.

Third, the fact that age differences are irrelevant in this context suggests that there is no obvious secular trend away from 'class consciousness', contrary to the arguments of Calvert and others who maintain that the idea of class has had its day. Our findings do not support the popular belief that we are witnessing a long-term decline in class loyalties and attitudes.[15] Just as the structural processes associated with class have persisted into the late twentieth century, in the face of sustained attempts at egalitarian reform by successive governments in post-war Britain, so too have the ideological differences associated with a class-based culture. Despite educational reform, the welfare state, and the growth of mass consumption, Britain is still, structurally and culturally, a class rather than a 'post-class' society.

Finally, and rather significantly, our analysis does not support John Goldthorpe's views about the marginality of gender to the process of socio-political class formation. One additional finding needs to be reported here in order to substantiate this claim. It will be remembered, from the discussion in Chapter 4, that Goldthorpe's view is that the class behaviour and demands of wives are a function of their husbands' class positions rather than their own occupational experiences. Class cleavages run between rather than through families. This is one of the reasons why Goldthorpe defends the 'conventional' approach to class analysis: the family is allegedly the basic unit of socio-political class formation, and since its socio-political characteristics seem to be determined by the family member having the greatest commitment to the labour market, then its class position is given by the occupation of putative 'heads of household' (the great majority of whom, as Goldthorpe sees it, are men). It was for this reason that the Oxford Mobility Study of the 1970s sampled only males. In fact our own data on 'class consciousness' suggest that matters may not be that simple. It is true, as we have already seen, that in some matters of class behaviour women's attitudes and actions are more closely related to their husbands' class positions than their own occupational experiences. Voting intention and (to a lesser extent) self-assigned class are the most obvious of these (see Tables 4.4 and 5.19 above.) These are, understandably, the dimensions of 'class consciousness' most commonly used to substantiate Goldthorpe's conventional view.[16] However, when a wider perspective is taken, the alternative strategy of sampling both men and women, and allocating class positions on an individual (rather than familial) basis, seems to be more convincing. The evidence comes from our analysis of the items in the class consciousness scale discussed above. The explanatory superiority of the Goldthorpe class schema over those devised by the Registrar-General and Erik Wright was apparent only when the version of Goldthorpe's classification based on *individual* respondents was used in the analysis: that is, when employed men and women were allocated to class positions, each according to his or her own occupation. As we saw this class scheme explained 12 per cent of the variation in the index scores. If, on the other hand, Goldthorpe's own approach is used then the explained variance drops to barely 2 per cent. In other words, if all the females in our study are given the class position of their husbands, then the variation explained by the Goldthorpe categories drops precipitously.

By converting the social class position of female respondents to that of their husbands we are effectively sampling only males – the strategy advocated and implemented by Goldthorpe himself. It was argued in Chapter 4 that this conventional approach restricts one's understanding of the processes of demographic class formation. Indeed, as the data in Table 4.12 showed clearly, this procedure yields a seriously misleading class map of modern Britain by underestimating the relative sizes of some class categories and overestimating others. We would now wish to add a corollary to our earlier observations. The conventional approach seriously restricts the understanding of socio-political class formation as well. This latter process is clearly more complex than Goldthorpe suspects. Some aspects of class behaviour (voting and class identities, for example) are, it seems, closely related to the class experiences of the male rather than the female in a couple. But others cannot be explained unless each individual's own class experiences are taken into account. A more complete understanding of socio-political class formation therefore demands that one allocates men and women to class positions according to their own employment. For this reason the Essex 'individualistic' version of the Goldthorpe classification is more robust than the Oxford 'familial' original.

III

Our analysis suggests, then, that modern Britain is a society shaped predominantly by class rather than other forms of social cleavage, no matter whether the phenomena under scrutiny are structural or cultural in nature. Further evidence to substantiate this claim is readily available from data elsewhere in our survey. These make it clear, for example, that awareness of class is not a function of class location. Among the factors that show no significant variation across classes (by whichever schema these are identified) are the proportions of respondents claiming a class identity; that class is an inevitable feature of modern society; and that there are important issues generating class conflicts. Nor is there significant variation in these items across sectors of the economy, by types of housing tenure, experience of cuts in public spending, dependence on state welfare benefits, or according to sex. Men show no signs of being more conscious of class than are women; private sector and public sector workers are, in this respect as in others we have examined, virtually indistinguishable; and home-ownership is not associated with a heightening or lessening of class awareness. Furthermore, our argument that the pursuit of distributional justice within capitalist economic arrangements would find fairly widespread support is confirmed by our finding that neither views on ascribed class membership, nor those on the putative ease of social mobility, show any signs of being structured significantly by class, or by any other obvious source of social cleavage. Those in relatively privileged class positions are no less inclined to perceive upward mobility as difficult, and no less likely to disapprove of class being ascribed by birth, than are their comparatively disprivileged peers.

These points are especially pertinent in the context of sociological discussions about the demise of social class. It has been argued recently that Britain is a society increasingly divided by sectoral and other cleavages which encourage the pursuit of narrow sectional interests in wholly instrumental fashion. These cleavages cut across social class boundaries and so have undermined older loyalties to class itself, and to class-related organizations, such as those of union and party. We would disagree with this interpretation of consensus and conflict in recessionary Britain on the basis of the twin findings reported in the previous paragraph. To repeat, our data suggest that, in so far as the identities, beliefs and values investigated in this study are socially structured, then the source of this structuring lies in social class differences rather than more fashionable sectoral cleavages. Moreover, instrumentalism towards class organizations coexists alongside a surprisingly widespread enthusiasm for social justice based on a redistribution of rewards in favour of those occupying disprivileged statuses, which suggests that the instrumental collectivism of our respondents may be based more on 'informed fatalism' than on a principled commitment to individual welfare as such. We have already suggested (and will argue again in Chapter 9) that this seeming fatalism most probably reflects a profound cynicism about present party politics. For the moment we will confine ourselves to pursuing the arguments about sectionalism and the social structuring of aspirations towards distributional justice.

The findings reported in Table 7.5 above offer a convenient starting point for considering these issues further. The factor analysis of normative items suggests that four of the items under inspection – those dealing with racial and sexual discrimination, the creation of jobs, and support for those on lower

184

incomes – load on to a factor which can reasonably be interpreted as a generalized attitude towards distributional issues concerning social justice. The analysis suggests that, taking our sample as a whole, people's attitudes towards the creation of jobs tend to be associated with their answers to questions on low pay, equal opportunities for women, and racial discrimination. Again we can bring multiple regression techniques to bear on the issue of how, if at all, support for this general principle of distributional justice varies across social groupings within the population at large. As before, an overall index was calculated by scoring the individual items, each of which offered an 'egalitarian' or 'inegalitarian' option. In this case the resulting index takes the values 4 (egalitarian on all items) to 8 (inegalitarian on all items). The best class indicator of overall attitudes to distributional justice, as measured by the index, is once more provided by Goldthorpe. His categories explain almost 7 per cent of the variation in the scores whereas those of the Registrar-General and Erik Wright explain only 4 or 5 per cent.[17] The mean scores for the seven Goldthorpe classes were as follows (beginning with class I): 6.2, 5.9, 5.5, 5.9, 5.5, 5.2, 5.2. This is in line with theoretical expectations. Members of the service class and the *petit bourgeoisie* are least likely to support a redistributive package of measures which increase the wages of the low paid more than those better off, which tax company profits so as to create jobs in declining industries, and which give special help to women and ethnic minorities. Members of the working class are most likely to do so. Routine administrative employees and supervisors of manual workers, occupying intermediate class positions, are also intermediate in terms of their support for these policies.

Among the additional variables that were tested against the index only that of sex proved to have significant explanatory power. Together with Goldthorpe class this raised the explained variance to almost 9 per cent. Males had a mean score of 5.7 whereas females average 5.4. This cannot be explained away as an artefact of the scale itself; that is, because it contains an item specifically about special help to give women equal opportunities outside the home. In fact, the basic cross-tabulation shows that men are not significantly less likely to support such measures than are women themselves, or at least are no less likely to do so in the rather artificial context of a survey interview. For whatever reason, women are somewhat more egalitarian than men, across the range of items in our index. That apart, no other significant variables emerged from the analysis, although the full range of sectoral differences (together with age and income) was again explored.

The differences between the mean 'egalitarianism' scores for the various classes, as measured by our simple index of four items, are consistent with those which emerge from more straightforward questioning about distributional justice and the system of monetary rewards. Respondents were asked directly whether or not they thought that the distribution of wealth and income in Britain was a fair one, and if not, what should be done to change things. There are no significant class differences in the responses to the initial question (see Table 7.10). A substantial majority in each class are convinced

185

Table 7.10 *Attitudes to distributional justice by Goldthorpe class*

A – Is distribution of wealth and income fair?

		Yes	*No*
	I	31	69
	II	34	66
	III	28	72
Class	IV	44	56
	V	24	76
	VI	25	75
	VII	22	78
	All	29	71
		(368)	(914)

B – Why not?

				Class			
	I	*II*	*III*	*IV*	*V*	*VI*	*VII*
Distribution favours those at the top							
Gap between haves and have nots is too wide	57	59	63	64	55	63	63
Pay differentials are too wide	21	19	19	19	26	21	19
Too much poverty, wages too low, too many reduced to welfare	13	17	20	16	13	17	18
Some people acquire wealth too easily (unearned income etc.)	31	16	13	13	20	10	9
The higher paid are not taxed severely enough	9	15	11	9	12	20	16
Welfare benefits are too low	6	5	6	2	8	9	6
The lower paid or working class are taxed too severely	2	3	3	5	3	0	2
Inequalities of opportunity (in education, for jobs, etc.)	2	2	2	0	0	1	2
Unequal regional distribution (of jobs, income, etc.)	4	3	3	0	2	1	2
Distribution favours those at the bottom							
There are too many scroungers around	6	5	12	9	15	8	10
Pay differentials are too narrow	5	4	1	3	4	4	4
The higher paid are taxed too severely	4	2	3	8	3	3	3
Other reasons							
Inequality of wealth and income inevitable	1	4	4	2	7	2	2
Key groups of workers can hold the country to ransom	1	1	0	0	0	0	0
Other reasons							

Note: Percentages in the 'Why not?' columns are based on respondents. Valid cases = 899.

that rewards are distributed unfairly – though the self-employed are here, as in other matters, somewhat distinct from employees of all ranks. However, as one would expect, those in higher class positions are somewhat more inclined to protect their relative privileges. For example, members of the service class are generally less likely than are those in working-class positions to claim that there is too much poverty, that the gap between the 'haves' and 'have nots' is too wide, that welfare benefits are too low, and that the rich are undertaxed. In other words, and as one might expect, there is some variation across social classes in the support for a more egalitarian income distribution.

Rather surprisingly, however, people in service-class locations are proportionately more likely than are members of the working class to oppose unearned income that is too easily acquired, and are no less likely to state that the distribution of rewards is unfair because pay differentials are too large. Indeed, surely what is striking about the results reported in Table 7.10 is the degree of uniformity in the responses across the different classes. A majority, even of those in the service class, feel that the gap between rich and poor is too wide; between 10 and 20 per cent of people in every class think that there is too much poverty; and very few in any class (generally less than 5 per cent of individuals) think either that the rich are overtaxed or that pay differentials are too small.

These findings can be considered alongside those in Chapter 6, where it was reported that 70 per cent of our sample think that the distribution of wealth and income in Britain is unfair, and well over 80 per cent of all assessments as to why this is so indicated a desire to redistribute wealth down the social hierarchy. Fewer than 10 per cent favoured redistribution upwards. We now see that, among those of our respondents in employment, there is a remarkable similarity in the distribution of the assessments across classes. It is not simply the case that those in the more privileged class positions endorse distributional inequalities while those with fewer privileges support egalitarian measures. Rather, there is a perhaps surprisingly widespread support for a more equal distribution of rewards, even among those who would on the face of it be relatively worse off as a result.

Again, however, this finding about similarities in the perception of income inequalities across classes must be seen in the context of the relative lack of concordance in the world-views of particular individuals. Support for a more egalitarian income redistribution need not imply support for racial or sexual equality, for Keynesian rather than monetarist economic policies, or for the idea that class inequalities are paramount to the structuring of social conflict. There is nothing in our data to suggest that the world-views of individuals typically display that degree of coherence and completeness. Rather, in so far as it is possible to generalize on the basis of our investigation, we should say that the 'class consciousness' of the majority of people in our sample is characterized by its complexity, ambivalence, and occasional contradictions. It does not reflect a rigorously consistent interpretation of the world with an underlying ideological rationale rooted in perceived class interest alone.

IV

This finding is hardly controversial but we believe it carries serious implications for Erik Wright's attempt to map so-called class consciousness.

In particular, the fact that the class-based world-views of so many of our respondents are characterized by ambivalence and inconsistencies suggests that 'class consciousness' is more a question of how classes are *organized* in pursuit of class objectives, than of the extent to which individuals are made *subjectively aware* of class structures and their importance.

The data themselves simply confirm the conclusions reached by many earlier studies of social consciousness. Most of these have dealt with working-class consciousness in particular but the picture they present of the ambivalence of proletarian world-views is rather similar to that painted by the evidence for our sample as a whole. Frank Parkin, for example, has characterized the subordinate meaning systems of advanced working classes as a form of 'normative ambivalence'. These represent a 'negotiated' version of the dominant values in particular societies. They are therefore ambiguous in their implications for class action: on the one hand, they are constrained by the overarching rules specified by the dominant value system, but on the other offer a latent possibility for class action by their limited resistance to the morality of the existing distributive order. Parkin suggests that the usage of dominant and subordinate frames of reference is situationally determined: more specifically,

it could be hypothesized that in situations where purely abstract evaluations are called for, the dominant value system will provide the moral frame of reference; but in concrete social situations involving choice and action, the negotiated version – or the subordinate value-system – will provide the moral framework.[18]

This argument for the ambivalence of working-class consciousness is similar to Michael Mann's view that the western working classes are characterized by their pragmatism. Mann views a mature class consciousness as comprising four elements; namely, class identity (a feeling of class), class opposition (to class enemies), class totality (the ability to analyse situations in class terms), and class alternatives (a conception of a better society). He finds that these elements exist in different degree and differing admixtures among working classes in the industrial west. This suggests, to Mann at least, that the social cohesion of liberal democracies rests on a lack of consensus which is sustained by 'pragmatic role acceptance' secured via 'manipulative socialization' conducted through schools, the media, and other ideological state apparatuses. As a result, most workers confront the realities of everyday life with only a very limited ability to relate these to abstract principles of political philosophy, so that 'the attachment of the lower classes to the distant state may be expected to be far less normative and more pragmatic than their attachment to the primary familial group'.[19]

Many studies of working-class consciousness reached similar conclusions during the 1970s so that, by the end of that decade, an impasse had been reached. The world-views, values, and beliefs – or 'social consciousness' – of most proletarians appeared to be ambivalent, volatile, even self-contradictory. Pragmatism, rather than either acceptance of or opposition to the dominant values, was the common conclusion arrived at by a generation of researchers.[20]

Our own findings would seem simply to add weight to this interpretation of the available evidence.

Of course it is true, as one of us has argued elsewhere, that this type of evidence is open to alternative interpretations and that it has sometimes been used to lend weight to conclusions which it cannot in fact substantiate.[21] Indeed both of these problems have also been encountered in the present study. An example of the former is provided by the answers given to several of the questions on social class. It is clear that most people have a multifaceted view of this phenomenon (see, for example, Table 6.3 above). That is, they do not conceptualize class as a unidimensional relationship or attribute, but rather tend to describe classes as characteristically complex in their make-up. Class is a phenomenon related to income, occupation, and education; or to occupation and life-style; and so on. Given this, it seems plausible to claim that popular perceptions of class conflict as a contest about the allocation of monetary rewards (see Table 6.10 above) should not be taken as unambiguous evidence of a widespread and simple pecuniary instrumentalism, since alternative interpretations cannot be ruled out. That so many people choose to answer questions about inequality in pecuniary terms is hardly surprising given the extent to which money has become the generalized medium of exchange in capitalist societies. The dictates of the market economy tend to reduce perceptions of inequality to statements about the relative size and security of different pay-packets. People tend to articulate their perceptions, together with their worries, ambitions, and aspirations for social justice in pecuniary terms, because these are almost always dependent on monetary considerations. Workers are, with good cause, concerned about the size of their income: few have any financial security beyond the next pay packet. So working-class pecuniary instrument-alism can be and has been identified in every era of capitalist development. However, it is entirely possible that statements about money are simply a shorthand form of offering wider assessments about social control, power, or social justice more generally. For example, Huw Beynon's study of the Ford Halewood plant in the 1960s showed that, on initial inspection, the 'strike-happy' line workers, with one eye on the clock and the other on their pay-packets, appeared to be interested in money alone. However, more detailed questioning about the role of management and the nature of work revealed that this apparently straightforward pecuniary orientation to work had a definite moral and political component, which could be uncovered only by extensive probing, and by situating the pecuniary responses in the context of the plant and its history. Yet context and meaning are precisely what must be sacrificed by survey researchers attempting to work towards more general and reliable conclusions. So it is quite possible (indeed evidence both from our own study and from research elsewhere suggests that it is highly probable), that the three-quarters of those asked the question who described class conflict as conflict about 'money' would have offered more complex and variable descriptions of such conflict, had our interviewers offered them the opportunity to do so.[22]

The limitations of survey-based research into the complexities of belief systems are also responsible for some researchers arriving at conclusions about the ambivalence and volatility of individuals' beliefs on the basis of methodological delusion rather than substantive proof. The debate about class consciousness has been plagued by the problems associated with ecological reasoning. Often, for example, the contradictions obvious from separate studies of working-class attitudes across a number of groups have been transferred to the individuals comprising the groups themselves. That is, from the inconsistent beliefs and values of different groups, researchers have sometimes concluded that the individuals within each group must themselves display inconsistency in their values.[23] The tendency to impute the correlations found among groups to the individuals comprising them is endemic to survey-based research into belief systems. The point is, of course, that associations computed from group means or proportions cannot be taken as valid estimates of the associations that would be arrived at on the basis of individual data. The ecological associations between social classes and a range of contradictory beliefs or values tell us nothing about the individual class member and his or her particular attitudes.[24] It is for this reason that we have addressed ourselves explicitly to the issue of attitudinal consistency among individuals. But we would be among the first to acknowledge the limitations of our analysis in this and in the previous chapter. While we can find no evidence for an underlying ideological or normative consistency in our sample, and have argued on this basis that Britain lacks a unified moral order, we are not suggesting that attitudes and beliefs are therefore wholly unstructured or random. Some beliefs are clearly related to social class location. Particular subgroups within these classes may show a high concordance in the case of specific values and beliefs. It may well be the case, for example, that highly educated and Labour-voting public sector employees are likely to share a great many attitudes in common that distinguish them from their Conservative, less educated, or private sector peers. We have not pursued these sorts of subgroupings in this particular volume, partly for lack of space, but mainly because our involvement in the international comparative project dictated our initial theme of class consciousness.

Nevertheless, despite these limitations, we feel that our analysis has provided sufficient data to substantiate two conclusions. First, there is little ideological consistency in the British population as a whole, and that most individuals seem content to hold conflicting and sometimes even contradictory beliefs about that society and their place within it. The limitations of our survey methodology notwithstanding, we suspect that few class subjects have a unified and unambiguous view of society, or interpret the world in terms of a coherent package of underlying values and principles. Second, in so far as there is a structure underlying people's attitudes towards the topics covered in our survey, it cannot be said to reflect a mature or developed class consciousness comprising class identity, class opposition, class totality, and the conception of an alternative society. It is true that class, rather than alternative sources of social cleavage, continues to structure ideological packages – or at least those ideological packages that were investigated in this particular study. But these class-structured ideological packages hardly amount to coherent class ideologies, either of a 'dominant' kind among those in privileged class positions, or of a 'radical' alternative among the workers and their possible class allies.

V

These twin conclusions suggest that we should look again at the concept of class consciousness that informs Erik Wright's analysis of the attitudinal data from the international project. Wright argues that it is important to distinguish two rather different usages of the term class consciousness. 'For some theorists it is seen as a counterfactual or imputed characteristic of classes as collective entities, whereas for others it is understood as a concrete attribute of human individuals as members of classes.'[25] Wright himself subscribes to the second of these. Class consciousness refers to those beliefs, ideas, preferences and theories which are 'discursively accessible to the individual's own awareness', and which have a distinctive class content to them. In other words, class consciousness is to be understood as 'the subjective processes that shape intentional choices', with respect to class interests and class struggles. That is why he (and we in turn) examine the scale characteristics of a selection of attitudinal items having a class content. This is an attempt to discover which individuals express preferences and choices that are consistent with working-class or capitalist class interests by looking at the 'patterned distribution of individual consciousness within the relevant aggregate'. Wright specifically rejects the idea that class consciousness refers to some imputed consciousness rather than the actual consciousness of individuals themselves. Lukacs, for example, seems to define class consciousness as a causally efficacious yet supra-individual set of beliefs corresponding to what people in a certain class position would believe were they to behave 'rationally'. Wright, quite correctly, judges this conception of class consciousness to be unwarrantably teleological. To put the matter somewhat differently, he dismisses the Hegelian view of class consciousness represented in the work of Lukacs, in favour of a methodological individualism which equates class consciousness with the subjective preferences of individual actors.

Our own view is that Wright has here thrown out the baby of collective capacities (or properties) with the bathwater of an objective teleology of history. His critique of the Hegelian view of class consciousness is extended, wrongly in our opinion, to all interpretations which view this phenomenon as an attribute of classes as such rather than of the individuals who make them up. In fact his own findings suggest the contrary. Comparing the variation in class attitudes in Sweden and the United States, Wright concludes that this is in line with theoretical expectations, since the values on the consciousness scale change as one moves across the class typology matrix. Despite the differences between the two countries, in terms of state expansion, income inequality, welfare state programmes and so on,

the basic pattern linking class structure to class consciousness is very similar in the two countries: they are both polarized along the three dimensions of exploitation, and the values on the consciousness scale basically vary monotonically as one moves along these dimensions.[26]

However, in order to explain the variation between the two countries Wright resorts to political rather than economic differences, and in particular to the activities of parties and unions in the two countries. As he puts it,

while the overall patterning of consciousness is structurally determined by class relations, the level of working-class consciousness in a given society and the nature of the class coalitions that are built upon those class relations are shaped by the organizational and political practices that characterize the history of class struggle.[27]

The Swedish Social Democratic Party and Swedish labour movement have pursued relatively universal welfare policies which have tended to incorporate wage-earners in contradictory class positions and so lessen the likelihood of their perceiving class interests which are opposed to those of the working class itself. In the United States, by way of contrast, the Democratic Party has displaced the language of class from political discourse and organized social conflicts around non-class bases. Welfare policies have divided rather than unified wage-earners. American unions, meanwhile, have tended to take a particularly narrow view of their objectives since so few American workers are unionized. Each union's special interests have displaced their common interest in relation to capital as a whole.

This conclusion points to the extent to which class consciousness is in fact best considered as a property of classes as such rather than of the individuals within them. It is an attribute which describes collective practices rather than individual preferences. Wright himself considers this alternative conception in passing but only in order to clarify his own view of class consciousness as comprising the beliefs and values of individuals:

There is one sense in which one could legitimately refer to class 'consciousness' as a property of a collectivity, namely when consciousness is used to describe the practices themselves and not simply the forms of subjectivity that shape the intentional choices implicated in those practices. Since the actual practices involve the use of organizational resources and various other kinds of collective capacities, when the term 'consciousness' is extended to cover the practices as such, then it is no longer strictly an attribute of individuals. I prefer to limit the expression consciousness to the subjective dimensions of the problem and use the term 'capacities' to describe the collectively organized resources used in struggles, and the term 'practices' to describe the individual and collective activities that result from the linkage of individual consciousness and collective capacities.[28]

However, the conclusions of Wright's own analysis of class consciousness in Sweden and the United States militate against this attempt to conceptualize a class attribute in terms of purely individual characteristics, since what is crucial to the explanation of class awareness and class action in the two countries is the activities of their respective trades union movements and left-wing political parties – that is, the organization and practices of classes *as collectivities*.

To define class consciousness as an attribute of organizations rather than individuals – as the capacity of a class to behave as a collective actor rather than the propensity of individual members to think in class terms – is simply to reiterate Marx's observations about the importance of parties and unions in the 'formation of the proletariat into a class'.[29] Class organizations play a crucial role in the formation of political perceptions. Wright's own analysis of the structuring of individual preferences in different countries points to precisely this conclusion. Yet his definition of class consciousness implies a rather simplistic relationship between class structure and politics. It suggests that the latter can be reduced to the former since 'mass consciousness' (of class) changes political (and thereby economic) structures. This form of reasoning is analogous to that used by psephologists who have recently argued that the electoral successes of the Conservatives in Britain since 1979 must reflect fundamental changes in the occupational structure of this country. (This particular thesis about the demise of class politics is dealt with in Chapter 9 below.) Yet all of the available evidence (including that introduced by Wright himself) suggests quite the opposite; namely, that powerful class parties are an essential condition for the transformation of latent feelings of class identity into class conscious activity on behalf of class, rather than sectional interests. Class identities are more salient to workers in Sweden than in the United States (and, as Duncan Gallie has shown, to workers in France rather than Britain)[30] precisely because of the ideological and political practices of the trades unions and left-wing parties in these countries. A centralized party and labour movement can, first of all, help constitute social identities in class rather than other terms; and, second, can control particular interest groupings within the class in the interests of the collectivity itself. Such a movement is a condition of class action. In its absence there is nothing to prevent the flourishing of groups which either 'free-ride' or in some other way pursue sectional interests at the expense of the class as a whole.

This is not to suggest that a strong party is a sufficient condition for the development of class consciousness. There must be a latent feeling of class which such parties can mobilize for class purposes. It is simply to point to the fact that the problems of forming class alliances in pursuit of democratic socialism – which is precisely the objective Wright sets for a class conscious proletariat – are problems of developing and co-ordinating centralized political initiatives rather than simply encouraging more and more powerful feelings of class in individual subjects. (And, in any case, the latter are in large part dependent on the former.) Perhaps this rather abstract point can best be illustrated by an empirical example. In the following chapter we will take a short excursion into British nineteenth-century history in order to show that our reconceptualization of the problems of class consciousness as an attribute of the collectivity (class practices organized by parties) rather than of individuals (the developing subjectivity of groups of class members) is no mere matter of definitional sophistry. If subjective factors remain more or less unchanged, yet the scope and intensity of class action varies greatly, then the importance of the organizational level to conceptions of class consciousness will have been forcefully demonstrated. As we shall see, this is in fact what happens. In effect, then, the following chapter is a critique of Wright's sociological determinism – his tendency (often contrary to his own evidence) to see ideological and political matters as determined by economic (that is class-structural) factors. Chapter 9 then complements this by looking at the reverse sociological determinism of psephologists who have argued for the demise of class politics by reducing ideological and political changes to putative shifts in the class structure. In neither case, as we shall now see, are matters really that straightforward.

Notes

1 Goldthorpe (1988) in fact extends these criticisms, rather convincingly, to three intellectual perspectives on the working class in Britain. First, that of 'liberals' such as Edward Shils, Daniel Bell, Clark Kerr and S. M. Lipset, who hold that class society is giving way to a 'post-industrial' mass society, with class conflict effectively contained by working-class integration into the structures of liberal democracy. Second, the view of 'organicists' such as F. R. Leavis, Raymond Williams, Richard Hoggart and others, who during the 1950s and 1960s 'rediscovered' the so-called working-class community, with its 'traditional' habits of collectivism and mutuality. Finally, that of 'the left' itself, notably the views of those such as Perry Anderson and Tom Nairn, who seem, to Goldthorpe at least, determined to unearth a working-class 'reason' and 'rationality' in the consciousness of proletarians, one that will (eventually) penetrate hegemonic ideologies rooted in traditionalism, deference, and egoism.
2 Wright (1985: 287).
3 Wright (1985: 288).
4 Wright (1985: 286, 289–90).
5 Wright (1985: 264, 278).
6 Wright (1985: 279).
7 Wright (1985: 280).
8 Wright (1985: 286).
9 See, for example, Scase (1977), Korpi (1983), Erikson et al. (1979, 1982).
10 On this issue see Heath (1986), from whose article on the subject the typology of logical, technical, normative and ideological consistency is taken.
11 Wright (1985: 251).
12 There is also a methodological point to be made here concerning Wright's reliance on Likert items alone in order to 'map' so-called class consciousness. The limitations of this technique are well known and we cannot accept that, considered in isolation, it tells sociologists much about anything. During the period in which the American survey was being designed, we (and others) tried to persuade the American team not to use Likert items as the primary means of measuring social consciousness, but in the event they were retained. In the interests of comparative research we included the items in the British pilot survey but respondents were clearly irritated by them. Around one-third of the interviews were unusable at this point, because respondents refused to answer Wright's items, didn't understand them, or persistently chose the 'Don't know' option. For example, the sixth of these items asks interviewees to:

Imagine that workers in a major industry are out on strike over working conditions and wages. Which of the following outcomes would you like to see occur: (a) the workers win their

most important demands; (b) the workers win some of their demands and make major concessions;
(c) the workers win only a few of their demands and make major concessions; (d) the workers go back to work without winning any of their demands?'

More than half of those to whom this question was put insisted (quite reasonably in our view) that they needed additional contextual information before they could reply.

13 The central item is here taken to be the one which had the highest loading on the relevant factor.

14 In his more systematic comparison across a much wider range of items Heath (1986) found that there was a 'definite structure' underlying people's attitudes to defence, conservation, equality, political liberty, and sexual liberty. In fact, however, his findings are not that different from our own. He describes as 'massive' a 50 percentage points difference between the logically 'consistent' and 'inconsistent' positions on two items about nuclear policy – by far the largest difference he encouraged in his data. We ourselves report a 47 percentage points difference between the consistent and inconsistent positions at Table 7.2. The differences between supporters and opponents of particular normative stances are much smaller: the highest is 40 per cent, but more typically Heath finds they are in the 20 to 30 per cent range, or below. Whether one elects to describe this degree of consistency as 'high' or 'low' is partly a matter of whether one describes the cup as 'half empty' or 'half full'. More than this, however, the difference in emphasis between Heath's account and our own is due to the fact that, in addition to calculating the percentage difference between those who agree and disagree with a particular item, (that is, looking at the column percentages in cross-tabulations), we have examined also the distribution of the total percentages in each of the cells for any given pair of items. It is arguable that, in some respects, the latter procedure gives a more accurate picture of 'overall concordance' or consistency, since it describes the situation across the sample as a whole, and not simply the differences between subgroups within it. It is also possible that, because the British Social Attitudes survey contains many more attitudinal items than our own, it offers interviewees greater opportunities to express relatively consistent packages of beliefs and opinions.

15 Compare, for example, Calvert (1982), Furbank (1985), and the currently fashionable thesis about the decline of class politics (which is discussed extensively in Chapter 9 below).

16 For example, see Goldthorpe (1984a: 493–4).

17 Again the Essex strategy of sampling and classifying individuals rather than families proved to be analytically superior here. If female respondents are reclassified to the class positions of their husbands, as is advocated by Goldthorpe, then the explained variation for the Goldthorpe class schema drops to less than 3 per cent.

18 Parkin (1972: 92–3).

19 Mann (1970).

20 For example, see Newby (1977), Pollert (1981), and the papers collected in Bulmer (1975).

21 See Marshall (1983).

22 Compare Beynon (1980). We are not the first survey researchers to have encountered this problem: see, for example, Platt's (1971) somewhat sceptical comment on the findings of the Affluent Worker Study. Similar problems of interpretation loom large at other points in our survey. For example, although three-quarters of those asked thought that 'birth' was the primary determinant of class membership (see Table 6.4), most respondents went on to mention another factor as well – hard work, education, income, occupation, and the like. It is clear from the interview schedules that many individuals hold possibly sophisticated (and certainly complex) views about the relationship between birth and these other factors. Unfortunately, because of the constraints of the interview situation, it was impossible for them to elaborate these.

23 Examples here include Mann (1970) and Roberts et al (1977).

24 See Robinson (1950).

25 Wright (1985: 242).

26 Wright (1985: 278).

27 Wright (1985: 278).

28 Wright (1985: 280, note 4).

29 Marx and Engels (1970b: 46). See also Panitch (1986: 16–21).

30 See Gallie (1983).

8 Goodbye to social class?

We began our study by noting clear signs of a developing consensus among social scientists about the changing basis and forms of distributional conflict in the United Kingdom during the past decade of economic recession. It is commonly argued nowadays that decisive shifts in the structuring of social inequalities have generated original forms of sectionalism to replace the long-standing solidarities associated with social class. Accompanying shifts in values and life-styles allegedly have encouraged individualism and privatism. Both processes are said to be discernable in a decline of class-based politics in Britain since 1979. Class analysis, according to its many critics, will therefore prove to be increasingly bankrupt in the explanation of social inequalities and schisms.

These arguments have been given additional credibility by the further consensus that exists among post-Parsonian social theorists to the effect that capitalism possesses, to use Fred Hirsch's celebrated phrase, a 'depleting moral legacy'.[1] Again this process is characterized as one of growing and excessive individualism. Daniel Bell, for example, maintains that the 'cultural contradiction' of western society,

is a widening disjunction between the social structure (the economy, technology, and occupational system) and the culture (the symbolic expression of meanings), each of which is ruled by a different axial principle. The social structure is rooted in functional rationality and efficiency, the culture in the antinomian justification of the enhance-ment of the self. . . . In the organization of production and work, the system demands provident behaviour, industriousness and self-control, dedication to a career and success. In the realm of consumption it fosters the attitudes of *carpe diem*, prodigality and display, and the compulsive search for play. But in both realms the system is completely mundane, for any transcendent ethic has vanished.[2]

Similarly, Jurgen Habermas speaks of a 'motivation crisis' in advanced capitalist societies, the effect of a contradiction between exorbitant demands for individual enhancement generated in the socio-cultural system, and the strictly limited redistributive aspirations of the bourgeois state, even in its welfare-reformist guise.[3]

Those on the political left then chart these developments as a depletion in the moral legacy willed to capitalism by earlier eras and lay bare the (as they see it) increasingly precarious residue of the cash nexus. Economic liberals, on the other hand, bemoan the revolution of rising expectations, pervasive envy, and irresponsible egoism that generates seemingly endless and, to them, irrational demands for pay increases and better living conditions.[4] For one group heightened distributional dissent is an expression of the moral bankruptcy of the old order and brings the system to the threshold of a new age of egalitarianism. For the other it marks a lamentable decline of traditional values, *civitas*, and responsible unionism into the anarchy of gang loyalties. Nevertheless, the common conclusion of commentators as diverse theoretically and politically as Habermas, Offe, Hirsch, Bell, Brittan, and Hayek is that dysfunctional effects of the market are no longer offset in advanced capitalist societies by consensus about a concrete morality for rendering distributive issues principled. Western liberal democracies lack *Sittlichkeit*; that is, an agreed morality or moral order. In the 'legitimation vacuum' thus created, distributional struggles become increasingly fragmented and intense, raising in due course serious problems of social integration.

In our view, however, there are good reasons to suppose that these structural and attitudinal features of British society are considerably less novel than proponents of the thesis of restructured distributional conflict would have us believe.

Sociological research on lower-class meaning systems has consistently identified a heterogeneity of circumstances, interests, and beliefs among manual workers during the period since 1945. Numerous accounts of post-war class segmentation identify a variety of 'new' and 'old' working classes based on a diversity of market and work situations. These structural cleavages have generally supported some form of intra-class schism. Moreover, it has also been argued that, during the so-called years of affluence in the 1950s and 1960s, 'expressive' orientations to manual work largely gave way to more narrow 'economistic' calculations, usually in association with declining job satisfaction, an increase in home-centredness and family-centredness, and corresponding privatism of hitherto communitarian working-class life-styles. It would seem, therefore, that neither sectionalism nor privatism are newly arrived among the proletariat.[5]

In fact, as we have seen, sustained research into the 'social consciousness' of British workers reached an impasse in the 1970s when the various studies converged on the conclusion that the great majority of respondents were normatively ambivalent and therefore content to make contradictory state-ments and act in inconsistent ways. Since, as Michael Mann puts it, 'only those actually sharing in societal power need develop consistent societal values' the dispossessed majority adopt a pragmatic stance towards existing socio-political arrangements. Their immediate concerns are contingent matters of everyday life. Normative attachments are to the proximate structures of family and community rather than the distant state. Lower-class meaning systems are correspondingly ambiguous and volatile. The social cohesion of liberal democracies therefore rests on the lack of consensus rather than its achievement.[6]

These findings have led some to argue that modern social theory places too much importance on the role of dominant ideologies and too little on the pressing necessities of material existence. That is, they question the

197

assumption that there exist in most societies a set of dominant beliefs, propagated by the ruling classes, which are absorbed into the consciousness of subordinate strata and so help block the development of radical political dissent.

For example, Bryan Turner and his colleagues maintain that dominant ideologies are rarely transmitted effectively throughout social structures, and that their principal effects are on superordinate rather than subordinate classes. In feudal and early capitalist societies such ideologies functioned to maintain the control of the dominant class over wealth – but at the level of the elites themselves. Both the feudal manor and the capitalist family firm depended on the conservation and accumulation of property. Private possession of land and capital required a stable marriage system, with unambiguous rules about inheritance, legitimacy, and remarriage. The 'dominant ideology' was a complex of legal, moral, and religious values which had the required effect of preserving wealth. Among feudal ruling classes, for example, Catholicism and the system of honour provided ideological guarantees that children would remain loyal to family holdings. By comparison the peasantry (and in early capitalism the factory work-force) were co-opted by the sheer exigencies of labouring to live – the 'dull compulsion of economic relations'. Even in late capitalism the 'iron cage' of everyday life offers a better explanation of working-class quiescence than does ideological incorporation. Moral pluralism and a great diversity of political, social, and cultural deviance can readily be tolerated because the compliance of subordinate strata is secured by economic constraint, political coercion, and the bureaucratic mechanisms of school, family, workplace, and prison. The 'structuralist' or 'materialist' position thus concurs with the perceived lack of *Sittlichkeit* in modern capitalist societies, but concludes that this raises no real problems for social integration since the meaning systems of subordinate classes have never been more than 'dualistic', embracing only a much modified version of any particular dominant ideology.[7]

It is beyond the scope of this book to explore in detail the full-blown and diverse theories of social order embraced by economic liberalism, Marxism, and the new versions of structuralism – far less arbitrate between these. Nevertheless, our interest in the putative demise of social class leads us to challenge two aspects of recent liberal and Marxist thinking, as this bears on the issue of distributional conflict in contemporary Britain. We shall argue, first of all, that left and right alike have exaggerated the extent to which current forms of distributional dissent can be said to be novel. Neither sectionalism nor instrumentalism are recent inventions of economic restructuring. Moreover, the tendency to connect changes in 'social consciousness' (or in electoral behaviour) directly to swings in values and/or shifts in the occupational structure greatly oversimplifies the relationship between the distributional order of societies, on the one hand, and the specific forms taken by distributional conflict, on the other. In particular it omits important issues that arise at the level of organizational capacity and collective action.

II

Before pressing these objections in terms of the evidence from distributional struggles in Britain, we can clarify the issues involved by considering the structure of distributional conflict in a more general sense. In principle, such conflict can be organized along inclusionary or exclusionary lines, and on the terrain of class or status orders. Four types of distributional conflict are then possible as can be seen from Table 8.1. This table represents one possible, though by no means the only, interpretation of Weber's remarks on class and status. In particular it embraces the central idea that classes and status groups are 'phenomena of the distribution of power within a community'.[8]

Table 8.1 *Types of distributional struggle*

| | | Principle of conflict | |
		Class	*Status*
Principle of organization	Exclusion	SECTIONAL	CONVENTIONAL
	Inclusion	SOLIDARISTIC	LEGAL

In the abstract, classes may be said to have their origins at the level of production so that 'property and lack of property are, therefore, the basic categories of all class situations'.[9] Organized on an inclusionary basis, class conflict would involve two collective actors: owners of capital and sellers of labour power. The obvious example is that of the solidaristic struggle between bourgeoisie and proletariat as analysed by Marx. However, at the level of what Marxists have termed 'social formation', certain complications appear. Principal among these are the complexities explored by Weber in terms of market situation and by subsequent neo-Weberians via the model of market, work, and status situations.[10] Empirically, class conflicts are shaped by the particular circumstances of market, work, and status factors. The market, which is not simply an economic but also a legal and conventional construct, serves to distribute life-chances differentially and, therefore, to circumscribe broad social classes. However these social classes are themselves further cross-cut by work and status factors. For example, the technical, sectoral, and social divisions of labour create a highly differentiated structure of roles and tasks. These divisions are made effective via market exchanges of the same order as those which actuate the distribution of property and, consequently, create a hierarchy of groups distinguished by the different types of skills and resources that each possess or control. Obviously, such considerations serve to render social classes less coherent empirically than they are theoretically, since they give rise to numerous sectional disputes. These disputes emerge as those differently placed in sectoral and technical terms attempt to maximize whatever advantages their particular position puts at their disposal. The wage advantage sought by workers strategically placed in a particular economy or

199

process of production is one characteristically sectional form of class action. Distributional struggles organized on the terrain of social class issues, whether sectional or solidaristic in tenor, contest in some way the control of property or allocation of rewards for marketable skills. Status conflicts also contest the structure of differential access to power and advantage. Again it is the allocation of life-chances that is in dispute and again such conflicts can be organized according to exclusionary or inclusionary principles. However, status conflicts are rooted in the moral rather than the material order of society. Exclusionary struggles occur when a group or groups of people differentiated from the wider society according to some conventional or symbolic criterion claim for themselves specific privileges of an honorific nature. All social relationships based on institutionalized deference are examples of status conflicts organized in this manner. Most commonly these are structured along lines of racial, ethnic, cultural, or life-style differences. Similarly, where inclusionary class struggles are an attempt to incorporate whole societies under a system of undifferentiated substantive rewards, status conflicts organized on the same principle seek to achieve universal membership in the privileges and responsibilities of citizenship. These may be oriented towards legal, political, or social equality.

Though analytically distinct, class and status struggles are, in practice, invariably intertwined and their precise relationship at any time becomes a matter for empirical research. Because the capitalist market has no moral dimension sociologists have sometimes seen the importance of the status order as that of legitimating the structure of power and advantage created by the system of production and exchange. Conventional status inequalities based on race, gender, and life-style, for example, are perceived by some as emergent properties of the class structure itself.[11] Others have observed, however, that in present-day plural democracies, legal rights of citizenship have been widely recognized, so that as long as these societies continue also to be organized economically on the basis of market exchanges they are subject to conflicts, arising out of the contradiction between axial principles governing class relationships on the one hand, and the status order on the other. Since the rights of citizenship determine the welfare of individuals independently of their market capacity, and in an egalitarian manner, they act as a barrier to the free play of exclusively capitalist social relations and are a constant reminder that the fundamental conflict between social justice and market value has not been resolved.[12]

One of the earliest commentators to appreciate the significance of this tension was T. H. Marshall writing about the 'realisation of citizenship' in western democracies. Citizenship for Marshall embraces civil, political, and social elements. The civil element is composed of individual rights to freedom of person, speech, association, and the right to justice in civil courts. Political citizenship is extended by participation in the exercise of political power via the universal franchise. By the social element Marshall means that form of economic welfare and social security that is accorded members of a society as a right and irrespective of their ability to pay. The various educational, health, and income-maintaining services of a welfare state, for example, are designed to ensure that all members of a society can 'live the life of a civilized human being according to the standards prevailing in the society', and to this end diminish inequalities that are specifically grounded in the market relations of a capitalist order.[13]

There are two aspects of this argument that are particularly important in the British context. The first is that the various citizenship rights tend not to have advanced in tandem. In the course of British history, for example, important civil and political rights were secured for males in the eighteenth and nineteenth centuries, and for females during the present century, while many of the rights to social citizenship have been a matter of contention for more than three-quarters of a century and remain so today.[14] The other important feature of Marshall's argument in relation to the British situation is the centrality of trades unions to struggles both for greater class equality and the extension of citizenship rights themselves. Marshall notes that the confirmation of civil rights in the economic sphere created a secondary system of 'industrial citizenship' complementary to that found in the realm of politics. Moreover, when exercised by workers, rights to collective bargaining became 'an instrument for raising their social and economic status, that is to say, for establishing the claim that they, as citizens, were entitled to certain social rights'.[15] In other words, collective bargaining presents the anomaly of civil rights, normally settled on individuals, being exercised collectively, as if such action were political in its intent. Historically, of course it is only political rights that have been so established – through elections to parliament and local councils.

For this reason the trades unions have been involved from the outset, not only in class, but also in status conflicts:

To have to bargain for a living wage in a society which accepts the living wage as a social right is as absurd as to have to haggle for a vote in a society which accepts the vote as a political right. Yet the early twentieth century attempted to make sense of this absurdity. It fully endorsed collective bargaining as a normal and peaceful market operation, while recognising in principle the right of the citizen to a minimum standard of living, which was precisely what the trade unions believed, and with good reason, that they were trying to win for their members with the weapon of the bargain.[16]

Wage disputes can pursue sectional or class interest by extracting whatever returns the market will bear at a given moment. But they can also appeal to the conceptions of social justice based on common citizenship – the notion of what constitutes a 'fair wage' for example. Indeed, the hierarchical wage structure of British society today is as much a reflection of differentially successful appeals to social rights, as it is a gradation according to strict market value. Conversely, from positions of market strength unions have bargained for the extension of rights of industrial citizenship itself, pursuing such objectives as security of employment, minimum wage guarantees, pension rights, and social service support during periods of ill-health.

In recent times, therefore, it has been the trades union movement which has formed the interface between class and status conflicts in this country. On many occasions unions have organized themselves along exclusionary lines and secured sectional gains at the expense of the working class as a whole. At other times more inclusionary class objectives have been to the fore. At one moment the struggle has been couched in class terms, at another in status terms, and often both simultaneously. In the following section we shall illustrate this argument by reference to the emergence of the so-called labour aristocracy in mid nineteenth-century England. Though necessarily sketched in broad terms, this example does confirm that working-class sectionalism and privatism are not peculiar to the present recession, and so casts doubt on the thesis that distributional conflict in Britain today has recently taken these novel forms. It also confirms that neither changes in the occupational structure nor shifts in individual values constitute adequate explanations for the patterning of distributional dissent.

III

The watchwords in the thesis of restructured distributional conflict are sectionalism, egoism, and privatism. Although proponents of the argument interrelate these in different ways their common perception is one of recent changes in social hierarchy (in particular the occupational structure), and in social values, each associated with the rise of a diffuse individualism embracing life-styles, politics, and ideology. The heterogeneous working class of contemporary Britain has absorbed capitalist economic values; it takes an instrumental stance towards class organizations so that pecuniary collectivism based on sectional self-interest has undermined worker solidarity; and it has retreated from class politics into the private world of home and family. Distributional dissent now centres on consumption and status rather than production and class. In this way sectionalism and privatism emerge as the obverse of class consciousness. The assumption is that they are not and cannot be associated with solidaristic or inclusionary forms of class-based distributional conflict.

This contrast forces the history of British labour into an implausible dualistic mould: solidaristic and class versus sectional and privatized. The reality is more complex. Consider, for example, the evidence from studies of the mid nineteenth-century work-force in rapidly industrializing Britain. Sectionalism is already evident, most obviously in the existence of a 'labour aristocracy' of traditional artisans and skilled manual workers, but for both groups the emergence of a culture of domesticity centred on the home and on privatized life-styles co-existed with solidaristic and class-based political activity in the context of the trades union movement.

It is true that there is little or no consensus about how to marshal these data under particular theoretical banners. At one extreme are those who accept an undiluted version of the classical Marxist theory of the labour aristocracy. At the other are critics who deny this term any analytical value and maintain that its retention, since it carries the implication of explanation, actually hinders the development of alternative frameworks within which to place changes in the social structure of Victorian Britain.[17] But the ongoing debate about the labour aristocracy is largely concerned with the circumstances surrounding its emergence and the precise parameters of the stratum itself. Why was the overt antagonism expressed in Chartism replaced in the mid nineteenth century by a working-class politics of moderate reformism? Precisely how deep were the divisions in political outlook between the different grades of factory workers?[18] If one suspends judgement on the various attempts to locate the documented changes in life-styles, politics and ideology within some wider theory of social order, it soon becomes apparent that there exists considerable overlap between the apparently competing accounts, at least in so far as the substance of the changes themselves is concerned.[19]

A common starting point is the observation that the culture of the artisan in the immediate pre-industrial era was trade-based, work-centred, and male-dominated. During the first half of the nineteenth century, for example, most London trades worked a twelve-hour day, six days each week, with people residing in the immediate vicinity of their work. Spare-time association, conviviality, and political discussion were centred on the workplace or an associated local hostelry, which served also as a house of call and centre of craft organization. Trade feasts, carnivals, intermarriage, and hereditary apprenticeships all served to reinforce trade solidarity. Homes were cramped, uncomfortable and, where they were not places of work, served as little more than somewhere to eat and sleep.

During the second half of the century, however, home and family became increasingly important both for artisans and the newly emerging skilled workers in the capital goods sector. For those who enjoyed secure employment and were able to restrict entry to the trade via apprenticeships the mid Victorian economic boom brought a new prosperity. Rising real wages and falling prices saw the emergence of a margin of comfort over subsistence. The rise in living standards was, in turn, associated with a shortening of the working week, improved housing, suburbanization, home-centred patterns of consumption, and new forms of 'family leisure', all of which increased the importance of home and family in working men's lives. Robert Gray, for example, documents the emergence of a 'culture of domesticity', of 'domestic responsibility', and the shifting focus of artisanal life away from work towards home-centred and family-centred life-styles. This period also sees the emergence of specifically artisanal housing areas as skilled workers moved away from the courts and alleys of the slums, where they shared facilities with unskilled and casual labour, to the often badly-built but nevertheless self-contained houses in superior suburbs. By 1870 the majority of skilled workers already commuted to work by tram or workers' train.

The concern for better housing was not simply a reflection of the desire for improved physical amenities. It was also an attempt to escape identification with the inhabitants of the older central slums and reflected the revaluation of home and family as a haven from work, source of dignity, and centre of recreation. Geoffrey Crossick, for example, describes the artisan elite as:

Separated from lower strata by a complex of social, economic and cultural characteristics, and to some extent divided internally amongst precisely demarcated crafts. This aristocray of labour, and the skilled workers who shared its aspirations if not its achievements, was defined by more than income alone. Social status, opportunity and behaviour reinfored the elitist potential offered by a stable and relatively adequate income. These artisans were conscious of their superiority over other sections of the working class, especially their labourers and the 'dishonourable' sections of their own trades, and they held an ambiguous position at the very time when they were the only organised section of the working class, organised within trade unions and, with those white-collar and petit-bourgeois groups with which they were seen by contemporaries to merge, dominating benefit societies, building societies, co-operatives and working men's clubs.[20]

This does not mean that there was wholesale conformity to middle-class ideals of domesticity. The outlook of the labour aristocracy was an ambivalent one. 'Dominant values changed their meaning as they became adapted to the conditions of the artisan world and mediated through autonomous artisan institutions.'[21] But a distinctively working-class conception of respectability did emerge and this was closely tied to a developing domestic ideal.

One consequence of this revaluation of family life that did in fact diffuse down the class structure was the emergence of a much stricter sexual division of labour, under which married women withdrew from paid employment outside the home. Men bargained for, and in effect secured, a 'family wage'. Wives who remained in paid labour shifted to 'genteel' occupations like shopkeeping or did homework such as laundering. The new division of labour was reinforced by the Education Act of 1870 which forced children into schools and left all household tasks in the hands of adult women. In due course the interiors of skilled working-class homes were transformed by cheap factory-produced commodities for home-based consumption. Wall-paper, floor coverings, furniture and ornaments turned front parlours everywhere into shrines of respectability. Finally, rising living standards and shorter working hours saw the development of new forms of family-centred recreation, including excursions and seaside holidays, although there remained considerable regional variation in this sphere with mining and heavy industry areas tending to retain more traditional sex-segregated patterns of associational activity.

These evolving home-centred and privatized life-styles nevertheless co-existed with high levels of participation in a range of voluntary associations, from sports clubs and churches to working men's clubs and trade unions. The labour aristocrats were unified outside family and workshop through their participation in local associations that were linked to claims both for respectability and citizenship rights. Skilled workers in particular were dependent on collective forms of organization and especially on the trades unions.

These could be, and were, simultaneously exclusionary and inclusionary in their activities. At one level, for example, the craft unions were concerned to protect the standard of living of their members by restricting apprenticeships and bargaining for higher wages. The instrumental use of trades unions by the skilled elite of manual workers differed from the individualistic instrumentality typical of the Victorian middle class in that the latter was concerned solely with personal or family benefit whereas the former rested principally on collective self-help. There was, in other words, an identification with craft or stratum, a feeling of mutuality and collective strength, a shared aspiration for economic betterment and social respectability to be achieved by the group as a whole. But this was, nevertheless, still instrumentalism. Many trades union struggles during the period were therefore exclusionary; that is, sectional and conventional. Their objective was to advance the interests of members in the areas of pay, hours, craft privileges, conditions of work and social benefits. At another level, however, these same craft unions were engaged in strenuous attempts to extend industrial and social citizenship by petitioning parliament on such issues as the ten-hour day, health and safety at work, formal rights for trades unions, and the vote for working men. Narrowly instrumental in pursuing sectional wage demands, the labour aristocracy in mid Victorian Britain was also considerably more radical than any other section of the working class, both in its class and its status aspirations. Of course it was the radicalism of social reform rather than wholesale revolution. As Crossick has observed:

This radicalism was circumscribed by a broad social acquiescence; an acquiescence not in this law or that law, not in this employer or that employer, not in this level of wages or that level of wages, but in the existing system of law, in the existence of employers, in the methods of wage determination. The oppositional efforts of working-class radicals in Kentish London during this period were based on an analysis of social ills that placed political inequality at its heart. . . . This radical position dovetailed with the social values of its adherents. Their liberalism concerned independence and respectability, acknowledgement of moral worth and value as citizens, and concern for justice and the ending of privilege. . . . Its central concerns can be summarised as universal suffrage, excessive taxation, opposition to the privileged establishment – especially the Church of England – and an opposition to landed privilege and the power of the great landowners that produced demands for reform of tax law and the ending of the national debt. To these must be added a Painite anti-authoritarianism built upon a traditional conception of an Englishman's liberties.[22]

Elsewhere in Britain, as studies by Foster, Tholfsen, and others have shown, working men's organizations developed at different times a labour conscious, class conscious and, according to some, even a socialist politics. Yet these were coincidental with a constant concern for respectability and the defence of craft privileges.

Among nineteenth-century labour aristocrats, therefore, sectionalism and privatism co-existed with solidarism and the growth of class institutions (trades unions, trades councils, the Trades Union Congress) which were commonly engaged in pursuit of civil, political, and social rights of citizenship that extended beyond particular crafts to the working class as a whole. As Gray concludes:

> The importance of craft control on the job meant that skilled trade unionists were often divided, not just from the unskilled, but also against each other. Such sectionalism can be found throughout the history of the working class. . . . [But] . . . the struggle to legalise union activity, and to achieve a wider recognition of the working class presence in the community fostered a common sense of identity among these skilled trades. . . . If the identity of trade unionists was narrowly based, it still reflected some common interests beyond immediate craft sectionalism. As at other times in the history of the movement, there was an uneasy co-existence of sectional and broader types of activity.[23]

Despite the apparent existence of great regional and sectoral variations, most unions were simultaneously (or at least sequentially) involved in what were earlier termed sectional, solidaristic, conventional, and legal forms of distributional struggle. At times they acted against the interests of unskilled and unorganized workers by defending craft privileges. But there is little doubt that, in their status aspirations, they were consistently the most forceful representatives of the interests of the working class as a whole – or, at least, the male portion of it. Neither the pecuniary motivations nor the burgeoning 'privatized' life-styles of their members seem to have precluded solidaristic forms of collective action.[24]

IV

Seen against this historical background, the current arguments suggesting that sectionalism, instrumentalism, and privatism are somehow novel results of a recent restructuring of distributional conflict seem less than convincing. These arguments are the probable consequence of a tendency towards dualistic historical thinking whereby a communitarian and solidaristic proletariat of some bygone heyday of class antagonism is set against the atomized and consumer-oriented working class of today. Not only is it the case that historical data suggest a less romantic reality: sectionalism, privatism, and instrumentalism have always been close to the surface of working-class life. It is also true that, conversely, class solidarities retain an importance that undermines many contemporary accounts of late capitalist societies in which sociability and altruism are reputed to have given way entirely to a 'one-dimensional' and atomized consumerism. The evidence of previous chapters confirms at least this much.

Our own data about so-called privatism, being cross-sectional rather than longitudinal, must also be set into this intellectual context. In considering these data it is pertinent to remind ourselves that the concept of privatism (or privatization) is itself rather nebulous. Three clear usages can be identified in the literature. First, there are those who have located privatism in a structural trend towards institutional and geographical non-coincidence as a general feature of modern societies, evident for example in the increasingly loose-knit characteristic of social networks. The argument here is that, with the emergence of capitalism and spread of the market economy, households become integrated into a web of economic relationships which undermine traditional extended kinship and community ties. Social relations in the different spheres are more and more discrete: the nuclear family household becomes an isolated, private sphere, separated from work and neighbourhood alike. Elsewhere, however, privatism has been characterized as a process reflected less in social relations than social consciousness. In contradistinction to the putative work-centred and expressive solidarism of 'class consciousness', privatism manifests itself in the location of central life interests firmly within the home, and in a corresponding instrumentalism towards social relations outside home and family. Finally, privatism in both its structural and cultural (or consciousness) variants has been linked to 'privatized politics'; that is, a preference for 'personal politics' said to be evident in the growth of political instrumentalism or issue-centred voting, and corresponding demise of class politics.[25] In this limited political sense the evidence for privatism will be discussed in the following chapter and will be found wanting. But the structural and cultural claims for the concept are more difficult to explore empirically since these take us far beyond the relatively straightforward terrain of voting behaviour.

One established way of broaching arguments about privatism as culture or consciousness is simply to ask people about central life interests and report their assessments of these. Respondents in our study were asked how they viewed their work (Question 89). Only 34 per cent of those in employment at the time of the survey saw their present job as nothing more than a means of earning a living. Sixty-six per cent claimed it meant more to them than that – and were then asked to explain why this was so. A variety of answers were offered, the most popular being that the work in question was somehow fulfilling or enjoyable (82 per cent of interviewees asked the question included this among their answers), that it offered sociability with colleagues, or that it provided an opportunity for using specific skills (Table 8.2). On the other hand, only 11 per cent of employees who claimed that work meant more than simply a means of earning a living went on to say that it was 'central to their life', so the argument can always be put that many of the seemingly positive attributes mentioned in this context are testimony to after the event rationalization rather than non-pecuniary attitudes to work. In other words, they are evidence merely of the extent to which people reconcile themselves to an unalterable and relatively unpleasant fact of life, literally by making the best of a bad job. In some instances this will undoubtedly be true. However, this does not seem to be generally the case, since our data also show that, among employees who stated that their jobs *were* simply a means of earning a living, only 36 per cent claimed that they would feel this way about *any* job they obtained. Other non-pecuniary explanations (relating to the character of the local labour market and limited skills of the respondent) were, by comparison, proffered by 31 per cent and 33 per cent respectively of these employees.

Table 8.2 *The meaning of work*

Way in which job is more than just a means of earning a living	N	% of responses	% of cases
Rewarding, fulfilling, worthwhile, enjoyable	634	37.0	81.6
Human contact, being with colleagues, getting out of house	279	16.3	35.9
Using or developing my skills	183	10.7	23.6
I enjoy working for the present organization	167	9.8	21.5
Job allows use of initiative	144	8.4	18.5
Variety in the work	128	7.5	16.5
Work is central to my life	85	5.0	10.9
Value of my work to the country	56	3.3	7.2
Work fits in with my family/I do it for my family	16	0.9	2.1
It is better than being unemployed	8	0.5	1.0
Other	12	0.7	1.5
Total	1712	100.0	220.3

(Valid cases = 777)

Not surprisingly these various responses are heavily structured by social class. As can be seen from Table 8.3, those who view their work merely as a means of earning a living are overwhelmingly to be found among the working class, no matter with which class schema one operates. (The seemingly high proportions of uncredentialled 'managers' and 'supervisors' who display this attitude are mere artefacts of Wright's revised procedures for allocating individuals to classes. These are the members of Goldthorpe's working class who work alongside a 'mate' or who exercise very limited supervisory authority over their peers. As was seen in Chapter 4 they can more plausibly be treated as part of the proletariat.) As this table also shows, women are somewhat more likely than men to find rewards other than mere money in their employment, even when they are engaged in unskilled manual work, and again this is to be expected, given the acknowledged attractions of sociability at work for erstwhile housewives. (Overall, 37 per cent of male employees stated that work was simply a means of earning a living, as compared to 29 per cent of employed females.) These attractions are confirmed by our data on class differences in expressed job satisfactions. They show that women across all class locations are much more likely than men to emphasize the sociability of formal employment as one of its rewards (see Table 8.4). Elsewhere in this table the expected class differences also materialize: service-class respondents can see more of value to the country in their work than can other employees, are more likely to experience the rewards of using their own initiative, and more commonly enjoy the variety in the work itself. Working-class respondents, on the other hand, tend to emphasize the sociability of work and, among males at least, the opportunity it offers to use or develop particular work skills. None of these findings are exceptional since all are consistent with data reported extensively elsewhere.

Table 8.3 *Meaning of job by social class and sex*

A – RG categories

Job is		I	2	3N	Class 3M	4	5	6
Just a means of earning	M	9 (3)	15 (27)	30 (24)	50 (135)	57 (59)	50 (11)	13 (1)
living	F	10 (1)	13 (16)	29 (55)	39 (16)	39 (33)	61 (19)	100 (1)
Much more than that	M	94 (31)	85 (150)	70 (57)	51 (136)	43 (44)	48 (11)	87 (7)
	F	90 (9)	87 (112)	71 (133)	61 (25)	61 (52)	39 (12)	0 (0)

B – Goldthorpe categories

Job is		I	II	III	Class IV	V	VI	VII
Just a means of earning	M	12 (11)	15 (19)	37 (16)	36 (31)	38 (28)	48 (58)	63 (97)
a living	F	15 (3)	11 (10)	29 (56)	12 (3)	38 (6)	42 (10)	47 (53)
Much more than that	M	88 (82)	85 (104)	63 (27)	64 (55)	62 (46)	52 (64)	37 (58)
	F	85 (17)	89 (83)	71 (135)	88 (23)	62 (10)	58 (14)	53 (61)

C – Wright original categories

Job is		B	SE	PB	Class MS	SAE	W
Just a means of earning a living	M	10 (2)	30 (15)	33 (17)	24 (51)	31 (21)	53 (154)
	F	0 (0)	11 (1)	13 (3)	16 (15)	12 (9)	41 (113)
Much more than that	M	90 (19)	70 (35)	67 (34)	76 (164)	69 (47)	47 (137)
	F	100 (3)	89 (8)	87 (21)	84 (80)	88 (67)	59 (164)

Key: B – Bourgeoisie; SE – Small employers; PB – Petit bourgeoisie; MS – Managers and supervisors; SAE – Semi-autonomous employees; W – Workers.

D – Wright revised categories

Job is		B	SE	PB	Class EM	ES	ENM
Just a means of earning a living	M	10 (2)	30 (15)	33 (17)	11 (5)	29 (4)	15 (3)
	F	0 (0)	11 (1)	13 (3)	14 (3)	0 (0)	13 (4)
Much more than that	M	90 (19)	70 (35)	67 (34)	89 (40)	71 (10)	85 (17)
	F	100 (3)	89 (8)	87 (21)	86 (18)	100 (11)	87 (13)

Job is		SCM	SCS	SCW	UM	US	P
Just a means of earning a living	M	18 (15)	24 (8)	34 (44)	50 (8)	48 (11)	60 (128)
	F	13 (2)	30 (3)	26 (11)	21 (4)	17 (3)	38 (107)
Much more than that	M	82 (68)	76 (25)	66 (84)	50 (8)	52 (12)	40 (84)
	F	87 (13)	70 (7)	74 (32)	79 (15)	83 (15)	62 (172)

Key: B – Bourgeoisie; SE – Small employers; PB – Petit bourgeoisie; EM – Expert managers; ES – Expert supervisors; ENM – Expert non-managers; SCM – Semi-credentialled managers; SCS – Semi-credentialled supervisors; SCW – Semi-credentialled workers; UM – Uncredentialled managers; US – Uncredentialled supervisors; P – Proletarians.

Interestingly enough, however, our survey also tends to suggest that the conventional wisdom about a pecuniary orientation to work being more

Table 8.4 *Meanings of work by Goldthorpe class and sex (%)*

Way in which job is more than just a means of earning a living		Service	Class Intermediate	Working
Rewarding, fulfilling, worthwhile,	M	90	89	80
enjoyable	F	84	73	68
Human contact, being with colleagues,	M	21	27	28
getting out of house	F	42	51	60
Using or developing my skills	M	25	21	31
	F	35	16	15
I enjoy working for the present	M	20	17	23
organization	F	19	27	21
Job allows use of initiative	M	27	21	9
	F	26	16	7
Variety in the work	M	20	21	11
	F	18	15	12
Work is central to my life	M	16	15	12
	F	8	7	4
Value of my work to the country	M	15	6	6
	F	8	2	3
Work fits in with my family/I do it for	M	0	2	2
my family	F	1	5	3
It is better than being unemployed	M	0	0	5
	F	0	0	3
Other	M	3	2	1
	F	3	1	0

(Valid cases, M = 434, F = 343)
Note: Figures in this table are percentages based on respondents. They are the percentage of respondents in each class (and sex) category who mentioned a particular item among their responses to Question 89c. (This is a multiple-response item.)

common among the working classes somewhat oversimplifies matters (see Table 8.5). The numbers in some of the cells are rather low, so the findings are of questionable reliability, and we would not wish to place too much importance on them. Nevertheless, comparing these figures with those in Table 8.3, our data suggest that, where proletarians do treat work simply as a source of income, more commonly they do so either because they lack sufficient skills to secure a more interesting job, or because they are trapped in labour markets offering only a restricted range of job opportunities. (Males and females exhibit the same pattern in this respect.) A straightforwardly pecuniary attitude is proportionately more characteristic of fairly privileged employees than of the relatively disprivileged.

In general, then, these findings lead us to conclude that only a relatively small minority of people are *strict* pecuniary instrumentalists with respect to their employment. Most people find some reward other than money in what they do. Of course these rewards are not evenly distributed since proportionately many more employees among the working classes are trapped in jobs that offer nothing other than a source of income to the incumbents. (It is perhaps worth making the point explicitly here that we could find no additional significant sources of variation in orientations to work other than those introduced by social class and, to some extent, sex. Among the factors that are not important in this regard are production sector, size of employing organization, and length of time in present employment.)

Of course it would be foolish to suggest that work was so important as to be

Table 8.5 *Respondents' explanations for pecuniary attitude to work by social class*

A – RG categories

				Class			
	1	*2*	*3N*	*3M*	*4*	*5*	*6*
No interesting jobs locally	25	22	18	32	38	46	50
Respondent lacks skills for interesting work	0	22	28	35	40	31	0
Respondent would feel the same about any job	67	56	54	33	22	23	50
Total	100	100	100	100	100	100	100
	(3)	(36)	(67)	(144)	(85)	(26)	(2)

B – Goldthorpe categories

				Class			
	I	*II*	*III*	*IV*	*V*	*VI*	*VII*
No interesting jobs locally	40	27	15	20	34	30	40
Respondent lacks skills for interesting work	10	11	32	40	32	33	38
Respondent would feel the same about any job	50	62	53	40	34	36	22
Total	100	100	100	100	100	100	100
	(10)	(26)	(62)	(30)	(32)	(66)	(140)

C – Wright original categories

			Class		
	SE	*PB*	*MS*	*SAE*	*W*
No interesting jobs locally	20	19	31	14	34
Respondent lacks skills for interesting work	27	50	19	32	36
Respondent would feel the same about any job	53	31	51	54	30
Total	100	100	100	100	100
	(15)	(16)	(59)	(28)	(248)

Key: SE – Small employers; PB – Petit bourgeoisie; MS – Managers and supervisors; SAE – Semi-autonomous employees; W – workers.

Table 8.5 (*cont.*)

D – Wright revised categories

	SE	PB	Class EM	ES	ENM
No interesting jobs locally	20	19	50	0	0
Respondent lacks skills for interesting work	27	50	0	0	14
Respondent would feel the same about any job	53	31	50	100	86
Total	100	100	100	100	100
	(15)	(16)	(6)	(3)	(7)

	SCM	SCS	SCW	UM	US	P
No interesting jobs locally	20	50	35	46	14	32
Respondent lacks skills for interesting work	13	20	26	18	36	39
Respondent would feel the same about any job	67	30	39	36	50	29
Total	100	100	100	100	100	100
	(15)	(10)	(54)	(11)	(14)	(215)

Key: B – Bourgeoisie; SE – Small employers; PB – Petit bourgeoisie; EM – Expert managers; ES – Expert supervisors; ENM – Expert non-managers; SCM – Semi-credentialled managers; SCS – Semi-credentialled supervisors; SCW – Semi-credentialled workers; UM – Uncredentialled managers; US – Uncredentialled supervisors; P – Proletarians.

the central life interest of many people. Neither committed 'organization men' nor heroically creative and gratified proletarians are much in evidence in our sample. On the other hand, while the great majority of our respondents clearly experience work as a less than wholly fulfilling activity which can give overall meaning and direction to their lives, it is not at all obvious that this has induced in them a compensatory fondness for some other activity outside work that forms a substitute for it. We asked everyone in our sample to nominate three activities that they enjoyed doing when they were not at work. These could include hobbies, sports, shopping, DIY, various aspects of family life, or indeed doing nothing at all. The responses were of course extremely diverse (we coded over ninety particular activities) and the details are not important here. What should be noted, however, is that very few people could think of some other aspect of their lives that was obviously 'more important' to them than work. Twenty-three per cent of the sample did give priority to such an item, but 73 per cent thought work was at least as important (or more so) than any non-work activity they had listed, with the remainder unsure. Employees showed no variation by social class on this pattern, with at minimum 16 per cent, and at most 24 per cent in any one class deeming some other activity to be more important to them than work.

There is no evidence here of widespread cultural privatism. The obvious absence of a stereotypical 'class consciousness' is not associated in our sample with a corresponding development of a social consciousness of 'privatism' centred on the home or on interests located elsewhere in the non-work sphere of life; nor, from the historical materials earlier examined, would we expect it to be.

This is not to say that family or home-life generally are unimportant to the people in our study. Just as there are relatively few individuals for whom a job means nothing beyond a source of income, so there are correspondingly few who see their homes as providing simply a roof over one's head. For most people (see Table 8.6) home means more than this: it is a centre of family life, a place to retreat where one can relax and 'be oneself', a place of freedom and independence. Note too, however, that just as relatively few individuals will locate a central life interest in their work, so also are there very limited numbers who will locate such an interest in their homes. If there is such a thing as 'alienation at work' then, clearly, it is not counterbalanced by a wholesale retreat into the home as an alternative or compensatory source of meaning and fulfilment. (Somewhat surprisingly, perhaps, there is no significant sex effect in the patterning of these responses. Ten per cent of women saw the home as 'merely a roof' over their heads, 54 per cent viewed it as the 'centre of family life', 14 per cent as a 'means of self-expression', while for 26 per cent it represented 'freedom and independence'. The comparable percentages among men were 14, 45, 9, and 21 respectively. On other items the distribution of responses was virtually identical.)

Just as there were class differences in expressed orientations to work so also can these be detected in expressed orientations to home. In this case, however, the differences are much smaller and much less significant (see Table 8.7). Indeed, they are generally so small as to make the table rather

Table 8.6 *The meaning of home*

Home is	N	% of responses	% of cases
The centre of family life	862	29	49
A place of retreat, to relax, to be oneself	745	25	43
Freedom, independence, a place of one's own	412	14	24
A financial asset, something to leave children	229	8	13
Simply a roof over my head	214	7	12
A means of self-expression, taste, style	207	7	12
The centre of my life, everything, very important to me	156	5	9
A place of security and safety	126	4	7
A place to clean and keep tidy, a job	6	0	0
Other	62	2	5
Total	3019	100	173

(Valid cases = 1749)

Table 8.7 *Meaning of home by Goldthorpe class (%)*

Home is	I	II	III	Class IV	V	VI	VII
Centre of family life	52	50	50	40	53	47	48
A retreat	55	49	48	42	43	35	39
Freedom, independence	16	24	22	21	18	21	27
A financial asset	19	15	13	19	18	12	11
Simply a roof	7	10	12	11	13	19	12
Self-expression	16	14	13	11	15	11	9
Centre of my life	6	5	7	13	10	7	8
Security, safety	7	8	13	6	4	8	6
A job	1	0	0	1	0	0	0
Other	2	7	4	4	2	3	5

(Valid cases = 1306)

Note: Figures in this table are percentages based on respondents. They are the percentage of respondents in each class category who mentioned a particular item among their responses to Question 121. (This is a multiple-response item.)

uninteresting, except for the item about 'home being simply a roof over one's head' itself. What the first row in this table shows is that there is in fact no systematic tendency among the working classes to 'retreat into the home' as some sort of private haven from communal and other sorts of social activities. If anything the reverse is true: working-class respondents are more likely to view their home-life in an instrumental way – and, it could be argued, are therefore less likely to develop home-centred and family-centred life-styles in preference to that associated with communal sociability. Is this in fact the case?

With this question we arrive at the issue of privatism in its structural sense. To what extent are social relationships centred on the family and the home, rather than on workplace or local community? Has there been a decline in neighbourliness or communal sociability, and corresponding growth in family-centredness or home-centredness in associational activity? Again our survey data bear on this question in a limited way only. We can show, for example, that of those activities nominated as being enjoyed outside of work, 35 per cent are undertaken with (extended and nuclear) family members, 31 per cent with friends, and 34 per cent by the respondent on his or her own. Forty-six per cent of these activities are centred on the home, 47 per cent take place elsewhere, and 7 per cent are pursued at home and elsewhere more or less equally. There is some tendency for working-class associational activities to be centred more on the home than are those pursued by the service class and *petit bourgeoisie*, but no stronger a likelihood of these being undertaken with family or on one's own than with friends, looking at the working class and service class as a whole (Table 8.8). Or, to express this rather differently, there is no significant difference in the sociability of the various classes, though working-class people more often entertain at home than do those in more privileged class positions. (Given the differential in average incomes

Table 8.8 *Associational activities by Goldthorpe class*

A – Who activities undertaken with (per cents based on responses)

		I	II	III	Class IV	V	VI	VII
With family	M	35	36	30	41	42	31	33
	F	31	32	31	51	43	38	36
With friends	M	37	30	44	35	33	41	35
	F	35	33	34	18	32	33	24
By oneself	M	28	34	26	24	25	28	32
	F	35	35	35	31	25	29	40

(N, activity 1 = 1305; N, activity 2 = 1275; N, activity 3 = 1166; Valid cases = Males 768; Females, 544)

B – Where activities mainly undertaken (per cents based on respondents)

		I	II	III	Class IV	V	VI	VII
At home	M	37	37	30	35	41	39	44
	F	41	45	47	41	53	51	55
Elsewhere	M	60	50	60	60	54	54	50
	F	52	46	46	55	45	43	39
Both equally	M	10	13	10	5	5	7	6
	F	7	9	7	4	2	6	6

(N = Males, 767; Females, 543)

within the classes this is perhaps not surprising.) Whatever their social class, women are somewhat more likely than are men to pass their leisure time by themselves, and are significantly more likely to spend it at home rather than elsewhere. Again these findings are not at all surprising given what is already known about the differences between the sexes.

However, it is worth making the point here that home-centredness and family-centredness are a function neither of home-ownership, nor of longevity of residence. The (slight) association between council tenancy and home-centred activities disappears, as one would expect, when a control for social class is introduced. Rather more surprisingly, perhaps, residential newcomers seem to exhibit more or less the same patterns of home-centredness and family-centredness in leisure activities as do long-established inhabitants (Table 8.9).

Approaching the issue of structural privatism from another angle, our data also show that there is a considerable overlap between the structure of spare-time association, and the friendships formed at work. About half of all employees (46 per cent) stated that none of those whom they would number among their friends actually worked alongside them at the present time. But no less than 82 per cent of those claiming to have some friends at work also met these individuals socially in other contexts. Again there is a strong relationship with social class here. Although members of the service class are no more likely to have friends among workmates than are members of the working class, they are significantly more likely to socialize with workmate friends outside work than are their proletarian counterparts (see Table 8.10). There might be all sorts of explanations for this: one obvious possibility is that members of the service class, tending to be geographically more mobile than other employees, will form restricted friendship networks based on the workplace rather than the local community and so invest proportionately more of their efforts in this direction. It would be wrong, therefore, simply to jump to the conclusion that this table provides evidence of some sort of movement towards traditional proletarian communal sociability through the looking-glass. What seems to us striking about the data is, instead, the extent of the coincidence between relationships formed at work and those pursued as spare-time activities. Given the degree to which residence has become dissociated from local sources of mass employment in post-war Britain, it is striking indeed to find that half of those in employment can number friends among their workmates, and that over 80 per cent of these friendships are subsequently pursued in non-work contexts. There is scant evidence for structural privatism in this finding at least.

V

We are fully aware of the limitations of our data in this chapter. The historical

Table 8.9 *Associational activities by longevity of residence*

A – Who activities undertaken with (per cents based on responses)

		Period of residence (years)						
	<1	*1–4*	*5–9*	*10–14*	*15–19*	*20–24*	*>25*	*Lifetime*
With family	41	46	43	42	39	41	42	35
With friends	37	33	32	37	34	35	28	44
By oneself	40	38	41	39	42	40	42	35

(N, activity 1 = 1763; N, activity 2 = 1713; N, activity 3 = 1554; Valid cases = 1763)

B – Where activities undertaken (per cents based on respondents)

		Period of residence (years)						
	<1	*1–4*	*5–9*	*10–14*	*15–19*	*20–24*	*>25*	*Lifetime*
At home	45	47	50	48	44	47	46	41
Elsewhere	47	44	43	46	48	45	46	51
Both equally	8	9	8	6	5	8	6	7

(N = 1757)

Table 8.10 *Work-based friendships by Goldthorpe class*

A – Proportion of his or her friends whom respondent works with at present

				Class			
	I	*II*	*III*	*IV*	*V*	*VI*	*VII*
None	38	45	49	76	37	34	46
1–10 per cent	38	28	30	14	31	37	30
11–50 per cent	17	15	12	5	19	18	13
51–100 per cent	7	12	9	5	13	11	11
Total	100	100	100	100	100	100	100
	(113)	(215)	(234)	(112)	(90)	(145)	(269)

(N = 1178)

B – Does respondent with friends at work see these people socially outside work?

				Class			
	I	*II*	*III*	*IV*	*V*	*VI*	*VII*
Yes	91	90	86	89	88	77	67
No	9	10	14	11	12	23	33
Total	100	100	100	100	100	100	100
	(69)	(117)	(120)	(27)	(57)	(95)	(144)

(N = 629)

context is derived entirely from secondary sources relating to somewhat contentious developments during the mid nineteenth century. Having ourselves undertaken research based on primary historical materials for other purposes we are alert to the assumptions about reliability that are implicit in our present strategy. Moreover, our survey data are inevitably constrained in what they can tell us about privatism as a process, and as authors also of studies elsewhere into the complex structure of social relationships in local communities we are fully conversant with the quite legitimate objections which can be raised against our rather insensitive questions about the structure and meaning of family life and of work. Nevertheless, with all their limitations, we submit that our data vindicate the argument that sectionalism, instrumentalism, and privatism among the British working class are not characteristics somehow peculiar to the recent years of economic recession.

There are no grounds to suppose that these phenomena have been increasing or changing in any significant way. It is true that the occupational structure has of late undergone considerable reshaping as a consequence of the decline in the manual work-force, proportionate expansion of white-collar employment, and growth of widespread and long-term joblessness. The evidence further suggests that the impact of this process, and of the recession itself, is indeed uneven. Certain regions, occupations, and sectors of the economy have fared markedly better than others. Lines of cleavage between those in public and private sectors, between men and women, between those employed in multinational and in national enterprises, merely compound this unevenness. But such sectionalism is no less apparent in data from the mid nineteenth century. The 'working class' has always been stratified internally: if not by 'sectoral cleavages' then according to industry or occupational grade. Today the owner-occupier may find it difficult to make common cause with the council tenant. The British Steel furnace-men in Sheffield may not see interests shared with the women assembling computer keyboards for Burroughs in Cumbernauld. But wasn't it ever so? The craftworkers, casual labourers, skilled and unskilled employees in the factories, small workshops, docks and quarries of mid Victorian Britain were no less segmented yet no less members of the same working class.

Nor are privatism – home-centredness or family-centredness – and pecuniary instrumentalism inventions of the last decade. In the 'affluent' 1960s, for example, Goldthorpe and Lockwood dismissed the thesis of working-class 'embourgeoisement' after research in Luton had shown the majority of workers to be 'privatized instrumentalists'. Attempting to put this world-view into its social context David Lockwood wrote that:

The social environment of the privatised worker is conducive to the development of what may be called a 'pecuniary' model of society. The essential difference of this ideology is that class divisions are seen mainly in terms of differences in income and material possessions. . . . Basically, the pecuniary model of society is an ideological reflection of work attachments that are instrumental and of community relationships that are privatised. It is a model which is only possible when social relationships that might provide prototypical experiences for the construction of ideas of conflicting power classes, or of hierarchically independent status groups, are either absent or devoid of their significance.[26]

As such, it explains, for the authors of the Affluent Worker Study at least, the lack of class consciousness among these workers, and their obviously instrumental attitude towards both trade unions and the Labour Party.[27] Lockwood, of course, argued further that the privatized instrumentalists of the age of post-war affluence were 'prototypical' of workers in general in advanced capitalist societies, and that their world-view was gradually replacing those of the traditional proletarians and deferentials of earlier eras. The evidence of the mid Victorian labour aristocrats suggests, however, that the three 'images of society' have long coexisted among employees who, at one moment have supported collective action on behalf of the class or stratum, yet, at another, subscribed to the conventional status politics of the privatized craftsman.[28]

The constant (and often seemingly disappointing) rediscovery of money-mindedness, sectionalism, and privatism among British workers by successive generations of researchers is largely a product of the tendency to treat class consciousness (the elusive quarry of most studies) as an attribute of individuals rather than collective actors. In fact, as we have seen, the

218

substantial literature on working-class consciousness is sufficiently open-ended for one to be able to read into studies of proletarian ambivalence, volatility, pragmatism and instrumentalism whatever theoretical – or political – conclusions one so desires. Thus, to cite only one rather obvious example from the literature on Britain, a wave of post-Braverman studies of the labour process have persistently drawn attention to what is taken to be resistance against managerial strategies of control at the point of production. Even in the face of the inexorable logic of capital accumulation, it is argued, labour cannot routinely be degraded and deskilled. In fact, the research in question confirms that the terrain of the workplace is still firmly in the grasp of the capitalist class, but the emphasis of the analysis is invariably placed on the extent to which this is contested by sections of the work-force.[29] Thus working-class kids might 'learn to labour', and so move painlessly from classroom to factory, but even then, in their subcultural beliefs and rituals (it is argued), they transform dominant values and recapture – if only symbolically – those of 'traditional' proletarians. The particular kids in question may appear to you and me to be racist, sexist, apolitical, and self-centred in both speech and behaviour – but they're still all right. They are still part of the rising class.[30]

The fallacy of explaining class consciousness solely in terms of workers' beliefs, attitudes, or values is then compounded by strenuous attempts to locate exclusively structural sources for the particular variant of consciousness that has been identified. A strict dualism is practised, whereby social consciousness becomes a spiritual reflection of social location. The analytical deficiencies of this position are only too obvious in the convergence about the electoral consequences of affluence and recession. During both boom and slump, it has been all too easy to see the various economic and political tendencies of the day in a neat relationship of cause and effect. In both contexts, changes in the occupational structure (induced this time around by recession rather than affluence) are seen to be the deep-rooted cause of electoral upheaval, and in both cases this has been affiliated to the growth of a 'new' sectionalism, privatism, and instrumentalism – and corresponding demise of social class.

Those who, in this manner, reason directly from shifts in the social or occupational structure to swings in values or changes in electoral behaviour, greatly oversimplify the relationship between the distributional order of society itself, and the specific forms of distributional conflict evident at any particular time. The reasoning is analogous to (and no less erroneous than) that which sees a simple transition between the mature class-in-itself and revolutionary class-for-itself. In both cases the phenomena of collective organization are omitted from the analysis and subsequent explanation.

As a corrective to this oversimplification we would argue that class action is not an automatic by-product of economic developments. It is not simply a function of changes in the structure of occupation or income. Class actions are shaped, not only by political and ideological as well as economic considertions, but also by the institutional frameworks of political democracy within which they occur. The various working-class organizations operating within this framework themselves help shape class conflicts. In Britain these organizations – notably the trades unions and Labour Party – have tended to pursue reforms via a social democratic rather than a class mode of action. The union movement is relatively decentralized and defends the exclusionary and market-reinforcing practices of free collective bargaining as a matter of principle. In a more or less separate political mobilization on behalf of the working class, the Labour Party persuades its constituents to pursue their political aspirations through exclusively electoral channels, and acts when in power as a court of last resort for conflicting sectional demands. Neither organization possesses the centralized authority to act as a positive force by organizing sectional demands into a coherent strategy for the benefit of the class as a whole.

Class consciousness, as we see it, is not mass consciousness. A class conscious movement is not the spontaneous product of a populace having progressed in linear fashion through feelings of class identity and opposition to those of class totality and the conception of an alternative society. Rather, a class conscious class is, as Jon Elster has so aptly put it, a class which has solved the free-rider problem. It is the ability of class organizations to pursue class and status objectives inclusively – to convert sectional and conventional struggles into solidaristic and legal ones – that constitutes class consciousness. Seen from this perspective class consciousness is an attribute of organizations rather than individuals: it is the capacity of a class to behave as a collective actor.[31]

We have already argued that, in the context of mid Victorian Britain, one such organizational entity – the trade union – was crucial in giving direction to struggles both for sectional and for class gains on behalf of British working men. Moreover, the exclusionary or inclusionary nature of these conflicts was, as far as the evidence permits us to judge, only in part explicable as a consequence of the 'social consciousness' of the craftworkers themselves. Privatized in life-style and fiercely sectional in defence of craft interests, their unions nevertheless pursued radical social and political objectives, not only on their members' behalf, but also in the name of the wider community of workers as whole.

The additional analytical purchase that is gained on the phenomenon of class consciousness by shifting the focus of study, from the individual, and his or her attitudes, to the dynamics of the collectivity, is evident in the debate about the significance of the apparent disintegration of the moral order of late capitalist societies for the maintenance of social consensus. When class consciousness, by which we mean collective action in pursuit of a coherent ideological strategy, is seen properly – as an attribute of organizations rather than of individuals – then the lack of *Sittlichkeit* in capitalist societies carries few immediate implications for social integration. What is important, rather, is the ability of class organizations to mobilize members behind centrally organized initiatives on behalf of class rather than particular interests; and, once mobilized, to hold in check groups who would 'free-ride' or pursue sectional gains at the expense of the collectivity as a whole. The fact is, of course, that the British Labour Party and trades unions have been relatively unsuccessful (compared with their counterparts in Sweden, for example) in precisely these terms: in constituting and mobilizing class interests, by presenting issues in class terms, and reinforcing the formation of collectivities with shared class identities.[32]

We suspect it is this realization that has led at least one leading participant in the debate to revise his position radically during the past decade. John Goldthorpe, in some of his writings, closely follows the arguments of Fred Hirsch and maintains that working-class sectionalism, with its allied intensification of distributional struggles, is a major threat to the stability of capitalist societies. His characterization of working-class consciousness as 'pecuniary instrumentalism' derives, of course, from the Affluent Worker Studies. It echoes David Lockwood's suggestions as to the 'prototypicality' of the new privatized instrumentalists among post-war British workers by settling this mantle upon the proletariat as a whole. The decline of locality-based status orders, extension of the sphere of citizenship, demographic and socio-political maturity of the working class, have encouraged members to exploit to the full such market advantages as they may possess. Workers are thus pecuniary in their attitude to labour, instrumental in support of working-class organizations, and privatized in their role as consumers. Central life-interests lie outside the workplace in the home. Pushful wage demands may be pursued aggressively but they testify only to the economic rationality of workers and imply nothing in the way of discontent that can be channelled in the direction of specifically socialist or even class objectives. Nevertheless, militant wage demands can generate uncontrolled distributional dissent and, in the form of inflationary pressure on the econonmy, bring the system to the point of crisis.[33]

In more recent publications however, and without altering this conception of the pecuniary and privatized instrumentalism of his working-class subjects, Goldthorpe has also argued that, under certain circumstances, sectionalism among employees operates to the advantage rather than the obvious disadvantage of the capitalist classes. Indeed it may even be actively encouraged by them. Faced with the problems of managing the economy under conditions of heightened distributional dissent, governments can choose to pursue corporatist solutions by organizing private economic interest groups and classes into the political arena, thus according them a role in the formation of (and in this way responsibility for implementing) public policy. The problem is that, in societies such as Sweden, Austria and Norway, which exhibit relatively stable corporatist arrangements, effective political bargaining to counter the economically dysfunctional effects of the market has required institutional recognition of real power shifts in the social structure. In short, the major interest groups, notably the centralized union movements, have become increasingly powerful and made real gains on behalf of their working-class constituents. Faced with the political costs of corporatist inclusion, therefore, governments and employers can opt instead to pursue an exclusionary strategy by creating disprivileged and disorganized collectivities of economic actors within the sphere of production itself. In other words they attempt to divide and rule. Economic dualism, such as is evident in the segmentation of labour markets and maintenance of 'industrial reserve armies', undermines organized labour by providing flexible, cheap, and organizationally weak work-forces engaged according to 'non-standard' employment arrangements, standing outside systems of industrial citizenship, and disposable as and when needs arise. From this perspective, which we ourselves would share, it is not lack of capitalist *Sittlichkeit* that poses the greatest threat to pluralist economies, but its achievement, since corporatist arrangements tend, where they have persisted, both progressively to undermine the free play of the capitalist labour market, and to reinforce class-based as opposed to sectional identities. Collectivism may still be instrumental but the collectivity is now the class as a whole rather than some fragment thereof.[34]

If, therefore, we accept the readily available data which suggest that there is little evidence of British working-class participation in a consensus about agreed principles governing distributional issues (be that testimony to instrumentalism, pragmatism, sectionalism, privatism, or whatever), this would seem to lend support to the claim made by Abercrombie, Hill and Turner that the social order in capitalist societies does not depend on agreement about a dominant ideology. The obverse is also true: lack of *Sittlichkeit* need not imply the absence of solidaristic and highly structured distributional conflicts. Privatized instrumentalism – so-called narcissism, egoism, individualism, and status awareness – can be consistent with collective action, social identities based on class, and therefore with class consciousness. The changing forms of distributional struggle are not a matter, at least primarily, of altering individual awareness but are, instead, more a question of straightforward organizational capacity. Lower-class meaning systems carry no particular implications for social integration unless these are seen in their changing organizational contexts. Modern British society lacks capitalist *Sittlichkeit* but it is not for this reason that social order will – or will not – be secured.

Notes

1 Hirsch (1977).
2 Bell (1976: 477–8). Gorz (1982: 80) arrives at the same conclusion, though by a slightly different route, observing that

> the 'freedom' which the majority of the overdeveloped nations seek to protect from 'collectivism' and the 'totalitarian' threat, is the freedom to create a private niche protecting one's personal life against all pressures and external social obligations. This niche may be represented by family life, a home of one's own, a back garden, a do-it-yourself workshop, a boat, a country cottage, a collection of antiques, music, gastronomy, sport, love, etc. Its importance varies inversely with the degree of job satisfaction and in direct proportion with the intensity of social pressures. It represents a sphere of sovereignty wrested (or to be wrested) from a world

governed by the principles of productivity, aggression, competition, hierarchical discipline, etc. Capitalism owes its political stability to the fact that, in return for the dispossession and growing constraints experienced at work, individuals enjoy the possibility of building an *apparently* growing sphere of individual autonomy outside of work.

3 Habermas (1975; 1979: Chapter 5).
4 Compare, for example, the views of Offe (1976, 1984) with those of Brittan (1978) or Hayek (1976). There are also those among the left who see the increasingly overt cash nexus as a stabilizing rather than destabilizing force in late capitalist societies. The class having the greatest potential for overturning capitalist production – the proletariat – has instead been seduced by its artefacts. Thus Gorz (1982: 40) complains that 'Working-class demands have turned into consumerist demands. An atomised, serialised mass of proletarians demand *to be given* by society, or more precisely the state, what they are unable to take or produce.' For a similar and more extended treatment see Marcuse (1972).
5 For an overview of this literature see Marshall (1983).
6 Mann (1970).
7 Turner (1983), Abercrombie *et al.* (1980). Moreover, the argument continues, in late capitalist societies changes in the forms of ownership and control of wealth (notably the rise of the multinational corporations and expansion of the state) mean that ideology ceases to be important for the coherence of the ruling class itself. Monopoly firms are not family firms and generally do not rely on inherited wealth for finance. Modern market economies do not depend on a coherent ruling class which retains capital within the family and there is correspondingly less need for coherent 'ruling ideas'.
8 Weber (1968: 927).
9 Weber (1968: 927).
10 See Lockwood (1958).
11 See, for example, Parkin (1972), Westergaard and Resler (1976), Miles (1982), and Kuhn and Wolpe (1978).
12 For example, see Goldthorpe (1978) and Lockwood (1974).
13 Marshall (1973).
14 Of course, this does not mean that civil and political rights are irrevocable, once granted; or that they are automatically bestowed on those entitled to them; or have ceased to be matters of dispute. The events of the miners' strike in Britain during 1984 offer sufficient proof of all three qualifications.
15 Marshall (1973: 94).
16 Marshall (1973: 111).
17 Compare, for example, the orthodox Marxist account in Foster (1974) and the critique by Joyce (1980).
18 See, for example, the discussion in the journal *Social History*: Moorhouse (1978, 1979, 1981), Reid (1978), and McLennan (1981).
19 The discussion that follows is based principally on the studies by Crossick (1978), Gray (1976), Kirk (1985), Alexander (1976), Davidoff (1979), Harrison (1965), Tholfsen (1976), Hobsbawm (1964), Daunton (1983), Walton (1981) and Pelling (1972).
20 Crossick (1978: 60-1).
21 Gray (1974: 26).
22 Crossick (1978: 230-1).
23 Gray (1981: 49).
24 See also Jones (1983), who tends to locate the 'remaking' of the (mass of the) working class during the final quarter, rather than the third quarter of the nineteenth century. Nevertheless, his substantive conclusions tend also to support our argument, in so far as he sees sectionalism and privatism preceding the mid Victorian period. Moreover, reviewing the interrelationships between the growth of trades unionism and that of working-class leisure, he describes the working-class culture of the 1880s and 1890s as defensive, stoical, fatalistic and politically sceptical. Yet, at the same time, the solidarity and organizational strength achieved in earlier struggles was channelled into union activity and, eventually, into support for a political party committed to union objectives. Unions, co-operatives, friendly societies and the music-hall all indicated 'a *de facto* recognition of the existing social order as the inevitable framework of action', and the rise of a 'culture of consolation' (pp. 236–7). Jones, like ourselves, points to the relative neglect of the organizational aspects of class analysis and goes so far as to suggest (p. 19) that it is not consciousness (or ideology) that produces politics but politics that produces consciousness. He observes that

> In general, the temporality of periods of heightened *political* conflict and political mobilization is determined, in the *first* instance, not by the conditions of the local economy nor by cultural factors, but by the activity of all those institutions of government and political order, both legislative and executive, central and local, which in short we call the state. . . . What sort of political dimension it acquires, other things being equal, depends upon the existence of a political organization or current with a capacity convincingly to portray the particular sequence of events as an instance of a coherent general position on the character of the state and of a strategy for its transformation (pp. 10–11).

This, in turn, raises the issue of state activity: the other side of the coin in the discussion of organizational capacities. (We comment on this very briefly below.)

25 For specific references and a more detailed discussion of the history and usages of the concept of 'privatization' see Newby *et al.* (1985). Recent proponents of the thesis of growing 'privatism' in industrial capitalist societies include Wilson (1985) and DeAngelis (1982). For a detailed critique see Pahl and Wallace (1988) who, justifiably, are also critical of some of the assumptions made in our own early position papers.

26 Lockwood (1975: 21–2).

27 Goldthorpe *et al.* (1969).

28 Morawska (1985) reaches a similar conclusion based on historical research into the social consciousness of labourers in an American mill town during the years 1890 to 1940. See also Hill's (1976) study of London dock workers.

29 See Littler and Salaman (1982); Wood (1982); and, for a particularly glaring example of socialist optimism belied by the sociological analysis on which it rests, Pollert (1981).

30 Compare Willis (1979).

31 Elster (1982: 467). For an elaboration of these ideas see the extensive discussions in Calhoun (1982) and Crouch (1982). Good empirical studies of the way in which organizational attributes and structures can not only mediate, but transform, constituency demands are Hemingway (1978) and Lash (1984).

32 See Scase (1977), Korpi (1983).

33 Goldthorpe (1978).

34 Goldthorpe (1984b).

9 Class politics

In previous chapters we have argued that the 'demise of social class' is a thesis not well supported by the evidence from the British survey of class structure and class consciousness. Sectionalism associated with possible sectoral cleavages is relatively unimportant when set alongside class phenomena, in particular the persistence of class identities, and the unequal class mobility chances associated with unchanging 'social fluidity' over the past half-century or so. To the extent that our respondents are instrumental in their attitudes to class organizations and privatized in their life-styles – and our evidence suggests that such claims must be qualified in important respects – then these are hardly novel developments somehow to be attributed to recent changes in the economic or social structure of this country. Studies undertaken by historians suggest that sectionalism, privatism, and instrumentalism are longstanding characteristics of British working-class life, yet have not prevented working-class organizations from pursuing class as well as sectional objectives. This suggests that class action is but partly a function of the 'social consciousness' of class members. Specific outcomes depend also upon the attributes of the organizations that represent class interests in the economic and political spheres. Class analysis should be extended to embrace this institutional level.

Such an interpretation of the recent history of 'class consciousness' in Great Britain would find few supporters among political scientists who have analysed voting behaviour in this country since the last world war. Among psephologists, according to one leading authority, 'the prevailing scholarly view' is that 'class is a diminishing political force in the electorate', a view that is allegedly supported by 'a wide range of data and analytic approaches'.[1] Processes of 'class dealignment' have resulted in a decline in class voting over successive post-war elections, and are evident particularly in falling support for the Labour Party, and in the rise of the Liberal/SDP Alliance. Most commentators have assumed that these electoral trends are associated with changes in classes rather than parties: that is, classes are somehow losing their cohesion as social entities, and as a result of this 'loosening of the class structure' social class has steadily assumed less importance as an influence on political partisanship.[2]

How can our own observations about the continuing importance of class processes possibly be reconciled with psephological arguments about the decline of class voting? On the one hand, we can find no evidence in our survey that class has lost its salience as the foremost source of social identity,

225

and have observed that differences in attitudes and values are structured more obviously by class than by other possible sources of social cleavage. On the other, evidence from most recent studies of electoral behaviour seems to suggest that there has been a steady decline in the class basis of politics, with the implication that the potential for collective political action by the various classes has been greatly reduced.

Our own explanation for this apparent discrepancy would be that the latter position rests on a serious misreading of the available evidence. The conclusions drawn by proponents of the class dealignment thesis do not, in fact, follow from the data offered in support of this argument. Curiously enough, the discussion here almost exactly parallels that in earlier chapters on social mobility, since the crucial point of difference between proponents and opponents of class dealignment concerns the relationship between absolute and relative class voting. This distinction is analogous to that between absolute levels of social mobility and relative mobility chances. Measures of absolute trends and of relative chances are equally valid but, as we have seen, they are appropriate to testing different sorts of propositions. Our contention about the so-called decline of class politics is that this thesis requires evidence about relative class voting whereas its proponents have examined only absolute levels of class voting. Or, to put the matter another way, arguments about class dealignment are rather more complex than might at first appear to be the case. Before presenting the evidence from our own survey it is necessary to consider these complexities somewhat further.

I

Class seems to have mattered in British political life over the years because nothing much else has. Other lines of social cleavage likely to be reflected in voting behaviour – urban–rural, religious, or ethnic–cultural[3] – have proved to be of little importance in recent history (Northern Ireland is the only obvious exception) or have been absorbed into class politics itself.

The connections between Britain's class structure and its party politics are in fact both manifest and multiform. The Labour Party was created by trades unionists specifically to represent working-class interests. Although periodic attempts to broaden its electoral appeal have swelled the numbers of middle-class Labour voters and Members of Parliament it is still seen as predominantly a trade union and manual workers' party. The modern Conservative Party is correspondingly perceived to be the party of profit, privilege, and property. Certainly it receives substantial financial support from business and landed interests. Political issues tend also to be presented in class terms: levels of welfare provision, transport and housing policies, the extension of comprehensive education, privatization and nationalization of industry are typical examples. Most commentators, therefore, would accept the proposition that British politics during the twentieth-century has been, or was until very recently, structured in social class terms.

Of course politics in this country is not and never has been reducible to class conflict.[4] Many issues are not viewed in obviously class-specific terms – defence and inflation might be two examples. And, more important to the concerns of this chapter, substantial minorities both of middle-class and working-class voters have always voted against their supposedly 'natural' class interest. It is generally accepted in psephological circles that about one-third of people who are 'clearly working class' regularly vote Conservative.[5] Statistics similar to those in Table 9.1 are commonly produced to show that, in the case of the general election of 1979 for example, some 22 per cent of the middle class and 36 per cent of the working class were 'deviant' cross-class voters. Lately, indeed, a consensus has emerged about the proposal that the class structuring of British politics decreased dramatically in the 1970s and shows every sign of continuing to do so.

Table 9.1   *Vote by class in Britain, May 1979 (%)*

| | | Party | | | |
		Con.	Lib.	Lab.	Total
Class	Middle	63	15	22	100
	Working	36	14	51	100

Source: Robertson, 1984, p. 20.

The decline of class politics is by no means a unified thesis. A common starting point for most versions of the argument is the shrinking Alford index for Britain during the past fifteen or so years (see Table 9.2). Some of the data offered in corroboration of this trend clearly overlap and they seem generally to depict an electorate now fragmented politically along unfamiliar lines. But beyond this there are substantial disagreements as to whether class-based support for the principal parties has been undermined specifically by partisan dealignment, the disaggregation of economic interests, cognitive consumer voting, or the development of sectoral cleavages.

It is beyond the scope of this study to comment in detail on the differences between these approaches. We need note only that the class politics orthodoxy has been subject to sustained challenge from several directions and

Table 9.2   *Alford indexes for Britain, 1955–79 (%)*

	1955	1957	1958	1959	1962	1964	1966	1970	1974	1979
Percentage of working class voting Labour	62	67	64	57	57	64	66	59	59	51
Percentage of middle class voting Labour	23	24	22	21	22	23	25	27	26	23
Alford index	39	43	42	36	35	41	41	32	33	28

Source: Robertson, 1984, p. 26.

together the various critiques amount to an apparently impressive case. Such consensus is particularly striking because it is cross-disciplinary and embraces a wide range of political beliefs and perspectives.[6] In any case, it is unnecessary for us to review the numerous contributions individually since the essence of the debate between proponents and opponents of the class dealignment thesis is crystallized in the disagreement between Ivor Crewe and Anthony Heath, each of whom has offered a quite different interpretation of the findings from the longitudinal series of British General Election Studies. This single exchange raises all of the relevant issues in a particularly trenchant manner.[7]

Crewe's argument is a simple one. Between the general elections of 1945 and 1983 the Conservative share of the middle-class vote fell from 63 per cent to 55 per cent, and the Labour share of the working-class vote from 62 to 42 per cent, so that the overall level of class voting (middle-class Conservative and working-class Labour taken together as a proportion of total votes cast) fell from 62 to 47 per cent. In other words, by the time of the 1983 election, fewer people voted along class lines than in fact declined to do so. The particularly pronounced decline in class voting since 1970 is evidence, for most commentators including Crewe himself, of a secular trend towards class dealignment; that is, a decrease in class solidarity linked to a general loosening of the class structure, which has caused a parallel decline in the Conservative and Labour vote and the rise of so-called 'centrist' parties such as those of the Alliance.

In defence of this 'conventional' interpretation of the data Crewe points to the weight of the scholarly opinion which informs it. Most political scientists investigating the problem have arrived at the same conclusion, irrespective of their political and methodological differences; namely, that British electors have become steadily less willing to express political preferences according to their putative class interests. Precisely how unwilling depends to some extent on how one chooses to measure class, political preference, and the relationship between them. Crewe himself favours an index of party identification, rather than vote, as a measure of partisanship, since the former is 'less sensitive to short-term political fluctuations and thus preferable for depicting underlying trends', though he maintains that his arguments are supported also by voting behaviour as such. Partisanship can be measured, therefore, by looking at the total percentages of Conservative and Labour identifiers (or voters); of nonmanual Labour minus manual Labour identifiers (the 'class index of Labour partisanship'); and nonmanual Conservative minus manual Conservative identifiers (the 'class index of Conservative partisanship'). Heath's use of (slightly modified) Goldthorpe categories to investigate patterns of class voting is welcomed in principle, although as a point of practice, Crewe invariably utilizes a straightforward manual/ nonmanual class distinction in his analyses. His principal objection to the Goldthorpe classification seems to be that it retains the 'ideologically-laden' term 'working class' for what is a sub-category of manual employees. This 'new-fangled' definition is allegedly rendered 'sociologically meaningless' by the fact that it embraces only some 32 per cent of the work-force – a 'distinct minority of the electorate'. If the 'middle class' is then confined to the salariat (another 28 per cent or so) then it seems, to Crewe at least, that conclusions about class voting must be drawn on the basis of the behaviour of only 60 per cent of the electorate. By comparison, his own definition of manual and nonmanual workers allows him to use the term 'working class' in 'contexts where its precise occupational definition is immaterial', and also yields a tidy 50:50 middle-class to working-class split in the total voting population.[8]

These seemingly esoteric matters of methodology are, in fact, crucial to the argument itself, since the principal substantive issue concerns the 'decline of class voting within the working class'; that is, whether or not there is 'a much lower proportion of manual workers voting Labour in 1983 than 1945', and, if so, how this is to be explained.[9] Other matters separating the protagonists are very much of secondary importance: the relative merits of competing measures of 'subjective class awareness' and of alternative political and social strategies for Labour's electoral salvation need not concern us here.

Heath himself places methodological issues squarely at the centre of his differences with Crewe and other observers who have identified a fall in the proportion of manual workers voting Labour with a long-term trend away from an older form of class politics. He accepts that, from the mid 1960s onwards, the Labour share of the overall vote has declined, while that of the Conservatives has increased marginally, and of the Alliance parties considerably. Long-term changes in the class structure, in particular the fact that the working class has shrunk from 47 per cent to 34 per cent of the electorate, might explain about half of the fall in the Labour vote over this period. However, these sociological changes cannot explain the rapid decline in the Labour vote between 1979 and 1983, or the rise of the Alliance parties over the period as a whole. The principal difference between proponents and opponents of class dealignment is in how they account for these developments. Heath argues that political rather than sociological factors are responsible. Prominent among these would be the disunity of the Labour Party in 1983, and the popular perception of the two major parties as moving away from the centre, so helping the Alliance to increase their share of the vote. In other words it is changes in parties rather than classes which explain these developments. Crewe, on the other hand, maintains that additional sociological factors have been at work. Over and above the contraction in the size of the proletariat there has been a 'precipitous decline in the ideological consciousness and solidarity of the working class'.[10]

These competing explanations are rooted in alternative interpretations of electoral trends since the late 1960s. More specifically, they reflect the difference between an analysis which rests exclusively on the measurement of absolute class voting (that of Crewe and many other leading psephologists), and one which includes a calculation of relative class voting chances alongside observations of aggregate movements (as conducted by Heath and his colleagues). Absolute class voting refers to the proportion of the electorate voting for its 'natural' class party. In effect, this measure of class voting is common to all accounts of class dealignment, including that offered by Crewe himself. Relative class voting, on the other hand, is an indication of the relative strength of the various political parties in different social classes. The difference between the two concepts is crucial and parallels that between the measurement of absolute and relative mobility. Thus, for example, a decline in the Labour vote which is due to both middle-class and working-class socialists switching to the Alliance means that absolute class voting has declined, though relative class voting has remained constant. If, on the other hand, Labour loses votes among the working class but retains its middle-class supporters then relative and absolute class voting will both decline.

Taking this difference into account, Heath finds that relative class voting exhibits 'trendless fluctuation' throughout the post-war period, with class voting stronger at some elections and weaker at others. In other words there is no evidence of a 'persistent and continuing decline of the kind that would have been expected if a gradual loosening of the classes had taken place'. It is true that absolute class voting was very low in the last general election but this was precisely because Labour, a major class party, did badly overall.

The crucial point is that in 1983 Labour fared badly in all classes alike. It remained relatively stronger in the working class than in the middle class – in other words it remained a class party, but in 1983 it was an unsuccessful class party.[11]

Thus, as Heath points out, a decline in absolute class voting is not necessarily an indication that classes have lost either their social cohesion or their political potential. If Labour moves to the left and loses support in all social classes to the Alliance, then absolute class voting will have declined because of political factors alone, without there having been any change in the class structure or in relative class voting.

The similarities between this dispute about class dealignment and discussions elsewhere about social mobility are readily apparent. We have seen that significant net upward mobility can result from changes in the shape rather than the openness of the class structure. An expansion of places at the top, exploited in equal proportion across the various social classes, will increase absolute rates of upward mobility but leave relative mobility chances unaltered. There will have been no movement in the direction of greater equality of opportunity. Under these circumstances, which match those prevailing in Britain during the past half-century and more, we can plausibly attribute more or less all observed upward mobility to the changing shape of the occupational structure itself. The argument that mobility from the lower to the upper classes indicates increased fluidity in the class structure, and so testifies to the efficacy of egalitarian social policies, can equally plausibly be rejected. The distinction between relative and absolute class voting is important in precisely the same way. If a class-based party loses support to a third party with the same relative frequency in all social classes then this will lead to a decline in absolute class voting while leaving relative class voting unchanged. That class party will still be stronger in one class than in another but will simply be less successful in all classes than was hitherto the case.

Under these circumstances one can plausibly claim that such a party has lost its electoral appeal because of political factors which have affected the overall levels of support for the different parties. It is not necessary to introduce putative sociological changes into the discussion, in order to explain the observed shifts in the distribution of votes, since the relative proportions in the class-specific support for the parties have not altered. In broad terms, according to Heath, this describes the situation with regard to the Labour Party in recent general elections.

In order to address the issue of whether political or sociological factors explain the failures of Labour and the rise of the Alliance, and so (implicitly at least) to assess the potential of classes for collective political action, it is necessary therefore to investigate the pattern of relative class voting using the techniques of odds ratios and loglinear modelling that were described in earlier chapters. The latter procedure allows one to examine the full set of odds ratios for class–party voting across a series of elections and so test the hypothesis that the strength of relative class voting has not varied over time. Using these statistical tools Heath offers a convincing demonstration of 'trendless fluctuation' in relative class voting. Modelling either party identification or reported vote one arrives at the same conclusion in respect of seven elections from 1964 to 1983; namely, that there are significant changes both in the sizes of the classes and in the fortunes of the parties, but the association between class and vote (defined in relative terms) does not vary systematically from one election to another.[12]

This finding renders highly suspect the additional sociological factors adduced by Crewe in order to explain his conclusion that Labour's decline since the 1960s is symptomatic of long-term changes in the situation of the working class.

If the classes had indeed become looser and had lost their social cohesion and potential for class politics then we would have expected the relationship between class and party to become more random. Instead of being relatively stronger in the working class than in the middle class, Labour might become equally strong (or weak) in both. In other words, a loosening of the class structure is likely to lead to a decline in relative class voting. While there may be other reasons too for a decline in relative class voting, the important point is that a decline in absolute class voting, if unaccompanied by a relative decline, is unlikely to have been caused by a loosening of the classes.[13]

Heath maintains, therefore, and rightly so in our view, that the findings from his more sophisticated analysis are consistent with this interpretation of the relevant survey data and cast serious doubts on the conclusions reached by theorists of class dealignment.

Of course trendless fluctuation in odds ratios provides only indirect evidence about the sociological processes at issue. Both Heath and Crewe accept that direct evidence would be better. It is here that the data from the class structure and class consciousness project allow us to make a modest contribution to the debate about class dealignment and so to wider discussions about the alleged demise of social class. Heath's analysis confirms that longitudinal data show a decline in absolute class voting. All commentators agree this much. What is at issue is how one explains this phenomenon. Does the decline of the Labour vote and rise of the Alliance parties indicate a long-term decomposition of social classes and, therefore, a reduced likelihood of collective political action in the future? Or can these developments be attributed to short-lived changes in the political fortunes of the parties? Unlike odds ratios, Crewe's *ad hoc* indices for examining the relationship between class and vote cannot control for overall changes in the sizes of the classes, or in the distribution of votes. The latter's conclusions therefore rest on analytic techniques which confound different effects and are suspect on these grounds alone.[14] Data from our own survey offer additional and direct evidence that arguments proposing a so-called loosening in the class structure lack empirical substance.

Unfortunately, however, as Heath himself points out, the precise nature of the additional sociological factors embraced under this rubric is by no means always clear. For some writers, such as Dunleavy, the development of politically relevant sectoral cleavages (about the consumption of housing, for example) have fragmented class interests and in this way undermined traditional class voting. Others, including Robertson and Franklin, attribute changing electoral patterns to the 'class secularization of society' – a decline in the social cohesion of classes, or in the salience of the idea of class, as a result of factors such as increased social mobility and the growth of cross-class marriages. Finally, there are those like Crewe himself who maintain that there has been a 'sea-change of attitudes within the proletariat', a wholesale movement from an ethos of collectivism to the values, norms (and hence voting behaviour) of self-interested individualism.[15] In fact our data indicate that all three accounts are implausible as explanations for the recent decline in absolute class voting. These findings therefore complement Heath's longitudinal analysis of electoral behaviour and suggest that his critique of the psephological orthodoxy is sound. The slump in the Labour vote and rise of the Alliance are due to political rather than sociological factors.

II

On initial inspection our data seem to lend a certain credibility to arguments about the breakdown of the class vote. Although, among our respondents, Labour continues to draw 40 per cent of its support from skilled manual workers, fully half such workers would vote for other parties, or not vote at all (Table 9.3). Twenty-eight per cent of partly-skilled workers and 22 per cent of the unskilled would also vote Tory; whereas, conversely, 14 per cent of professionals, 22 per cent of those in intermediate occupations, and 23 per cent of skilled nonmanual workers would vote Labour. 'Deviancy' in class voting patterns is, in short, more or less in line with that recorded in Table 9.1.

Moreover, support for arguments about the electoral significance of consumption sectoral cleavages in particular is evident from data on sectoral dependency, as for example in Table 9.4. Respondents were asked which

Table 9.3 *Voting intention by Registrar-General's social class*

		Class						
		1	*2*	*3N*	*3M*	*4*	*5*	*6*
Vote	Conservative	43	46	49	28	28	22	89
	Labour	14	22	23	50	45	53	0
	Alliance	38	23	19	16	15	17	0
	Would not vote	7	9	9	6	12	7	11
	Total	100	100	100	100	100	100	100
		(42)	(283)	(247)	(317)	(178)	(58)	(9)

(N = 1134)

Table 9.4 *Voting intention by state benefits*

A – Voting intention by number of state benefits received in household

		Benefits			
		None	*One*	*Two*	*Three or more*
Vote	Conservative	40	38	29	22
	Labour	31	35	49	65
	Alliance	21	20	12	7
	Would not vote	9	8	9	6
	Total	100	100	100	100
		(478)	(731)	(217)	(99)

(N = 1525)

B – Voting intention by proportion of gross household income received from state benefits

Row % Column %		Income		
		Less than 5 per cent *from state benefits*	*More than 5 per cent* *from state benefits*	*Total*
Vote	Conservative	78	22	100 (517)
		42	25	
	Labour	55	45	100 (530)
		30	52	
	Alliance	71	29	100 (262)
		19	16	
	Would not vote	72	28	100 (118)
		9	7	
	Total	100	100	
		(962)	(465)	(1427)

state benefits they received and what proportion of household income came from these sources. Even a simple count of benefits reveals that those receiving more frequent state support are more inclined to vote Labour. Recipients of three or more benefits were approximately three times more likely to vote Labour than Conservative. On the other hand, those receiving no state benefits, or only one payment, were more likely to be Tory voters. Actual dependence on state benefits is probably more important than the symbolic act of receiving them. More than three-quarters of all Conservative voters in our sample live in households where less than 5 per cent of gross income is in the form of state benefits. Forty-five per cent of Labour voters are in households where more than 5 per cent of income is so constituted. The greater the proportion of household income derived from welfare payments the greater the likelihood of respondents voting Labour. Further calculation (not shown here) confirms, as one would expect, that these effects are additive. Among those who are more dependent, therefore, at every numerical level of benefits the proportion voting Labour is increased. The Alliance vote is more or less evenly distributed throughout.

If one then considers data on home-ownership, the aspect of consumption at the centre of many recent debates about new sources of cleavage among the electorate, arguments about the demise of class voting seem particularly convincing. There is a clear association between housing tenure and voting intention evident in Table 9.5. Sixty per cent of council tenants indicated they would vote Labour in contrast to 30 per cent of home-owners. Forty-four per cent of the latter would vote Conservative: only 14 per cent of council tenants would do so. Furthermore, among respondents who were homeowners, those who owned their properties outright were rather more inclined to vote Tory than those paying off a mortgage or loan. Forty-nine per cent of outright owners would vote Tory, 29 per cent Labour, and 16 per cent for the Alliance parties, with the balance not intending to vote at all.

Turning from the sphere of consumption to that of production, a relatively neglected but nevertheless significant dimension of the argument about sectoral cleavages, differences are also observable between the voting

Table 9.5 *Voting intention by housing tenure*

		Owner occupation	Tenure Local authority rented	Privately rented
	Conservative	44	14	38
Vote	Labour	30	60	31
	Alliance	20	16	18
	Would not vote	7	11	14
	Total	100	100	100
		(1010)	(393)	(128)

(N = 1531)

patterns of those in public sector as against private sector employment. Table 9.6 shows voting intentions according to the sectoral location of people's present jobs. It will be seen that, among those employed in the public sector, Labour voters form the largest category followed by Conservative and, not far behind, Alliance supporters. Private sector employees, on the other hand, are more likely to vote Conservative, with the Labour and Alliance parties both losing support in this direction.

Table 9.6   *Voting intention by sector of employment*

| | | Sector | | | | |
| | | Public | | | Private | |
	Non-industrial	*Nationalized industrial*	*Total public*	*Multinational corporation*	*British national*	*Total private*
Conservative	31	20	28	43	37	40
Labour	37	56	42	34	36	35
Vote Alliance	23	18	22	16	18	17
Would not vote	9	5	8	7	9	8
Total	100	100	100	100	100	100
	(288)	(93)	(381)	(221)	(401)	(622)

(N = 1003)

On the face of it, therefore, social class – at least as conceptualized in terms of the Registrar-General's schema – is no more important a determinant of voting behaviour than are a range of other variables. In fact class has a seemingly less impressive association with vote than do some measures of what has come to be known, following Dunleavy's usage, as sectoral dependency. Sectoral cleavages are evident in the spheres of production and consumption that would seem to vindicate claims for the declining significance of social class in structuring electoral behaviour.

III

Few class analysts would accept this argument without comment, since few would deem unproblematic either the Registrar-General's schema or the social grading of occupations used by market research companies, one or other of which invariably forms the starting point for psephological analyses of so-called class politics. Sarlvik and Crewe, Finer, and Dunleavy, for example, all launch their critiques of the class politics orthodoxy from the platform of an analysis of voting patterns in terms of the opinion poll 'social grades', and the evidence for political dealignment that this allegedly generates.[16] Yet the social grades approach, no less than that of the Registrar-General, allocates occupations to 'social classes' on the basis of unreliable if not arbitrary judgements about life-style and general social standing.[17] Crewe's assessment of the Goldthorpe class categories as 'sociologically

235

meaningless' is particularly ironic when seen in the context of his own reliance of these conventional classifications and the obsolete manual/nonmanual dichotomy that they embrace. It would seem minimally desirable, therefore, to examine the data against a more coherent social class schema. In fact the analysis of voting intentions in terms of Goldthorpe class categories suggests that class politics is far from exhausted.

Table 9.7 shows the distribution of voting intentions by the Goldthorpe class positions of respondents in our sample. More than 50 per cent of those in the upper echelons of the service class will vote Conservative. Conversely, more than 50 per cent of semi-skilled and unskilled manual workers will vote Labour, a figure rising to 62 per cent among the skilled working class. The distribution of votes within other classes is rather as one might have expected: a majority of the self-employed vote for the Conservative Party, which also receives the largest single share of the vote among lower service-class (II) and routine white-collar (class III) employees; while supervisors of manual workers (class V) given an equal share of their votes to each of the two major parties and a significant minority (21 per cent) to the parties of the Alliance. Indeed it is obvious from this table that the Alliance is not a class party at all since (with the partial exception of skilled manual workers) about 20 per cent of those in each class location will give their votes to this 'third force'.

For the sake of completeness Table 9.7 includes cross-tabulations of voting intention by each of Erik Wright's neo-Marxist class schemes. The class effects on vote are significant in both cases. Employers and the *petit bourgeoisie* tend to vote Conservative, Labour voters are the largest single category within the working class, and the balance of the votes given to each of the major class parties tends to favour the Conservatives as one moves up the class structure and away from the working class and proximate class groupings. However, no further reference will be made to Wright's class frameworks in the course of this chapter, since direct comparison with Goldthorpe's neo-Weberian categories shows that the former are less useful than the latter for the explanation of voting behaviour. Applying analysis of variance techniques to the data we find that the F ratio for Goldthorpe classes is significantly higher than those for either of the Wright classifications in the case both of Labour and Conservative voters. (Of course, since the Alliance is not a class-based party, no class schema helps explain voting intentions here.) Another reason for preferring Goldthorpe to Wright class categories in this particular context is that the former facilitate systematic investigation of the effects of social mobility on partisanship. As we saw in Chapter 3, the Wright categories are inferior in this respect, given the practical difficulties associated with the acquisition of data necessary to allocate parents to the appropriate Wright classes.

There are two other aspects of the basic class voting data presented in Table 9.7 that are also worthy of comment. The first is that, when they are recoded to the same base as those taken from the British General Election Studies used by Heath and Crewe, they confirm the former's finding of a trendless fluctuation in relative class voting. This is evident from Table 9.8

Table 9.7 *Voting intention by Goldthorpe social class, and by Wright social classes*

A – Goldthorpe class

		I	II	III	IV	V	VI	VII	Total
Vote	Conservative	53	47	41	55	38	19	25	38 (427)
	Labour	17	24	27	14	35	62	51	35 (394)
	Alliance	23	23	20	20	21	12	17	19 (216)
	Would not vote	8	7	12	12	6	7	8	8 (97)
Total		100 (106)	100 (208)	100 (210)	100 (102)	100 (100)	100 (141)	100 (267)	100 (1134)

B – Wright original classes

		B	SE	PB	MS	SAE	W	Total
Vote	Conservative	67	66	48	44	39	29	38 (427)
	Labour	13	11	15	26	29	47	35 (394)
	Alliance	8	15	24	23	26	15	19 (216)
	Would not vote	12	8	13	7	6	9	8 (97)
Total		100 (24)	100 (53)	100 (71)	100 (308)	100 (127)	100 (551)	100 (1134)

C – Wright revised classes

		B	SE	PB	EM	ES	ENM	SCM	SCS	SCW	UM	US	P	Total
Vote	Con.	67	66	48	45	54	24	50	31	25	58	23	33	38 (427)
	Lab.	13	11	15	16	18	33	28	42	50	13	37	42	35 (394)
	All.	8	15	24	30	25	29	15	20	18	24	31	16	19 (216)
	WNV	12	8	13	9	4	14	8	7	7	5	9	9	8 (97)
Total		100 (24)	100 (53)	100 (71)	100 (67)	100 (28)	100 (42)	100 (93)	100 (45)	100 (163)	100 (38)	100 (35)	100 (475)	100 (1134)

Key to Wright social classes: see Table 3.5, p. 49.

which shows the distribution of votes in British general elections since 1970, together with our own data on voting intentions, cross-tabulated by social class. The model which assumes a constant set of class/party odds ratios over this period fits rather well. That is, loglinear analysis shows a relationship

Table 9.8 *Partisanship by Goldthorpe social class, 1970–84*

A – Partisanship and class (%)

	All	Salariat	Routine nonmanual	Petit bourgeoisie	Foremen/ technicians	Working class
1970						
Conservative	44	60	47	63	37	32
Labour	46	29	43	19	55	62
Liberal	10	12	10	18	9	7
	100 (1155)	101 (235)	100 (190)	100 (78)	101 (98)	101 (447)
1974 (Feb.)						
Conservative	39	55	42	70	36	24
Labour	45	24	39	19	43	63
Liberal	16	21	19	12	21	13
	100 (2208)	100 (436)	100 (406)	101 (184)	100 (149)	100 (837)
1974 (Oct.)						
Conservative	38	51	40	63	32	23
Labour	44	24	39	17	47	64
Liberal	18	25	21	20	21	13
	100 (2126)	100 (467)	100 (404)	100 (162)	100 (156)	100 (785)
1979						
Conservative	44	57	43	72	38	27
Labour	42	25	38	18	47	61
Liberal	15	18	19	10	15	13
	101 (1629)	100 (401)	100 (303)	100 (125)	100 (161)	100 (509)
1983						
Conservative	42	54	42	67	46	26
Labour	36	18	32	19	34	57
Alliance	22	28	26	14	20	16
	100 (3383)	100 (878)	100 (778)	100 (254)	100 (237)	101 (1098)
1984 (Essex survey)						
Conservative	38	52	47	60	35	23
Labour	41	22	29	18	41	60
Alliance	21	26	24	22	24	17
	100 (1439)	100 (361)	100 (195)	100 (128)	100 (121)	100 (489)

Table 9.8 (*cont.*)

B – Loglinear analysis of class and partisanship data

Model	G^2	df	p
1 Grand total	7938.9	89	
2 [C] [P] [E]	1712.2	78	<.001
3 [CP] [E]	298.0	70	<.001
4 [CP] [EP]	147.2	60	<.001
5 [CP] [EP] [CE]	42.6	40	>.05

Key: C – Class; E – Election; P – Party identification (voting intention in Essex survey).

Note:
1 Data for 1970–83 are based on the British General Election Studies and taken from Heath (1987: Table 5). At Crewe's suggestion party identification rather than reported vote is used in the analysis.
2 Liberal (and Alliance) includes supporters of 'other' parties.
3 Respondents who are formally employed are assigned a class according to their own occupation and employment status. Otherwise, they are assigned to their spouse's class, provided they are married, or living as married, and have a spouse who is formally employed.
4 The 'all' column includes respondents who could not be assigned to a class.
5 Heath's class schema is simply Goldthorpe's relabelled. The salariat are Goldthorpe classes I and II, the working class are classes VI and VII, while the routine nonmanual, petit bourgeoisie, and foremen/technician classes are Goldthorpe classes III, IV, and V as before.
6 To maintain comparability with Heath's own study the loglinear analysis is here laid out in full rather than (as elsewhere in this book) showing simply the principal parameters under test. For the same reason a *G square* rather than a *Y square* is reported.

between class and party (CP), class and election (CE), and election and party (EP), but no significant variation in the association between class and party over successive elections (the CPE interaction term is not required). Model 5 provides a satisfactory fit to the data. In other words, there are significant changes over time both in the sizes of the classes and the fortunes of the parties, but the level of class voting (in the relative sense) has not varied significantly over the years. The strength of the class–party alignment is undiluted over successive surveys. Heath's critique of the class dealignment thesis is clearly well founded.[18]

The second observation is perhaps more contentious. It is arguable that the influence of class on voting behaviour is somewhat underrepresented by these findings. The basic data in Table 9.7 do not distinguish the sexes. Both men and women have been allocated to class locations on the basis of their own occupations. Heath's longitudinal analysis modifies this practice somewhat by assigning, additionally, a social class location to those respondents who are economically inactive but married to employed partners. (The class standings of economically active men and women are determined, as before, according to their own occupations and employment statuses.) In order to preserve the integrity of the comparison we have followed this procedure in Table 9.8. Yet, as has already been demonstrated in earlier chapters, the voting intentions of married women in employment depend mostly on their spouses' rather than their own jobs. The relationship between an employed wife's class and her own vote is much less important than that between her vote and the class of her husband (see Tables 4.5 and 5.22 above). This suggests that, if anything, the strong association between Goldthorpe class and voting intention reported above actually underestimates the extent of class-based voting behaviour.

Moreover Goldthorpe has always maintained that an exclusively structural approach to class is inadequate to the explanation of solidarity, schism, and class action. In his view a satisfactory class analysis must take seriously the issues of process and agency, hence class formation. Class analysis within a neo-Weberian 'action frame of reference' therefore calls for explicit consideration of the question of social mobility.

The social backgrounds of the various factions within the electorate are indeed revealing. Table 9.9 shows the distribution of votes by respondents' present class positions, distinguishing those who are intergenerationally stable from the socially mobile. It can be seen clearly that certain kinds of intergenerational stability reinforce class voting. For example, among those from service-class origins presently in service-class locations, 53 per cent vote Conservative while only 13 per cent vote Labour. Members of the service-class from working-class backgrounds, on the other hand, are far more likely to vote Labour: in fact 39 per cent vote Tory while not many fewer, 31 per cent, vote for the Labour Party. Similarly, no less than 59 per cent of the intergenerationally stable working class vote Labour, with only 20 per cent inclined to the Conservatives. Note also that those upwardly mobile into the intermediate class are almost as likely to vote Labour as Conservative. Among those downwardly mobile to intermediate locations, Tory voters outnumber those supporting Labour by well over two to one. The Alliance vote seems largely unaffected by these patterns except to the extent that those upwardly mobile into intermediate-class positions who do not vote Labour are less likely to vote Tory and more likely to vote for the political centre than those downwardly mobile into this class.

In other words, the 'more than one-third' of the 'clearly working class' electorate who allegedly vote against their class interest by supporting the Tories (compare Table 9.1) are in reality barely one-fifth of unambiguous proletarians; that is, those who are at least second generation working class. Conversely, only 13 per cent of the demographically mature service class vote Labour, while almost one-third of those upwardly mobile into the service class from working-class locations retain their class of origin vote and not much more than one-third vote Conservative. The proportion of the electorate who are genuine cross-class voters is therefore considerably smaller than dealignment theorists would have us believe.

Again these findings tend to vindicate Heath's interpretation of the class voting data. Social mobility does not operate unambiguously to the benefit of the Conservatives. The socially mobile are simply cross-pressured.

People appear to be influenced both by their social origins and by their current class

Table 9.9 *Voting intention by Goldthorpe social class by Goldthorpe class of origin*

A – Class of origin = service

| | | Present class | | | |
		Service	Intermediate	Working	Total
	Conservative	53	53	41	51 (71)
	Labour	13	21	27	17 (24)
Vote	Alliance	25	16	27	23 (32)
	Would not vote	9	11	5	9 (12)
	Total	100	100	100	100
		(79)	(38)	(22)	(139)

B – Class of origin = intermediate

| | | Present class | | | |
		Service	Intermediate	Working	Total
	Conservative	53	51	22	43 (144)
	Labour	19	15	55	28 (93)
Vote	Alliance	22	22	16	20 (67)
	Would not vote	6	13	7	9 (29)
	Total	100	100	100	100
		(109)	(128)	(96)	(333)

C – Class of origin = working

| | | Present class | | | |
		Service	Intermediate	Working	Total
	Conse;vative	39	38	20	30 (133)
	Labour	31	33	59	44 (195)
Vote	Alliance	23	21	14	18 (81)
	Would not vote	7	8	8	8 (35)
	Total	100	100	100	100
		(83)	(163)	(198)	(444)

position. Where these influences work in opposite directions the outcomes are less clear-cut than when they are congruent. . . . There is little sign that the mobile as a whole either reject or are rejected by their class destinations.[19]

Moreover, and rather importantly, the fact that those upwardly and downwardly mobile tend to divide their votes in proportions more equal than are evident among the socially immobile does not mean that mobile individuals actually feel divided in their loyalties. Those from working-class backgrounds who move into service-class employment, yet nevertheless vote Labour, may be as committed to that particular party as are its second generation working-class suppporters. The tendency to read individual proclivities into overall proportions betrays an ecological reasoning that undermines at least some versions of the class dealignment thesis.[20] The relationship between 'looseness' in the class structure and any lessening of partisanship, if indeed it exists, is not that simple.

Ecological reasoning also undermines the claim that, because the *proportions* of Conservative and Labour votes in 'mixed-class' families tend to be more evenly balanced than those for 'single-class' households, *individual* voters in the former situations are somehow more fickle and volatile than those in the latter. In fact our data show clearly that electors in cross-class families are no less partisan than those in class-homogeneous households. Nor does a mixed-class situation erode the salience of class itself to the construction of social consciousness and world-views.

For example, we have already seen (in Table 5.18 above) that people in cross-class households are no less likely to define themselves in class terms than are men and women in class-homogeneous households; that is, they show no signs of being confused or ambivalent about their class identities. Consider, in addition, the data in Table 9.10. These suggest that, contrary to the assertions of class dealignment theorists, class does not lose its salience among mixed-class couples. Those living in cross-class households are no less

Table 9.10 *Salience of class, and political partisanship, by family type of respondent*

| | | | % who claim that . . . | |
		Class conflict is important	Class is an inevitable feature of society	It makes a difference which party runs the country
Family type:	S–S	69	75	67
Class	I–I	58	86	51
homogeneous	W–W	54	76	42
Respondent in	S–I	63	71	73
higher class	S–W	64	79	68
than spouse	I–W	49	83	48
Respondent in	W–S	74	80	75
lower class	W–I	63	79	48
than spouse	I–S	63	87	56
Respondent	U–U	69	71	55
unemployed or	U–S	77	62	68
keeping house	U–I	55	75	50
	U–W	40	81	56

Note: Family types are as in Chapter 5, Tables 18–22, though no distinction is here made between male and female respondents. In each type the class position of the respondent is stated first.

likely to claim that there are important issues causing class conflict in Britain, or that class is an inevitable feature of modern society, than are those resident in single-class households. There is simply no systematic difference between the perceptions of respondents in the two different types of class situations. In both cases the percentages are rather high across almost all household types. Moreover, partisanship does not seem to decline as the class purity of the household is dissolved, since (as this same table shows) voters from cross-class households are just as likely as those from class-homogeneous households to claim that it 'makes a great deal of difference' which party runs the country. Of course there is an obvious class effect in the figures for this particular column of the table. Those in higher classes are more likely than those further down the hierarchy to claim that parties matter. Disillusionment or indifference is more common among working-class individuals. But the pattern of responses does not vary between class-homogeneous and cross-class household types. In other words the two groups are equally partisan. Indeed, as the data in Table 9.11 show, they are not at all distinct in the pattern of their responses to questioning about electoral partisanship itself. Individuals in cross-class situations are as likely as those in class-homogeneous circumstances to vote for a particular party because they like its policies, believe in who or what it stands for, and so forth. The responses given by the two groups are almost identical.

These findings suggest strongly that individual voters from cross-class households are not distinct from their class-homogeneous counterparts. Those in both groups are equally likely to identify themselves as belonging to a class, to see the world as structured in class terms, and to be partisan in their political allegiance. It is true that greater proportions of men and women vote

Table 9.11 *Reasons for choice of party by family type of respondent*

	Family type	
Reasons why respondent votes for the [. . . .] party	*Homogeneous*	*Mixed*
Likes general policies of the party	34	42
Because of who the party stands for ('the businessman', etc.)	21	17
Likes general features of the party (unity, style, etc.)	16	17
Supports fundamental beliefs of the party ('socialism', etc.)	14	16
Dislikes general policies of another party	14	13
Likes leading members of the party	12	12
Dislikes general features of another party	12	11
Always voted for this party	8	7
For a change	6	5
Dislikes leading members of another party	4	6
No particular reason	3	2
Personal reasons	2	1
Other reasons	8	9

Note: Per cents are based on respondents. Valid cases = class homogeneous, 325; cross-class, 500.

243

Conservative or Labour in class-homogeneous households than is the case for households where spouses have different occupational class standings. Our own data have already confirmed this finding (see Table 5.22 above.) However the association between 'mixed' family types and a more equally divided Labour and Conservative vote does not mean that each individual within a cross-class family is somehow divided in his or her loyalties. These same data also show that, contrary to the assumptions made by dealignment theorists, people in cross-class households are as partisan and 'class conscious' as those in 'pure' class situations. So there is no reason to suppose that recent electoral shifts can be attributed to a 'loosening in the class structure' effected by the emergence of mixed-class households. Neither increased social mobility, nor a rise in the numbers of cross-class families, implies a necessary 'class secularization of society'.

IV

What conclusions can then be drawn about the reality of class politics from these data? Goldthorpe's own observations are based on recent mobility analyses which show that the working class is largely self-recruiting in most western societies – certainly in Britain – and that the expanding service class, heterogeneous in composition so far as the social origins of its members are concerned, nevertheless preserves a high degree of intergenerational stability among subsequent generations.[21]

The demographic maturity of the working class leads him to conclusions about its socio-political maturity and in particular to the notion of collective instrumentalism. The decline of locality-based status orders, extension of the sphere of citizenship, together with the self-recruiting characteristics of this class and its long tradition of Labourism, has encouraged members to exploit to the full such market advantages as they may possess. Workers are thus pecuniary in their attitude to labour, instrumental in support of working-class organizations such as the trades unions and Labour Party, and privatized in their role as consumers.[22] This means that, although they may pursue wage demands aggressively both within and outside the framework of trades union organization, such militancy implies nothing in the way of discontent that can be channelled in the direction of support for specifically socialist or even Labour Party policies. Working-class support for Labour is of a calculative rather than affective kind: it is 'an attachment likely to be more dependent on Labour clearly and consistently demonstrating that it *is* the party of the working man'.[23]

The service class, on the other hand, exhibits a low degree of class formation. Paradoxically, this means that voting proclivities are no less open here than among manual workers, although Goldthorpe expects that this class, as it consolidates, will form a conservative and Conservative force within society.

244

The expectations must . . . be – unless powerful countervailing influences can be identified – that these employees will in the main act in the way that is characteristic of members of privileged strata: that is, that they will seek to use the superior resources that they possess in order to *preserve* their positions of relative social power and advantage, for themselves and their children.[24]

The fact that collective action by managerial and administrative employees has consistently sought to maintain favourable differentials in pay, conditions, and life-chances generally is, for Goldthorpe, indicative of future political sympathies.

Our data are not inconsistent with both these conclusions. The demographically mature working class are majority Labour voters – with the evidence cited in previous chapters suggesting an instrumental attachment of the kind claimed by Goldthorpe. And the distribution of service-class votes confirms, as the data on social mobility would suggest, a low degree of class formation – for the moment. But one cannot draw firm conclusions about the parameters of class politics from this evidence alone. It is also important to consider here the arguments of those like Stewart and his colleagues who argue that class structure in fact consists of typical life-history trajectories between different occupational positions. Consequently a great deal of mobility, especially that which is in and out of intermediate classes, is of a career rather than intergenerational form.[25] Again this raises the question of volatility in the votes of individuals in intermediate positions. Can the Labour Party win (or win back) the support of those from working-class origins?

There seems no reason to suppose that it cannot. It is clear from Table 9.9, for example, that present members of the working class whose class of origin was in fact intermediate are proportionately almost as likely to vote Labour as are the demographically mature working class themselves. Indeed the voting profiles of the two groups are virtually identical. Similarly, those who have arrived at intermediate-class locations from working-class backgrounds are much less likely to vote Conservative than are those among their class peers who have service-class origins, or who are from established intermediate-type backgrounds. These findings suggest that, contrary to the assertions of many class dealignment theorists, there is no straightforward association between increased rates of social mobility and the changing electoral fortunes of the political parties. Some of those upwardly mobile into the service and intermediate classes from working-class backgrounds have, as it were, taken their Labour vote with them; working-class sons and daughters of intermediate-class parents show the same relative voting proclivities as those having proletarian backgrounds; and we know from evidence elsewhere that somewhere between one-quarter and one-third of the children of intermediate-class parents will themselves arrive at working-class destinations (see, for example, Table 4.8 above). Of course we would not dispute the fact that recent changes in the shape of the occupational structure have affected the distribution of votes. The class composition of the electorate has been changing, as the relative sizes of the working and service classes have become more equal, and the proportion in routine nonmanual employment has

245

steadily grown. But this is not the same thing as saying that class differences as such have declined. Class dealignment suggests that classes have become fragmented so that class issues are now of secondary importance to the structuring of voting behaviour. In other words parties should stop appealing to putative class interests. We, on the other hand, maintain that the alteration to the shape of the structure has not undermined the distinctiveness of the classes or the salience of class issues to voters. Parties should continue to appeal to class interests since, as Heath and his colleagues rightly insist, 'they remain the fundamentals of electoral choice'.[26] This may present the Labour Party with a difficult dilemma for the future: its class base is shrinking, but since the majority of its votes still come from the working class, it must devise an electoral appeal which attracts support from elsewhere without abandoning its class appeal. However, it does not signal the 'end of class politics', for there is nothing in these findings to suggest that class interests have ceased to be the principal focus for political partisanship.

Indeed, pursuing a class analysis within the action frame of reference, we can offer additional evidence that the class basis of politics is not experiencing some long-term process of secular decline. Social action theory takes explicit cognizance of issues not only of social process, hence social mobility and class formation, but also those of social meanings. That is, actors' definitions of situations are taken seriously in explanations of their social behaviour and relationships, at least in so far as the interpretation of motives is concerned.[27] Given the variety of meanings that the world may possess for individuals, even those within the same class location, it would seem to make good theoretical sense to inquire about beliefs, values, and attitudes before drawing conclusions about supposed class interests and their likely effects on electoral behaviour. Of course one possible source of meaning with likely electoral consequences is that of class identification itself. Do people identify with social classes or see the world as structured in class terms? As we have already seen, fewer than 3 per cent of our respondents refused to assign themselves a specific class location, and only 6 per cent couldn't say to which class they belonged. If one then examines the impact of class identification on party preference one can readily see the importance of social identities for voting behaviour. As Table 9.12 shows, class identification is particularly important for the Labour vote, since even among those presently in service-class positions Labour has a majority at the polls – providing these individuals identify themselves as working class. Affiliation to the working class greatly increases the proportion of Labour voters in every class category. Again, this table probably understates the importance of class identities for electoral behaviour, since it does not control for sex, and we know from evidence elsewhere (see Table 5.19 above) that economically active women living in cross-class households are somewhat more likely to take their class identities from their husbands, than from their own occupations.

More striking evidence as to the importance of class meaning systems can be observed in Table 9.13. We have seen that respondents to our survey were asked about the salience of class as a source of social identity, the persistence

Table 9.12 *Voting intention by Goldthorpe social class by self-assigned class*

A – Self-assigned middle class*

		Service	Social class Intermediate	Working	Total
Vote	Conservative	58	53	34	52 (240)
	Labour	14	13	40	19 (86)
	Alliance	23	23	18	22 (103)
	Would not vote	5	11	8	8 (37)
	Total	100 (199)	100 (177)	100 (90)	100 (466)

B – Self-assigned working class

		Service	Social class Intermediate	Working	Total
Vote	Conservative	28	38	19	27 (159)
	Labour	36	35	59	47 (277)
	Alliance	25	17	15	17 (102)
	Would not vote	10	11	7	9 (51)
	Total	100 (88)	100 (208)	100 (293)	100 (589)

* Includes 'Upper'.

Table 9.13 *Voting intention by self-assigned class by attitudes to class (%)*

			Con.	All.	Lab.	Vote Will not vote	Total	Cons. % minus Lab.%
Self-assigned middle class	Class identity	Yes	52	21	20	7	100	32
		No	48	21	22	9	100	26
	Class structure	Stayed same	36	21	32	11	100	4
		Changed	61	21	12	6	100	49
	Class conflict	Yes	52	24	17	7	100	35
		No	49	17	26	8	100	23
Self-assigned working class	Class identity	Yes	26	16	52	6	100	−26
		No	25	19	45	11	100	−20
	Class structure	Stayed same	18	14	59	9	100	−41
		Changed	36	21	38	5	100	−2
	Class conflict	Yes	25	18	50	7	100	−25
		No	27	16	48	9	100	−21

of class inequalities, and importance of class divisions to the structuring of social schism. Simple Yes/No answers to each question can be cross-tabulated against voting intention while controlling for self-assigned class position. The extreme right-hand column of the table shows the percentage of Conservative votes minus those for Labour in each category and is most revealing. Among middle-class identifiers the Tories have in all cases a clear majority of votes. But this majority is increased among those who normally think of themselves as belonging to a particular social class, do not believe class inequality has persisted undiminished over the ages, but are convinced of the existence of class conflict in Britain today. This same pattern persists among working-class identifiers – although, of course, Labour voters are here in the majority. Those who normally identify themselves as working class, can see no amelioration of class inequalities, and view British society as structured in class conflict terms, are more likely to vote Labour.

The salience of class identities to voting behaviour is also obvious in perceptions of the parties themselves. It will be remembered that respondents were asked who they thought voted for the particular party which they supported and for the same reasons as themselves. No less than 40 per cent of all Labour supporters nominated 'the working class' among their answers. Indeed another 20 per cent mentioned 'working people', 13 per cent the unemployed, and 12 per cent 'the poor'. Perceptions of the Conservative vote were rather more dispersed although 12 per cent of Tory supporters offered 'the middle class' among their replies, 23 per cent mentioned the self-employed, and 10 per cent 'those well off'. Interestingly enough, almost equal numbers of Alliance voters cited the working and middle classes among their replies (11 per cent and 14 per cent respectively), although by far the largest proportion (37 per cent) felt that others voting Alliance for the same reason as themselves would simply be 'fed up with the other two parties'.

In short, therefore, not only does social class in the objective sense of location within the social relationships of production have a generally undiminished effect on voting behaviour, but, furthermore, this is reinforced by the effects of class identity and beliefs in the salience of class processes to the structuring of modern British society. Neither the data on social mobility nor those on self-assigned class support the contention of class dealignment theorists that 'the old classes have ceased to be cultural communities, witness the decline in class consciousness and class loyalty'.[28] To the contrary, classes have not withered away, and class identities exert a powerful influence on electoral choice.

V

What then is the relative importance of social class as compared to that of sectoral cleavages in the explanation of voting intentions? We can find no evidence of a loosening of class processes themselves, no matter whether class is considered in its objective or subjective aspects, but perhaps these class processes are now fragmented by additional cleavages which have important consequences for party politics?

These are difficult questions to answer in a cross-sectional study such as ours, since the various class and sectoral variables are heavily interrelated. Not only is it the case that vote is associated with both class and housing tenure: housing tenure and class are themselves strongly correlated. Fewer than 6 per cent of those in the upper echelons of the service class live in accommodation rented from a local authority. This figure rises to almost 40 per cent among the semi-skilled and unskilled manual workers of class VII (Table 9.14). Similarly, there are significant associations between class and dependence on welfare benefits, class and self-assigned class, present class and class of origin. Thus, for example, 93 per cent of Goldthorpe class I respondents live in households where less than 5 per cent of the total income is obtained from welfare benefits, while 34 per cent of class VII respondents are in households receiving more than 5 per cent of total income in this way. Sixty-nine per cent of those in service-class positions claim a middle-class identity whereas 76 per cent of the working class claim proletarian identities. The strong association between present class and class of origin has been commented on at some length. The relationship between class and production sector is more uneven but still pronounced (Table 9.15). Forty-four per cent and 48 per cent of classes I and II respectively are in the public sector, but this figure falls to 26 per cent and 33 per cent for clases VI and VII. (The unevenness comes in the intermediate classes: only 35 per cent of class III are in public sector employment as compared to 47 per cent of class V. The *petit bourgeoisie* are by definition entirely within the private sector.)

Table 9.14 *Housing tenure by Goldthorpe class*

		I	II	III	IV	V	VI	VII	Total
					Class				
House tenure	Owner-occupied	93	83	74	81	65	61	53	70 (918)
	Local authority, rented	6	9	17	8	25	31	38	21 (276)
	Privately rented	2	9	9	11	10	8	8	8 (110)
	Total	100 (122)	100 (234)	100 (254)	100 (114)	100 (107)	100 (162)	100 (311)	100 (1304)

Given this degree of interconnectedness among our key variables, one strategy might be to construct a series of three-way cross-tabulations of vote, class and sector, similar to those already offered with respect to voting intention and the several class variables (self-assigned class, class of origin, and present class). In this way it can be demonstrated that, for example, present social class is still strongly associated with vote even when a control is introduced for housing tenure (see Table 9.16). This table also reveals some of the interaction between these three variables. The association between vote and class is not uniform across housing tenures. Among owner-occupiers

Table 9.15 *Production sector by Goldthorpe class*

			I	II	III	Class V	VI	VII	Total
Prod. sector	Public	Non-Ind.	34	45	30	28	10	25	29 (335)
		Nat. Ind.	10	3	5	19	16	8	9 (103)
		Total Publ.	44	48	35	47	26	33	38 (438)
	Private	Multi. Corp.	26	19	21	21	21	26	22 (261)
		Brit. Nat.	31	33	44	33	53	41	40 (470)
		Total Priv.	57	52	65	54	74	67	62 (731)
		All	100 (101)	100 (225)	100 (256)	100 (107)	100 (165)	100 (314)	100 (1168)

Table 9.16 *Voting intention by Goldthorpe social class and housing tenure*

			I	II	III	IV	Class V	VI	VII	Total
Vote/ house tenure	Owner-occupied	Con.	55	49	46	61	41	23	27	43 (340)
		Lab.	14	22	21	11	35	54	47	29 (228)
		All.	24	23	22	18	22	14	19	21 (165)
		WNV	7	6	10	10	2	9	7	7 (60)
		Total	100 (99)	100 (168)	100 (154)	100 (81)	100 (63)	100 (86)	100 (142)	100 (793)
	Local authority rented	Con.	0	21	21	25	23	10	18	17 (57)
		Lab.	75	32	53	38	50	73	59	57 (133)
		All.	0	32	15	13	19	12	13	15 (35)
		WNV	25	16	12	25	8	5	11	11 (25)
		Total	100 (4)	100 (19)	100 (34)	100 (8)	100 (26)	100 (41)	100 (102)	100 (234)
	Privately rented	Con.	50	50	33	33	55	18	43	40 (39)
		Lab.	50	30	24	17	0	82	38	32 (31)
		All.	0	15	14	33	18	0	19	16 (16)
		WNV	0	5	29	17	27	0	0	12 (12)
		Total	100 (2)	100 (20)	100 (21)	100 (12)	100 (11)	100 (11)	100 (21)	100 (98)

(N = 1125)

Key: Con. – Conservative; Lab. – Labour; All. – Alliance; WNV – Would not vote.

there is a largely unaffected class–vote relationship. Local authority tenants, on the other hand, seem to be more influenced by their housing situation than by objective social class. Indeed, the association between class and vote is not significant among either council or private tenants, with the majority of the former voting Labour whatever their class situation. Around 60 per cent of all council tenants would vote Labour – a figure that rises to almost 70 per cent if those who would not vote are excluded from the total. But, of course, such tenancy is predominantly a characteristic of the working rather than the middle classes.

Similarly, the association between class and vote is still evident when production sector is controlled for, with Conservative voters being more common in classes I to III and Labour voters a majority in classes V to VII (Table 9.17). Again, however, this table shows an unevenness in the sector-vote correlation. The impact of sectoral location on vote is confined almost entirely to the nonmanual occupations. Members of the service class employed in the public sector are significantly less likely to vote Conservative than their private sector counterparts. Among class III employees, those involved in private firms are majority Conservative voters, whereas in the public sector, the party preferences are reversed, with Labour voters being the more common. Sectoral location also has a significant impact on the Alliance vote among the more privileged members of the service class, with those in the public sector more inclined to vote for the political centre, than are their counterparts who are involved in private businesses.

Table 9.17 *Voting intention by sector of employment by Goldthorpe social class*

			I	*II*	*III*	Class *V*	*VI*	*VII*	*Total*
	Public	Con.	32	26	28	33	16	21	28 (108)
		Lab.	27	31	39	35	74	50	42 (159)
		All.	32	26	21	27	5	20	22 (86)
		WNV	8	7	11	4	5	9	8 (30)
Vote/sector of employment		Total	100 (37)	100 (95)	100 (74)	100 (48)	100 (38)	100 (91)	100 (383)
	Private	Con.	63	56	48	42	20	27	40 (246)
		Lab.	12	17	20	35	57	50	35 (216)
		All.	16	22	19	15	15	15	17 (106)
		WNV	8	5	13	8	8	8	8 (52)
		Total	100 (49)	100 (105)	100 (136)	100 (52)	100 (103)	100 (175)	100 (620)

Key: Con. – Conservative; Lab. – Labour; All. – Alliance; WNV – Would not vote.

These general patterns also emerge when the Registar-General's and Erik Wright's class categories are substituted for those of John Goldthorpe. (For this reason it seems superfluous to include the corresponding tables.) They suggest to us that, in so far as sectoral cleavages in housing and employment are associated with voting intention, these are merely surrogates for social class. Or, at best, class voting is mediated by sectoral differences. Only among council tenants is the class–vote pattern significantly altered. This group are more likely to vote Labour whatever their class situation. But these tenants are overwhelmingly found among the working classes. It is reasonable to claim, therefore, that the association that shows up between housing and vote is simply a proxy for the familiar class–vote linkage. A similar situation prevails in production. Only among public sector nonmanual employees (classes I, II and III) does sectoral location have a significant impact on the class voting patterns. Public sector employees in these classes are less likely to vote Conservative than are their private sector peers. However, proportionately more of these three classes (certainly of classes I and II) are in public sector employment than is the case for classes VI and VII, and the working classes are in any case majority Labour voters. Again, therefore, it seems reasonable to claim that the association between vote and production sector is simply a surrogate for the more fundamental relationship between vote and class.

A somewhat less tedious method of exploring the interrelationships between these variables is to fit a series of loglinear models to our data. It would be superfluous to report this analysis in full. A variety of models were fitted and the findings can be summarized in the results reported in Table 9.18. The best fitting model in the table (model 6) indicates the relationship between voting intention and the combination of class and housing, together with self-assigned class, and class of origin. Among these, self-assigned class is the single variable having the strongest association with vote, although the significant interaction between vote, class, and housing tends to confirm our earlier conclusion that the association between housing and vote is in fact a class effect, with the impact of class mediated through the class composition of housing areas. Note that one putative source of sectoral cleavage – dependence on state benefits – can be removed from the model without worsening the degree of fit. The relationship between vote and class of origin also seems to be weaker than that between vote and the other class variables.

Of course loglinear models specify only the strength of the associations between variables. Causal analysis remains a matter of interpretation and therefore debate. Nevertheless we would argue that our data and analysis are sufficiently robust as to sustain the conclusion that class politics, though not immediately apparent on the surface of British political life at present, is certainly not in abeyance. It is true that the relationship between (say) class location, housing tenure, and voting intention can be specified in any one of three different ways. It can plausibly be argued that people who buy their own houses will tend to switch votes to the Conservatives; that class mobility encourages home-ownership and Tory voting; or even that Conservative voters are more highly motivated to buy their own homes and pursue upward mobility itself. A life-course analysis would be required to arbitrate on the more complex matters of causality here. (Do people who purchase property then switch votes? Or is it the case that Conservative voters are disproportionately inclined to buy their own homes?) In the absence of appropriate longitudinal data from our own study we can pursue the issue of causality little further here.[29]

Table 9.18 *Interrelationship of voting intention, class, class of origin, class identification, housing tenure, and state benefit dependency*

Model	df	Y^2	Difference			Y^2/df	p
1 [DOIHB][VD][VO][VI][VH]	456	473.6					
2 [DOIHB][VO][VI][VH]	465	506.9	⇒ VD	9	33.3	3.7	<0.0005
3 [DOIHB][VD][VI][VH]	462	490.4	⇒ VO	6	16.8	2.8	<0.01
4 [DOIHB][VD][VO][VH]	459	503.0	⇒ VI	3	29.4	9.8	<0.0005
5 [DOIHB][VD][VO][VI]	462	523.7	⇒ VH	6	50.1	8.3	<0.0005
6 [DOIHB][VDH][VO][VI]	439	437.6	⇒ VDH	17	36.0	2.1	<0.005

Key: V = Voting intention; D = Social class (Goldthorpe categories collapsed); O = Class of origin (Goldthorpe categories collapsed); I = Self-assigned class; H = Housing tenure; B = Dependence on state benefits (none, low, high).

Note: When modelling on this scale there is an obvious problem in the relationship between increasing cell numbers and decreasing observations to fill them. The above table is significant, not so much on its own, but as part of a general pattern that emerges across various modelling exercises. For example, in the full seven-way analysis that includes variables V to B, together with production sector (P), we find very strong evidence of the association between vote and class, strong evidence of that between vote and self-assigned class, and marginal evidence of a relationship between vote and housing and (even more slight) between vote and production sector. State benefit dependency is irrelevant. If this table is then collapsed over benefit dependency, associations are clear between vote and (in decreasing order of importance) class, self-assigned class, production sector and housing tenure. The relationship between class of origin and vote is marginal. Of course, with an increase of numbers both in absolute terms and relative to the availability of cells, it is not surprising that most relationships appear more significant (in a statistical sense) in this analysis of the data. Nevertheless, class and self-assigned class certainly are relevant, and more so than the sectoral items. If we then collapse over class of origin as well we find very strong evidence of a relationship between vote and self-assigned class, and vote and housing. There seems to be no need to include production sector in this model. Taken together then, these results suggest that housing is a surrogate for class, given that in the initial analyses vote with class is the dominant association.

In any event, we have certainly provided evidence sufficient to establish the case that class remains an important factor closely allied with voting intentions, more so in fact than are the newer sectoral cleavages that allegedly have replaced it, since our data also suggest that these are themselves proximate class variables. Our own understanding of these results can perhaps best be represented diagrammatically (as in Table 9.19). As before the number of heads on the arrows represents the broad magnitude of the effects involved. The associations are suggested by our data: the interpretations of direction and therefore of causality are, of course, our own. The persistence of class identities, and their apparently undiminished effect on electoral preferences, suggests that the lines of class cleavage that are highlighted by the present recession – between those employed in public sector and private sector enterprises, those self-sufficient on wages and welfare claimants, home-owners and council tenants – are likely to prove no more an obstacle to the continuance of class-based politics than were earlier forms of sectionalism among the electorate. The 'working class' has always been stratified according to industry, locality, grade and occupation, and was so long before the

Table 9.19 *Relationship between voting intention, class variables, and sectoral variables*

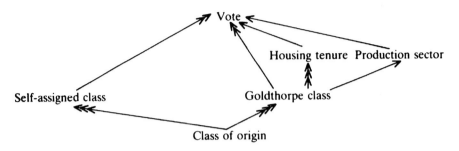

emergence of Labour as a political force. Yet this prevented neither the emergence of a specifically working-class party on to the political stage nor the subsequent structuring of politics in Britain along class lines. The source of recent fluctuations in this party's electoral fortunes must therefore be sought elsewhere.

VI

If Labour's particularly poor performances at the polls during the past decade are not testimony to the decline of class politics, and cannot be traced to the emergence of new cleavages in the structure of social hierarchy, how then are these to be accounted for? Like Heath and his colleagues we are inclined to search for the answer in the direction of electoral politics itself. Our data suggest that Labour voters in particular respond to the language of social class and see the world about them structured by class processes. It would seem, then, that Labour gains to the extent that it succeeds in constituting and mobilizing class interests by presenting issues in class terms, and reinforcing the formation of collectivities with common class identities. The fact is, of course, that the Labour Party and trades unions alike have been relatively unsuccessful at mobilizing members in precisely these terms, especially when compared with their counterparts in countries such as Sweden, Austria and Norway where, in any case, much smaller populations have rendered this task markedly more simple.

The extent to which constituents, even those in the ideological heartland, are disillusioned with the party itself is evident even from our own rather limited survey data. (The limitation here, of course, is that our questions were not focused exclusively on the complex issues of political culture. The British General Election Studies, among other sources, offer more detail on these matters.) For example, our results show that members of the working classes – from whom Labour continues to draw most of its support – are less inclined to see any differences between the various political parties, than are those in more privileged class positions (see Table 9.20). In other words cynicism or

Table 9.20 *Attitude to party differences by Goldthorpe social class*

	I	II	III	Class IV	V	VI	VII	Total
Makes no difference which party runs the country	30	29	46	40	51	49	53	43 (554)
It does make a difference which party runs the country	70	72	54	60	49	51	47	57 (727)
Total	100 (119)	100 (229)	100 (244)	100 (113)	100 (104)	100 (164)	100 (308)	100 (1281)

disillusionment is most common among the classes that provide the base for the socialist vote. Of course those who continue to vote Labour (whatever their class position) are no less committed (or, perhaps more accurately, no more committed) than are those who support the Conservatives. Rather, what seems to happen (see Table 9.21) is that the disillusioned voters switch to the Alliance parties, or state their intention simply to refrain from voting altogether. Thus, for example, if we look at the patterns of vote switching (Table 9.22) among those who expressed a positive party preference, noting also their present class locations, we find that the largest movement in party support is from Labour to the Alliance among the working classes (though almost as many have switched from Labour to Conservative). Of course these figures must be treated with caution. Because of the way the relevant questions were asked they represent aggregate changes of votes over several elections. But they are certainly not inconsistent with our earlier analysis. Labour, a class party, has lost votes across all classes alike. But there is no naive sociological determinism at work here: half as many Labour voters have switched back from the Alliance parties as have defected to them. Similarly, as many Alliance voters have switched to the Conservatives, as have Conservatives to the Alliance. Again this tends to suggest that Labour's decline, and the rise of the Alliance, reflect relatively ephemeral changes in the political fortunes of the various parties rather than underlying trends in the class structure.

Table 9.21 *Attitude to party differences by voting intention*

	Con.	Lab.	Vote All.	WNV	Total
Makes no difference which party runs the country	32	35	53	83	41 (620)
It does make a difference which party runs the country	68	65	47	17	59 (890)
Total	100 (547)	100 (566)	100 (270)	100 (127)	100 (1510)

Key: Con. – Conservative; Lab. – Labour; All. – Alliance; WNV – Would not vote.

Table 9.22 *Patterns of vote switching by Goldthorpe social class*

Previously voted	Present voting intention	Social classes	%	N
Labour———→(switched to)——→Conservative		I and II	22	
		III	13	
		IV	16	
		V	12	
		VI and VII	39	(106)
Labour———→(switched to)———→Alliance		I and II	32	
		III	13	
		IV	7	
		V	14	
		VI and VII	34	(111)
Conservative———→(switched to)———→Alliance		I and II	38	
		III	21	
		IV	5	
		V	16	
		VI and VII	20	(81)
Conservative———→(switched to)———→Labour		I and II	25	
		III	13	
		IV	3	
		V	9	
		VI and VII	50	(32)
Alliance———→(switched to)———→Labour		I and II	27	
		III	13	
		IV	6	
		V	11	
		VI and VII	43	(53)
Alliance———→(switched to)——→Conservative		I and II	41	
		III	24	
		IV	9	
		V	7	
		VI and VII	19	(75)

Note: That this table includes only those respondents who expressed a positive party preference. Those who stated that they 'would not vote' were not asked to indicate how (if at all) they had voted previously.

However, as was observed in previous chapters, despite the cynicism about present party politics, people are not generally fatalistic about what governments could achieve, were there sufficient political will. The majority of our respondents have not abandoned their concern for social justice or their belief that significant economic and social change is possible. Those who expressed a party preference continue to justify their choice according to principled reasons of party policy and belief (Table 9.23). Parties tend, on the whole, to be selected for positive rather than negative reasons, and in particular because supporters like the general policies of the party, subscribe to its fundamental beliefs, or wish to further the interests of the particular social group that it purports to stand for. However, there are some interesting differences between the parties, in terms of the typical motivations of their supporters. Almost 40 per cent of those in our sample who intended to vote

Table 9.23 *Reasons for choice of party*

A – Among voters in the sample as a whole

Are there any particular reasons why you
   would vote for the [. . .] party?

	N	% of responses	% of cases
Like general policies of party	550	24.4	38.3
Who the party stands for ('the businessman', etc.)	275	12.2	19.2
Like general features of party (unity, style, etc.)	243	10.8	16.9
Believe in fundamental beliefs of party ('socialism', etc.)	203	9.0	14.1
Dislike general policies of another party	203	9.0	14.1
Dislike general features of another party	165	7.3	11.5
Like leading members of the party	159	7.1	11.1
Always voted for this party (no other reason given)	112	5.0	7.8
For a change	85	3.8	5.9
Dislike leading members of another party	82	3.6	5.7
No	45	2.0	3.1
For personal or family reasons	19	0.8	1.3
Other	112	5.0	7.8
Total	2253	100.0	156.9

(Valid cases = 1436)

B – By voting intention

	Conservative	Labour	Alliance
Like general policies of party	49	33	30
Who the party stands for ('the businessman', etc.)	6	39	4
Like general features of party (unity, style, etc.)	22	9	25
Belief in fundamental beliefs of party ('socialism', etc.)	10	21	7
Dislike general policies of another party	19	9	17
Dislike general features of another party	15	8	14
Like leading members of the party	17	6	10
Always voted for this party (no other reason given)	4	15	2
For a change	1	2	25
Dislike leading members of another party	5	7	5
No	3	3	3
For personal or family reasons	2	2	0
Other	10	5	10

Note: Per cents in Table B are based on respondents. Valid cases = 1409.

Labour stated that they would support the party because of 'who it stood for'.
One-third of Labour supporters liked party policies while one-fifth subscribed
to the fundamental beliefs of its political philosophy. The Conservative vote,
by comparison, is rooted less in fundamental beliefs and support for who that
party 'stands for', and rather more in Conservative policy, the unity and style

257

of Conservatism, the personal appeal of Tory politicians, and an active dislike of the policies and style of other parties. Similarly, the Alliance parties are most commonly supported because of their policies and style, because of an active dislike of the policies and style of other parties, or simply because voters would 'like a change'. Taken in conjunction with our findings about the extent to which class identity remains a pronounced feature of British society, these data would seem to suggest that people have moved away from Labour for political and largely instrumental reasons, and not because there is a loosening of class processes. The Conservatives and Alliance are more likely to be supported because their policies are popular, their style and unity are appealing, and because respondents positively dislike the style and policies of other parties, than because voters endorse either the 'fundamental beliefs' of these parties or who they stand for. In that sense Crewe's earlier thesis of *partisan* dealignment is more convincing that his subsequent account of *class* dealignment. The electorate as a whole may have a generally declining attachment to the Conservative and Labour parties. People may well be more likely now than in the past to vote for reasons of perceived self-interest (that is instrumentally) rather than out of inalienable partisanship.[30] However, the crucial point that has been missed by theorists of class dealignment is that perceptions of self-interest can be shaped by class awareness as well as the individualized concerns of the isolated political consumer. Indeed our results suggest that this is in fact still the case.

Whether those members of the service class who are from working-class origins and vote Labour would continue to do so if their relative life-chances were likely to be diminished by socialist policies securing a redistribution of wealth is, as Goldthorpe himself admits, an open question. Speculation on this matter tends to go beyond our data although it is worth noting that the proportion of the service class which votes Labour shows no signs of decreasing even under the impact of diminishing life-chances. Table 9.24 shows voting intentions for those currently in the service class according to the frequency with which they have suffered during the present recession. Neither among those personally affected by a worsening economic climate, nor among those in households so affected, does the proportionate Labour vote diminish. (In fact it increases.) Research elsewhere also suggests that, even among relatively privileged Labour voters, there is a widespread and solid support for a more egalitarian distribution of power, wealth, and opportunities in the country. Indeed Labour supporters generally seem to be more committed to egalitarian principles than do those voting for either of the other major party groupings.[31] Goldthorpe's predictions concerning service-class 'electoral closure' about the Conservative Party may yet come undone.

All of which leads us to conclude that a common failing of those who have announced the demise of class politics is their refusal to take the political process seriously. It is indeed ironic that so many political scientists are among their number. Class dealignment theorists seem to us to share in a remarkably simplistic conception of the relationship between the distributional order of society itself, on the one hand, and the specific forms of

Table 9.24 *Goldthorpe service class voting intention by impact of economic recession*

		Number of effects experienced personally			
		0	*1*	*2*	*3 or more*
Vote	Conservative	55	54	34	41
	Labour	20	21	20	32
	Alliance	18	17	39	27
	Would not vote	7	8	7	0
	Total	100	100	100	100
		(114)	(104)	(71)	(6)

		Number of effects experienced by other members of household			
		0	*1*	*2*	*3 or more*
Vote	Conservative	55	42	34	36
	Labour	18	25	34	14
	Alliance	22	23	23	43
	Would not vote	5	10	9	7
	Total	100	100	100	100
		(177)	(79)	(35)	(14)

Note: Effects of economic recession are taken from answers to Question 5 of the interview schedule.

distributional conflict evident at any particular time on the other. In most versions of the argument there is a tendency to connect changes in electoral behaviour directly to putative shifts in the class structure and to associated alterations in values, consciousness, or culture. Thus it is commonly argued that changes in the nature of social hierarchy (increased social mobility, the extension of home-ownership, or whatever) have generated a new sectionalism and individualism to displace formerly solidaristic struggles. This tendency to trace each and every transitory movement in the electoral landscape to major upheavals in the class structure displays unwarranted contempt for important issues that arise at the level of organizational capacity and political mobilization. Most obviously it neglects the lesson taught by Michels; namely, that organizations count. Between the perception of common interests or consciousness of shared values, and joint pursuit of these in co-ordinated action, lies the necessity of collective organization. But the dynamics of organization itself intervene between the shared experience or consciousness and the collective actions of particular members. Leaders may pursue goals that are personal and differ from those of the membership in general. Bureaucratic procedures can stifle the objectives sought by the rank and file. Conversely, those at the top of the organizational hierarchy may invoke democratic principles to impose the wishes of the majority on a reluctant or dissenting minority. In this way the organizational process intervenes between tendencies immanent in social structures and whatever patterns of social action are consequent upon these.[32]

Or, indeed, and this brings us directly to our own argument, dispositional shortcomings on the part of national class organizations (in this case the Labour Party and trades unions) can disguise a shared identity of class, and frustrate commonly held class objectives. There is nothing in our data to support Crewe's thesis that there has been a 'sea-change of attitudes among the proletariat'. Social class and social class identities are no less salient today than during earlier periods commonly acknowledged as being characterized by 'class voting'. We can find no evidence to sustain the thesis of class dealignment; that is, the interpretation of shifts in class voting as a consequence of long-term loosening or fragmentation of the class structure, rather than more ephemeral political factors. In order to explain the observed decline in absolute class politics it is not necessary to invoke fundamental social changes on the basis of speculative sociological arguments. Contemporary sectional struggles are, instead, testimony to the failure of national class organizations to mobilize members behind centrally organized initiatives on behalf of general rather than particular interests. But, and this is the crucial difference between our argument and those of the various class dealignment theorists, class background and class attitudes remain a powerful influence on electoral behaviour.

There is no reason to suppose, therefore, that present patterns of voting will prove any more permanent than earlier seeming departures from the British class voting orthodoxy. During the long post-war boom, for example, as during the present recession, it was tempting to see the various economic and political tendencies of the day in a tidy relationship of cause and effect. Butler and Rose linked changes in the occupational and social structures of affluence directly to patterns of voting behaviour and concluded of the 1959 General Election that 'The swing to the Conservatives cannot be dismissed as an ephemeral veering of the electoral breeze. Long-term factors were also involved. Traditional working-class attitudes had been eroded by a steady growth of prosperity.'[33] Twenty-five years later Crewe depicts the consequences of recession in almost identical terms, claiming that 'the decline in the absolute class vote recorded since the 1960s cannot . . . be dismissed as the mere reflection of Labour's electoral misfortunes'.[34] Of course the return of the Labour Party to power in 1964 effectively discredited the embourgeoisement arguments of the 1950s and 1960s. But contemporary dealignment theorists are equally convinced that the shifts they have identified are fundamental and enduring. We, on the other hand, see the future to be as open as ever. Certainly the evidence suggests it is premature to conclude we are witnessing the demise of class-based politics. We strongly suspect, therefore, that the great debates within psephology, and on the left itself,[35] about the recent failures of Labour at the polls would sound more convincing if rather more attention was paid to such factors as the unpopularity of much of Labour's electoral programme, and the party's lack of credibility during successive election campaigns, and rather less to the search for novel cleavages in the social structure that make either Thatcherism or the Liberal/SDP Alliance harbingers of entirely novel electoral arrangements.

Notes

1 Crewe (1986: 620).
2 The phrase 'loosening of the class structure' is used by Butler and Kavanagh (1984: 8) in their analysis of the British General Election of 1983. Like most other commentators who have resorted to sociological determinism by way of explaining changes in the distribution of votes, these authors neither state explicitly what they mean by this term, nor offer any evidence to support the claim itself.
3 Lipset and Rokkan (1967).
4 Even at its most forceful, the impact of social class on voting behaviour has been mediated by other factors – in particular the sense of national identity (see Vogler, 1985).
5 For example, see Robertson (1984: 6).
6 See the reference cited at Chapter 1, Note 3 above. The convergence of the political left and right about the decline of class-based politics is particularly striking. Compare, for example, the almost identical accounts in Hobsbawm (1981) and Lipset (1981). For similar arguments about other western democracies see Worre (1980), Haranne (1980), Hildebrand and Dalton (1978), and Abramson et al. (1982).
7 Crewe (1987). Heath (1987), Lengthier formulations of the same arguments can be found in Sarlvik and Crewe (1983) and Heath et al. (1985).
8 Crewe (1986: 623–4).
9 Crewe (1986: 624).
10 Compare Heath (1987: 2–3) and Crewe (1986: 633).
11 Heath (1987: 4).
12 This is a somewhat simplified account of Heath's argument though it by no means distorts its meaning. Briefly, his data show that the strength of the class–party alignment (relative class voting) does vary significantly from one election to another, if the period 1964–70 is considered as a whole. The model which assumes a constant set of class/party odds ratios over successive elections does not give a good fit to these data. However, inspection of the residuals shows that the remaining deviations show a 'trendless fluctuation', rather than steady class dealignment. The biggest residuals occur in 1964 and 1970, whereas those for 1983 show that the election of that year was not exceptional, and that the assumption of constant odds ratios gives a good fit to the 1983 data. Loglinear analysis of the three elections between 1964 and 1970 confirms that a significant difference in relative class voting occurred during this period alone. There are no signs of any continuing dealignment during the five elections between 1970 and 1983. As Heath and his colleagues conclude, 'there is thus no evidence of a long-standing secular trend towards class dealignment. All that has occurred is a change of doubtful meaning between 1964 and 1970.' This change is especially doubtful since subsequent analysis confirms, not only that housing has not become more important than class in explaining voting behaviour over time, but also that the addition of housing tenure to the loglinear analysis removes the necessity to include the class/party/election interaction term in the fitted model. In other words a control for changes in housing tenure shows that the assumption of no change in relative class voting is sound. See Heath et al. (1985: 35, 41–2, 57) and Heath (1987: 12). However one looks at the class voting data from the British General Election Studies, there can be no doubting that they seriously undermine the dealignment thesis. The principal reason for the disjuncture between Crewe's interpretation of this material and that proposed by Heath is that the former mistakenly assumes that relative class voting is measured solely through the calculation of a salariat/working-class odds ratio. Heath, of course, examines the full set of class–party odds ratios using loglinear techniques.
13 Heath (1987: 3).
14 This criticism also applies to the similarly ad hoc indices used by several other proponents of the class dealignment argument. For example, Rose and McAllister's (1986) 'Standardized Index of Determination', like the Alford Index itself, is sensitive to changes in the marginal distributions of class size and party share of the vote over time. In attempting to reduce the

class–vote association to a crude single statistic these measures inevitably confound effects emanating from different sources of change.

15 See Dunleavy (1980: 70–86), Robertson (1984: 85–6, 222), Franklin (1985), and Crewe (1984: 198–9; 1986: 633).

16 Dunleavy does so despite an open admission that the market research A–B–C schema 'cannot be assimilated to an adequate concept of social class' (1979: 436). Another critic (Franklin, 1985) claims to chart the demise of class voting in Britain yet nowhere actually states what he intends by 'social class'. The structure of his key variables (parental class and present class occupation) is wholly unclear, though one can surmise that the multiple regression techniques employed in the study have forced the author to treat classes as manual and nonmanual occupations. If this is indeed the case then it is hardly surprising that 'class' explains relatively little of the variance in voting behaviour. Perhaps, as his frequent references to 'initial class status' and 'class modified by occupation' suggests, Franklin has no clear conception of social class underpinning his analysis.

17 See Marsh (1986).

18 The additional irony in these findings is that Crewe, in common with most class dealignment theorists, treats the decade of the 1970s as particularly significant because the Alford Index, and other similar such measures, suggest that 'until 1970 the overall amount of class voting remained fairly stable' (Crewe, 1984: 193). Class dealignment is particularly obvious, so it is claimed, in the precipitous decline of Labour and upturn in the fortunes of the Alliance from 1970 onwards. (See also Himmelweit et al. 1985: 87ff.; Franklin, 1985: 153ff.; Rose and McAllister, 1986: 53; Robertson, 1984: 28.) In fact, however, longitudinal analysis confirms that, while there has been no significant variation in the class/party alignment since 1970, there was a slight (though statistically significant) difference in relative class voting prior to that date. Our own loglinear analysis of the three elections in 1964, 1966 and 1970, fitting the model [CP] [EP] [CE] produces a G^2 of 28.7 with 16 degrees of freedom (p = <.05). In other words the data show exactly the opposite of what class dealignment theorists claim to have been the case. There was a slight decline in relative class voting before 1970 but this was reversed in the 1970s and 1980s. In the light of our findings elsewhere in this chapter, and the more extensive analysis of the General Election Studies conducted by Heath and his colleagues, it is (as the latter claim) simply not clear what the meaning of the slender decline in class/party alignment during the 1960s actually indicates.

19 Heath (1981: 235–6).

20 Compare, for example, Heath (1981: 236), Rose and McAllister (1986: 109–11), and Robertson (1984: 72–9).

21 See Erikson et al. (1979).

22 Goldthorpe (1978).

23 Goldthorpe et al. (1969: 191).

24 Goldthorpe (1982: 180).

25 Stewart et al. (1980).

26 Heath et al. (1985: 36).

27 Weber (1968: 4–26), Parsons (1968: 43–51, 731–7), Goldthorpe et al. (1968).

28 Robertson (1984: 222). See also Heath (1987: 16–17), whose data on self-assigned class over successive election surveys confirm that there has been a remarkable constancy of subjective class awareness in the working class throughout the years 1964–83, certainly by comparison to the large swings in its political behaviour over the same period. The findings for other classes are similar. The hypothesis of a constant association between objective and subjective class therefore gives a good fit in loglinear terms. The small fluctuations, which are not statistically significant, are again entirely trendless.

29 In the 1983 British General Election Study owner-occupiers were asked if they had previously rented their properties as council tenants. Those who had were no more likely than other council tenants to switch votes away from the Labour Party. Moreover, purchasers of council properties were more likely than other tenants to have been Conservative voters in 1979, which suggests that they differed at the outset in their political preferences. These findings support the argument that 'housing tenure, at least in the short run, probably reflects rather than causes differences in party preference' (see Heath et al., 1985: 49–51).

30 Compare Crewe et al. (1977) and Crewe (1986).

31 See Robertson (1984: 133–58). This conclusion is also broadly consistent with that reached by Heath and his colleagues. Their much more detailed and highly sophisticated study of British general elections over the past quarter of a century leads them to an 'interactionist' interpretation of electoral behaviour. They conclude that,

On the one hand, we do not hold that group membership or social background determines vote but that it provides a *potential*. . . . On the other hand, we also accept that a party's ideological stance will affect the level of support it can command. . . . However we would wish to add . . . the idea that the parties themselves can help to shape and realize these potentials. . . . In principle, we would argue . . . class inequalities provide a potential for class ideology. The conception of social class which reduces it to income differences and lifestyle suggests that Labour must shift its ground towards the affluent centre. Our conception, which emphasises the more enduring differences of interest suggests that Labour might be able to revive whilst remaining a class party. Just as the petty bourgeoisie was receptive to a free market ideology, so the working class might still be receptive to an egalitarian one. The Labour party does not have to take the existing distribution of values and attitudes as given. Nothing in our evidence indicates that the shift to the right on the class values was an inevitable or irreversible phenomenon. But we would suggest that the language of class struggle is unlikely to be successful in securing an ideological move back to the left. Class inequalities persist but the classes have not been polarised in their values at any time in the postwar period. We doubt if they will become so. An appeal to social justice rather than to class struggle has more hope of success (Heath *et al.*, 1985: 174).

32 Michels (1962).
33 Butler and Rose (1960: 15).
34 Crewe (1986: 626).
35 See, for example, Curran (1984), Hall and Jacques (1983).

10 Conclusion

I

This book results from our collaboration in an international project aiming at the comparative study of class structure and class consciousness. Our objective within the international effort was straightforward and rather modest. As authors of the UK survey we were required simply to produce a 'class map' of contemporary Britain in terms of neo-Marxist categories devised by our colleague Erik Wright. We have tried to retain maximum comparability with affiliated projects in other countries and have reproduced the methodology of the original United States survey as accurately as possible in the British context. In due course our detailed results will be compared with those obtained for countries elsewhere, similarities and differences will be explored, and we shall attempt to formulate a clearer picture of the generic characteristics of class structures in the various capitalist societies of late twentieth-century Europe, America, and Australasia.

In the particular case of the British survey, however, we set ourselves two additional objectives as our research proceeded: namely, to assess the relative merits of alternative approaches to class analysis, specifically those unlikely to be explored by our Marxist colleagues abroad; and, so far as this was possible within our limited budget, to investigate the thesis that social class was an increasingly obsolete tool for describing the structure of solidarity and schism in recessionary Britain.

The first of these involved us in a prolonged discussion of the neo-Weberian class scheme devised by John Goldthorpe for the Oxford study of social mobility in England and Wales. In the early chapters of this book we contrasted the findings of the Goldthorpe and Wright schemata across a range of issues in demographic class analysis. As a result of the comparison we are sceptical about the value of Wright's neo-Marxist approach. Its logic is that classes are defined by social relations of production, as these are evident in ownership and non-ownership of productive means, and in relationships of domination (supervision, decision-making, and autonomy) in the workplace. (Of course, in the revised version of his class scheme, Wright translates the latter dimension into effective control over organization and skill assets – though, in terms of research strategy, this has limited implications since it is still relationships of supervision, decision-making, and autonomy that are being measured.) Wright's argument throughout is that such an approach is analytically superior to one which operationalizes class in terms of occupational titles. Yet, as we have seen, there are a number of reasons for suspecting that Wright's framework is less useful than that proposed by John

Goldthorpe, which rests precisely on an occupational conception of social class. For Goldthorpe, classes are defined in terms of market situations and work situations, as indicated by occupational titles and employment statuses alone.

Our reservations about Wright's schema refer both to the construction of the class categories themselves and to the results of the analyses generated by them. We have strong doubts about the validity and reliability of his research procedure. Numerous problems have been documented: difficulties in measuring skill assets, for example, so that people performing radically different tasks nevertheless appear in the same categories of 'expert' or 'uncredentialled employee' because of arbitrary solutions to coding decisions; or conversely, individuals sharing identical occupations and employment situations who (because of differences in their self-reported autonomy and participation in decision-making) are assigned to quite different class locations; all of which, when taken together with Wright's other measurement and coding problems, yield large numbers of proletarians who (even in Wright's own terms) are not really proletarians, managers who are not really managers, and so forth. More than his theoretical and methodological difficulties, however, it is the incoherence of Wright's empirical findings that casts serious doubts on the utility of his approach. These suggest that the class structure of Britain is in an advanced state of 'polarization'; that is, large numbers of routine white-collar employees have been proletarianized, while others have been upwardly mobile into unambiguously managerial positions. Of course it is not surprising that a Marxist should want to demonstrate the validity of such a thesis. But, as we have seen, there is scant evidence to support this claim. Demographic materials, from the study of work situations and social mobility trajectories, show that the picture is altogether more complex. On the one hand, the British class structure is not as open as Wright's class maps suggest, since relative mobility rates show no signs of changing over the years. Nor has the expansion of managerial, professional, and administrative ('service-class') positions been as great as these maps indicate, since many so-called managers and supervisors in fact perform such minimal supervisory and managerial tasks that, even in terms of Wright's own theory, it makes more sense to locate them among the proletariat, with whom they share largely indistinguishable conditions of employment. A fitter working with a couple of 'mates' is hardly a manager. On the other hand, routine white-collar workers are not uniformly proletarianized, since both their working conditions and their socio-political characteristics are rather different from those of the manual working class. The picture here is complicated by the fact that women in routine administrative employment tend as a whole to have different working conditions to similarly located men, and tend also to display socio-political characteristics appropriate to the social class of their husbands, if these women are married. But in neither case do the observed differences between the sexes substantiate a thesis of proletarianization among routine nonmanual employees. Clerical workers, even female ones, are not necessarily working class.

265

In short, the class structure is not polarized in the manner suggested by Wright's class maps, since a more reliable and empirically convincing class analysis reveals 'intermediate' categories which are, both demographically and socio-politically, located between the working and service classes. The boundaries between manual workers, routine administrative, and skilled nonmanual workers cannot be dissolved by either theoretical sophistry or methodological guile, because the boundaries themselves are real. Consequently, in subsequent comparisons between our own findings and those of our colleagues abroad, we shall be focusing analyses as far as possible on Goldthorpe's neo-Weberian rather than Wright's neo-Marxist class categories.

In reaching this conclusion we have, nevertheless, not endorsed John Goldthorpe's strategy for class analysis *in extenso*. Though his conception of class in terms of market situations and work situations seems to us to be generally sound, there are difficulties in applying Goldthorpe class categories to the analysis of women's employment, and these suggest that the scheme should be modified for use where females are classified by reference to their own occupations. Of course, it is about this last issue that we are most obviously at odds with Goldthorpe himself, since his 'conventional' and our own 'individual' approaches each treat married women quite differently. There is no need to reiterate here the rather complex arguments of Chapters 4 and 5, which offer a defence of our strategy of sampling both sexes, and so allocating employed women to social classes in accordance with their own jobs. The differences between Goldthorpe and ourselves are in fact relatively straightforward. He wishes to place sex segregation in the labour market beyond the legitimate concerns of class analysts. We, on the other hand, would extend our interests to embrace the study of factors which might explain the sexually segregated social division of labour, if for no other reason than that the class experiences of men are largely unintelligible without reference to those of women. If in fact John Goldthorpe agrees with this prognosis, then we are separated only by the programmatic issue of defining the terrain for study, and are left wondering simply why he would want to exclude from class analysis information that surely facilitates understanding of the processes in which we are both interested.

The second half of our report addresses the thesis that class conflict has somehow been restructured. In particular we concentrate on the themes of sectionalism, egoism, privatism, and fatalism. These have been well summarized by, among others, Lukes and Hobsbawm. The argument here, it will be remembered, is that technological change, the increased participation of women in paid labour, and 'politicization of the market' via state intervention in economic processes, together with the shift from manufacturing to service industries, have made the distinction between manual and nonmanual labour largely irrelevant. Indeed, with the rise of mass production and consumption, labour or work itself has become less central to the identity and consciousness of workers. More and more the working class is concerned with issues of consumption – of housing and of state benefits for example. According to Lukes, Hobsbawm and others, recent events show Britain to be a society divided against itself in new ways: those with a stake in private property and those without; the self-sufficient on wages versus welfare claimants; the populations of declining regions against those resident in economically buoyant areas; those in relatively secure occupational or company career-ladders against the unemployed and subemployed who are on the economic margins of society. These new sectional interests are reflected, so the argument goes, in the growth of instrumental, pecuniary, egoistic (that is capitalist) values and attitudes, and in a corresponding decline in older forms of solidarity based on community, unionism, or class itself. British workers, having come to terms with the acquisitive society, now seek their private satisfactions at home and in leisure. Disillusioned with their class organization they pursue conflicting sectional demands in the workplace.

Our investigation of these arguments (the issues of socio-political class formation) is less thorough than the study of demographic class formation conducted in the first part of the book because our data are rather less full. The relevant findings are correspondingly more tentative. We have argued that sectionalism, privatism, and instrumentalism among the British working class are not characteristics somehow peculiar to recent years of economic recession. The working class has long been stratified internally yet this has not prevented it from developing class organizations in order to pursue solidaristic as well as sectional objectives. Nor has its longstanding privatism necessarily been associated with status rather than class concerns. The so-called labour aristocracy, for example, supported collective action on behalf of the working class and sectional or individualized status politics in more or less equal measure. Of course there are well-documented difficulties of interpretation here, especially where pecuniary orientations to distributional struggles are concerned, but an historical perspective suggests that section-alism, privatism, and instrumentalism have always been close to the surface of working-class life.

Conversely, data from our own survey confirm that class solidarities retain an importance that undermines recent accounts of the alleged demise of class consciousness and class politics, and associated rise of aggressive con-sumerism. Social class is to the fore among conceptions of collective identity. It is still the case that important differences in shared beliefs and values are structured more obviously by class than by other sources of social cleavage. It is true that the commitment to class organizations seems to be instrumental rather than expressive in tenor. However, this can be explained as an evaluative rather than cognitive phenomenon, the result of a realistic appraisal – based on past experience – of the likely outcome of the economic and social policies pursued by all political parties. This 'informed fatalism' is reflected in an overt cynicism about *party* politics. *Class* politics is far from exhausted. Social class still structures voting intentions in complex though quite definite ways and does so no less today than in the recent past. Labour and Conservative supporters continue to vote, on the whole, for principled reasons of party policy. Many of the disillusioned say that they will vote for the political centre or else not vote at all. But this is not the demise of class politics. It is, rather, class politics with a volatile and perhaps none too permanent protest option. The protest is not against class politics as such – so, as Heath has shown, there has been no secular and persistent decline in relative class voting. Changes in the pattern of voting reflect political factors rather than a long-term loosening of class processes.

Of course class awareness and class-based voting are not what most sociologists intend by the term 'class consciousness'. Among our interviewees, class was a salient source of social identity, but few were inclined to the systematic pursuit of clear class objectives. This would require a degree of logical, technical, and normative consistency in world-views for which we can find no evidence in our data. Our replication of Erik Wright's study of 'class consciousness' must be set in this context, as well as that of our historically grounded observations. We would argue that there has been no secular decline in the tendency for collective identities and collective action to develop on a class basis. But class consciousness is not, and never has been, mass consciousness. Rather, class consciousness becomes evident in the propensity to take collective action in pursuit of class objectives, rather than purely personal or sectional gains. Such actions are shaped by the institutional and organizational frameworks within which they occur. They will be successful only to the extent that free-rider problems are solved. Our evidence suggests that there is a rather widespread support for a greater measure of social justice within capitalist socio-economic arrangements. This is consistent with the predominant view of class inequalities as differences in income and life-style. There is no obvious polarization in the values and attitudes of the different classes. Class ideologies are not that neatly packaged. Rather, the longstanding absence of class consciousness in Britain lies in the failure of class organizations to convert sectional and conventional struggles into solidaristic and legal ones. The decentralized structure of free collective bargaining in this country militates against such a process. The failure of successive Labour governments to pursue a more generalized social justice by controlling union sectionalism makes many sceptical of the party's ability or even its willingness to do so.

But these are speculations which take us far beyond our data and are the subject of detailed study elsewhere. Our own objectives have been much more limited. Examining 'class consciousness' in modern Britain we can find no evidence of the demise of class identities. As Weberians we find this result somewhat gratifying. It confirms the general principle that the frame of reference within which action takes place – the 'definition of the situation' – carries significant implications for social conduct. Certainly, as far as Britain is concerned, perceptions of class identity are at least as important to any plausible explanations of the patterning of votes as are the more objective aspects of social class. The class structure does not determine social outcomes. People are not simply bearers of class relationships. Moreover, in so far as class locations are associated with voting behaviour (as clearly they are), class effects are more obvious if class is derived from a conception of market situation and work situation rather than relationship to the means of production. 'Semi-autonomous employee', 'expert non-manager', and the like are less coherent and meaningful class categories than are John Goldthorpe's more straightforwardly named alternatives, when judged according to the criterion of analytical utility.

II

Our one remaining task in this volume is to attempt, however briefly, to relate these rather disparate findings – about the class schemata of Erik Wright and John Goldthorpe, on the one hand, and the structuring of social consciousness on the other – to more general statements about class processes in advanced western societies. Our rather specialized research monograph has concentrated, for reasons that are by now well documented, on a strictly limited number of issues and perspectives. But there are more things in class analysis than have been thought of by our theoretical mentors – no matter how convincing their respective contributions may seem to be. How then, if at all, can our conclusions about social mobility, class identities, attitudes to distributional justice and the like, be fitted into the broader canvas of debates in class analysis as a whole?

These debates have been very broad-ranging. In recent years, for example, close attention has been given to a large number of perceived and alleged changes in the class structures of western societies. These include the decline of traditional proletarian occupations and communities; the expansion of working-class 'affluence'; the growth of service sector and white-collar employment; the professionalization of certain nonmanual occupations and routinization or deskilling of others; and the increasing participation of women in paid employment. Commonly, however, these processes have been interpreted within one or other of two overarching theoretical frameworks. These make rather different predictions about long-term transformations in the class stratification of advanced western societies.

One perspective is typified by the work of liberal theorists such as Daniel Bell. The image that is presented here is one of societies in which the labour process is decreasingly proletarianized, requiring a higher proportion of workers with technical expertise, in occupations demanding less routinization of tasks and more responsibility. Tendencies intrinsic to production itself – in particular the sectoral shifts in economic activity due to technological change – are seen to accord workers greater control over their conditions of work and more freedom within it. This 'upgrading' of employment leads to a shrinkage of the working class – the proportion of the employed population involved in routine manual activities for which no specialized knowledge is required – and the emergence of a 'new middle class' of salaried and highly qualified nonmanual employees. Necessarily, therefore, the transformation in the structure of employment – the move from manufacturing to services and unskilled to skilled occupations – creates high levels of class mobility. Since the demand for highly trained administrators, managers, and professionals cannot be met by self-recruitment, the structure itself generates substantial net upward mobility, as those from working-class origins move into the new middle-class positions. Additionally, however, the widespread use of more 'meritocratic' criteria in selection procedures enhances the rates of mobility as the new 'post-industrial' society becomes more open and egalitarian. Class structures give way, at least in some liberal accounts, to gradational and fluid socio-economic hierarchies.[1]

The other framework is distinctively Marxist in provenance and most recently has been evident in debates about the work of Harry Braverman. This perceives changes in the labour process as being almost the complete opposite of those outlined by the theorists of post-industrialism. Work is regarded as becoming generally more proletarianized, real technical expertise is thus confined to a smaller proportion of the labour force, routinization of activities is more pervasive and responsibilities less meaningful. Far from the material basis of alienation being undermined it is here argued that deskilling is prevalent and alienation correspondingly intensified. The expansion of middle-class positions is therefore more apparent than real, since many of the new nonmanual jobs are 'degraded' or 'deskilled' to such an extent that they are indistinguishable from those performed by manual workers, for whom those in the 'proletarianized' or 'contradictory' middle layers form a natural class ally. The reality of all wage labour under capitalism is that it is necessarily exploitative and is organized only in the interests of capital. Putative rates of upward mobility out of manual into nonmanual employment therefore serve only to mystify the class struggle and obscure the continuing dynamics of class stratification.[2]

Different conclusions about the nature of 'working-class consciousness' follow from these contrasting accounts. Liberals argue that the openness of modern industrial societies undermines class identities and so lessens the potential for collective action in general and class confict in particular. As consciousness of class steadily declines, so workers become more individualistic, more consumer-oriented, and correspondingly less inclined to pursue any form of class politics. In meritocratic post-industrial societies they strive for pleasure and status in a strictly personal fashion. The transition from 'class' to 'mass' society dissolves all sub-cultural particularisms in favour of the hitherto middle-class norms of individualism, consumerism, and privatism. Marxists, on the other hand, maintain that the newly proletarianized workers of late capitalism will be pushed to collective resistance against the managerial strategy of deskilling tasks and policing the labour process ever more closely. In their view, work (and in particular the process of production) is still central to the creation of class-based images of society, and so to the development of oppositional social consciousness. In due course the inherent tendency of workers towards workplace and communal solidarism will re-emerge from the alienation induced by social relationships that rest exclusively on the cash nexus. Class-based action, in the political and industrial spheres, will eventually challenge the structures of property and power which underpin late capitalism.[3]

270

To some extent the contrast between these frameworks simply reflects the changed economic circumstances of the long post-war boom as compared with those of the recessionary 1970s and 1980s. As the age of affluence has given way to economic stagnation so the liberal perspective has become less fashionable among class theorists. In part, however, the contradictory interpretations arise as a consequence of determined efforts by the two groups of social theorists to shackle the activities of certain social groups (most commonly the working class) to their own socio-political goals. For this reason the two perspectives actually converge in their logic – despite wide-ranging and explicit substantive disagreements. Both have taken the western working classes as the essential means to achieving liberal or (conversely) socialist political and social goals; both are prone to implicit historicism since they share a common tendency to view present events as part of a predetermined long-term historical trend; and, in consequence, both are inclined to wishful rather than critical thinking in the interpretation of empirical materials.

As will already be obvious our own findings about class structure and class consciousness vindicate neither perspective. For those with no particular political axe to grind the picture seems somewhat more complicated than is allowed for by straightforward arguments about embourgeoisement or proletarianization.

It is true that, at first sight, much of the evidence presented in the above chapters seems to substantiate the liberal position. In recent years there has been a marked expansion of the salariat and corresponding decline in the working class. Perhaps as many as one-third of those presently in service-class positions have arrived there from working-class origins. Around 10 per cent of those from working-class backgrounds whose own initial class at entry to employment was itself working class will nevertheless arrive at service-class destinations during the course of their occupational careers. Meanwhile, the working class has itself shrunk by about one-third during the years covered by our mobility data, perhaps somewhat less if one treats routine 'sales and service' employees as proletarians. Upward mobility on this scale is clearly at odds with Marxist theories about the rigidity of class structures in advanced capitalism. Nor can these theories be salvaged by recourse to arguments about the proletarianization of the middle layers of the structure. There is nothing in our data to suggest that routine nonmanual jobs, or those who perform them, are somehow degraded or deskilled. The jobs themselves characteristically allow more autonomy to their incumbents than do manual occupations. Very few of those involved report any deskilling of the associated tasks. In any case, even where the working conditions for routine nonmanual jobs *are* largely indistinguishable from those found in manual employment, it is clear that socio-political proletarianization does not necessarily follow. Most of those recruited to routine sales and service or administrative jobs have been women, and as we have seen, they tend to take the socio-political lead from their male partners – only about one-third of whom are themselves in the working class. Finally, we might note that the

271

individuals performing the various routine 'middle layer' jobs are themselves not subject to a process of proletarianization, since there is no evidence that relative mobility rates for this stratum have changed over the years – even when these are calculated separately for men and women. It would seem, then, that during the post-war periods of economic growth and recession alike, the numbers involved in specialized and routine nonmanual activities have continued to grow at the expense of those involved in traditional (manual) working-class occupations.

However, despite this seemingly extensive corroborating evidence there are serious flaws in the liberal account of advanced western societies, at least where the case of modern Britain is concerned. The notion of relative mobility provides the key to these. Our data show clearly that, calculating the likely transitions from class of origin to class destinations as a series of odds ratios, the chances of someone from a service-class background securing service-class rather than working-class employment for himself or herself are somewhere between seven and thirteen times greater than those for someone arriving at service-class employment rather than working-class employment from working-class origins. Moreover, since there is no evidence that the degree of 'social fluidity' or equality of opportunity has altered over successive mobility cohorts, then it is reasonable to conclude that the expansion of the salariat that is evident in the comparison between the class distribution of parents and children is almost entirely due to structural factors. That is, the 'room at the top' created by the transformation in the occupational division of labour has not been accompanied by greater equality in the chances of getting there, since the most privileged groups have shown themselves to be more rather than less successful at using their relative advantages to prevent downward mobility among their offspring. As a result, the association between an individual's class of origin and his or her eventual destination has proved remarkably stable, despite economic expansion, egalitarian social policies, and educational reform. Moreover, whether one looks at mobility trajectories or conditions of employment, women tend to be generally disadvantaged when compared to men. They are no less divided by class differences, but tend to have inferior market situations and work situations to those of class-comparable men, and to receive proportionately fewer rewards for their educational achievements. Finally, nowhere in liberal theories is it envisaged that the expansion of professional and skilled occupations will be accompanied by large-scale unemployment, yet this is precisely what has happened in recessionary Britain. Our concern with class theories and employment as such has meant that, in this volume at least, we have had relatively little to say about joblessness. We intend to rectify this in subsequent publications. For the moment, it is sufficient merely to note that extensive evidence from research elsewhere points overwhelmingly to the conclusion that unemployment and subemployment are predominantly working-class fates, and that many both inside and outside this class have only a precarious employment in 'secondary' labour markets based on non-standard types of work.[4] We have reserved the study of this phenomenon – of part-time work, subemployment, and 'dualism' or 'segmentation' of labour markets – for a separate volume. Already, however, there is more than sufficient evidence from other economic and sociological studies to cause serious doubts, in our minds at least, about the optimistic scenario for long-term changes in the structure of stratification that is presented in liberal theories of industrialism.

Not surprisingly, therefore, these theories are equally suspect in their predictions about the progressive disappearance of classes and increasing stability of western industrial societies. There is nothing in our data to suggest that collective identities and collective action of a class-based kind are in the process of long-term decline. It is true that individualism, consumerism, and privatism are readily apparent. But there is no evidence to support the claim that these tendencies indicate a decomposition of classes resulting from social mobility or the extension of meritocratic criteria to processes of occupational selection. Our own belief is that the explanation for working-class instrumentalism in Britain is to be found in the strategies and policies of working-class movements rather than putative changes in the structure of inequality itself. Naturally, we cannot directly substantiate this belief here, since a study of organizational dynamics, class strategies, and political processes would take us far beyond the confines of our particular data set. What we can do, however, is rule out the alternative possibility that any obvious changes in 'class consciousness' can be attributed to a long-term 'loosening of the class structure'.[5]

The debate about the so-called decline of class politics provides a good illustration of this. Class dealignment – a weakening in the association between class and vote – has popularly been advanced as an explanation for the recently poor performances of Labour at the polls and corresponding rise of the Liberal/Social Democratic Alliance. The Labour Party was said to be in decline precisely because it was a class party: it did not appeal to the growing numbers of white-collar workers and failed to detect a 'sea-change' in the attitudes of manual employees away from traditional class loyalties and concerns. In fact, however, longitudinal data support the countervailing claim advanced by Heath and his colleagues that relative class voting has remained more or less constant throughout the period of so-called dealignment. The fact that such variations as can be found to exist in the association between vote and class take the form of 'trendless fluctuations' suggests that Labour's electoral failures have a political rather than a sociological source. It has performed badly as a party across its entire electoral base, and not simply among the working class, because (among other things) many of its policies (such as those on defence) have been unpopular, it lacks coherence as a movement, and it has failed to convince voters as a whole that a Labour government could offer credible alternatives to Thatcherite 'realism' in the economic sphere. True, the decline in the relative size of the working-class electorate has damaged the Labour vote, since the largest proportion of its support comes from this quarter. But neither of these factors suggest that there has been a decline in the political cohesiveness or class identity of the working class. Class interests are seemingly still central to the political process. There has been no transition to a post-industrial society in which the structure of class inequalities, together with class-based political action, have given way to the purely status politics of the open society. There is, seemingly, no 'logic of industrialism' to which our data lend credibility.

On the other hand there is nothing in our findings to support the claims of Marxist authors that the working class share in an intrinsic commitment to communal rather than individual concerns. Historical evidence suggests that class and status politics have always coexisted. Only a determinedly historicist reading of instrumentalism among the working class can impute an 'objective' collectivism – socialist 'resistance' – to the beliefs and values of our respondents. Wright's assertion that the overall trajectory of historical development is 'progressive' is no more plausible than Kerr's supposition that there is a 'logic of industrialism'.[6]

Thus, to take up the specific concerns of class analysts, routine nonmanual employees cannot be regarded as a new proletariat in the making. The systematic degradation of labour is Marxist myth. Rather, as our evidence confirms, the proletarianization of intermediate layers in the class structure is historically contingent. Routine clerical and sales and service workers are not an undifferentiated mass soon to be shackled to the historical destiny of the proletariat. On the other hand, they can no more plausibly be described as part of a 'new middle class', willing to endorse unambiguously the reward structure embraced by existing socio-political arrangements. In fact these workers have widely varying worklife trajectories. If class differences and interests are therefore to be mobilized for political purposes, as Marxists claim, then this will result from political will rather than a spontaneous process of class polarization. In the British case, the Labour Party must find some means of transcending its class constituency, without losing the support of manual workers. Our data suggest that a broad-based appeal to social justice would attract support, not only among those routine nonmanual employees whose market and work situation is similar to that of manual workers, but also among many in more privileged class positions. Previous Labour governments have in fact succeeded in achieving Wright's political objective. That is, they have created class alliances around social democratic issues having popular suppoort across manual and nonmanual groupings alike, particularly those issues associated with the extension of the various rights of citizenship – education, social welfare, and the like. Our own belief is that the party's best hope for the future lies in precisely the same direction – but this is to let our personal political beliefs spill over into our sociological analysis. We can claim, from sociological reasoning alone, that whatever happens will not be the result of some underlying logic or dialectic in the development of industrial-capitalist societies. Our analysis of demographic and socio-political class formation offers no support to historicists either on the left or the right.

Notes

1 See, for example, Bell (1976), Blau and Duncan (1967), and Kerr *et al.* (1960). Naturally, there is considerable variation in these (and the many other) liberal accounts of industrial society, but it is not necessary to explore this here.

2 As with liberal theories of industrial or post-industrial society there is considerable variation in Marxist accounts of late capitalism. Recent statements include Braverman (1974), Carchedi (1977), and Mandel (1978).

3 Compare, for example, Zweig (1961) and Willis (1979).

4 See, for example, Goldthorpe and Payne (1986a), Showler and Sinfield (1981), and the papers on labour markets in Roberts *et al.* (1985).

5 For a more detailed account which reaches the same conclusions see the forthcoming revised edition of Goldthorpe's *Social Mobility and Class Structure in Modern Britain* (especially Chapter 12).

6 Compare Wright (1985: 114–18) and Kerr (1983: 18–19, 89).

Bibliography

Abercrombie, Nicholas *et al.* (1980), *The Dominant Ideology Thesis*, London: George Allen and Unwin.

Abercrombie, Nicholas and Urry, John (1983), *Capital, Labour, and the Middle Classes*, London: Allen and Unwin.

Abramson, P. R. *et al.* (1982), *Change and Continuity in the 1980 Elections*, Washington: CQ Press.

Ahrne, Goran and Wright, Erik Olin (1983), 'Classes in the United States and Sweden: a comparison', *Acta Sociologica*, **26**, p. 211–35.

Alexander, Sally (1976), 'Women's work in nineteenth-century London: a study of the years 1820–1850', in Juliet Mitchell and Ann Oakley (eds), *The Rights and Wrongs of Women*, Harmondsworth: Penguin, pp. 59–111.

Alt, James E. (1979), *The Politics of Economic Decline*, Cambridge: Cambridge University Press.

Althusser, Louis (1977), 'Marxism and humanism', in his *For Marx*, London: New Left Books, pp. 219–47.

Amin, S. (1973), *Unequal Development*, London: Monthly Review Press.

Barbalet, Jack M. (1980), 'Principles of stratification in Max Weber: an interpretation and critique', *British Journal of Sociology*, **31**, pp. 401–18.

Bauman, Zygmunt (1982), *Memories of Class*, London: Routledge and Kegan Paul.

Bell, Daniel (1976), *The Coming of Post-Industrial Society*, Harmondsworth: Penguin.

Bell, Daniel (1979), *The Cultural Contradictions of Capitalism*, London: Heinemann.

Beynon, Huw (1980), *Working for Ford*, Wakefield: EP Publishing.

Binns, David (1977), *Beyond the Sociology of Conflict*, London: Macmillan.

Blackburn, R. M. and Mann, Michael (1979), *The Working Class in the Labour Market*, London: Macmillan.

Blau, P. M. and Duncan, O. D. (1967), *The American Occupational Structure*, New York: Wiley.

Blom, Raimo (1985), 'The relevance of class theory', *Acta Sociologica*, **28**, pp. 171–92.

Braverman, Harry (1974), *Labour and Monopoly Capital*, London: Monthly Review Press.

Brewer, Richard I. (1986), 'A note on the changing status of the Registrar-General's classification of occupations', *British Journal of Sociology*, **37**, pp. 131–40.

Brittan, S. (1978), *The Economic Consequences of Democracy*, London: Temple Smith.

Britten, Nicky and Heath, Anthony (1983), 'Women, men and social class', in Eva Gamarnikow *et al.* (eds), *Gender, Class and Work*, London: Heinemann, pp. 46–60.

Brown, Richard *et al.* (1983), 'Changing attitudes to employment?', *Department of Employment Research Paper No. 40*, London: HMSO.

Brown, W. (1981), *The Changing Contours of British Industrial Relations*, Oxford: Basil Blackwell.

Bulmer, Martin (ed.), *Working-Class Images of Society*, London: Routledge and Kegan Paul.

Butler, David, and Kavanagh, Dennis (1984), *The British General Election of 1983*, London: Macmillan.

Butler, David, and Rose, Richard (1960), *The British General Election of 1959*, London: Macmillan.

Calhoun, Craig (1982), *The Question of Class Struggle*, Oxford: Basil Blackwell.

Calvert, Peter (1982), *The Concept of Class*, London: Hutchinson.

Carchedi, G. (1977), *On the Economic Identification of Classes*, London: Routledge and Kegan Paul.

Carter, Robert (1985), *Capitalism, Class Conflict and the New Middle Class*, London: Routledge and Kegan Paul.

Cashmore, E. Ellis (1984), *No Future*, London: Heinemann.

Clarke, Simon (1982), *Marx, Marginalism and Modern Sociology*, London: Macmillan.

Cohen, G. A. (1978), *Karl Marx's Theory of History: A Defence*, Oxford: Clarendon Press.

Crewe, Ivor (1984), 'The electorate: partisan dealignment ten years on', in H. Berrington (ed.), *Change in British Politics*, London: Frank Cass, pp. 183–215.

Crewe, Ivor (1986), 'On the death and resurrection of class voting: some comments on *How Britain Votes*', *Political Studies*, **34**, pp. 620–38.

Crewe, Ivor *et al.* (1977), 'Partisan dealignment in Britain, 1964–1974', *British Journal of Political Science*, **7**, pp. 129–90.

Crompton, Rosemary (1979), 'Trade unionism and the insurance clerk', *Sociology*, **13**, pp. 403–26.

Crompton, Rosemary, and Gubbay, Jon (1977), *Economy and Class Structure*, London: Macmillan.

Crompton, Rosemary, and Jones, Gareth (1984), *White-Collar Proletariat*, London: Macmillan.

Crompton, Rosemary, and Sanderson, Kay (1986), 'Credentials and careers: some implications of the increase in professional qualifications amongst women', *Sociology*, **20**, pp. 25–42.

Crossick, Geoffrey (1978), *An Artisan Elite in Victorian Society*, London: Croom Helm.

Crouch, Colin (1982), *Trade Unions: The Logic of Collective Action*, London: Fontana.

Curran, James (ed.) (1984), *The Future of the Left*, Cambridge: Polity Press.

Cutler, Anthony *et al.* (1977), *Marx's 'Capital' and Capitalism Today*, London: Routledge and Kegan Paul.

Dale, Angela (1986), 'Social class and the self-employed', *Sociology*, **20**, pp. 430–34.

Dale, Angela *et al.* (1985), 'Integrating women into class theory', *Sociology*, **19**, pp. 384–408.

Daniel, W. W. (1975), 'The PEP Survey on Inflation', *Political and Economic Planning*, **41** (no. 553).

Daniel, W. W. and Millward, Neil (1983), *Workplace Industrial Relations in Britain*, London: Heinemann.

Daunton, M. J. (1983), *House and Home in the Victorian City*, London: Edward Arnold.

Davidoff, Leonore (1979), 'The separation of home and work? Landlords and lodgers in nineteenth- and twentieth-century England', in Sandra Burman (ed.), *Fit Work for Women*, London: Croom Helm, pp. 64–97.

DeAngelis, Richard A. (1982), *Blue-Collar Workers and Politics*, London: Croom Helm.

Dex, Shirley (1985), *The Sexual Division of Work*, Brighton: Wheatsheaf.

Duke, Vic, and Edgell, Stephen (1984), 'Public expenditure cuts in Britain and consumption sectoral cleavages', *International Journal of Urban and Regional Research*, **8**, pp. 177–201.

Dunleavy, Patrick (1979), 'The urban bases of political alignment: social class, domestic property ownership, and state intervention in consumption processes', *British Journal of Political Science*, **9**, pp. 403–43.

Dunleavy, Patrick (1980a), 'The political implications of sectoral cleavages and the growth of state employment', *Political Studies*, **28**, pp. 364–83, 527–49.

Dunleavy, Patrick (1980b), *Urban Political Analysis*, London: Macmillan.

Dunleavy, Patrick, and Husbands, Christopher T. (1985), *British Democracy at the Crossroads*, London: George Allen and Unwin.

Edwards, Richard (1979), *Contested Terrain*, London: Heinemann.

Elger, Tony (1982), 'Braverman, capital accumulation and deskilling', in S. Wood (ed.), *The Degradation of Work?*, London: Hutchinson, pp. 23–53.

Elster, Jon (1982), 'Marxism, functionalism, and game theory', *Theory and Society*, **11**, pp. 453–82.

Erikson, Robert (1984), 'Social class of men, women and families', *Sociology*, **18**, pp. 500–14.

Erikson, Robert *et al.* (1979), 'Intergenerational class mobility in three western European societies', *British Journal of Sociology*, **30**, pp. 415–41.

Erikson, Robert *et al.* (1982), 'Social fluidity in industrial nations', *British Journal of Sociology*, **33**, pp. 1–34.

Finer, S. E. (1980), *The Changing British Party System, 1945–1979*, Washington: American Enterprise Institute for Public Policy Research.

Foster, John (1974), *Class Struggle and the Industrial Revolution*, London: Methuen.

Fothergill, Stephen, and Gudgin, Graham (1982), *Unequal Growth*, London: Heinemann.

Franklin, Mark N. (1985), *The Decline of Class Voting in Britain*, Oxford: Clarendon Press.

Friedman, Andrew L. (1977), *Industry and Labour*, London: Macmillan.

Furbank, P. N. (1985). *Unholy Pleasure: The Idea of Social Class*, Oxford: Oxford University Press.

Gallie, Duncan (1983), *Social Inequality and Class Radicalism in France and Britain*, Cambridge: Cambridge University Press.

Garnsey, Elizabeth (1978), 'Women's work and theories of class stratification', *Sociology*, **12**, pp. 223–43.

Garnsey, Elizabeth (1981), 'The rediscovery of the division of labour', *Theory and Society*, **10**, pp. 337–58.

Giddens, Anthony (1973), *The Class Structure of the Advanced Societies*, London: Hutchinson.

Goldthorpe, John H. (1978), 'The current inflation: towards a sociological account', in J. H. Goldthorpe and Fred Hirsch (eds), *The Political Economy of Inflation*, London: Martin Robertson, pp. 186–216.

Goldthorpe, John H. (1980), *Social Mobility and Class Structure in Modern Britain*, Oxford: Clarendon Press.

Goldthorpe, John H. (1982), 'On the service class, its formation and future', in Anthony Giddens and Gavin Mackenzie (eds), *Social Class and the Division of Labour*, Cambridge: Cambridge University Press, pp. 162–85.

Goldthorpe, John H. (1983a), 'Women and class analysis: in defence of the conventional view', *Sociology*, **17**, pp. 465–88.

Goldthorpe, John H. (1983b), 'Social mobility and class formation: on the renewal of a tradition in sociological theory', *Working Papers of the CASMIN Project*, no. 1, Mannheim.

Goldthorpe, John H. (1984a), 'Women and class analysis: reply to the replies', *Sociology*, **18**, pp. 491–9.

Goldthorpe, John H. (1984b), 'The end of convergence: corporatist and dualist tendencies in modern western societies', in John H. Goldthorpe (ed.), *Order and Conflict in Contemporary Capitalism*, Oxford: Clarendon Press, pp. 315–43.

Goldthorpe, John H. (1988), 'Intellectuals and the working class in modern Britain', in David Rose (ed.), *Social Stratification and Economic Change*, London: Hutchinson.

Goldthorpe, John H. *et al.* (1968), *The Affluent Worker: Industrial Attitudes and Behaviour*, Cambridge: Cambridge University Press.

Goldthorpe, John H. *et al.* (1969), *The Affluent Worker in the Class Structure*, Cambridge: Cambridge University Press.

Goldthorpe, John H., and Hope, Keith (1974), *The Social Grading of Occupations*, Oxford: Clarendon Press.

Goldthorpe, John H., and Payne, Clive (1986a), 'Trends in intergenerational mobility in England and Wales, 1979–1983', *Sociology*, **20**, pp. 1–24.

Goldthorpe, John H., and Payne, Clive (1986b), 'On the class mobility of women: results from different approaches to the analysis of recent British data', *Sociology*, **20**, pp. 531–55.

Gorz, Andre (1982), *Farewell to the Working Class*, London: Pluto Press.

Gray, Robert Q. (1974), 'The labour aristocracy in the Victorian class structure', in Frank Parkin (ed.), *The Social Analysis of Class Structure*, London:Tavistock, pp. 19–38.

Gray, Robert Q. (1976), *The Labour Aristocracy in Victorian Edinburgh*, Oxford: Clarendon Press.

Gray, Robert Q. (1981), *The Aristocracy of Labour in Nineteenth-Century Britain*, London: Macmillan.

Habermas, Jurgen (1975), *Legitimation Crisis*, Boston: Beacon Press.

Habermas, Jurgen (1979), *Communication and the Evolution of Society*, London: Heinemann.

Hall, Stuart, and Jacques, Martin (eds) (1983), *The Politics of Thatcherism*, London: Lawrence and Wishart.

Haranne, M. (1980), 'Dialectics between occupational and party structures: Finland since World War II', *Acta Sociologica*, **23**, pp. 83–96.

Harrison, R. (1965), *Before the Socialists*, London: Routledge and Kegan Paul.

Hartmann, Heidi (1979), 'The unhappy marriage of Marxism and Feminism: towards a more progressive union', *Capital and Class*, **8**, pp. 1–33.

Hayek, F. (1976), *The Mirage of Social Justice*, London: Routledge and Kegan Paul.

Heath, Anthony (1981), *Social Mobility*, London: Fontana.

Heath, Anthony (1986), 'Do people have consistent attitudes?', in Roger Jowell et al. (eds), *British Social Attitudes: the 1986 Report*, Aldershot: Gower, pp. 1–15.

Heath, Anthony (1987), 'Trendless fluctuation: relative class voting 1964–83', *Political Studies*, forthcoming.

Heath, Anthony et al. (1985), *How Britain Votes*, Oxford: Pergamon.

Heath, Anthony, and Britten, Nicky (1984), 'Women's jobs do make a difference: a reply to Goldthorpe', *Sociology*, **18**, pp. 475–90.

Hemingway, John (1978), *Conflict and Democracy*, Oxford: Clarendon Press.

Hildebrand, K., and Dalton, R. I. (1978), 'The new politics: political change or sunshine politics?', in M. Kaase and K. von Beyme (eds), *Elections and Parties: Socio-political Change and Participation in the West German Federal Election of 1976*, London: Sage.

Hill, Stephen (1976), *The Dockers*, London: Heinemann.

Himmelweit, Hilde T. et al. (1985), *How Voters Decide*, Milton Keynes: Open University Press.

Hindess, Barry (1973), *The Use of Official Statistics in Sociology*, London: Macmillan.

Hirsch, Fred (1977), *Social Limits to Growth*, London: Routledge and Kegan Paul.

Hobsbawm, Eric (1964), *Labouring Men*, London: Weidenfeld and Nicolson.
Hobsbawm, Eric (1981), 'The forward march of Labour halted?' and 'Observations on the debate', in M. Jacques and F. Mulhern (eds), *The Forward March of Labour Halted?*, London: New Left Books, pp. 1–19, 167–82.
Holmwood, J. M., and Stewart, A. (1983), 'The role of contradictions in modern theories of stratification', *Sociology*, **17**, pp. 234–54.
Hunt, Alan (ed.) (1977), *Class and Class Structure*, London: Lawrence and Wishart.
Ingham, Geoffrey (1984), *Capitalism Divided?: The City and Industry in British Social Development*, London: Macmillan.
Jarvie, I. C. (1972), *Concepts and Society*, London: Routledge and Kegan Paul.
Jones, Gareth Stedman (1983), *Languages of Class: Studies in English Working-Class History 1832–1982*, Cambridge: Cambridge University Press.
Joyce, Patrick (1980), *Work, Society and Politics*, London: Macmillan.
Kerr, Clark (1983), *The Future of Industrial Societies*, Cambridge, Mass.: Harvard University Press.
Kerr, Clark *et al.* (1960), *Industrialism and Industrial Man*, Cambridge, Mass.: Harvard University Press.
Kirk, N. (1985), *The Growth of Working-Class Reformism in Mid-Victorian England*, London: Croom Helm.
Korpi, Walter (1983), *The Democratic Class Struggle*, London: Routledge and Kegan Paul.
Kreckel, Reinhard (1980), 'Unequal Opportunity Structure and Labour Market Segmentation', *Sociology*, **14**, pp. 525–50.
Kuhn, Annette, and Wolpe, AnnMarie (eds) (1978), *Feminism and Materialism*, London: Routledge and Kegan Paul.
Lash, Scott (1984), *The Militant Worker*, London: Heinemann.
Lazonick, William (1979), 'Industrial relations and technical change: the case of the self-acting mule', *Cambridge Journal of Economics*, **3**, pp. 231–62.
Lee, D. J. (1981), 'Skill, craft and class: a theoretical critique and a critical case', *Sociology*, **15**, pp. 56–75.
Leete, R., and Fox, J. (1977), 'Registrar-General's social classes: origins and uses', *Population Trends*, **8**, pp. 1–7.
Lipset, Seymour Martin (1981), 'Whatever happened to the proletariat?', *Encounter*, **56**, pp. 18–34.
Lipset, Seymour Martin, and Rokkan, Stein (1967), 'Cleavage structures, party systems and voter alignments', in their *Party Systems and Voter Alignments*, London: Collier-Macmillan, pp. 1–65.
Littler, C. R., and Salaman, G. (1982), 'Bravermania and beyond: recent theories of the labour process', *Sociology*, **16**, pp. 251–69.
Lockwood, David (1958), *The Blackcoated Worker*, London: George Allen and Unwin.
Lockwood, David (1964), 'Social integration and system integration', in

G. K. Zollschan and W. Hirsch (eds), *Explorations in Social Change*, London: Routledge and Kegan Paul, pp. 244–57.

Lockwood, David (1975), 'Sources of variation in working-class images of society', in Martin Bulmer (ed.), *Working-Class Images of Society*, London: Routledge and Kegan Paul, pp. 16–31.

Lockwood, David (1981), 'The weakest link in the chain? Some comments on the Marxist theory of action', *Research in the Sociology of Work*, **1**, pp. 435–81 reprinted in David Rose (ed.) (1988), *Social Stratification and Economic Change*, London: Hutchinson.

Lukes, Steven (1984), 'The future of British Socialism?', in Ben Pimlott (ed.), *Fabian Essays in Socialist Thought*, London: Heinemann, pp. 269–83.

Mandel, Ernest (1978), *Late Capitalism*, London: Verso.

Mann, Michael (1970), 'The social cohesion of Liberal Democracy', *American Sociological Review*, **35**, pp. 423–31.

Mann, Michael (1973), *Consciousness and Action Among the Western Working Class*, London: Macmillan.

Marcuse, Herbert (1972), *One Dimensional Man*, London: Sphere.

Marglin, Stephen A. (1974), 'What do bosses do? The origins and functions of hierarchy in capitalist production', *Review of Radical Political Economy*, **6**, pp. 60–112.

Marsh, Catherine (1986), 'Social class and occupation', in Robert G. Burgess (ed.), *Key Variables in Social Investigation*, London: Routledge and Kegan Paul, pp. 123–52.

Marshall, Gordon (1982), *In Search of the Spirit of Capitalism*, London: Hutchinson.

Marshall, Gordon (1983), 'Some remarks on the study of working-class consciousness', *Politics and Society*, **12**, pp. 263–301 reprinted in David Rose (ed.) (1988), *Social Stratification and Economic Change*, London: Hutchinson.

Marshall, Gordon (1984), 'On the sociology of women's unemployment, its neglect and significance', *Sociological Review*, **32**, pp. 234–59.

Marshall, Gordon et al. (1985), 'Class, citizenship, and distributional conflict in modern Britain', *British Journal of Sociology*, **36**, pp. 259–84.

Marshall, Gordon et al. (1988), 'Political quiescence among the unemployed in modern Britain', in David Rose (ed.), *Social Stratification and Economic Change*, London: Hutchinson.

Marshall, T. H. (1973), 'Citizenship and social class', in his *Class, Citizenship and Social Development*, Westport, Conn.: Greenwood Press, pp. 65–122.

Marx, Karl (1970a), 'Die moralisierende Kritik und die kritisierende Moral', in T. B. Bottomore and Maximilien Rubel (eds.), *Karl Marx: Selected Writings in Sociology and Social Philosophy*, Harmondsworth: Penguin, pp. 208–9.

Marx, Karl (1970b), *Capital I*, London: Lawrence and Wishart.

Marx, Karl (1970c), 'Preface to *A Contribution to the Critique of Political Economy*', in Karl Marx and Frederick Engels, *Selected Works*, London: Lawrence and Wishart, pp. 180–4.

Marx, Karl (1970d), 'The Eighteenth Brumaire of Louis Bonaparte', in *Selected Works*, pp. 96–179.

Marx, Karl (1970e), 'Theses on Feuerbach', in *Selected Works*, pp. 28–30.

Marx, Karl (1972), *Capital III*, London: Lawrence and Wishart.

Marx, Karl (1973), *Economic and Philosophical Manuscripts of 1844*, London: Lawrence and Wishart.

Marx, Karl, and Engels, Frederick (1970a), *The German Ideology*, London: Lawrence and Wishart.

Marx, Karl, and Engels, Frederick (1970b), 'Manifesto of the Communist Party', in *Selected Works*, pp. 31–63.

Massey, Doreen (1984), *Spacial Divisions of Labour*, London: Macmillan.

McLennan, Gregor (1981), ' "The Labour Aristocracy" and "Incorporation": notes on some terms in the social history of the working class', *Social History*, **6**, pp. 71–81.

McRae, Susan (1986), *Cross-Class Families*, Oxford: Clarendon Press.

Michels, Robert (1962), *Political Parties*, New York: Free Press.

Miles, Robert (1982), *Racism and Migrant Labour*, London: Routledge and Kegan Paul.

Moorhouse, H. F. (1978), 'The Marxist theory of the labour aristocracy', *Social History*, **4**, pp. 481–90.

Moorhouse, H. F. (1979), 'History, sociology, and the quiescence of the British working class', *Social History*, **4**, pp. 481–90.

Moorhouse, H. F. (1981), 'The significance of the labour aristocracy', *Social History*, **6**, pp. 229–33.

Moorhouse, H. F. (1983), 'American automobiles and workers' dreams', *Sociological Review*, **31**, pp. 403–26.

Morawska, Ewa (1985), 'East European labourers in an American mill town, 1890–1940: the deferential-proletarian-privatized workers?', *Sociology*, **19**, pp. 364–83.

Murphy, R. (1986), 'The concept of class in closure theory: learning from rather than falling into the problems encountered by neo-Marxism', *Sociology*, **20**, pp. 247–64.

Nef, J. U. (1934), 'The progress of technology and the growth of large scale industry in Great Britain, 1540–1640', *Economic History Review*, first series, **5**, pp. 3–24.

Newby, Howard (1977), *The Deferential Worker*, Harmondsworth: Penguin.

Newby, Howard et al. (1984), 'From class structure to class action: British working-class politics in the 1980s', in Bryan Roberts et al. (eds), *New Approaches to Economic Life*, Manchester: Manchester University Press, pp. 86–102.

Newby, Howard et al. (eds) (1985), *Restructuring Capital*, London: Macmillan.

Offe, Claus (1976), *Industry and Inequality*, London: Edward Arnold.

Offe, Claus (1984), *Contradictions of the Welfare State*, London: Hutchinson.

Offe, Claus (1985), 'Work: the key sociological category?', in his *Disorganized Capitalism*, Cambridge: Polity Press, pp. 129–50.

OPCS [Office of Population Censuses and Surveys] (1970), *Classification of Occupations 1970*, London: HMSO.

OPCS (1980), *Classification of Occupations 1980*, London: HMSO.

OPCS (1985), *1981 Census Post-Enumeration Survey*, London: HMSO.

Ossowski, Stanislaw (1963), *Class Structure in the Social Consciousness*, London: Routledge and Kegan Paul.

Page, Charles H. (1969), *Class and American Sociology*, New York: Schocken.

Pahl, R. E. (1984), *Divisions of Labour*, Oxford: Basil Blackwell.

Pahl, R. E., and Wallace, Claire (1988), 'Neither angels in marble nor rebels in red: privatization and working-class consciousness', in David Rose (ed.), *Social Stratification and Economic Change*, London: Hutchinson.

Panitch, Leo (1986), *Working-Class Politics in Crisis*, London: Verso.

Parkin, Frank (1972), *Class Inequality and Political Order*, London: Paladin.

Parkin, Frank (1979), *Marxism and Class Theory*, London: Tavistock.

Parsons, Talcott (1968), *The Structure of Social Action*, New York: Free Press.

Pelling, Henry (1972), *A History of British Trade Unionism*, London: Macmillan.

Penn, Roger (1981), 'The Nuffield class categorization', *Sociology*, **15**, pp. 265–71.

Penn, Roger (1983), 'Theories of skill and class structure', *Sociological Review*, **31**, pp. 22–88.

Penn, Roger (1986), 'Where have all the craftsmen gone?', *British Journal of Sociology*, **37**, pp. 569–80.

Platt, Jennifer (1971), 'Variations in answers to different questions on perceptions of class', *Sociological Review*, **19**, 409–19.

Polanyi, Karl (1957), *The Great Transformation*, Boston: Beacon Press.

Polanyi, Karl (1977), *The Livelihood of Man*, New York: Academic Press.

Pollert, Anna (1981), *Girls, Wives, Factory Lives*, London: Macmillan.

Poulantzas, Nicos (1978), *Classes in Contemporary Capitalism*, London: Verso.

Pratten, C. F. (1976), *Labour Productivity Differentials Within International Companies*, Cambridge: Cambridge University Press.

Purcell, Kate (1982), 'Female manual workers, fatalism and the reinforcement of inequalities', in David Robbins *et al.* (eds), *Rethinking Social Inequality*, Aldershot: Gower, pp. 43–64.

Rattansi, Ali (1982), 'Marx and the abolition of the division of labour', in Giddens and Mackenzie, *Social Class and the Division of Labour*, pp. 12–28.

Reid, A. (1978), 'Politics and economics in the formation of the British working class', *Social History*, **3**, pp. 347–61.

Roberts, Bryan *et al.* (eds) (1984), *New Approaches to Economic Life*, Manchester: Manchester University Press.

Roberts, K. *et al.* (1977), *The Fragmentary Class Structure*, London: Heinemann.

Robertson, David (1984), *Class and the British Electorate*, Oxford: Basil Blackwell.

Robinson, W. S. (1950), 'Ecological correlations and the behaviour of individuals', *American Sociological Review*, **15**, p. 351-7.

Rose, David (ed.) (1988), *Social Stratification and Economic Change*, London: Hutchinson.

Rose, David *et al.* (1984), 'Economic restructuring: the British experience', *Annals of the American Academy of Political and Social Science*, **475**, pp. 137-57.

Rose, David *et al.* (1987), 'Goodbye to supervisors?', *Work, Employment, and Society*, **1**, pp. 7-24.

Rose, Richard, and McAllister, Ian (1986), *Voters Begin to Choose*, London: Sage.

Routh, Guy (1980), *Occupation and Pay in Great Britain, 1906-1979*, London: Macmillan.

Rubery, Jill (1978), 'Structured labour markets, worker organisation, and low pay', *Cambridge Journal of Economics*, **2**, pp. 17-36.

Runciman, W. G. (1966), *Relative Deprivation and Social Justice*, London: Routledge and Kegan Paul.

Runciman, W. G. (1983), 'Capitalism without classes', *British Journal of Sociology*, **34**, pp. 157-81.

Salaman, Graeme (1986), *Working*, London: Ellis Horwood/Tavistock.

Sarlvik, Bo, and Crewe, Ivor (1983), *Decade of Dealignment*, Cambridge: Cambridge University Press.

Saunders, Peter (1978), 'Domestic property and social class', *International Journal of Urban and Regional Research*, **2**, pp. 233-51.

Saunders, Peter (1981), 'Beyond housing classes: the sociological significance of private property rights in means of consumption', *International Journal of Urban and Regional Research*, **8**, pp. 202-27.

Scase, Richard (1977), *Social Democracy in a Capitalist Society*, London: Croom Helm.

Scott, Alison (1986), 'Industrialization, gender segregation and stratification theory', in Rosemary Crompton and Michael Mann (eds), *Gender and Stratification*, Cambridge: Polity Press, pp. 154-89.

Scott, John (1979), *Corporations, Classes and Capitalism*, London: Hutchinson.

Scott, John (1982), *The Upper Classes*, London: Macmillan.

Showler, Brian, and Sinfield, Adrian (eds) (1981), *The Workless State*, Oxford: Martin Robertson.

Sinfield, Adrian (1981), *What Unemployment Means*, Oxford: Martin Robertson.

Singelmann, J., and Browning H. L. (1980), 'Industrial transformation and occupational change in the US, 1960-1970', *Social Forces*, **59**, pp. 246-74.

Singelmann, J., and Tienda, M. (1985), 'The process of occupational change in a service society: the case of the United States', in Bryan Roberts *et al.*, *New Approaches to Economic Life*, pp. 48-67.

Sparrow, P. (1983), 'An analysis of British work values', *Work and Society*, Discussion Paper Series, Report no. 8, London: Work and Society.

Stanworth, Michelle (1984), 'Women and class analysis: a reply to Goldthorpe', *Sociology*, **18**, p. 159–70.

Stewart, A. *et al.* (1980), *Social Stratification and Occupations*, London: Macmillan.

Stone, K. (1974), 'The origins of job structures in the steel industry', *Review of Radical Political Economy*, **6**, pp. 113–73.

Szreter, Simon R. S. (1984), 'The genesis of the Registrar-General's social classification of occupations', *British Journal of Sociology*, **35**, pp. 522–46.

Taylor-Gooby, P. (1982), 'Two cheers for the welfare state: public opinion and private welfare', *Journal of Public Policy*, **2**, pp. 319–46.

Taylor-Goodby, P. (1983), 'Legitimation deficit, public opinion and the welfare state', *Sociology*, **17**, pp. 165–84.

Thatcher, A. R. (1979), 'Labour supply and employment trends', in F. Blackaby (ed.), *Deindustrialisation*, London: Heinemann, pp. 26–48.

Tholfsen, Trygve R. (1976), *Working-Class Radicalism in Mid-Victorian England*, London: Croom Helm.

Thompson, E. P. (1965), 'The peculiarities of the English', in his *The Poverty of Theory and Other Essays*, London: Merlin Press, pp. 35–91.

Thompson, E. P. (1978), 'The poverty of theory: or an orrery of errors', in *The Poverty of Theory and Other Essays*, pp. 193–397.

Thompson, Paul (1983), *The Nature of Work*, London: Macmillan.

Turner, Bryan S. (1983), *Religion and Social Theory*, London: Heinemann.

Upton, G. J. G. (1978), *The Analysis of Cross-tabulated Data*, Chichester: Wiley.

Vogler, Carolyn M. (1985), *The Nation State: The Neglected Dimension of Class*, Aldershot: Gower.

Walton, John (1981), 'The demand for working-class seaside holidays in Victorian England', *Economic History Review*, second series, **34**, pp. 249–65.

Warner, W. Lloyd *et al.* (1960), *Social Class in America*, New York: Harper.

Weber, Max (1968), *Economy and Society*, New York: Bedminster Press.

Wesolowski, W. (1979), *Classes, Strata and Power*, London: Routledge and Kegan Paul.

Westergaard, J. H. (1984), 'Class of '84', *New Socialist*, January/February, pp. 30–6.

Westergaard, J. H., and Resler, H. (1976), *Class in a Capitalist Society*, Harmondsworth: Penguin.

Willis, Paul E. (1979), *Learning to Labour*, Westmead, Hants.: Saxon House.

Wilson, Bryan R. (1985), 'Morality in the evolution of the modern social system', *British Journal of Sociology*, **36**, pp. 315–32.

Wood, Stephen (ed.) (1982), *The Degradation of Work?*, London: Hutchinson.

Worre, T. (1980), 'Class parties and class voting in the Scandinavian countries', *Scandinavian Political Studies*, **3**, pp. 299–320.

Wright, Erik Olin (1979), 'The class structure of advanced capitalist societies', in his *Class, Crisis and the State*, London: Verso, pp. 30–110.

Wright, Erik Olin (1980a), 'Varieties of Marxist conceptions of class structure', *Politics and Society*, **9**, pp. 323–70.

Wright, Erik Olin (1980b), 'Class and occupation', *Theory and Society*, **9**, pp. 177–214.

Wright, Erik Olin (1985), *Classes*. London: Verso.

Wright, Erik Olin *et al.* (1982), 'The American class structure', *American Sociological Review*, **47**, pp. 709–26.

Wright, Erik Olin, and Singelmann, Joachim (1982), 'Proletarianization in the changing American class structure', *American Journal of Sociology*, **88**, supplement, pp. 176–209.

Zweig, Ferdynand (1961), *The Worker in an Affluent Society*, London: Heinemann.

Appendix Technical details of the British survey

(Prepared with the assistance of Patricia Prescott-Clarke)

Agencies

The survey on which this book is based was sponsored by the Economic and Social Research Council. The Project Directors (and joint grant holders) were Gordon Marshall, Howard Newby, and David Rose. Carolyn Vogler was Senior Research Officer from January 1983 until August 1985. The Survey Research Centre at Social and Community Planning Research assisted with the questionnaire design, carried out the fieldwork, edited and coded the data, under the Research Directorship of Patricia Prescott-Clarke.

The sample

The sample was designed to achieve 2000 interviews with a random selection of men aged 16–64 and women aged 16–59 who were not in full-time education. The Electoral Register was used as a sampling frame. As with most academic surveys of this type electors in Northern Ireland and the Scottish Highlands and Islands north of the Caledonian Canal were excluded. A three-stage design was employed. This involved the selection of parliamentary constituencies, polling districts, and finally individuals.

Parliamentary constituencies were stratified by four variables in order to maximize the efficiency of the sample: standard region, density per hectare, party voted for in last general election, and percentage owner-occupation. Constituencies were ordered by standard region (of which there are eleven), then allocated within region to one of three density bands (more than ten persons per hectare, five to ten persons per hectare, less than five persons per hectare). Each of these subgroups was then re-ordered by the party voted to represent the constituency at the last general election (Labour, Conservative, Alliance, Other). The resulting subgroups were listed in ascending order of percentage owner-occupation. One hundred parliamentary constituencies, then two polling districts from each sampled constituency, were selected with probability at both stages proportionate to size of electorate.

The sampling procedure adopted was one which minimizes the amount of weighting required. (The electoral registers, though reasonably complete as a frame of addresses, cannot satisfactorily be taken as a frame of individuals.) Nineteen addresses from each sampled polling district were then selected by taking a systematic sample through the list of elector names and noting the address of the elector on which the sampling interval landed. A note was

288

made, for weighting purposes, of the number of electors listed for each address selected. One person at each address was then selected from those eligible for the survey. This selection was made by interviewers who were given the set of rules laid out in the respondent selection sheet that forms the frontispiece of the questionnaire. Since at any address the number of names on the register is closely related to the number of eligible persons at that address the weight to be applied tends to be one.

When deciding on the size of the starting sample of addresses two forms of sample loss, in addition to non-response, had to be taken into account. The smaller of these losses is the 'deadwood' contained in a sample of addresses selected via electoral registers. This comprises addresses which are found to be no longer occupied as residential properties. The usual allowance of 4 per cent was made for this factor. The other form of loss was related to the population to be surveyed – persons of working age who were not in full-time education. It was known that a proportion of sampled addresses would contain no such persons and therefore no interviews could be conducted at these addresses. (Some addresses, for example, would contain only persons of pensionable age.) Data from the 1981 Census were used as a basis for estimating the number of such ineligible households. These suggested that around 20 per cent of sampled addresses would be outside the scope of the survey and this too was allowed for in the sample size calculation. It was decided, on the basis of these estimates and an anticipated net response rate of 70 per cent, to issue 3800 addresses (19 in each of the 200 selected polling districts).

Of the addresses issued, 165 were found to be non-residential, vacant, or demolished. At 805 of the 3635 occupied residential addresses in the starting sample, interviewers established that none of the occupants were eligible for the survey. A successful interview was conducted at 1770 of the remaining addresses (a response rate of 62.5 per cent). Table A.1 gives details of the out-of-scope addresses and types of non-response. The response rate of 62.5 per cent in this table is, however, likely to be an underestimate of the 'true' response rate. This is because of the high proportion of addresses about which no information is known. (At 204 addresses the occupants refused to provide

Table A.1 *Basic statement of response*

	N	Percentage of achieved sample
Addresses issued	3800	—
Out of scope (premises vacant, derelict, demolished; institutional and business premises; premises containing no eligible persons)	970	—
Total in scope addresses	2830	100.0
Addresses at which interview conducted	1770	62.5
Reasons for non-response		
– Refusal	819	28.9
– Non-contact or away for survey period	174	6.1
– Other reasons (illness, inadequate English etc.)	67	2.4
Interview not achieved	1060	37.5

289

any information whatsoever and at 83 it was not possible to make any contact at all.) The response calculation shown in the table is based on the assumption that all of these 287 addresses contained someone eligible for interview. This is extremely unlikely, particularly as it is known that establishing contact is most problematic at one-person addresses, many of which are pensioner-only households. It therefore seems reasonable to argue that a higher proportion of the 287 addresses at which no information was obtained contained no-one eligible for the survey than was found at the 3348 addresses where eligibility was established. Even if the more cautious assumption is made that addresses where no information was obtained were identical to those where eligibility was established, then the number of addresses containing no eligible persons increases by 69, giving 2761 'in-scope' addresses. The 1770 interviews then represent a response rate of 64 per cent.

Table A.2 *Basic response by standard region*

Registrar-General's standard regions	Addresses issued N	Total in scope N	Interviews N	Achieved %
Scotland	342	274	184	67
North	228	176	121	69
North West	456	337	203	60
Yorkshire and Humberside	342	248	169	68
West Midlands	380	288	192	67
East Midlands	228	164	104	63
East Anglia	152	119	67	56
South West	304	220	133	60
South East	722	512	315	62
Greater London	456	351	182	52
Wales	190	141	100	71
Total	3800	2830	1770	63

Regional variations in response are shown in Table A.2. Using the figures in Table A.1 as the basis for calculation, the lowest response rate was in Greater London (52 per cent), and the highest in Wales (71 per cent). The difficulty of obtaining a high level of response in London now seems to be a problem encountered universally among survey researchers, the combined result of a higher rate of refusal than elsewhere, and marked difficulty in contacting respondents. Nevertheless, the regional variations in response rate indicated in Table A.2 do not seem seriously to have affected the representativeness of our sample, as can be seen from Table A.3. The differences observed are within the limits of acceptable sampling error and this is confirmed in a chi-square test of set sample against achieved sample by region. Applying this formula to our sample yields the value 13.194 which shows it to be consistent with the hypothesis that the sample is random at the 0.05 (95 per cent) tolerance level.

Table A.3 *Socio-economic characteristics of the sample (%)*

RG social class	Essex Survey			1981 Census		
	Male	Female	Total	Male	Female	Total
Professional	4.8	2.0	3.7	5.5	1.0	3.7
Intermediate	24.6	25.2	24.9	21.4	20.2	20.9
Skilled nonmanual	11.0	38.4	22.4	11.2	38.6	21.9
Skilled manual	39.7	9.6	27.2	34.6	8.1	24.3
Partly skilled	14.9	17.8	16.1	16.1	21.0	18.0
Unskilled	3.9	6.8	5.1	6.1	6.8	6.4
Armed Forces, nec	1.0	0.2	0.7	5.1	4.3	4.8
Total	100.0	100.0	100.0	100.0	100.0	100.0

Socio-economic group	Male	Female	Total	Male	Female	Total
Employers and managers, government	8.2	2.0	5.6	5.5	2.1	4.1
Employers and managers, industry	11.3	4.6	8.5	8.7	4.3	7.0
Professionals, self-employed	1.6	0.2	1.0	0.9	0.1	0.6
Professionals, employees	3.2	1.7	2.6	4.5	0.9	3.1
Intermediate nonmanual	9.7	21.9	14.8	7.3	14.4	10.1
Junior nonmanual	7.3	32.0	17.5	9.5	37.3	20.3
Personal service	0.8	12.1	5.5	1.1	12.2	5.4
Foreman and supervisors, manual	8.9	2.2	6.2	3.6	0.7	2.5
Skilled manual	24.6	3.5	15.9	26.3	4.0	17.6
Semi-skilled manual	12.8	8.6	11.1	13.6	10.4	12.3
Unskilled manual	3.5	6.8	4.9	5.8	6.7	6.2
Own account (other than professional)	5.2	3.7	4.6	5.3	1.8	4.0
Farmers, employers and managers	0.4	0.0	0.2	0.7	0.1	0.5
Farmers, own account	0.6	0.2	0.5	0.7	0.1	0.5
Agricultural workers	0.8	0.4	0.6	1.2	0.5	1.0
Armed forces	1.0	0.2	0.7	1.6	0.2	1.0
Inadequately described, not stated	0.0	0.0	0.0	3.5	4.2	3.8
Total	100.0	100.0	100.0	100.0	100.0	100.0

Fieldwork and quality control

Fieldwork was carried out during the period 1 March to 3 July 1984. One hundred and twenty-three interviewers were employed on the survey. Six full-day briefing sessions were held, all of which were attended by a member of the Essex team, and interviewers were also given a full set of written instructions. The first three interviews conducted by each interviewer were subjected to an immediate thorough checking in order that critical comments, where appropriate, could be conveyed. During the course of fieldwork the work of interviewers was subject to personal recall. Ten per cent of issued addresses were re-issued for recall (13 per cent of productive interviews). In addition, 36 interviewers were accompanied in the field by supervisors, as part of SCPR's standard supervision process. The mean length of interviews was 77 minutes.

Coding and data analysis

The data were coded by SCPR in two waves. The first wave concentrated on answers to all precoded questions plus occupation codes. The questionnaires were subject to a full manual edit before precoded data were transferred to punched cards. A computer edit then checked the data for both range and logic errors. The second wave was concerned with coding the open-ended questions and 'other' answers to precoded questions. Coding frames were devised by the Essex team from listings made by SCPR from 100 questionnaires. These frames were then subjected to a pilot in which the Essex team coded the answers recorded in a 10 per cent sample of questionnaires. These questionnaires were in turn passed to the SCPR data processing team who also coded the same answers. A comparison of codes identified any problems and the code frames were then revised at Essex. The open question codes were then recorded on coding sheets, edited by computer, and integrated with the precoded data. Data analysis was carried out at Essex.

Questionnaire

Note: For the sake of brevity only the principal items from the interview schedule are here reproduced. For example, a number of questions were dealt with by using 'show cards', and details of these are excluded. Instructions to interviewers and clarification for interviewees (for example the definition of 'significant promotion' at question 43b) are not shown. Various short, entirely factual, prolegomena to the various sections of the interview are also omitted. Nor have we included details of the numerous additional probes or of the (fairly complicated) filtering instructions. Which group within our sample answered which questions should be fairly obvious from the items themselves. Interviewees who were keeping house or were unemployed were not asked questions 38 to 94. Only the self-employed, and those who were senior partners or directors in their employing organizations, were asked questions 76 to 85. Filters on particular questions are self-evident. For example, only those answering 'No' to question 15 are asked question 16, which itself contains alternative items depending on how part (b) is answered. There is a standard package of questions asked each time occupational information is sought. This has been reproduced once, at questions 39 to 41, which ask about the respondent's present employment. The rubric 'occupational data' indicates those places at which the same information was gathered about his or her previous jobs or the jobs of spouse and parents.

I shall start by asking you a couple of questions about where you live now and where you grew up.

1   How long have you lived in this area?

2   In what part of Britain did you grow up?

Now questions about the economy, the recession, and some general social issues.

3(a) First, Britain's economic problems. People have different opinions about the reasons for these problems. What would you say are the main reasons for Britain's economic problems in recent years?
(b) Which of these is the most important reason?
(c) Do you think anything can be done to change things for the better?
(d) What could be done?; or
(e) Why not?

4 Does (this reason for Britain's economic problems) affect you personally?

5(a) Which [of the items on show card] has happened to you personally as a direct result of the economic recession?
(b) And which of these things has happened to other members of your household as a direct result of the economic recession?

6(a) Do you think unemployment will ever fall below 1 million, the level it was in 1975?
(b) Why do you think it will fall below 1 million again?; or
(c) Why do you think it will never fall below 1 million again?

7 It has been said that the main conflicts in Britain today are between those who run industry and those who work for them. Do you agree or disagree with this?

8 What do you think are the issues that cause conflict between those who run industry and those who work for them?

9(a) Do you think there are any important issues which cause conflicts between those who run industry and those who work for them?
(b) What conflicts are these?

10(a) Do you think there are any issues over which those who run industry and those who work for them share the same interests?
(b) What are these issues?

11(a) Apart from conflicts between those who run industry and those who work for them, do you think there are any (other) important conflicts in Britain today?
(b) What are these (other) important conflicts?

12 A number of ideas have been put forward in order to overcome Britain's economic problems. [For each one indicate whether agree or disagree.]
(a) Leaving it to market forces to revive the economy.
(b) Income policies which increase the wages of the low paid more than those of the high paid.
(c) Increasing income tax in order to increase welfare benefits.
(d) Import controls to protect Britain from competition from abroad.
(e) Increased taxes on the profits of successful companies in order to maintain jobs in declining industries.
(f) Increased government spending to revive the economy.

(g)   Policies which make multinational companies reinvest in Britain all the profits they make here.

(h)   Special help for ethnic minorities over jobs and housing.

(i)   Special help to give women equal opportunities outside the home.

13(a)   Would you be prepared to pay more tax in order to create jobs for the unemployed?

(b)   Would you be prepared to pay more in tax so that more money could be spent on the welfare state?

14   Would you say that over the last five years you have been improving your standard of living, falling behind, or staying about the same?

15   Do you think the distribution of income and wealth in Britain is a fair one?

16(a)   Why don't you think it's fair?

(b)   Can anything be done about this?

(c)   What could be done?; or

(d)   Why can nothing be done?

17   In recent years there have been considerable changes in government spending patterns. Have you or your immediate family been affected by changes in government spending on the National Health Service; education; law and order; public transport; council housing; unemployment benefit; supplementary benefit? Which of these has affected you or your immediate family most?

18(a)   Do you approve or disapprove of this?

(b)   Have you done anything about it?

(c)   What have you done?; or

(d)   Why haven't you done anything?

19   Do you think it makes a great deal of difference which party runs the country?

20   Why do you feel it makes no difference?

21   If there were a general election tomorrow who would you vote for?

22(a)   Are there any particular reasons why you would vote for this party?

(b)   What other kinds of people do you think vote for (this party) for the same reasons as yourself?

(c)   Have you ever voted for another party at a general election?

(d)   Which other party or parties have you voted for at past general elections?

23   Outside of your normal work-time, do you take part in any of the types of groups on this [show card]?

24   Which ones?

Now some questions about social class.

25(a)   In the past there was a dominant class which largely controlled the economic and political system, and a lower class which had no control over economic or political affairs. Some people say that things are still like this, others say it has now changed. What do you think, has it changed, or stayed the same?

(b) In what ways have things changed?

26 When you hear someone described as 'upper class' what sort of people do you think of?

27 When you hear someone described as 'middle class' what sort of person do you think of?

28 When you hear someone described as 'working class' what sort of person do you think of?

29(a) How is it that people come to belong to the class that they do?

(b) How do you feel about people belonging to a class because of birth, do you approve or disapprove?

(c) Do you think it is easy or hard for a person to go from one social class to another?

(d) Under what circumstances do you think a person could move from one class to another?

30(a) Do you think there are any important issues which cause conflicts between social classes?

(b) What conflicts are these?

31 Do you think class is an inevitable feature of modern society?

32 Do you think of yourself as belonging to any particular social class?

33 Suppose you were asked to say which class you belonged to, which would you say?

34 Apart from class, is there any other major group you identify with?

35(a) What sort of group are you thinking of?

(b) Do you normally think of yourself as a member of that grouping or as a member of a social class?

Now some questions about work.

36(a) At the present time are you in work, including part-time work, free-lance work, and working through a government scheme? (Do you work 30 or more hours a week? Are you looking for work, looking after the house, or what?)

(b) Are you available for paid employment if it was offered to you?

(c) Are you registered with a Jobcentre or Employment Office? (For a full-time or part-time job?)

37(a) Have you ever had a regular paid job of 10 or more hours a week, including working through a government scheme or working unpaid in a family business?

(b) How long is it since you last had a job of 10 or more hours a week?

(c) Was your last job full-time or part-time?

(d) Since you left full-time education have you ever had a full-time job of 30 or more hours a week?

38(a)   Can I check, is your present job through a government scheme like the Community Programme and Youth Training Schemes?

(b)   How long have you worked for your present organization?

39(a)   What is the name or title of your job?

(b)   What kind of work do you do in your job?

(c)   What training or qualifications are needed for your job?

(d)   Do you supervise or have management responsibility for the work of other people? How many?

(e)   Are you an employee; working as a temp for an agency; or self-employed?

(f)   Can I check, is your business a professional practice, a farm, or some other type of business?

(g)   Is that a single business (practice/farm) or do you own more than one?

40(a)   How many people are employed at the place where you work?

(b)   Now, think of the immediate work group, that is the people you work directly with on a regular basis. How many would that be?

(c)   What does your employer make or do at the place where you usually work (from)?

41   Which type of organization on this [show card] do you work for?

42(a)   Is this organization part of a larger company or organization?

(b)   Is the larger company a multinational one, that is does it own companies in other countries as well as the UK?

(c)   Does the organization you work for have any subsidiary companies?

(d)   In addition to where you work, does the organization have other offices, plants, branches and so on elsewhere?

(e)   About how many people are employed altogether in the organization for which you work, including all other branches, plants, companies and organizations involved?

(f)   Is the organization you work for owned by someone in your family?

(g)   Are you an owner or part owner of the organization in which you work? That is, do you own shares in it, or are you entitled to a share of the profits?

(h)   Are you a senior partner, a director on the main board, or in an equivalently placed position in the organization?

43(a)   On average how many hours a week do you work in this job, including overtime whether paid or unpaid?

(c)   Use this [show card] to tell me why you left that job.

44(a)   Use this [show card] to say how high you think your chances are of being given a significant promotion within your present organization.

(b)   Is this (zero chances) because you are already in the highest type of job for people who do your sort of work?

45(a)   Use this [show card] again to say how high you think your chances are of being promoted by changing employers.

(b) When a better job comes available in your organization, for people like yourself, how much of an advantage is already working for the organization?

(c) Generally speaking, when it comes to getting a significant promotion, do you think people like yourself are better off staying put with the same employer, or moving around between employers?

(d) Thinking about getting promotion or going up a career ladder, is your present job a step in a recognized career or promotion ladder within your organization?

(e) Does your sort of work have a recognized career or promotion ladder, even if it means changing employers to go up it?

46 Which of the ways on this [show card] best describes how you are paid in your present job?

47(a) Officially, how many hours per week must you work in order to receive your basic wage or salary?

(b) Are you required to clock or sign yourself in and off?

(c) Are you paid for any overtime you work?

(d) Which of the amounts on this [show card] comes closest to your gross pay in this job; that is pay before tax and other deductions are made.

48 Thinking about the immediate future, in which of the ways on this [show card] are you most likely to increase your present level of pay?

49(a) Is this the most likely way of increasing pay in the immediate future for other people in the same sort of job as yourself?

(b) Is this the main way you have increased your pay in the past?

(c) What has been the main way you have increased your pay in the past?

50 Thinking ahead a few years, which of the ways on this [show card] do you think is most likely to lead to you getting an increased level of pay?

51 Is your rate of pay or pay scale decided by an agreement between your management and a trade union or staff association?

(b) Is this agreement made here locally or is it made elsewhere? (Is the agreement made between your company and the trade union or your industry and the trade union?)

(c) (d) Are you on a recognized pay scale with specified annual increments?

(e) Is your pay regularly reviewed each year?

(f) Can you ask to discuss the possibility of a pay rise at any time in the year?

52(a) Would you be prepared to take lower wage increases to allow those earning less than you to catch up?

(b) Would you be prepared to take lower wage increases if it meant your organization could then provide extra jobs for the unemployed?

53(a) As an organization to work for, how does your present organization compare with others? It is better than most, about average, or worse than most?

(b) Why do you say that it is better than most?

(c) Why do you say that it is about average?

(d) Why do you say that it is worse than most?

54 Does your present job require more skill, less skill, or about the same amount of skill as when you first started to do it?

55(a) Is yours a job which allows you to design and plan important aspects of your own work or is your work largely defined for you?

(b) Would you say yours was a job which required you to design or plan important aspects of your own work or is this something you have done on your own initiative?

56(a) Do you decide the specific tasks or jobs you carry out from day to day or does someone else?

(b) Does someone else decide how much work you do or how fast you work during the day?

(c) Can you decide, officially or unofficially, the time you arrive and leave work?

(d) Is that because of official rules, the system of supervision, or the nature of the work itself?

(e) Can you considerably slow down your pace of work for a day when you want to?

(f) Is that because of official rules . . . ?

(g) Can you decide on your own to introduce a new task or work assignment that you will do on your job?

(h) Is that because of official rules . . . ?

57 Can I check again, as part of your job do you supervise or manage the work of other employees?

58(a) Are you directly responsible for deciding the specific tasks or work assignments of your subordinates?

(b) Are you directly responsible for deciding what procedures, tools or materials your subordinates use in their work?

(c) Are you directly responsible for deciding how fast they work, how long they work, or how much work they get done?

(d) Do you have any influence on the granting of a pay rise or promotion to any of your subordinates?

(e) Do you have any influence in preventing someone having a pay rise or promotion because of poor work or misbehaviour?

(f) Who has the greatest influence, you or someone higher up in the organization?

(g) Who makes the final official decision, you or someone else? (Who?)

59(a) Do you have any influence on the sacking or suspending of a subordinate?

(b) Who has the greatest influence . . . ?

(c) Who makes the final official decision . . . ?

298

60(a) Do you have any influence on issuing a formal warning to a subordinate?

    (b) Who has the greatest influence . . . ?

    (c) Who makes the final official decision . . . ?

61 On this [show card] are a number of decisions to do with policy-making at places where people work. Do you participate in making any of these kinds of decisions or in providing advice for them?

62 I shall read out each type of decision in turn. Please tell me whether or not you personally are involved in that decision. If you are, use the card to say how you usually participate in the decision [makes decision on own authority; participates as voting member of a group which makes the decision; makes decision subject to approval; provides advice to person who actually makes the decision].

    (a) Are you personally involved in decisions to increase or decrease the total number of people employed in the place where you work?

    (b) How do you usually participate in this decision?

63(a) . . . . decisions affecting the number of people employed in your own department or section? (How?)

64(a) . . . policy decisions to significantly change the products or services delivered by the organization for which you work? (How?)

65(a) . . . decisions to change the policy concerning the routine pace of work or the amount of work performed in your workplace, or some major part of it? (How?)

66(a) . . . decisions to significantly change the basic methods or procedures of work used in a major part of your workplace? (How?)

67(a) . . . decisions concerning the budget at the place where you work?

    (b) Do you participate in deciding the overall size of the budget?

    (c) (How?)

    (d) Do you participate in general policy decisions about the distribution of funds within the overall budget of the place where you work?

    (e) (How?)

68(a) . . . major investment decisions to expand or contract significantly the size of your business? (How?)

69(a) Now, thinking back over all the time you have been working, do you think employer/employee relations in general have changed in any significant way in that time?

    (b) In what ways have they changed?

70 Are you a member of a trade union concerned with pay and working conditions?

71(a) Is this union recognized by your management for pay and working conditions negotiations?

    (b) Why do you belong to a union?

72(a)   Have you ever been a member of a union concerned with pay and working conditions?

(b)   Why did you leave?

(c)   Why have you never belonged to a union concerned with pay and working conditions?

73   On this [show card] are a number of things trade unions try to achieve for their members. Which of these do you think your union should concentrate on at the present time?

74(a)   Would you say your union is effective or ineffective when it comes to dealing with (this issue)?

(b)   Would you say that the recession has made any difference to your union's ability to deal effectively with this issue?

(c)   In what way?

75(a)   Which best describes your position within your organization, are you in a managerial/supervisory/non-managerial or non-supervisory position?

(b)   Is that a top, upper, middle or lower management position?

76   On average, about how many hours a week do you work in this job, including overtime whether paid or unpaid?

77(a)   Do you have fellow directors or partners?

(b)   How did you come by the capital to have your own business?

78   What are the advantages of being an owner (partner) or senior manager rather than an ordinary employee?

79   And what are the disadvantages of being an owner . . . ?

80   Do you think owning (or being a senior manager in) a business gives you a particular outlook on life? Do you see yourself as significantly different in any way from, say, someone who works in someone else's business? In what ways?

81   Which of the amounts on this [show card] comes closest to your gross pay in this job; that is, pay before tax and other deductions are made?

82(a)   In total, about how many people do you employ in your organization on a permanent basis, including members of your family?

(b)   Do you employ people on a casual or seasonal basis?

(c)   How many of these are members of your family?

83(a)   I want to find out how much of your time is spent in management rather than directly in producing the goods or service your business is about. Use this [show card] to say how you divide up your time between management and producing goods or services yourself.

(b)   Do you employ other people whose job is solely a management one?

84(a)   Thinking back over the time you have been an employer (or senior manager) do you think employer/employee relations have changed in any significant way in that time?

(b)   In what way have they changed?

85 Are any of your non-management employees members of a union concerned with pay and working conditions?

86(a) Do you have a second job, including freelance or casual work, or any other kind of work? [Occupational data.]

87(d) Use this [show card] to say what percentage of your personal income comes from this second job.

Now some more general questions about how you see your job.

89(a) For some people their job is simply something they put up with in order to earn a living. For others it means much more than that. Is your present job just a means of earning a living, or does it mean much more to you than that?

(b) Is that because there are no interesting jobs around here; or you don't have the right skills to get a more interesting job; or because you would feel the same about any job that you had?

(c) In what ways does your job mean more to you than just a means of earning a living?

90(a) What proportion of your friends work with you at the present time?

(b) Do you see any of these people socially outside work?

91(a) If, for any reason, you were to leave your job, would you find it easy or difficult at the present time to get a comparable job elsewhere?

(b) In the last five years, do you think getting a comparable job has become more difficult, less difficult, or remained about the same?

(c) Could anything be done to alter the situation?

92(a) Compared to other people with the same kind of skill and doing similar kinds of work, do you think your job is more secure, less secure, or about the same as theirs?

(b) Why do you think it is more/less secure?

93(a) Has the current recession had any noticeable effects on the organization in which you work?

(b) What effects has it had?

94 Since leaving full-time education, have you had any other full-time jobs of 30 or more hours a week, including different jobs with the same employer?

95 How many?

96 [Occupational data on first full-time job after leaving full-time education.]

(i) How long did you work in that job?

(j) Use [show card] to tell me why you left that job.

98, 99 [Occupational data on last full-time job held by respondent; that is, job before present one.]

(e) How long did you work in that job?

(f) Use [show card] to tell me why you left that job.

101 [Occupational data on penultimate job; that is, job before last job.]

(j) How long did you work in that job?

(k)   Use [show card] to tell me why you left that job.

102(a)   Have you ever been unemployed between jobs for more than 4 weeks at a time?

(b)   How many times?

103   Have household or family responsibilities ever prevented you from (a) looking for a job; (b) accepting a full-time job; (c) accepting a promotion or a transfer; (d) changing jobs; or required you (e) to change your job; (f) leave paid employment for more than a year?

(g)   Has your work ever required you to move home?

(h)   How many times?

Now your leisure time.

104(a)   What three things do you most enjoy doing when you are not working (or looking for a job)? [Establish for each who this is mainly done with – friends, family, or alone; where it is mainly done – at home or elsewhere.]

(b)   Are any of these things more important to you than work?

(c)   Which?

Turning to school days.

105   What type of school did you last attend full-time?

106(a)   What age were you when you left school or sixth-form college?

(b)   Before you left school, did you pass any examinations or obtain any qualifications?

107   Use [show card] to say what qualifications you obtained before leaving school.

108   Have you passed any examinations or obtained any qualifications since leaving school?

109   Use [show card] to say what is the highest qualification you have obtained since leaving school.

110   Why did you study for this qualification?

111   Thinking back to when you were aged about 14, what job did your father have then? [Occupational data on father's job.]

112   When you were about 14, did your mother have a paid job or work in a family business? [Occupational data on mother's job.]

113   Generally throughout your childhood up to the time you left school, who provided most of your family's financial support – your father, your mother, or someone else?

114   [Occupational data on chief childhood supporter at respondent's age 14.]

115   When (chief childhood supporter) was your present age, was he/she in the same job as when you were about 14, or was he/she in a different job?

116 [Occupational data on chief childhood supporter's job when he/she was same age as respondent is now.]

Back to the present time

117(a) Are you married and living with your husband, living as married, widowed, separated, divorced, or single?
(b) How long have you been married/living as married?

118 [Employment status of spouse or partner – as at questions 36 and 37.]

119 [Occupational data on spouse or partner.]

120 [Details of children: numbers, financial dependency, their paid work.]

Turning now to your home.

121 For some people a home is simply a roof over their heads. For others it means more than that. What does your home mean to you?

122(a) [Sex of respondent.]
(b) [Ethnic group.]

123 Including yourself, how many people live in your household?

124 [Household grid of other household members: numbers; relationship to respondent; age.]

125(a) Is this accommodation owned or rented in your or your husband/wife's name?
(b) Who is responsible in your household for owning or renting it?

126 Does the person responsible for it own it or rent it?

127(a) Do you own or rent your home?
(b) Who does own your home?

128(a) Do you own your home outright or are you paying off a mortgage or other loan on it?
(b) If you were to sell your home, how much do you think you would get for it?
(c) If you were to sell your home, how much do you think you would get after paying off your mortgage or loan?

129(a) When you bought your first home how did you raise the part of the purchase price that was not covered by a mortgage?
(b) What made you decide to become a home-owner?
(c) Apart from what you've just told me, what does home-ownership mean to you? Is it important in any other ways?
(d) Can I check, did you buy your present home from the council as a tenant?

I want to talk now about income from sources other than work.

130(a) At present, are you or any other members of your household receiving any of the state benefits, state pensions or payments on this [show card]?

(b)   Which ones?

(c)   At the present time, what proportion of your household's total income comes from these sources?

131(a)   At the present time, do you or other members of your household receive income from any of the sources on this [show card], or from any other source, other than earnings or state benefits?

(b)   What are these?

(c)   At the present time, what proportion of your household's total income comes from these sources?

132(a)   Are any other households other than the one you live in wholly or partly financially dependent on you?

(b)   What proportion of your gross personal income goes to this other household?

133(a)   How many people in your household are in paid employment at the present time?

(b)   About what proportion of your household's total income comes from earnings?

134   Which of the amounts on this [show card] comes closest to your household's total gross income – I mean income before tax and other deductions and from all sources for everyone in the household?

135   Finally, suppose someone you had not met before asked you 'What do you do for a living?', what would you say? (Suppose, for example, the brother of a friend asked you what you did?)

136   [Consent for follow-up interview.]

Coda Constructing the Goldthorpe classes

The employment data from the Essex Class Project were collected in such a way that respondents could be allocated a social class standing according to three different class frameworks – those of the Registrar-General, John H. Goldthorpe, and Erik Olin Wright. Chapters 2 and 3 of our text make it clear that the first and last of these frameworks have changed over the years. The procedure for constructing Registrar-General's classes was altered at the time of the 1981 Census, when the schema ceased to group occupations according to 'social standing', and switched to the alternative (though no less contentious) criterion of 'occupational skill'. More radical changes were effected in the Wright class categories while our survey was actually in the field. Both the theoretical rationale for Wright's whole approach and the operational definitions for the various class categories themselves were entirely revised. It was probably too much to expect that our research report would be published before John Goldthorpe also decided to reformulate his class framework. In fact, a revised version of the Goldthorpe scheme was announced late in 1986, just as the present text was being prepared for publication. The purpose of this short coda, therefore, is to describe the revision itself and to examine briefly its possible implications for our analysis. Fortunately, as we shall see, there is nothing in Goldthorpe's reworking of his schema that would lead us to amend any of the arguments that are offered above. Indeed, to the contrary, the change in question entirely vindictes our own assessment of the strengths and weaknesses of the Goldthorpe scheme.

That scheme, it will be remembered, attempts to combine occupational categories whose members share similar market situations and work situations. Goldthorpe, following Lockwood, takes these to be the two major components of class position. They are observable in occupational title and employment status respectively. Somewhat confusingly, the original sevenfold class schema, which appeared in the late 1970s, was constructed by aggregating categories from the 36-category version of the much earlier Hope–Goldthorpe (H–G) occupational scale, itself a scale of the *social desirability* of occupations. For example, in *Social Mobility and Class Structure in Modern Britain* (1980), Goldthorpe and his co-authors report that Class II (the cadet level of the service class) comprises H–G categories 5, 6, 8, 9, 10, 12, 14 and 16. However, and rather crucially, the actual scale values (the social desirability) of these H–G categories are entirely ignored in allocating them to Goldthorpe social classes since the H–G scale does not rank occupations according to market situation and work situation. Coincidentally, however,

305

the 36-category version of this scale groups together individual occupations without amalgamating across either employment status divisions (employer, manager, employee) or broad occupational divisions (such as those of professionals, technicians, skilled and unskilled manual and nonmanual workers). It is possible, therefore, to use the fairly high degree of differentiation of occupational function and employment status within the H–G scale to construct a class schema based on market and work situations. In devising his class scheme, John Goldthorpe simply ignored the 'social desirability' of the 36 basic units in the H–G scale and grouped them together, instead, into (seven) categories comprising occupations whose incumbents appeared, 'in the light of the available evidence', to be typically comparable in terms of income, economic security, chances of economic advancement, and job-autonomy.[1]

In this way Goldthorpe arrives at the familiar sevenfold class scheme used to analyse the data from the Nuffield social mobility inquiry. Two aspects of his procedure are particularly noteworthy from our point of view. First, the class categories that are arrived at were explicitly designed for a study of social mobility among men only, with women being excluded for various theoretical and practical reasons. It is the pay and conditions (market and work situations) of men whom Goldthorpe has in mind in constructing his schema.[2] Second, Goldthorpe's procedure for operationalizing his notion of market situation and work situation is not fully explained, since we are never shown the 'available evidence' according to which occupational categories are judged to be similarly placed in these terms.

Over the years the original scheme has been modified in order to meet specific research objectives. Agricultural workers were distinguished so as to facilitate comparative studies of social mobility involving countries with sizeable proportions of the workforce on the land. The *petit bourgeoisie* was subdivided for the same reason.[3] Moreover, the basic units for the class categories themselves have been changed, from those of the Hope–Goldthorpe scale, to the occupation groups and employment statuses devised by the OPCS in 1980. In this way, all permissible combinations of occupation group and employment status could be allowed for in Goldthorpe's class framework, thus making the revised version more sensitive to variations in market situations and work situations and so 'implementing the principles of the schema more precisely'. Once again, in undertaking the revision,

each such combination was assigned to the schema in the light of the available information from official statistics, monographic sources etc. regarding the typical market and work situations of the individuals comprised: e.g. on levels and sources of income, other monetary and non-monetary benefits, degree of economic security, chances of economic advancement, and location in systems of authority and control.[4]

Finally, in order to make the schema 'more suited to the allocation of women where it is found desirable to do this by reference to their own employment', class III was split into IIIa and IIIb,

so as to bring as far as possible into the latter category occupations which are very largely filled by women and which, in terms of their characteristic employment relations and conditions, would seem to entail straightforward wage-labour rather than displaying any of the quasi-bureaucratic features of the remaining positions in Class III.

Late in 1986 Goldthorpe and Payne announced that,

when applying the schema to women in virtue of their own employment, it would in fact seem to be generally more realistic – and to give a better comparison with men – to combine Class IIIb with Class VII, that of semi- and unskilled manual workers.[5]

As we have seen, this new strategy for extending the scheme to cover women's own employment would appear to be well founded, since the reported job-autonomy of those in class IIIb (shop assistants, receptionists, and the like) seems to be closer to that of manual workers generally than to the routine nonmanual employees comprising class IIIa. Our own data about work situation seem to vindicate the conclusion arrived at by Goldthorpe and his colleagues. In some of the tables presented above, those where the logic of the analysis required it and the numbers involved permitted, we actually distinguish the two component parts of class III. However, on learning of this latest revision to the schema, we are not inclined to re-analyse our data accordingly by reclassifying class IIIb females alongside class VII in all tables involving the Goldthorpe categories. We have three reasons for presenting our findings as they stand. First, and least substantially, our text was more or less completed when John Goldthorpe published his conclusions about classes IIIa and IIIb. Having already revised the manuscript thoroughly in order to accommodate Erik Wright's reformulation of his class categories, we were (perhaps understandably) reluctant to revise the analysis yet again, this time in the light of Goldthorpe's latest suggestion. To have one of the two class frameworks that was central to our project changed during the course of the study itself was unfortunate; to have the other revised as well begins to look like a conspiracy.

Second, and more importantly, we intend to investigate the whole question of market situations and work situations much more thoroughly in a subsequent publication. We are convinced that John Goldthorpe's Weberian approach to the analysis of class processes is generally correct. However, we have a great deal of information in our study that is relevant to the construction of class categories based on the principles outlined above, and so can subject Goldthorpe's claims about market and work situations to detailed and systematic scrutiny. In this way we can determine whether or not his interpretation of the 'available evidence' is in fact generally sound. It may well be the case, for example, that rather more extensive revisions are required before Goldthorpe class categories can cope fully with the peculiarities of women's employment situations.

Finally, and most significantly, it is also clear that the reclassification of class IIIb alongside class VII would not lead us to alter the conclusions we have arrived at in this volume. Only 4 per cent of employees in our sample actually appear in Goldthorpe class IIIb. If they are considered as part of the

307

working class, then class III shrinks from 19.5 per cent to 15.1 per cent of those employed, while class VII increases from 23.9 to 28.3 per cent. We have already seen (from Chapter 5) that a shift of this magnitude does not eliminate the discrepancy between Goldthorpe and Wright classes since well over three-quarters of class III are in routine clerical employment – and still, therefore, outside the proletariat as far as Goldthorpe is concerned. If we then reconstruct the basic mobility data (origin to present job) to take account of Goldthorpe's suggestion, as in Table C.1, we can determine the implications of treating sales and personal service employees as working class for arguments about social mobility in general and proletarianization in particular. This table should be compared with Tables 4.8 and 5.1 in the text. Scarcely any effect is evident in the case of class origins, while in the marginal distribution of female destinations the proportion in class III falls from 38.1 to 28.7 per cent, as that in class VII increases from 22.1 to 31.5 per cent. This would not lead us to revise our arguments about proletarianization: the dominant movement is still one of upward mobility into professional, administrative, and managerial positions. Proportionately more women than men will now arrive at class VII destinations (31.5 as against 23.1 per cent). Even so, it is still not the case (despite Erik Wright's claim to the contrary), that a majority of proletarians are women. In fact, the sexes are more or less

Table C.1 *Class distribution by sex and class of chief childhood supporter at same age as respondent – Goldthorpe class categories revised*

| | | | | | Males | | | | |
| | | | | | Class of respondent | | | | |
		I	II	IIIa	IV	V	VI	VII/IIIb	Total
Class of	I	27.7	31.9	10.6	6.4	4.3	10.6	8.5	7.4 (47)
chief	II	20.8	39.6	3.8	11.3	1.9	13.2	9.4	8.4 (53)
childhood	IIIa	24.0	24.0	0.0	8.0	12.0	24.0	8.0	4.0 (25)
supporter	IV	14.4	15.6	5.6	28.9	10.0	11.1	14.4	14.2 (90)
	V	14.4	18.9	4.5	7.2	13.5	13.5	27.9	17.6 (111)
	VI	8.6	12.9	9.4	6.5	14.4	23.0	25.2	22.0 (139)
	VII/IIIb	12.6	8.4	4.2	11.4	9.6	20.4	33.5	26.4 (167)
Total		14.6	17.2	5.9	11.6	10.4	17.2	23.1	100.0
		(92)	(109)	(37)	(73)	(66)	(109)	(146)	(632)

| | | | | | Females | | | | |
| | | | | | Class of respondent | | | | |
		I	II	IIIa	IV	V	VI	VII/IIIb	Total
Class of	I	13.8	27.6	37.9	3.4	0.0	0.0	17.2	6.8 (29)
chief	II	14.3	42.1	28.6	0.0	0.0	0.0	14.3	6.6 (28)
childhood	IIIa	5.0	40.0	30.0	5.0	0.0	5.0	15.0	4.7 (20)
supporter	IV	9.1	25.5	21.8	9.1	3.6	1.8	29.1	12.9 (55)
	V	0.0	27.5	32.5	6.3	1.3	6.3	26.3	18.8 (80)
	VI	3.6	15.3	35.1	2.7	5.4	8.1	29.7	26.1 (111)
	VII/IIIb	2.0	8.8	19.6	7.8	5.9	4.9	51.0	24.0 (102)
Total		4.7	21.2	28.7	5.4	3.5	4.9	31.5	100.0
		(20)	(90)	(122)	(23)	(15)	(21)	(134)	(425)

evenly balanced within Goldthorpe class VII/IIIb, while men make up (as before) more than 80 per cent of skilled manual workers (class VI). Nor are our conclusions about relative mobility rates affected by this change. If the model of common social fluidity is fitted to the data in Table C.1, then we find (as when it was fitted to the original data in Table 4.8) that there are strong and significant associations between both origins and destinations and sex and destinations (and of these the latter is the stronger), but no evidence that the former association itself varies with sex. (In fact the Y^2/df ratios for the various parameters hardly change from those given at note 12 in Chapter 5 above.)

In short, Goldthorpe's recent suggestion that, where women are classified by reference to their own employment, those in class IIIb should be considered as part of the working class, seems to us, at this stage, to fulfil its intended objective. It makes his schema more suitable to the class allocation of women. However, taking cognizance of this fact simply strengthens our finding that, within *all* class categories, women are more commonly to be found in the lower or relatively disprivileged levels: in class II rather than class I, in class VII rather than class VI. It also strengthens our conviction that, Goldthorpe to the contrary, it is indeed desirable to classify both men and women as individuals in undertaking a systematic class analysis. True, class analysts have yet to devise a satisfactory means of coping with gender differences, and because we do not exclude ourselves from this generalization we shall have a good deal more to say about this issue in the future.

Notes

1 Compare Goldthorpe and Hope (1974: 131–43) and Goldthorpe (1980: 39–42). From the 36-fold version of the H–G scale, it is also possible to determine the precise occupational titles and employment statuses that are covered by each Goldthorpe class category, by reference to the OPCS *Classification of Occupations 1970.*
2 See Goldthorpe (1980: 287–8).
3 See Erikson *et al.* (1979; 1982).
4 See Goldthorpe and Payne (1986a: 21).
5 Goldthorpe and Payne (1986b: 533, 550–1).

Index

Abercrombie, Nick 12, 13–14, 29, 30, 222, 223, 276
Abramson, P. R. 261, 276
Ahrne, Goran xv, 276
Alexander, Sally 223, 276
Alt, James E. 12, 276
Althusser, Lewis 29, 276
Amin, S. 12, 276
Anderson, Perry 194
autonomy 23–4, 40–2, 117–22

Barbalet, Jack M. 29, 30, 276
Bauman, Zygmunt 12, 276
Bell, Daniel 194, 196, 197, 222, 269, 275, 276
Beynon, Huw 189, 195, 276
Binns, David 30, 276
Blackburn, R. M. 12, 44, 47, 61, 141, 276
Blau, P. M. 275, 276
Blom, Raimo xv, 276
Braverman, Harry 16, 17, 29, 99, 116, 140, 141, 270, 275, 276
Brewer, Richard I. 30, 276
Brittan, Samuel 197, 223, 276
Britten, Nicky 65–7, 84, 95, 122–6, 130, 136, 141, 280
Brown, Richard 7, 12, 277
Brown, W. 12, 277
Browning, H. L. 140, 285
Bulmer, Martin 195, 277
Butler, David 260, 261, 263, 277

Calhoun, Craig 224, 277
Calvert, Peter 29, 182, 195, 277
Carchedi, G. 275, 277
Carter, Robert 12, 277
Cashmore, E. Ellis 12, 277
citizenship 200–2
Clarke, Simon 29, 277
class boundaries 21–6, 36–8, 98–142
class consciousness 6–10, 168–95, 216–24, 268–75 passim
class dealignment (see social class and electoral behaviour)
class formation (see also entries under Goldthorpe and Wright) 21–2, 31–2, 39, 44–6, 50, 63–97
class imagery 145–7
class interests 44–5, 37–88, 96–7
Cohen, G. A. 29, 277
credentials 35–8, 47
Crewe, Ivor 12, 228–32, 236, 260, 261, 262, 263, 277, 285
Crompton, Rosemary 12, 13, 29, 30, 61, 100, 115, 140, 141, 277
Crossick, Geoffrey 204–5, 227, 277
Crouch, Colin 224, 278
Curran, James 263, 278
Cutler, Anthony 29, 278

Dale, Angela 95, 96, 278
Dalton, R. I. 261, 280
Daniel, W. W. 12, 278
Daunton, M. J. 223, 278
Davidoff, Leonore 223, 278
DeAngelis, Richard A. 224, 278
deskilling of work 115–22, 270–5
distributional conflict 196–224 passim
dominant ideology thesis 197–8
Duke, Vic 12, 278
Duncan, O. D. 275, 276
Dunleavy, Patrick 9, 12, 232, 262, 278

Edgell, Stephen 12, 278
educational qualifications (see credentials)
Edwards, Richard 29, 100, 140, 278
Elger, Tony 29, 278
Elster, Jon 220, 224, 278
Erikson, Robert 95, 141, 194, 262, 278, 309

fatalism 143–67 passim
Finer, S. E. 12, 278
Foster, John 205, 223, 279
Fothergill, Stephen 12, 279
Fox, J. 20, 30, 281

Franklin, Mark N. 232, 262, 279
Friedman, Andrew L. 29, 279
Furbank, P. N. 195, 279

Gallie, Duncan 193, 195, 279
Garnsey, Elizabeth 12, 29, 30, 279
gender: and class consciousness 182-3;
  and class identity 130-4; and class
  perceptions 134; and class
  structure 83-4, 103-12, 115-26; and
  class position 72-81, 138-9; and
  proletarianization 103-12, 115-26;
  and social mobility 75-7; and voting
  behaviour 71-2, 129-30, 135-6
Giddens, Anthony 29, 279
Goldthorpe, John H.: on class
  consciousness 168, 194, 218, 221-2,
  244-5; on class formation 21-2, 45,
  82-5; on class and gender 63-8, 81-
  7, 106-15, 138-9; on class model
  of 21-3, 26-9, 30, 43, 266, 305-9;
  class model compared with
  Wright's 27-8, 48-60, 89-95, 101-3,
  139-40, 264-5; on class structure 21-
  3, 45, 98-100, 137-8; on instrumental
  collectivism 6-7, 8, 12; on
  proletarianization 98-100, 137-8; on
  social mobility 21-2, 45; on unit of
  class analysis 63-4
Gorz, Andre 2, 12, 222, 223, 280
Gray, Robert Q. 203, 206, 223, 280
Gubbay, Jon 13, 29, 30, 277
Gudgin, Graham 12, 279

Habermas, Jurgen 196, 197, 223, 280
Hall, Stuart 263, 280
Haranne, M. 261, 280
Harrison, R. 223, 280
Hayek, F. 197, 223, 280
Heath, Anthony 65-7, 84, 95, 122-6,
  130, 136, 141, 194, 195, 228-32, 236,
  239, 240, 246, 254, 261, 262, 263, 280
Hemingway, John 224, 280
Hildebrand, K. 261, 280
Hill, Stephen 224, 280
Himmelweit, Hilde T. 12, 262, 280
Hindess, Barry 21, 30, 280
Hirsch, Fred 196, 197, 221, 222, 280
Hobsbawm, Eric 1-2, 12, 223, 261, 281
Hoggart, Richard 194
Holmwood, John 30, 281
homecentredness (see privatism)
Hope, Keith 21, 30, 279, 305, 306, 309
Hunt, Alan 141, 281
Husbands, Christopher T. 12, 278

Ingham, Geoffrey 12, 281
instrumentalism 143-67 *passim*, 202-4
  passim

Jacques, Martin 263, 280
Jarvie, I. C. 95, 281
Jones, Gareth 12, 140, 141, 277
Jones, Gareth Stedman 223-4, 281
Joyce, Patrick 223, 281

Kavanagh, Dennis 261, 277
Kerr, Clark 194, 274, 275, 281
Kirk, N. 223, 281
Korpi, Walter 194, 224, 281
Kreckel, Reinhard 12, 281
Kuhn, Annette 223, 281

labour aristocracy 202-6
Lash, Scott 61, 224, 281
Lazonick, William 29, 281
Leavis, F. R. 194
Lee, David 12, 281
Leete, R. 20, 30, 281
Lipset, Seymour Martin 12, 194, 261,
  281
Littler, C. R. 29, 224, 281
Lockwood, David 29, 30, 96, 141, 166,
  218, 221, 223, 224, 281, 282, 305
Lukacs, Georg 191
Lukes, Steven 1-2, 12, 282

McAllister, Ian 261, 262, 285
McLennan, Gregor 223, 283
McRae, Susan 141, 283
Mandel, Ernest 275, 282
Mann, Michael 6, 12, 141, 188, 195,
  197, 223, 276, 282
Marcuse, Herbert 223, 282
Marglin, Stephen A. 29, 282
Marsh, Catherine 30, 262, 282
Marshall, Gordon xv, 12, 29, 95, 96,
  195, 223, 282
Marshall, T. H. 200-2, 223, 282
Marx, Karl 13-18, 29, 195, 199, 282,
  283
Massey, Doreen 12, 283
Michels, Robert 259, 263, 283
Miles, Robert 223, 283
Millward, Neil 12, 278
Moorhouse, H. F. 9, 12, 223, 283
Morawska, Eva 224, 283
Murphy, R. 96, 283

Nairn, Tom 194
Nef, J. U. 29, 283

Newby, Howard   xv, 12, 195, 224, 283
Offe, Claus   12, 197, 223, 283
Ossowski, Stanislaw   29, 284
Page, Charles H.   29, 284
Pahl, R. E.   12, 224, 284
Panitch, Leo   195, 284
Parkin, Frank   30, 47, 141, 188, 195, 223, 284
Parsons, Talcott   262, 284
Payne, Clive   30, 95, 96, 140, 141, 275, 280, 307, 309
Pelling, Henry   223, 284
Penn, Roger   30, 140, 284
Platt, Jennifer   195, 284
Polanyi, Karl   29, 284
political behaviour   9–10, 149–50, 161–4, 225–63
Pollert, Anna   195, 224, 284
'post-industrial' theories   196–7, 269–75
Poulantzas, Nicos   96, 284
Prandy, K.   44, 47, 61
Pratten, C. F.   12, 284
privatism   8–10, 196–7, 202–24
privatization (see privatism)
proletarianization   42, 98–137, 265, 270–5
Purcell, Kate   12, 284

Rattansi, Ali   29, 284
Registrar-General (see social class)
Reid, A.   223, 284
Resler, Henrietta   223, 286
Roberts, Bryan   12, 275, 284
Roberts, K.   195, 284
Robertson, David   12, 227, 232, 261, 262, 284
Robinson, W. S.   195, 284
Roemer, John   33–5, 61
Rokkan, Stein   261, 281
Rose, David   xv, 12, 285
Rose, Richard   260, 261, 262, 263, 277, 285
Routh, Guy   12, 285
Rubery, Jill   29, 285
Runciman, W. G.   29, 166–7, 285

Salaman, W. G.   29, 224, 281
sample design   288–90
Sanderson, Kay   61, 227
Sarlvik, Bo   12, 261, 285
Saunders, Peter   12, 285
Scase, Richard   194, 224, 285
Scott, John   12, 96, 285

sectoral cleavages   181, 182, 184, 232–5, 248–54, 266–7
Shils, Edward   194
Showler, Brian   275, 285
Sinfield, Adrian   12, 95, 275, 285
Singelmann, Joachim   12, 97, 140, 285, 287
social attitudes: class conflict   153–4; consistency of   171–9; distributional justice   156–8, 184–7; the economy   158–60; industry   151–3; politics   161–3; sectionalism   202–24 *passim*, 266–7
social class: alleged demise of   1–10, 182, 184, 196–216, 225–63 *passim*; definitions of   13–26; and electoral behaviour   9–10, 225–63; and gender   63–97, 103–12, 182–3; Goldthorpe's model of   21–3; Marxist models of   5, 14–16, 23–6, 29, 31–61; and occupation   18–23, 42–3; Registrar-General's model of   18–21 26–9; self assignment to   143; and social identity   6–10, 143–5, 148–50, 225–6; structure of   3–5, 13–26, 31–2, 36–8, 44–6, 98–142; subjective perceptions of   145–7, 189; and unit of analysis   63–8, 85–7; Weberian models of   16–18, 21–3, 30, 44, 45, 199–201
social identities   6–10, 148–50, 216–24
social mobility   21–2, 39, 45–6, 63–97, 101–26, 269–75
social status   18, 35, 199–201
Sparrow, P.   12, 285
Stanworth, Michelle   66–7, 68, 72, 82, 85, 95, 104, 106, 108, 141, 285
Stewart, A.   30, 44, 47, 61, 245, 262, 281, 285
Stone, K.   29, 286
Szreter, Simon R. S.   29, 30, 286

Taylor-Gooby, Peter   12, 286
Thatcher, A. R.   12, 286
Tholfsen, Trygve R.   205, 223, 286
Thompson, E. P.   29, 96, 286
Tienda, M.   140, 285
trades unions   128–9, 154–5, 161–4, 200–2, 204–6
Turner, Bryan S.   222, 223, 285

Upton, G. J. G.   141, 285
Urry, John   12, 13–14, 29–30, 61, 277, 281

Vogler, Carolyn 261, 286
voting behaviour 9–10, 149–50, 232–63

Wallace, Claire 224, 286
Walton, John 223, 286
Warner, W. Lloyd 29, 286
Weber, Max 13–18, 29–30, 47, 61, 199, 223, 262, 286
Wesolowski, W. 29, 286
Westergaard, John 12, 223, 286
Williams, Raymond 194
Willis, Paul E. 224, 286
Wilson, Bryan R. 224, 286
Wolpe, AnnMarie 223, 281
Wood, Stephen 141, 224, 286
work attitudes 207–12
Worre, T. 261, 286

Wright, Erik Olin: on class consciousness 168–73, 191–5; on class formation 39, 44–6; on class and gender 87–8; class model (1979) 23–9, 30, 265; class model (1985) 31–61, 265; on class structure 36–8, 44–6, 98, 99–100, 136–7; class models compared with Goldthorpe's 27–8, 48–60, 89–95, 101–3, 139–40, 264–5; comparative class analyses xiii, xv; on Marxist class analysis 5, 12, 31–2; on proletarianization 98, 99–100, 136–7; on social mobility 44–6; on unit of class analysis 88

Zweig, Ferdynand 275, 287

Lightning Source UK Ltd.
Milton Keynes UK
09 February 2011

167166UK00002B/29/A

9 780415 098762